Mammal Tracks & Sign

The Falcone

Family

0 11557 02626 9

Mammal Tracks & Sign

A Guide to
North American Species

Mark Elbroch

STACKPOLE
BOOKS

Copyright © 2003 by Stackpole Books

Published by
STACKPOLE BOOKS
5067 Ritter Road
Mechanicsburg, PA 17055
www.stackpolebooks.com

Printed in China

10 9 8 7 6 5

First edition

Cover design by Caroline Stover
Cover photos by Mark Elbroch

All photographs and illustrations by
Mark Elbroch unless otherwise noted.

Library of Congress Cataloging-in-Publication Data

Elbroch, Mark.
    Mammal tracks & sign : a guide to North American species /
Mark Elbroch.—1st ed.
        p.   cm.
    Includes bibliographical references and index (p.   ).
    ISBN 0-8117-2626-6
    1. Mammals—North America—Identification.   2. Animal
tracks—North America.   I. Title: Mammal tracks and sign.   II. Title.

QL725.N7 E43   2003
599′.097—dc21   2002010549

ISBN 978-0-8117-2626-9

For my mother, Victoria Elbroch,
who delivers unrivaled support for me and my work,
my grandmother, Liz Gorst,
who made sure to walk me in the sea air just after my birth
and who has supported this project in so many ways,

and in memory of Olaus Murie,
whose work in tracking in North America has touched
untold thousands, if not millions—including me.

CONTENTS

Editor's Note: Abbreviations for the states in which the photographs were taken follow the captions.

Introduction

*In wildness is the preservation
of the world.*
HENRY DAVID THOREAU

The snow began to fall well after dark and finished just after midnight. It was a light spring snow, made moist by the morning's warm temperatures—perfect for tracking. I woke, stretched, and grabbed a blueberry muffin on my way out the door. I strolled into the woods to assess tracking conditions. Just beyond the yard, I crossed her fresh trail. I knew this red fox very well. She often holed up in the network of cavities created when stumps had been bulldozed to the west to create my driveway. She seemed quite content there, sharing her quarters with numerous cottontails that also sought cover amidst the root tangles and dirt mounds. I knew her usual rounds and the limits of her territory, and I knew what she hunted and where. I followed her trails no fewer than five days a week, constantly sharing in her life since I had moved there the previous October.

On this glorious morning, every track in her eastward trail was perfect. She moved in her natural rhythm, a direct registering trot, and I envisioned her gliding through the undergrowth, likely heading to the tiny wetland just east of my home, where she hunted voles and other small mammals. I decided to follow her for a while, as I was in no hurry to leave for work and her trail was so fresh.

Shortly after I joined her, she slowed to a walk. Any time she switched from her natural rhythm to another gait, I paused to look deeper. Why was she walking? It was only a few steps, really; she moved close to one of her regular stumps and scented. I could smell her urine before I leaned down— a pungent odor, similar to that of a skunk.

Kneeling, I attempted to absorb every detail laid before me. The snow was such that each footprint registered perfectly: the small toe pads; the great, blurry gap between the toes and palm pad created by the abundance of fur; the chevron-shaped depression where the only portion of exposed

1

A moose walked in the direction of the camera in the forefront of the spectacular Teton Mountains. (WY)

palm pad had registered clearly. I studied her tracks with my eyes and felt the ridges and depressions lightly with my fingers. I could not help but smell her scent post, as well as listen to the wind move in the hemlocks and pines above me. And I could taste my blueberry muffin. While consciously using all my senses, I felt it.

Most people have experienced the feeling of someone looking at them from across a room, only to turn and catch the person in the act. That's what I felt—the gut feeling of being watched. I searched the surrounding woodlands for prying eyes. I thought that the couple I rented from might be in the yard, or worse, their dog, who loved to accompany me into the woods. But there was no one, nothing. I stood and looked around again. Still nothing. Hmm. I decided to continue on.

She returned to her natural rhythm and in short order circled to her wetland, just as I had predicted. She hunted some, but there was no evidence of successful kills and she quickly looped back toward my home. I followed her into a tight, young hemlock stand, where I was forced to a crawl. Eventually I arrived at a spot where she had sat down. I knelt beside the spot, envisioning her as best I could and judging where her gaze would fall. That's strange, I thought to myself; she seemed to be looking at the very place she'd come from earlier—where I'd just been.

Following her further, I found that she had trotted right up to my recent boot prints. She followed my trail for several yards, finally selecting one of my knee prints in which to squat and urinate. After several more steps she squatted again, leaving a brown splat in a boot track, a disgusting ooze I've yet to see the likes of to this day. Then she galloped off into the deep woods, at which point I turned toward home.

Tracking is about real relationships with real animals in the real world. Much of what I learned about red foxes that year is absent in the literature. Tracking provides such amazing opportunities to learn and interact with our homes, our environments, and our neighbors the wild creatures. Tracks and signs bring woodlands, deserts, and suburbs to life, revealing the presence of the dynamic lives that perpetually surround us. Tracking also leads to self-knowledge, because you cannot increase your awareness of the world around you without becoming more aware of your role in it.

Tracking is also the meeting place between storytelling and science—both are required in advanced levels of tracking. Louis Liebenberg reminds us in his *Art of Tracking,* "Tracking is not strictly empirical, since it involves the tracker's imagination." Yes, tracking involves science—collecting evidence, testing hypotheses, and researching animals and their habits. But at some point you will interpret the data collected in the field, bringing the numbers and measurements to life as they tell the story of animals in some piece of woodland you've been frequenting.

The competent tracker is both scientist and storyteller. You must critically observe, collect good data, and avoid rash conclusions, as well as use your imagination to interpret and celebrate the signs you've discovered. Attempt to track without making any judgments. Experience completely the signs of animals for as long as possible, using all your senses to absorb the many details and ecological clues.

I also encourage you to become the animal and try to decipher how it was moving and what it was doing. The only rule I enforce with my students is flexibility. We must all be

Wolf tracks carpet Lamar Valley in Yellowstone National Park, and somehow the park seems wilder. (WY)

Cultural Tracking

If we followed our lineages back far enough, we would find the trackers from whom we came. During the long era that preceded agricultural society, the art and science of tracking were necessary skills for survival. One glance at a track, and a story of incredible richness and complexity unfolded.

Real tracking is the work of more than one lifetime. Tracking, as our ancestors knew it, was a body of knowledge handed down from generation to generation. Each person added to this knowledge base and expanded it. I call this *cultural tracking.* Here in North America, the arrival of the Europeans brought churches, governments, and the limited perspective of "science," severing the cultural connection responsible for passing on the stories held by wildlife tracks and signs. As American native cultures and mountain men were devastated and mainstreamed, we lost not one lifetime's knowledge but many.

Today there is renewed enthusiasm for tracking. Scientists, researchers, and naturalists are beginning to understand what tracking and trackers have to offer. Ordinary folks are also taking to the woods to reconnect with wilderness, to engage in real relationships with wild creatures, and to gain a sense of place by reading the signs left in their own environments. Tracking is really about a greater awareness, a way of living more fully. Tracking centers us in the world and slows us down. It reminds us that there are alternate ways of living on earth that were successful for thousands of years.

Those of us who are passionate about this subject are beginning to reclaim what was lost. The material in this book is one contribution in the effort to rebuild our cultural knowledge of tracking and share it with others. May all of you, the readers, add to this knowledge and advance it ever further.

Animal tracks, animals, and people cover Newspaper Rock, estimated to be several thousand years old. (UT)

Nothing is so insignificant that it does not leave tracks or should be ignored: a blister beetle. (MA)

willing to let go of our hypotheses as quickly as we make them, for 15 feet down the trail, further evidence may disprove our current thinking. And this is not the end of the world; we should just create a new and improved hypothesis. This is the lot of both scientist and tracker—to often be wrong but learn from the experience regardless.

Tracking Applied

As I write this, tracking is being applied across the country for various purposes. One study in Montana collects data on bear sign, stockpiling scats and waiting for DNA testing to drop in price. This avoids having to capture bears, pull their teeth, drug them, collar them, or habituate them to human scent. Another research project in Maine is

A brown bear's trail follows a bloated river full of glacial silt. (AK)

Maine's Lynx Project

I volunteered for a short period with Maine's Department of Inland Fisheries and Wildlife in the North Woods, where one of the first extensive studies of lynx is being coordinated. Backtracking collared animals in snow is just one component of the project, but it allows for tremendous learning. Below are the data and route I recorded using a GPS unit while following L25, a two-year-old female, for one day during the mating season. The waypoints in the picture correspond with the numbers below.

1. Coordinates from flyover the previous day
2. Two day beds, 5 feet apart. The second was in denser cover—disturbed by flyover?
3. Scent marking—squat
4. Scent marking—raised leg
5. Scat—uncovered and no scrape
6. Hunting lay

7. Scent marking—backward squirt
8. Scent marking—backward squirt
9. Scat—uncovered and no scrape
10. Road crossing
11. Hunting lay
12. Hardwood under- and overstory
13. Hunting lay
14. Scat—uncovered and no scrape
15. Scent marking—backward squirt; unsuccessful snowshoe hare chase
16. Scent marking—backward squirt
17. Road crossing
18. Unsuccessful snowshoe hare chase
19. Traveling with male—he separates from her at this point
20. Mating
21. Male walking separate
22. Mating
23. Short-term bed
24. Moving in a tight spruce grove
25. Romp—mating?
26. Romp—mating?
27. Scent marking—backward squirt
28. Hunting lay
29. Romp and final coordinate
30. Same couple crossing wood road

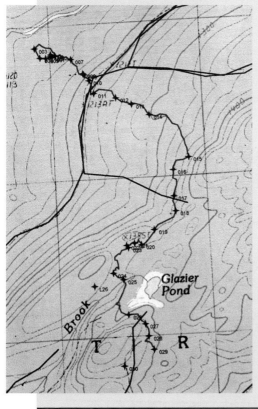

developing snow survey techniques to discover the presence of lynx in a given area. Wildlife inventories are beginning to rely on track and sign, which provides an accurate snapshot of wildlife in an area, rather than depending on theoretical assumptions about inhabitants based on vegetative analysis.

The potential applications of tracking are limited only by our creativity. Skalski (1991) points out that all that is needed to turn tracking into quantified species density estimates is a known rate of sign production. Deer pellet counts have been used for decades in deer density counts, but this is only the beginning of what could be done with further research and training.

Ecology and Education

Tracking is field ecology; I know of no better way than studying tracks and other signs to see and experience the relationships among wildlife species, between wildlife and herbaceous plants, and between wildlife and the ecosystems in which they live. A study of relationships offers a much better view of the whole, interconnected animal than a compartmentalized and therefore limited experience of a wild creature. Tracking also brings us beyond species study. The personalities and tendencies of individuals soon become evident in the field, emphasizing that each individual is a contributing member of the ecological community.

Tracking also offers holistic lessons in natural history, animal behavior, biology, and ecology in such a manner that knowledge is unconsciously absorbed and lasts forever, rather than rote memorization from textbooks that lasts just long enough to pass exams. Several academic and nontraditional schools have brought tracking into the cur-

The perspective of a climbing bear, on an aspen wallpapered with old bear claw marks. (WY)

A grizzly bear's digs for glacier lily bulbs in the high country of Glacier National Park. (MT)

riculum already, but it is my hope that more academics will embrace tracking in the future. Tracking offers direct experiential learning to students of any age.

Keith Badger has been teaching high school students biology, botany, and ecology through the traditional skills of bow making, buck skinning, and tracking for 10 years at the High Mowing School in Wilton, New Hampshire. He also preaches tracking at educational conferences in the area. He claims that tracking is the pinnacle skill, for it combines naturalist skills that ground students in their environment while bringing them to a far greater level of awareness; they recognize the interconnectedness of all things in their ecosystem. He believes that tracking is the most appropriate metaphor for the human journey, from sublime to spiritual: "It should be a core requirement in education, kindergarten through graduate school."

Walker Korby has been sharing tracking with middle school students at the Hartsbrook School in Hadley, Massachusetts, and students at the Uplook School in Greenfield, Massachusetts, for several years. He believes that tracking is an excellent way to force students to "break from their normal realms of thought" and to encourage more dynamic independent thinking. Nancy Birtwell has found similar benefits and success teaching tracking to her preschool class. "They love it! It teaches them to be more observant and to stretch their thinking skills." And Joan Regan has created a tracking curriculum for her gym class at the Pike School in Andover, Massachusetts. She is thrilled with her students' progress—

Etiquette

We must be respectful while out tracking and exploring, because unfortunately, our natural resources are a limited commodity. This is becoming even more apparent with the further development of our country and the greater need for people to post "No Trespassing" signs to keep people out. Here are some suggestions for trackers to contemplate while in the field:

• Promote the welfare of all wildlife and its environment and support the protection of important wildlife habitat.

• Be respectful of active dens, rendezvous sites, display areas, and important feeding sites.

• Respect the interests, rights, and skills of fellow trackers, as well as those people participating in other legitimate outdoor activities.

• Be especially supportive of beginning trackers, sharing freely our knowledge and experience.

• Consider stepping next to, rather than on the trail, so that others may enjoy what we have found as well.

• Be honest in recording what we find in the field, and let us acknowledge when we cannot interpret what we've found. These moments point out potential future research projects.

• Speak well of others who work in the field. We are a newly emerging science.

There is always the question of whether you should fore- or backtrack an animal. If you can age the trail and know that it has been some time since the animal passed, it doesn't matter. Many people believe that we should always backtrack, to avoid disturbing the animal. I do both, but when I'm foretracking, if I sense that I may be stressing the animal or the trail shows signs that the animal has become aware of me, I turn back. Either way, forward or back, you are bound to discover amazing things.

An active red fox den. Note the bed at the entrance. (MA)

they're active and completely engaged in learning. Many people across the country are integrating tracking skills into their curricula, as schools are recognizing the amazing potential in a tracking education. Some universities are also offering tracking courses, often disguised under titles such as "Wildlife Inventory Techniques" or "Field Mammalogy."

Tracking on a Larger Scale

Louis Liebenberg created the CyberTracker, a visually based handheld computer program for GPS units, for Bushman trackers in South Africa. Liebenberg has tapped an incredible and rich source of knowledge—a wealth of natural history, tracking, and behavioral information that dates back to the roots of science and beyond. In doing so, he has also created a value for tracking in a modern society that gnaws at the Bushman culture. Also, tracking has intrinsic worth, much more so than the other jobs available in the towns at the edges of the remaining wild African bush. His work saves people and the roots of tracking and wildlife knowledge within them.

Jon Young, Dr. Jim Halfpenny, and Kurt Rinehart are among those who have developed a North American sequence for the CyberTracker. Now this new technology can be used to plot wildlife movements in North America, as well as to document vernal pools, salamander migrations, and a host of other exciting possibilities—the limits of its applications seem endless. But we need trackers to implement this new

A kit fox den in dune habitat. (CA)

Gulf Coast kangaroo rat trails and a ghost crab's trail share a coastal dune. (TX)

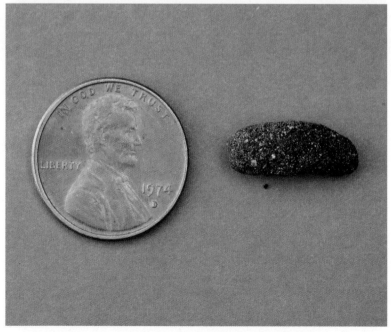

An aplodontia scat. (WA) Photo by Paul Houghtaling and Tim Selim.

The Shikari Tracking Guild and the CyberTracker Program

by Jon Young

To simulate and facilitate the processes that helped trackers emerge in native societies and to guide modern learners in these ancient skills, a group of trackers formed the Shikari Tracking Guild. The guild gets its name from the late Jim Corbett, the great *Shikari* (big-game tracker) from the Kumoan region of India. It is dedicated to preserving and enhancing the science and art of tracking.

Part of its mission is to serve the community through the application of tracking science. Data integrity is the backbone of science, and professional tracking must support this through exacting methodologies and peer review, both of which are core traditions of science and tracking practice in the native sense. Through international networks of conservation and land management, citizen science has become an important force in the inventory of nature's shrinking diversity. The Shikari Tracking Guild helps trackers develop professional skills that help them become invaluable assets to stewardship efforts in their communities.

Recently, scientific researchers discovered the value of trackers through Louis Liebenberg's CyberTracker program. In South Africa, authentic, holistic wildlife trackers such as Bushmen are gathering data in unprecedented quantities—without sacrificing the quality so important to the integrity of science. The Bushmen trackers working with CyberTracker software in handheld computers have been lauded by land managers, wildlife scientists, and park officials as the most efficient and cost-effective means of collecting data.

What makes the CyberTracker program so effective is the Bushmen's tracking ability—and the ability of the CyberTracker program to evaluate the skills of a master tracker. Without competent track-

technology, for its applications are restricted only by the skills and knowledge of those who use it.

Susan Morse's nonprofit Keeping Track in Vermont teaches members of a community to identify the tracks and signs of several keystone species in their own area, such as otter, black bear, and moose. When local people scientifically document the presence of these species in their towns, they can better weigh and consider the influences of new construction, land trust acquisitions, rock quarry lease renewals, and many other important activities. Susan's work base at Keeping Track is also creating something larger still, incorporating all the data for every

A bushy-tailed woodrat nest and surrounding rocks stained by urine accumulations. In the foreground is a Handspring Visor linked with a Magellan GPS unit, which in combination with CyberTracker software allowed me to record and map this and numerous other signs for a private ranch owner. (ID)

ers operating the system, the handheld computer is just another piece of field technology.

Thus, if tracking is to go the same route in America and elsewhere, there must be a similar program to train and evaluate trackers. Another part of the Shikari Tracking Guild's mission is the development of training and evaluation standards for students that replicates those created by Louis Liebenberg in Africa and provides a template for training—much the way any field of specialty has its core curriculum.

town and thus allowing a bird's-eye view of wildlife movements and corridors in New England and elsewhere.

The work of identifying and protecting wildlife corridors is incredibly exciting. Biologists have known for some time that the preservation of healthy, complete ecosystems and the wildlife within cannot be done in scattered nature preserves and parks; it requires protecting the strips of land that connect these preserves. This is the critical goal of the Wildlands Project: to link these "islands" of protected land with corridors. M. Rupert Cutler writes in *In Defense of Wildlife: Preserving Communities and Corridors,* "the prompt identification and protection of wildlife movement corridors may spell survival and extinction for such diverse species as the spotted owl and the Florida panther." He goes on to write, "The time is right to win political support for the wildlife habitat-connection approach to the preservation of biological diversity." I couldn't agree more, and trackers can help in the identification of existing corridors.

Time and again, in my wildlife inventory work and personal studies, the identification and mapping of wildlife track and sign have made wildlife corridors jump out of the landscape. Certain ridges, certain tracts of land, and certain water systems are better than others. These are existing wildlife corridors that need immediate protection. Work completed by Sue Morse's trained communities and the technology prepared by Louis Liebenberg will help us identify existing corridors across North America. But we need volunteers—we need competent trackers. Thus the creation of this book to stimulate interest and further your education.

What follows is a visual presentation of the tracks and signs of most North American mammals. The careful reader can extract subtleties from the illustrations that are difficult to express with the written word but are vital to competent interpretation in the field. Together with *Bird Tracks & Sign* (2001), this book provides the researcher, educator, hunter, and naturalist with the most comprehensive study of tracks and signs to date.

Getting Started

I was feeling particularly confident that February day, comfortable in my ability to interpret what I encountered in the field. I was walking in a place I knew well and explored regularly, out on the ice of a large, frozen pond, where several inches of snow made for easy tracking. I'd been following an otter most of the morning when I came across a new trail out on the ice. But rather than the familiarity and recognition I was accustomed to when I looked at animal tracks and trails, nothing registered. I needed a closer look. The snow was fluffy, and the trail had been blown a bit as well, making individual track recognition difficult. The animal seemed to be moving in a gait that obscured the tracks. I did my best to differentiate front from rear, but conditions were better suited to a study of the overall pattern.

I backed away a bit, to study the obvious groups of marks in the trail. There was a circular impression at the center of each grouping, as well as four additional marks just outside the circle, like the four corners of a box; the trail width varied from 5 to 5¹/₂ inches (12.7 to 14 cm). This pattern was repeated over and over as far as I could see. Still nothing was clicking. What would be out and about on a cold February morning in a northern hardwood forest in central New England? I considered all the species associated with the forest type, but still I was confounded.

I decided to follow the trail further—I needed more clues. In a few minutes the animal changed gaits completely, leaving a very different pattern. The tracks were paired, and groups of two zigzagged from side to side, like a small deer trail. Hmm, an animal that both hops and walks. The individual tracks were a bit better, too. The tracks were large, considering the stride and trail width, and their distinctive shape could no longer be denied. Ha! I'd refused to consider the obvious, blinded by my assumptions about February in New England. It was a bullfrog.

Left: A bullfrog trail in shallow snow. (MA) *Right:* You don't even need to get out of your car to appreciate this roadside feral hog sign. Signs of wildlife constantly surround us. (NC)

I backtracked the creature several hundred yards to where it had emerged from a hole in the ice made by otters at the edge of a large lake just east of the pond. I don't know what became of the bullfrog, nor what stirred it awake and sparked the need for travel in the dead of winter. But that frog taught me humility and reminded me to remain flexible in my interpretation and to acknowledge all the clues presented.

Tracks and signs are never found alone in the world; they are always related to an ecosystem. The location of tracks and signs and the surrounding environment provide as much information about behavior, habits, and ecology as the signs themselves. You cannot become a student of tracking without becoming a well-rounded ecologist—a naturalist, if you will. Are you aware of the forest types near your home and the

animals that typically inhabit them? Do you know the dietary preferences of local animals? Do you know which species hibernate, and for
how long? Can you visualize local wildlife using your imagination? Can
you identify animals when you see them? Do you know the names of the
trees and shrubs in your yard? The more ecological information we
absorb and teach ourselves, the easier track and sign interpretation
becomes, for signs, when understood in ecological relation to their environment, are bursting with clues for species identification.

You don't need to travel far to begin your study of tracking—start in
your own backyard. Animals live secret lives all around us. Tracks and
signs are everywhere, but some places are better than others. Consider
cover, water, and food resources when you go out in search of animal
sign. Look for diversity in vegetation, because that's often a feature of a
healthy ecosystem. Investigate forested passes between peaks; low,

Naturalist Training

by Jon Young

Since 1978, I have worked as a professional tracker and as a coach
and trainer for trackers to preserve and restore the art and science
of tracking. It is vital that mentoring systems to facilitate the development of holistic wildlife trackers be preserved and adapted to
modern needs. Holistic wildlife tracking is based on full sensory
development and the knowledge of hazards, mammals, ecological
indicators, trees, shrubs, and low-growing plants that provide food,
forage, cover, medicines, and other necessities for people living
close to the land.

Along with other naturalists and trackers, I developed a training
system known as the Shikari Tracker Training Program, but the students' lack of nature knowledge caused them to flounder in their
tracking studies. We realized that the foundation that native trackers
receive in their early years was missing. So we went back to the draw-
ing board and created the Kamana Naturalist Training Program,
designed to simulate the sensory awareness immersion and natural
history training that children in hunter-gatherer tribes receive.

There are now thousands of Kamana students worldwide, and
tracking teachers report that advanced Kamana students and gradu-
ates have measurably better skills than others. Trackers don't learn
the basic skills by accident; they learn by being mentored in a way
that helps them develop the necessary base knowledge of nature.
The tracking journey is a long one; it can take ten to fifteen years to
develop the skills of a master tracker. Naturalist training can be a
good two to three years of this journey. (See the appendix.)

The mark of a black bear on an American beech. Also look closely for recent signs of climbing bears and the older scars made by climbing porcupines. (VT)

forested ridgelines; wetland systems; and river valleys, all of which are natural wildlife corridors.

You are always surrounded by the signs of wild creatures. Tom Brown discusses the "self-inflicted blindness" of beginning students in his field guide to nature observation and tracking. I have had long discussions on this subject with Fred Vanderbeck, a blossoming tracker in Massachusetts, and he uses the words "giving oneself permission." This is what you must do from the outset. Be confident that signs surround you, and give yourself permission to see, feel, listen to, sense, and know them intimately.

Journals and Documentation

Documenting your discoveries and your in-the-field collecting activities increases the speed with which you absorb tracking knowledge and enhances the learning process; it's also great fun. Journaling of any kind is invaluable—whether it be writing, sketches, photography, or a combination of all three. I recommend that you use a good sturdy notebook. Paste in photos, leaves, and feathers; draw freely; write everything down. Note the weather, the season, the time of day, and the environment. I explain the "three perspectives" approach below, which is the process I recommend when students begin to keep journals and study tracking, but any way is great. If it feels right and you're enjoying yourself, stick with it.

Clare Walker Leslie's *Keeping a Nature Journal* is a wonderful introduction to field journaling. Jon Young has created a tracking curriculum, the Shikari Tracker Training Program, that provides, among other things, a specific approach to track and sign journaling.

The Three Perspectives

The three perspectives—lying, standing, and flying—approach to tracking forces us to look carefully and acknowledge all the information surrounding every track and sign. First, lie down and look at the track or sign very closely. Second, stand and look at the track pattern or the immediate context of the sign. Third, imagine soaring high above to study the ecology of the environment within which the track or sign sits. And don't just look—listen, feel, taste, smell. Engage your whole body and ask as many questions as possible as you constantly vary your focus from the big picture to the immediate context to the individual track or sign and then back to the big picture again.

In the beginning, I suggest that you journal or illustrate each of these perspectives when you encounter track and sign in the field. Much can be learned when you slow down and study a track or other sign from multiple perspectives.

Perspective 1: a mystery track.

Lying, an Intimate Perspective

Perspective 1 is a close and intimate study of the track or sign you have discovered, best done while lying down with your nose as close to your find as you can get with your eyes still in focus. Be a nature detective; ask yourself useful questions that will help you visualize the animal. What could large claws be used for? Would a smaller or larger animal leave most of the nut intact? Because the feet are the point of contact between the earth and the animal, a track gives lots of clues about how a mammal exists in the world. All sign is bursting with relevant information, ready to unfold a story based on your own creativity, questions, awareness, and, most important, imagination.

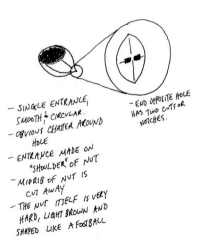

Perspective 1: a mystery nut.

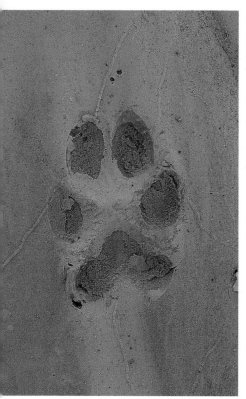 

Left: The perfect front track of a coyote in infrequent mud on the floor of Death Valley. (CA) *Right:* Meadow vole sculpture; an entire locust sapling was debarked while deep snow blanketed the ground in winter. (MA)

This book is intended to provide written and visual reference materials for what you find in the field. Consider cross-referencing the information in this guide with other field guides, such as those written by Olaus Murie (1954), Paul Rezendes (1999), Jim Halfpenny (1986), or Marcelo Aranda (2000). You should also seek out people in your community who have knowledge of tracks and signs—maybe an old hunter or the local postman. Or sign up for a tracking course with one of the schools listed in the resources section of this book. Mammal guides also help you visualize the entire animal you are tracking.

Standing, a Contextual Perspective

While standing (Perspective 2), it is easy to assess the trail in which your track fits or the immediate context surrounding the sign in question. What you've discovered is probably part of a larger group or area of sign.

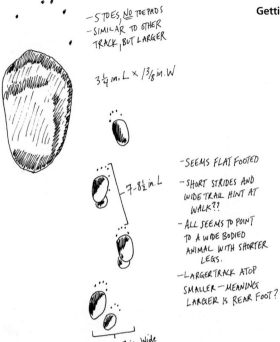

- 5 TOES, NO TOE PADS
- SIMILAR TO OTHER TRACK, BUT LARGER

3 ¼ in. L × 1 ⅜ in. W

- SEEMS FLAT FOOTED
- SHORT STRIDES AND WIDE TRAIL HINT AT WALK??
- ALL SEEMS TO POINT TO A WIDE BODIED ANIMAL WITH SHORTER LEGS.
- LARGER TRACK ATOP SMALLER — MEANING LARGER IS REAR FOOT?

7 - 8 ½ in. L

6 - 7 in. Wide

Perspective 2: a mystery track.

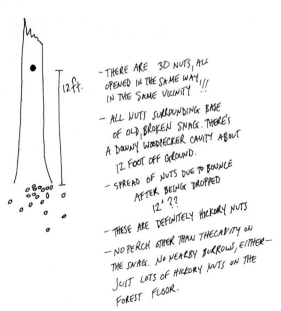

12 ft.

- THERE ARE 30 NUTS, ALL OPENED IN THE SAME WAY!!! IN THE SAME VICINITY!!
- ALL NUTS SURROUNDING BASE OF OLD, BROKEN SNAG. THERE'S A DOWNY WOODPECKER CAVITY ABOUT 12 FOOT OFF GROUND.
- SPREAD OF NUTS DUE TO BOUNCE AFTER BEING DROPPED 12'??
- THESE ARE DEFINITELY HICKORY NUTS
- NO PERCH OTHER THAN THE CAVITY ON THE SNAG. NO NEARBY BURROWS, EITHER — JUST LOTS OF HICKORY NUTS ON THE FOREST FLOOR.

Perspective 2: a mystery nut.

Track Casting

Track casting allows us to bring home what we've seen in the field. Casts are the trophies of track hunters. They are also wonderful tools for education and research, allowing others to touch and see actual life-size tracks; they can also be referred to for measurements or species comparison.

Track casting takes a bit of practice, but the process is simple. Mix plaster of paris and water in a container (I use 1-gallon Ziploc bags) until you have a milk shake–like consistency, pour, and wait 20 to 40 minutes. If the mixture is too watery, it prolongs the drying process, is more difficult to control, lays down thinner, and produces a weaker final result. If it's too thick, you may squash the track as you pour the plaster, or the liquid may not enter all the tiny cracks and fissures, so you lose detail.

There are a number of alternatives to plaster. Just about any compound used to fill holes in walls will create casts. Dental stone is more expensive and harder to come by, but it creates very sturdy casts of incredible detail—excellent for small mammals. There is also a product on the market to aid in snow casting. The chemical reaction between plaster and water gives off heat, which distorts a track in snow as it dries. Snow Wax Print (Kinderprint Co., [800] 227-6020) can be sprayed on first to hold the track shape, followed by plaster to create the cast.

I prefer to use frames when casting. These can be made in the field by pinching dirt around the track, laying down sticks, or creating a circle with stiff paper and a paper clip. Frames remove the worry of overall cast shape and give you some leeway in plaster consistency. More liquid mixes can be controlled and poured, and frames also allow for thicker casts, which are sturdier in the long run. You may want to consider adding a wire hoop during the drying process, which allows you to hang the results on the wall.

Cleaning the cast is crucial. If you wash everything from the cast, you will be left with a glowing white ornament, but the lack of contrast makes the track very hard to see. Some people paint casts to bring out the track, but I'm wary of this process; it's too easy to slip and distort the shape of the actual track or lose subtle pressure differences across the foot. I always leave a thin layer of the original substrate on the cast to provide the necessary contrast.

This book offers visual and written information on trail patterns and circumstances in which you find specific sign. Along with the resources mentioned for Perspective 1, you will probably need tree and plant guides to identify what elk have browsed or what sort of nut a fox squirrel has opened. Any books on the natural history of specific animal species are also invaluable. They are full of behaviors and clues for trackers.

Flying, an Ecological Perspective

If you could leap high enough, catch a breeze, and maintain flight, you would be allowed a bird's-eye perspective of the larger context within which sign sits. Perspective 3 is the whole environment encompassing the trail in the mud puddle, the snag, and the scattered nuts. At this level of tracking, you incorporate what you know about the area—where there is cover, water, and food resources, and where there are roads and areas that dogs or people

Moose feeding on the cambium of mountain ash. (NH)

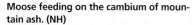

Track Plates

Another great way to collect tracks is to use carbon-sooted aluminum track plates, which are the modern version of Lord and coauthors' (1970) "tracking board." This can be done in two ways. You can place a completely sooted and baited track plate in an area of high traffic, and then read tracks directly from the plate. (Tracks will appear as negative space, the area where soot has been removed.) Alternatively, sooted plates can be used in conjunction with white Con-Tact paper. The second method is a bit more complicated, but the tracks can be kept and compared as others are collected. The animal must first step on the soot and then on the sticky side of the Con-Tact paper, where the track is recorded.

Regardless of the method, use thin sheets of aluminum as the base. I use the sooty flames of acetylene torches to cover my track plates, which creates superb results. I have also heard that glass can be sooted by running sheets over candle flames, with decent results. But be careful not to burn yourself or shatter the glass. Remember: Two-dimensional tracks on Con-Tact paper look quite different from tracks made on natural surfaces; remain flexible in your analysis.

Experiment with different setups, and make sure to include cover if your neck of the woods receives regular rain. For further details on track plates, refer to USFS General Technical Report (PSW-GTR-157), *American Marten, Fisher, Lynx, and Wolverine: Survey Methods for Their Detection.*

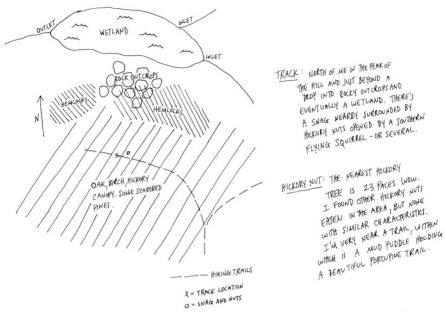

TRACK: NORTH OF ME IN THE PEAK OF THE HILL AND JUST BEYOND A DROP INTO ROCKY OUTCROPS AND EVENTUALLY A WETLAND. THERE'S A SNAG NEARBY SURROUNDED BY HICKORY NUTS OPENED BY A SOUTHERN FLYING SQUIRREL - OR SEVERAL.

HICKORY NUT: THE NEAREST HICKORY TREE IS 23 PACES. WOW. I FOUND OTHER HICKORY NUTS EATEN IN THE AREA, BUT NONE WITH SIMILAR CHARACTERISTICS. I'M VERY NEAR A TRAIL, WITHIN WHICH IS A MUD PUDDLE HOLDING A BEAUTIFUL PORCUPINE TRAIL.

— — — — HIKING TRAILS

X = TRACK LOCATION
O = SNAG AND NUTS

Perspective 3: a mystery track and nut.

Aerial view of a site where wolves killed a white-tailed deer. (MN)

Contextual view of a grizzly scat. You are standing in Denali National Park on an overgrown riverbank, where pea vines thrive and bears swarm in late spring to dig up and eat their roots. (AK)

frequent. You consider the forest type and which animals are generally associated with it.

Although some of the information in this book will be useful for Perspective 3, there are numerous other resources to help improve your knowledge of nature and the ecosystem. John Kricher and Gordon Morrison have written wonderful books—in the Peterson's field guide series—to help people identify forest types as well as learn which birds, mammals, and plants are associated with each one. My favorites are *Ecology of Eastern Forests* and *Ecology of Western Forests*, but their newer and more specific regional guides are also good.

Consider trying the Kamana program, a home-study course designed by Jon Young to train people to be naturalists wherever they happen to live. The school will recommend books applicable to your area, put you in contact with other students, and provide support for a more structured learning process. The more you learn, the more you realize how much there is to learn.

Tom Wessels's *Reading the Forested Landscape* adds a whole new dimension to multiple-perspective tracking. It will help you read the history of a forested landscape and track at an ecosystem level. Also consider reading works in conservation biology and articles on wildlife corridors, both of which emphasize an ecosystem perspective.

Ideal light conditions enhance this black bear's hind track. (WA)

Photography

With some reading and the help of professional photographer and tracker Paul Rezendes, I have learned to take quality pictures of wildlife track and sign. Any camera will work, and so will any film, but if you're serious, you may want to invest in a manual camera and shoot slower film. I use the slide film Fuji Velvia (50), which is so slow that it requires the use of a tripod. Those who want to publish quality results should consider a camera with mirror lock and depth-of-field preview.

Two components affect the quality of each picture: the aperture, which controls the depth of field, and the shutter speed, which controls how long the film is exposed to light. (Read John

Sensible Field Technique

Field samples are a great way to continue your studies at home and share what you're learning with others. For example, I have an extensive collection of nuts opened by various species, as well as a collection of sticks, so the teeth marks of feeding voles can be compared with those of feeding porcupines in the classroom as well as in the field. Almost everything can be collected, but be respectful in your collection techniques. I collect live saplings only if they have been completely girdled or cut free by the animal feeding. In this way, I remove only what would die in the upcoming growing season.

You need to be aware of the risks in handling wild animal scat. Leptospires, found in mammal urine, are dangerous to humans. The roundworm, *Baylisascarius procyonis,* which may be found in raccoon scat,

Shaw's *The Nature Photographer's Complete Guide to Professional Field Techniques* for a thorough explanation of cameras and their functions.) Camera meters rarely read sand, snow, or mud correctly, so use the meter only as a general guide. In snow, one must "open up" 1 1/2 to 2 stops, lowering the shutter speed, to accurately capture the scene. For example, if the camera meter suggests a shutter speed of 60 at an aperture of 13, opening 1 stop means shooting at 30, 1 1/2 means shooting at 20, and opening 2 full stops means shooting at 15. In sand, 1/2 stop above what the meter suggests is generally the right exposure. This is also true in mud, except in very dark brown or black mud, in which case you need to do the opposite and close down 1/2 stop. *The Keeping Track Guide to Photographing Animal Tracks and Signs* contains wonderful hints, suggestions, and guidelines for beginning photographers (see the appendix).

Remember that film is relatively cheap, so shoot several angles if you're not sure which is best. And bracket your exposures; for example, in snow, I shoot the same picture three times—opening up 1 stop more than the meter suggests, then opening up 1 1/2 stops, and finally opening up 2 stops. I'll probably toss one or two exposures after they're developed, but I won't have missed the opportunity. Tracks and signs are temporary—they'll never be the same again.

I prefer to shoot in shade or on cloudy days. Small areas can be shaded with the body. Shadows made by direct sun tend to distort the shape of tracks, and areas of mixed sun and shade are difficult to capture on film. Only under perfect lighting conditions will shadows enhance a track or trail—generally early in the morning or as the sun is going down.

and hantavirus, which is carried in rodent scat, can be deadly when inhaled. Dry scats break down easily, allowing particles to become airborne, so they should be treated with caution. Also be aware that in tight enclosures, such as caves and summer cabins, particles from dry feces can be suspended in air. Use sticks or gloves, rather than your bare hands, to break up and study scats.

Having sounded the warning, note that Jim Halfpenny (1986) writes, "I have never known a naturalist to pick up a disease from scat." Neither have I.

The first step in scat collection is to dry the scat, which is best done in a paper bag or by just leaving it outside; scat tends to grow mold in plastic bags. When completely dry, thickly coat the scat with a clear polyurethane or similar product to protect yourself during handling and to keep it from falling apart. Others suggest first soaking scats in alcohol, then drying, and then coating as an added protection against parasites and bacteria.

Hickory nuts opened by a red squirrel, which has left scats behind to help in the interpretation. (MA)

You may want to go further than just journaling, documenting, or collecting what you find in the field. You may want to create better tracking surfaces (I often smooth and rake areas where I know animals move), leave food in areas of good substrate, or use baited track plates where perfect tracks are rare. The learning only stops when your imagination stops thinking of ways to continue to learn.

Tracks and Trails

2

I spent a summer working in the Adirondacks of northern New York several years ago. The density of black bears was a great attraction for me. In fact, that summer I gained the trust of a female bear near the lodge where I worked. Given time and patience, she allowed me to walk with her as she moved about checking dumpsters, digging up roots, and the like.

But my story is not about this bear; it is about another bear, her mate. One of the staff members burst into the kitchen with the news that a massive bear had just strolled by with just several feet and a quarter inch of glass between himself and dozens of gaping teenagers. I was out the back door in a flash.

The long driveway to the lodge curved just before the building and headed west, paralleling the nearby lakeshore. It was a dirt drive, and if conditions were right, it would show clear tracks. The bear had come onto the road just beyond the edge of the building and headed west, toward some cabins and the potential for carelessly stored trash and food scraps. Right away I knew that this was not my bear but the larger male who wandered through the area sporadically. I hadn't seen him since the previous summer but desperately wanted to see him again. Kneeling next to a large rear track, I touched it. The pads of the toes and palm were more exposed than many black bear tracks I'd seen and left a remarkably crisp print. The wind rustled the spruce canopy, and smells from the kitchen lingered in the air. I really wanted to see this bear, but all of a sudden an image of the staff parking lot flashed in my mind. The lot lies east of the building—exactly opposite of where the bear had gone and where I wanted to follow. The bear would be easy to track, as a string of dog alarms was set off as he moved steadily past various summer homes.

Reluctantly, I turned away from the bear and made my way toward the parking lot, curious as to why it had suddenly come to mind. As I walked, I convinced myself that there would be beautiful fresh bear tracks in the *soft, fine sands of the parking lot. They would certainly be worth casting, and a decent consolation prize for missing the bear himself. I searched the sands and found fresh turkey, old bear, old fox, and coyote tracks, but no new bear tracks. So I sat on a hemlock log at the edge of the lot and frowned at the oncoming darkness and the beauty that surrounded me.*

About 30 minutes passed, during which the sunlight faded and disappeared. The lot remained illuminated by an overhead lamppost, a bright plot within the vast spruce and red maple forest on all sides. There had to be a reason why I was there, but I hadn't figured it out. I decided to leave. As I stood and stepped forward, I heard the first twig snap, and froze. The sound had originated off in the wetlands west of the drive, betraying the passage of something quite large. Eventually, he was close enough for me to hear his rhythmic breathing, and then I could make out the black silhouette of his head swaying from side to side as he moved. The bear paused at the edge of

the lot to assess the area and then, not 5 feet from where I stood like a new telephone pole, he stepped out of the darkness into the light. His luxuriant coat sparkled in the lamplight, his health and vigor radiating. He looked both ways and then began to walk up the drive toward the locked shed where we stored our trash. I'd seen my bear after all.

Tracks and trails bring environments to life. How much wilder does a canyon feel when you see and recognize the footprints of a mountain lion or wolf? Mud, snow, sand, and even debris offer us glimpses of our environment's inhabitants—our neighbors, the wild creatures. Tracks enhance the wilderness experience and also bring wilderness closer to home. I've tracked red foxes and skunks through the streets of Boston, and stepped out my door in central New England to discover the trail of a bobcat across my porch.

Tracks and trails also allow you to interpret animal behavior and discover what wild animals are up to. Many tracking books use the

An otter slide cuts an expanse of Idaho wilderness, reminding us of the incredible wildlife all around us. (ID)

analogy of the earth as paper, the animals as writers, and the tracks and trails as the letters and words left behind for those who are fluent in the language and willing to pause and read. Tracks and trails are truly a script for those with trained senses, and they tell many stories rich in drama, suspense, mystery, love, and sometimes horror.

Foot Morphology

Thousands of years ago, the first mammals moved about with five toes on each foot. Over a long time, through evolution and specialization, feet and legs evolved and became more varied. Insectivores, such as shrews, are believed to retain a foot structure similar to that of the first mammals.

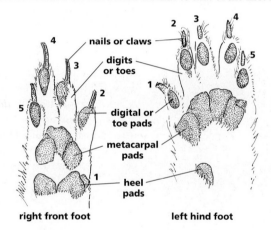

Gray squirrel (numbers refer to digital formula).

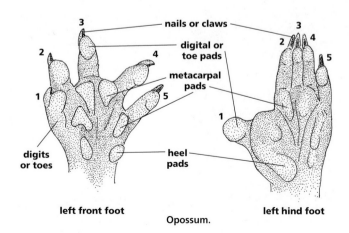

Opossum.

Scientists who study the anatomy of mammals have devised descriptive means by which to categorize their feet. Digits, or toes, are numbered 1 to 5, beginning with the inside (analogous to our thumb) and moving outward. In most species, toe 1 is the smallest and toe 3, the central toe, the largest. But with evolution, some species developed structures and natural movements that required different foot structures. In some animals toe 1 is completely gone, and in others it is greatly reduced. Bang and Dahlstrom (1974) note that many species began to evolve longer bones to aid in running while losing toe 1 altogether.

Tough, horny layers of skin protect bones and other foot structures from rough ground. The thick toe and metacarpal (palm) pads are covered in sweat glands, so that every track holds the scent of the animal that created it. In most animals these pads are naked (hares are one exception), and the spaces between these pads are usually filled with fur (striped skunks are an exception).

Mammals also diversified in how they place the foot on the ground while moving about on the land. Animals that are plantigrade, such as humans and bears, place all the bones of their feet on the ground when moving. Animals that are digitigrade, such as cats and dogs, place only their toes on the ground.

A perfect fisher track shows the claws, the toe pads, ample fur, the metacarpal region, and an additional heel pad at the posterior edge of the track. (MA)

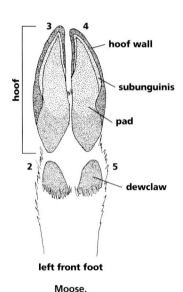

left front foot

Moose.

Unguligrade animals, such as deer and bison, and odd-unguligrade mammals, such as horses, walk on the ends of their toes, the equivalent of our toenails. Note that many mammals can vary between moving in both plantigrade and digitigrade fashion.

Track Morphology

Most mammal tracks are composed of claws, toe pads, metacarpal pads (the palm), and the negative space in between. Many tracks also show one or two additional pads at the posterior edge of the track, behind the

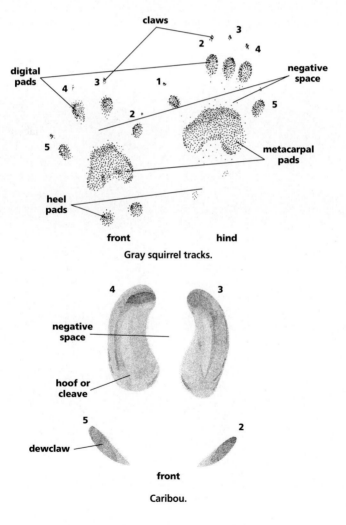

Gray squirrel tracks.

Caribou.

palm pads; I refer to these pads as heel pads. (There is ongoing discussion on the technical names for the pads on mammal feet, which requires a study not only of anatomy but also of evolutionary physiology.) Still others involve webbing.

Hoofed, or cleaved, tracks generally register two toes but may also show dewclaws, the small toes 2 and 5 found higher on the leg and covered by a horny sheath. Odd-unguligrade mammals (horses) register only one toe.

Important Track Features

Symmetry. Symmetry refers to the balance between the right and left sides of the track. Using your imagination, cut the track directly down the center and flip one side onto the other. Do the left and right sides align

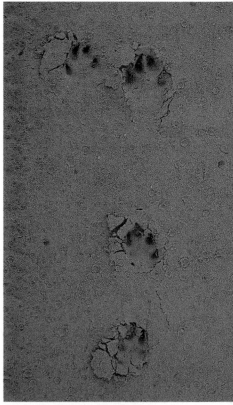

Left: Compare symmetry in the front and rear (above) tracks of this cougar. The front track is far more asymmetrical than the hind track. (MT) *Right:* Carefully count the toes on these perfect desert cottontail tracks: Each front track has five toes (the innermost toe is just a dot), and each hind track has four toes. (UT)

front   **hind**

Bobcat. Note the teardrop-shaped digital pads.

and match perfectly? If not, to what degree is the track asymmetrical, or different? In bobcats, the front track is often very asymmetrical, while the rear tracks tend to be more symmetrical. The opposite is true in otters, with the front track being far more symmetrical than the rear track.

Number and placement of toes. How many toes does your animal have? Shrews have five toes on both the front and rear feet, and hares have four toes only on their hind feet. All canine tracks tend to register four distinct toes, even though they have five toes on their front feet; one sits on a higher plane on the inside of the leg.

The smallest toe is found on the inside of most mammals' feet, and in the rear feet of weasels, it is found farther back in the track than the four other toes. This helps differentiate left from right tracks, as well as front from rear. In coyotes, the outer toes, numbers 2 and 5, are farther back and tucked in behind toes 3 and 4, whereas toes 2 and 5 of the bobcat are nearer the top of the track and somewhat alongside toes 3 and 4.

Toe pad shape. What is the shape of the digital pads? Teardrop-shaped toes are a feature of feline tracks, as well as those made by minks and smaller weasels. In fisher tracks, the bulbous toe pads are separate from the metacarpal pads, whereas in raccoon tracks, the cigar-shaped toes tend to be connected to the palm.

Nails. Are claws present? If so, what is their shape, and where do they come from? Are they sharp or blunt? Are they coming straight out from the toes, or do they curve down from the top of the toe? In deep snow, bobcat tracks often show claws, which register in the wall of snow in front of the track on a *higher* plane than the tracks themselves. Domestic dog tracks tend to have large, blunt nails, in comparison with the sharp, thin nails of coyotes. The outer nails of coyotes often register so close to the inner toes that the tracks appear to have only two nails.

Fur. Has fur registered in the track, and if so, where? Certain species, such as rabbits, have completely furred feet, while others have very small

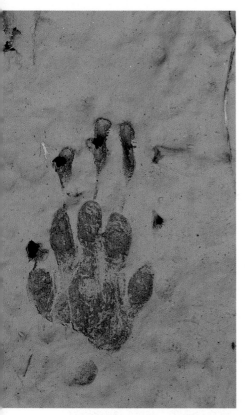

toe pads surrounded by lots of hair. Still others have no hair in between their toes at all, and striped skunk tracks are completely hairless. Hair greatly influences the appearance of tracks. Red fox and kit fox tracks appear blurry in sand, and the toes seem unusually small and spread farther apart than in other canines—all effects of extremely furry feet.

Metacarpal pad shape (palm). In some animals, including canines and felines, the metacarpal pads have fused together to form one palm pad. The shape and size of these pads are important in species identification. Also note the proportion of palm in the overall track—this is a great way to distinguish cat fam-

Left: The front track of a striped skunk with long, prominent nails. (NH) *Below:* In this amazing front track of a kit fox, the furred sole is absolutely clear. Kit foxes may or may not have furred soles, depending on region and individual variation. (CA)

Compare the shape and proportion of the metacarpal pad with the overall track size in the front tracks of this bobcat (left) and coyote. (CA)

ily tracks from dog family tracks. If the top of the palm pad, the anterior edge, has two lobes (termed *bilobate*), and the back of the same pad, the posterior edge, has three, you've found a feline track.

Heel pads. All mammals in the order Rodentia, from mice to beavers (except the porcupine), register two distinct pads behind their metacarpal

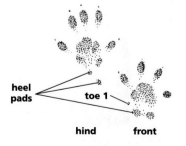

White-throated woodrat tracks.

Study the heel pads of both the front and hind tracks of this coati. (Mexico)

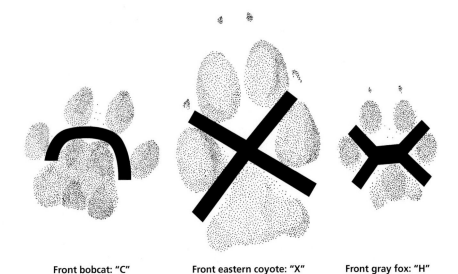

Front bobcat: "C"   Front eastern coyote: "X"   Front gray fox: "H"

pads in front tracks, just as all weasels, ringtails, and bears register at least one pad in complete front tracks. Mammalogists and zoologists are still in the process of studying the function of many of these pads.

Negative space. The spaces between the toes, between the toes and palm pads, and between the individual interdigital pads form shapes that are incredibly useful to track detectives. I often look for an X, H, or C shape to help distinguish feline and canine tracks. The front tracks of gray foxes and domestic dogs tend to show an H, while those of red foxes and coyotes show an X. Look for a C in the front tracks of cats.

Substrate

Substrate is a catchall word for what an animal has stepped in, whether it be sand, mud, snow, or grass. The depth of substrate, which is reflected in the depth of the print, has an enormous influence on the appearance, size, and shape of the track, as well as on how the animal moves. In shallow substrates, such as moist, hard sand, animals move easily and therefore tend to use their natural gaits, but in deep or slippery substrates, animals tend to move in ways that best suit the circumstances, sometimes crawling or floundering. Always note the substrate characteristics as you look at tracks and trails so that you'll be able to predict the substrate's influence on track patterns and gaits.

The conditions of the substrates in which animals step are infinite, creating great challenges for trackers. So if a beginner is taught to rigidly rely on memorizing each experience and track, like a file or archive of frozen images, track identification will be more difficult. It is better to ask yourself diagnostic questions about a track and avoid quickly labeling it with a species name. Ask, Why is this a coyote? not, Is this a coyote? Your questions will help you understand the subtleties of why it is one particular species and not another; those characteristics that remain consistent across substrates and speeds are obviously the most important. With time in the field, you will absorb these nuances without even knowing it. Just continue practicing the three perspectives introduced in the previous chapter, and avoid identifying a track or trail at first glance.

To begin to understand the effects of substrate on an animal trail, start with your own body. Compare your barefoot track on firm ground with one made in several inches of mud. The mud track will likely look larger, and your toes will be spread farther apart. Trackers often use the word *splay* to indicate track spread due to depth of substrate, speed, shifts in weight, change of direction, and so forth. Often, the deeper the substrate, the larger the track—up to a certain point. In very deep substrates, however, the track appears smaller, because the foot has slid into and under a layer of substrate, or the top layers may be so soft that they fold in on the foot as it sinks deeper. Also keep in mind that the depth of the substrate is relative to the size and weight of the creature—what is deep for an ermine is not deep for a black bear.

Now compare the trails you leave when walking in 1 inch of snow and 2 feet of snow (or in dry sand if you don't live in snow country). It is likely that the length between your tracks decreases in deeper snow and

Splayed front and rear tracks of a red fox. (ID)

that the width of the entire trail pattern increases. This is a wonderful lesson in the effects of substrate depth on trail characteristics. Now, let's add another variable: speed.

When looking at trail characteristics in relation to depth of substrate, it may be more accurate to discuss *energy output* rather than *speed*. Let us return to our two trails in snow. If you were to use the same amount of energy in each trail, you would move slower in the deeper conditions. If you wanted to move at the same speed in both trails, it would take a greater energy output to maintain that speed in 2 feet of snow. Consider running in the two snow conditions. Could you run at the same speed in 2 feet of snow as in 1 inch of snow? Would the energy output be equivalent while maintaining a run in these two different conditions? The effects of depth of substrate on an animal trail are dramatic and should be approached with a flexible, imaginative, and patient mind.

A coyote uses a direct register walk to traverse an open expanse in 3 feet (91.4 cm) of snow. (MT)

Just as we adapt to changing conditions, so do other mammals. As you track across varied substrates, you will begin to note gait changes and behaviors in deeper substrates that reflect an awareness of energy efficiency. Trotting in deep snow is difficult if not impossible, so coyotes are often found walking or bounding for short distances in deep snow conditions. Fishers, which tend toward a 3×4 or rotary lope, change to a 2×2 or transverse lope in deep soft conditions and often walk longer distances as well.

If you've ever been hiking with friends in deep snow, it was likely only a short time before you fell into single file, each taking advantage of the person who took the lead and broke the trail. Other mammals also take advantage of each other's trails, making tracking in deep snow difficult. I've followed what appeared to be one coyote, only to find that the trail split into five animals in shallower snow under evergreen canopies; four other coyotes had stepped exactly in the tracks of the first. I've followed a walking coyote and found that it had been stepping in the tracks of a bobcat until it decided that the trail was no longer heading in a convenient direction. Human trails are also utilized. I've returned on my own trails to find that a bobcat had followed my footprints for a while. Bobcats can stretch to match the strides of deer and then cut off and shrink their strides to match a porcupine trail. On one spectacular trail, I found a red fox in a 2×2 lope matching perfectly the fisher trail he followed.

Substrates also change over time due to weather. This can be truly appreciated only in the field. Watch and be aware of how things change over time. Learning to identify fresh tracks is a start, but begin to challenge yourself with older tracks and trails. *Tom Brown's Field Guide to Nature Observation and Tracking* offers some excellent exercises to practice aging. My favorite is "The Wisdom of the Marks."

This grizzly established runs to move about in search of food when snow began to accumulate. This trail has been used many times, but most recently, the bear has moved away from the camera. (MT)

Visualization

Sue Mansfield, tracker and bear enthusiast, invited me out to see some bear trails she'd discovered in the frozen surface of a beaver pond, preserved as those made in wet cement. We arrived on the scene, and it was just as she'd told me: A mature sow and cub had crossed the slushy surface of the pond as the temperatures dropped, and their movements from the week before were held in suspension, awaiting a thaw.

As I interpreted the trail, the bears had come from the north, bumbling downhill and out onto the wetland, pulling at winterberries as they passed through the shrubby border. The cub was soon off exploring on its own, still within sight of its mother. They progressed out over deeper and more open water. The cub went straight across, even daring to venture toward the open water near the beaver dam itself. The sow tried to follow, picking up her pace a bit, but on approaching the dam, she suddenly slipped and, in a flurry of legs and feet, danced to regain her balance and keep from landing

A black bear trail frozen into a beaver pond's surface. After nearly falling, this sow slowly moved off the slippery ice in an understep walk. (NH)

on her head. *The thought of an experienced sow caught break-dancing as she tried to keep up with junior was too much for me, and I chuckled. Sue asked why, and I explained my interpretation of the trail.*

Having managed to stay upright, the bear slowly moved off the ice, avoiding the dam altogether. She placed each foot very carefully, leaving the print of a perfect understep walk, which also spread her weight on the thinner ice. Soon she was on firmer ground and was rejoined by junior as she ascended the hill beyond.

An understanding of gaits and track patterns opens the door to interpreting animal behaviors. Each time I follow a trail, I attempt to visualize the animal moving before me, rather than following the prints on the ground. The tracks help me do this, and so do the patterns. I also draw on my cumulative knowledge of the animal gained from reading, past tracking, and discussions with others. And I use any visual experience I've had with that particular species, whether personal encounters or clips from National Geographic specials. This combination of resources is what I need to fully envision a species moving before me, as well as lots of practice.

More than visualizing the animal, it is my goal to become the animal. Louis Liebenberg, who studies tracking with the Kalahari Bushmen, writes in his book *The Art of Tracking,* "To interpret tracks and signs trackers must project themselves into the position of the animal in order to create a hypothetical explanation of what the animal was doing. Tracking is not strictly empirical, since it also involves the tracker's imagination." And in *Field Guide to the Animal Tracks of Southern Africa,* he states, "To be able to anticipate and predict the movements of an animal, trackers must know the animal and its environment so well that they can identify themselves with that animal. They must be able to visualize how that animal was moving around, and place themselves in its position." Although following and identifying tracks are crucial—as well as recognizing patterns and learning the corresponding vocabulary—visualization and imagination play greater roles in advanced levels of tracking. !Ngate Xgamzebe, a traditional Bushman tracker, teaches us, "When you track an animal, you must become the animal . . . you jump when the track shows it jumps!"

Once I led a workshop in southern New Hampshire, where we followed a black bear trail in the first snow. At one point, he broke a branch of a downed snag and began running in tight circles at full speed. He rolled on his back and slid down a small hill, where he flipped on his side; the shape of the stick was impressed with his head in the snow. He then got up, dropped the stick, and resumed his walk in the woods. To have missed that glimpse inside a bear's life—the burst of play while alone in the woods—would have been to miss a joyful experience. Track pattern interpretation brings trails to life.

Can you visualize this female cougar and her three kittens, one of whom is filled with energy, gliding across this open area and disappearing into the horizon? (ID)

Evolution and Energy Efficiency

Energy efficiency is a tremendously important variable in interpreting trails, as well as in predicting how a given animal will move in a given depth of substrate. Generally, the slower an animal moves, the less energy expenditure required, but it's a bit more complicated than this. Although it is true that a walking weasel is saving more energy than a galloping weasel, we should not expect weasels to walk whenever possible. All mammals have evolved in ways that balance energy intake (food collection) and energy output (the ground covered to locate and/or

Visual Thinking

One way to develop visualization skills that allows you to become the animal is to switch from linear thinking to visual thinking. For example, rather than thinking to myself, "I left my keys on the kitchen table," I actually see in my mind's eye a picture of my keys on the kitchen table. Here are some suggestions for becoming a more visual thinker, fostering imagination, and "seeing" and "feeling" how animals move.

• Practice storytelling—but visualize the story like a movie playing in your imagination, and then voice what you are watching.

• Study something, and then turn away and draw it from memory. I grew up playing a game based on this simple exercise. My mother would lay out a number of items on a tray, my friends and I would take 10 seconds or so to look at everything, and then she would take them away. We would try to list all the things on the tray. It's even better to reconstruct what you saw with rough sketches, which forces you to include the items' relationships to one another.

• Watch animals as often as possible—however briefly—and then replay the movements in your mind over and over again, memorizing the gait for future reference. Rent videos, watch nature specials, and visit zoos and sanctuaries—anything that provides visual ammunition.

• Read everything you can find on an animal's natural history and behavior. The more you know about an animal, the easier it is to see it in your imagination.

• Practice moving like an animal—alone, in a group, on two legs or four. This is especially useful in sand, where you can study the track patterns left behind.

• Role-play trails and how signs were created. Take an extra three seconds each time you think you've successfully interpreted a trail to step back and envision the animal creating the sign (e.g., trotting, digging, or biting a tree).

• Take a course in American Sign Language, a language based in space. It will completely alter the way you think.

pursue that food). Each animal species also has a natural rhythm, a gait that best expresses the harmony between energy intake and output for the particular niche inhabited by that animal. For example, weasels have a very high metabolism, an insatiable appetite that fulfills their energy needs, and a gait preference that propels them over the ground quickly and carries them long distances. A weasel that walks too often may save a bit of energy, but it is denying that which makes it a weasel, and it will die of starvation in the long run. Animals must submit to their natural rhythms to be truly energy efficient.

Now let's compare the bobcat and the coyote. Bobcats *walk*. Cats move through the forest slowly and stealthily, pausing and sitting frequently to study their environment, hoping to see or sense potential prey before they themselves are noticed. They may even lay up and wait for prey to come to them. They do not generally cover large distances while hunting. When a prey animal is chosen, they stalk it and then, when close enough, explode with speed that allows them to catch their intended victim before it is aware of them or before it can escape. Their sheathed claws come out and curve down, close in front of the toes—designed to hold their prey.

Now consider the coyote, which hunts in a very different manner. Coyotes *trot* through the woods, hoping to catch the smell, sound, or sight of potential prey or to startle something into fleeing before them. Coyotes occasionally stalk, and they even eat tremendous amounts of fruit, which doesn't move at all. But in general, coyotes cruise long distances through the woods, allowing scents and sounds to betray the presence of prey species. When opportunities appear, coyotes run their intended prey down, gripping it and pulling it down with their teeth. Their claws, which are never sheathed, project straight out from their toes and aid in traction while running.

These two very different examples of how animals earn a living in the woods are the result of different adaptations to different niches of the same environment. These different lifestyles and strategies for survival explain the differences in their natural rhythms: Bobcats tend to walk, and coyotes tend to trot. But can coyotes walk? Of course. Can bobcats trot? Yes. Every animal is capable of a variety of gaits and speeds, but each animal has one or two gaits that are most energy efficient for it, and that is what it uses the majority of the time.

Gait Analysis

A *gait* describes the way an animal moves; it is *not* a description of a specific track pattern. Each gait has numerous track patterns, depending on the speed and behavior of the animal, as well as the physiology of the species.

Language often complicates matters, with trackers around the world using different words to describe the same thing. This book uses the widely accepted vocabulary coined by Eadweard Muybridge many years ago to describe how animals move. Muybridge began his intensive study and photography of animal gaits when former California governor Leland Stanford asked for his help in settling a wager: whether all four feet of the horse are airborne in midgallop. His terminology provides

Walking trail of a mule deer. (TX)

visual information about how an animal moves, which is crucial in envisioning and becoming that animal in advanced levels of tracking.

I separate all gaits into two large categories: (1) those with continuous, consistent rhythms, created by keeping the spine straight, with most of the motion in the legs, and (2) those with a broken but consistent rhythm, moving in such a way that the whole body is flexed, and motion results from the spine and legs moving together. Animals may move any way they wish, and they certainly will move on occasion in ways that are not described below. However, for the most part, wild mammals of North America stalk, hunt, chase, and hide using the gaits described here.

Gaits with an Unbroken, Consistent Rhythm
Walking

Walking is a slow gait in which each foot moves independently, and at no point during the cycle of footfalls does the animal lose contact with the ground. Arbitrarily beginning with the right rear foot, that leg moves forward, and just before touching down, the right front foot lifts up and moves forward. For a moment, both feet are off the ground, and then the right rear touches down. The right front continues forward and then

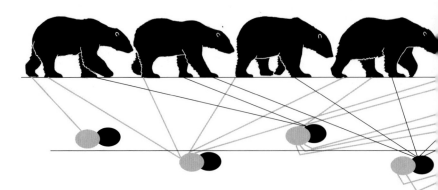

touches down. The left rear moves forward, and just before it touches down, the left front picks up and moves forward. For a second time in the cycle of footfalls, there are only two feet in contact with the ground, and then the left rear touches down. The left front continues forward and then touches down. Immediately the cycle begins again, and the right rear picks up and moves forward. Musically, this would sound like 1, 2, 3, 4, 1, 2, 3, 4, 1, 2, 3, 4 . . . , where each number is an independent footfall. Note that the rhythm is continuous, and there is no break.

The rear foot may land in any relation to the front track and still be considered a walk. Because the front foot picks up before the rear one touches down, the rear may land exactly where the front had been, called a *direct register,* or it may even touch down beyond where the front had been, called an *overstep.*

A good portion of time during each cycle of footfalls, only one leg is lifted from the ground; the other three maintain contact with the ground and support the animal while it is in motion. These three legs act like the legs of a tripod—a very sturdy arrangement—efficiently balancing heavy objects, including wide animals with short legs.

Walking is common among almost all animals. For many wide-bodied animals, such as beavers and bears, it is their natural rhythm, as it is for deer, moose, and members of the cat family. Other species walk when exploring or while traveling in deep substrates, such as snow, to save energy.

A variation of the walk is the *stalk.* In the stalk, only one limb moves at a time, but the order is the same as for the walk. The right rear moves forward and touches down; the right front moves forward and touches down; then the left rear, followed by the left front. The resulting trail is often an *understep* walk, which means that the rear tracks in each pair register behind the front tracks.

There are numerous variables to consider when interpreting speed from a trail and track pattern, but one general rule

● = Front

● = Hind

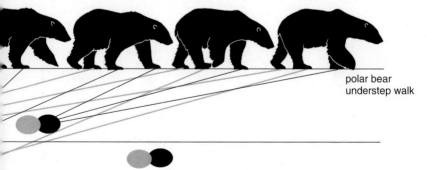

polar bear
understep walk

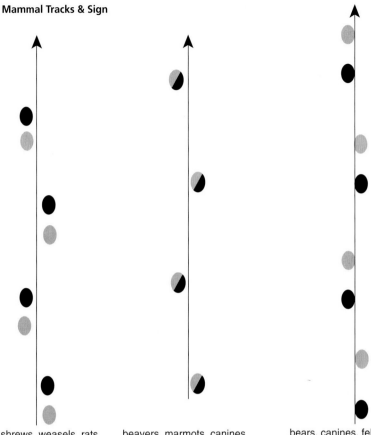

voles, shrews, weasels, rats, woodrats, stalking carnivores, opossums, polar bears

Understep Walk

beavers, marmots, canines, felines, ringtails, bears, skunks, opossums, porcupines, muskrats

Direct Register Walk

bears, canines, felines, muskrats, coatis, skunks, porcupines

Overstep Walk

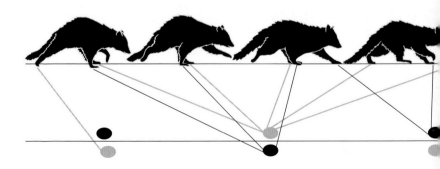

holds true for all walking gaits: As an animal walks faster, its rear track moves over and beyond the front track in each pair. Therefore, an understep walk (rear track behind the front track) is probably a slower gait than a direct registering walk (rear track on top of the front track), and both are likely slower than an overstep walk (rear track beyond the front track). A fast walk is also called an *amble*. Remember, there are other variables to consider as well, such as depth of substrate and physiology of the specific animal. But as a general rule, speed can be inferred by considering the placement of the rear foot in relation to the front.

There are several variations of the walk that add some confusion. For example, raccoons prefer to walk in such a way that the front and hind legs on one side of the body move

Typical overstep walk of a bobcat. (MA)

nearly simultaneously. The resulting track pattern is one in which the tracks are paired—a front and the opposite side's rear—and they flip-flop from one pair to the next. That is the front sits on the left side in the first set, and on the right side in the second (see the illustrations). However, moving the legs nearly simultaneously is not enough to create such a radi-

● = Front

● = Hind

cally different track pattern. Walker Korby and I have discussed this at length, and he believes that the animals also shift their weight to the hind legs. When I walk this way, it shortens my stride and seems to create similar track patterns, especially when I stretch my arms to their fullest potential.

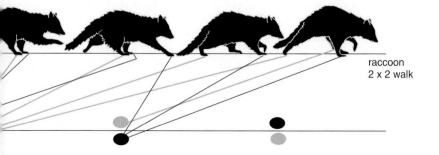

raccoon
2 x 2 walk

Slow, raccoon-like walk of a large brown bear. (AK)

Northern raccoon. Slow 2x2 walk.

This variation of the walk can also be altered by adding or subtracting speed. Look at each pair of tracks and note whether the rear track registers ahead of, on the same plane as, or behind the opposite front track, thus giving you an indication of speed in the same way as discussed for typical walking gaits. Raccoons use all three variations. Brown bears and occasionally black are partial to the slowest version, where the hind tracks register behind the opposite fronts. Coatis may use any of the three, and opossums occasionally create similar track patterns.

I've watched raccoons creating the fastest version of this walking gait, with the legs moving nearly simultaneously. The animal stretches forward so far with its front and hind feet that it nearly becomes airborne

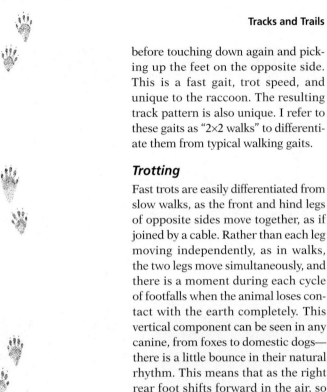

Northern raccoon. Fast 2x2 walk.

before touching down again and picking up the feet on the opposite side. This is a fast gait, trot speed, and unique to the raccoon. The resulting track pattern is also unique. I refer to these gaits as "2×2 walks" to differentiate them from typical walking gaits.

Trotting

Fast trots are easily differentiated from slow walks, as the front and hind legs of opposite sides move together, as if joined by a cable. Rather than each leg moving independently, as in walks, the two legs move simultaneously, and there is a moment during each cycle of footfalls when the animal loses contact with the earth completely. This vertical component can be seen in any canine, from foxes to domestic dogs—there is a little bounce in their natural rhythm. This means that as the right rear foot shifts forward in the air, so does the left front. Just before the right rear and left front are placed down, the right front and left rear feet push off, maintaining forward momentum. Then the right rear and left front make contact with the ground again, and the cycle begins again. Musically, the beat is a continuous, unbroken 1, 2, 1, 2, 1, 2 . . . , where each number is two diagonally placed feet landing simultaneously.

The natural rhythm of canines, voles, and short-tailed shrews is the trot. Many other species also use trots as a travel gait, from woodchucks to black bears to members of the cat family, and bighorn sheep tend to trot on flat ground.

Direct register trots, in which rear tracks are superimposed on the front tracks of the same side, are common in many species. Rear tracks land exactly on the recently made front prints, as the front foot and opposite rear pick up just before the alternate pair touches down. The

● = Front

● = Hind

◗ = Hind atop Front Track
(direct register)

forward momentum of the animal carries the rear foot directly over the front track. This is commonly seen when trailing canines, woodchucks, voles, short-tailed shrews, and many ungulates.

As with walking, speed can be inferred by the position of the rear foot in relation to the front. Direct register trots are theoretically slower than overstep trots, in which the rear tracks in a given pair register beyond the front tracks. Overstep trots are achieved by species in different ways. The rear foot can move forward only so far before it collides with the front foot on the same side. The two most common overstep trot patterns clearly show how mammals overcome this obstacle. Canines tend toward the *side trot*, where they continue to move in a trot, but the entire body is angled (also referred to as a *crab*), with the rear end kicked out to one side. In this way, the rears pass to one side of the fronts to stretch out farther. All the front tracks appear on one side of the trail, and all the rears, beyond the fronts, appear on the other side of the trail.

Direct register trot of a mule deer. (TX)

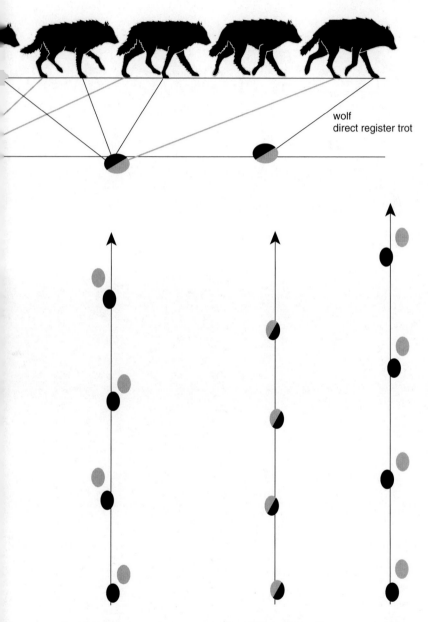

wolf
direct register trot

canines, lynx, shrews, voles,
elk, moose, caribou

canines, felines, deer, elk,
moose, short-tailed shrews,
voles, fishers

canines

Straddle Trot

Direct Register Trot

Side Trot

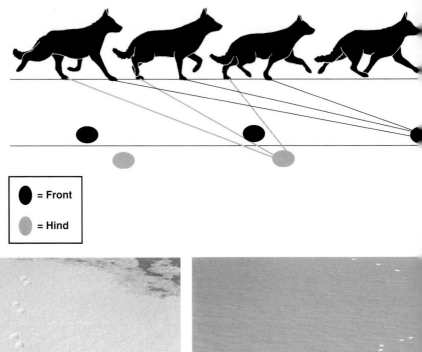

● = Front

● = Hind

Left: A red fox's side trot. (NH) *Right:* Straddle trot of a red fox. (MN)

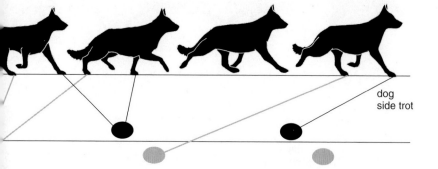

dog
side trot

The Speed of a Red Fox

Inspired by the work of J. D. Henry with red foxes in the Canadian
Rockies, I sought to walk with a wild fox where I lived. My first
opportunity came while biking one morning on a back road in the
Adirondacks. I came across a red fox feeding on a road-killed mammal—what appeared to be a fisher. The fox noticed me and pulled
his prize off the road into some spruce trees, but still within view.
There he continued to feed, using his back carnassial teeth to shear
off manageable chunks and swallowing vigorously. I walked in quite
close, and eventually the fox gathered what remained of the carcass
and trotted off into the woods. I followed closely, and the fox
stopped to look at me several times. Eventually, he trotted through
someone's yard—right in front of the bay window where the family
was eating breakfast. I did not follow.

I returned to the spot the next day and encountered the fox on
the road. Ditching my bike, I followed him at a distance. He paused
once to look over his shoulder at me. I froze, and then he continued, never acknowledging me again during the several hours we
spent together. He trotted silently along the pavement, using his
ears to locate voles and other small mammals in the tall grasses
that lined the road. From time to time he stopped, located the prey,
and pounced. He was successful more often than not and gulped
down a number of voles.

The real lesson was in the speed of this fox, which trotted almost
continuously, with occasional walking steps when adjusting and
preparing for a spring. I could not keep up by walking and had to
jog slowly to keep the distance between us constant. This can easily
be studied with a leashed dog. A trotting dog pulls and jerks the
leash, but when a dog walks, it stays at its master's side.

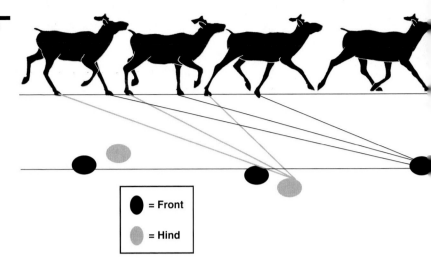

● = Front

● = Hind

Lessons from a Bobcat

Differentiating walks from trots can be challenging. With this in mind, I journaled the trails of a bobcat I found several years ago on a steep hill near my home.

A recent snowstorm had changed to ice and freezing rain just before the temperatures plummeted, allowing a thick crust to form and lock in 2 feet of snow beneath its surface. Nothing but moose and occasionally a deer and myself left visible tracks on that hill for nearly a week, until an inch of fresh powder fell one afternoon and covered everything.

The unique weather conditions and a willing bobcat provided a wondrous opportunity. I came across her trail early the next day and quickly backtracked her to her bed, where she'd waited out the storm. There were few obstacles on the thick crust above the forest floor—no logs or tangles of young saplings—and she moved with little restriction. The pitted crust gave remarkably good traction, and the inch of snow barely influenced her movement.

Following her downhill, I watched as she moved from a direct register walk to an overstep walk and then for a short while to a direct register trot, before returning to a fast overstep walk and finally a slower direct register walk. I took comparison measurements and sketches all the way, hoping that they would illustrate the differences between her walks and trots.

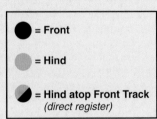

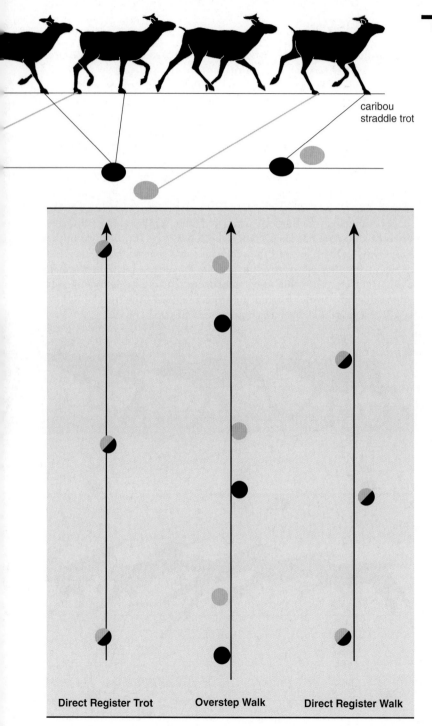

caribou
straddle trot

57

Direct Register Trot   **Overstep Walk**   **Direct Register Walk**

This unique track pattern is easy to find along coyote, wolf, and red fox trails; gray foxes very rarely side trot.

The second common option is to kick the rear legs out to either side of the fronts, termed a *straddle trot*. All the canines use this gait, but usually only for short sections of trail, and most often in transition from a direct registering trot to a side trot. However, gray foxes use this gait very often, as do caribou, moose, mule deer, and several shrew species. There is also a third overstep trot that involves a longer air time, allowing the rear feet to glide over the front tracks with forward momentum, as seen in lizards and occasionally other animals. This last option is rare in mammals.

According to my definition, turtles and other reptiles and amphibians do not trot (some lizards are an exception). Their limbs move in the same way—a front leg and the opposite side's rear leg move simultaneously—but they never leave the ground. I'd suggest the term *diagonal walk* to differentiate this movement from trotting. This is why it is impossible for a turtle to completely direct register—the right front foot is still on the ground when the right rear comes up behind.

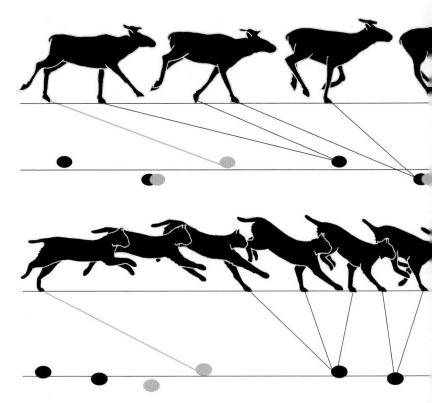

Gaits with Broken Rhythms

Loping and Galloping

Lopes and gallops are very similar and are the fastest gaits for animals. Each foot lands independently of the others, as in walks, but in rapid succession. During both gaits, the animal becomes momentarily airborne, just after pushing off with the front legs. But during gallops, there is a second point when the animal is in the air, just after pushing off with the rear legs. It is difficult to catch this second, short flight when watching an animal move, and it is difficult to decipher when interpreting track patterns on the ground.

There are two variations on the order in which the feet touch the ground during lopes and gallops. If they land in a circular fashion—left front, right front, right rear, left rear—it is a *rotary* lope or gallop. If the order cuts across the body—left front, right front, left rear, right rear—it is called a *transverse* lope or gallop. Musically, there is a four-beat as each foot falls independently, followed by a pause: 1, 2, 3, 4, pause, 1, 2, 3, 4,

● = Front

● = Hind

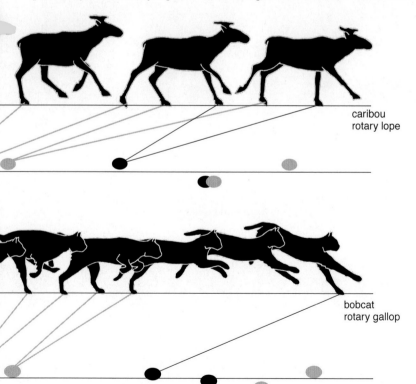

caribou
rotary lope

bobcat
rotary gallop

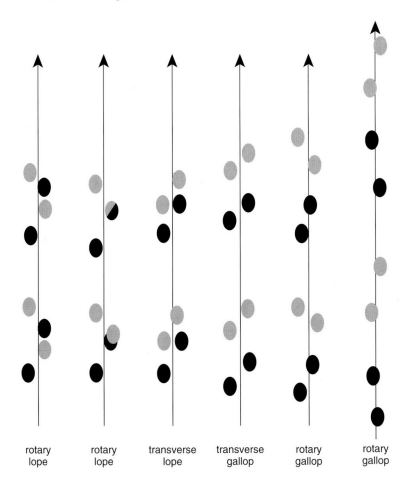

| rotary lope | rotary lope | transverse lope | transverse gallop | rotary gallop | rotary gallop |

Lopes and Gallops

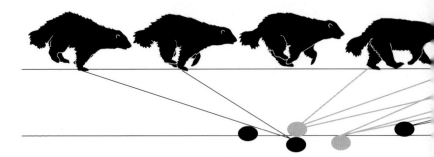

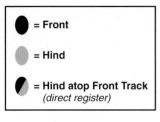

pause, 1, 2, 3, 4 . . . This is not a continuous rhythm like that found in walks and trots.

When looking at track patterns on the ground, a lope typically becomes a gallop when both rear feet land beyond both front feet. If the order of tracks on the ground in a single set of four is front, rear, front, rear, it is a lope. If the order is front, front, rear, rear, it is a gallop.

Similar to walks and trots, the placement of the rear track in relation to the front track is a factor in speed interpretation. In this case, consider how the pair of front tracks is placed in relation to the pair of rear tracks. As the pair of rear tracks moves beyond the pair of front tracks, this indicates a faster lope or gallop. Also note the distance between the groups of four tracks. In general, the greater the length spanned by the four tracks in a series and the shorter the distance between groups of four tracks, called the *stride*, the faster the animal is moving. At all-out speeds, some mammals leave track patterns that casually look like trots—in that the tracks are placed regularly and in a straight line. But each mark is a single track, and careful measurements can differentiate between the two.

Two particular lopes are characteristic of the weasel family: the 3×4 lope and the 2×2 lope. The 3×4 lope is a rotary lope, in which a front and rear foot on the same side of the body may land in the same space, giving the impression of only three tracks in a set rather than four. Milton Hildebrand's research showed that weasels still have a front foot on the ground when the first rear foot touches down; therefore, this gait is a true lope.

The 2×2 lope is a transverse lope, although other than the order of footfalls, the body mechanics are similar to those of a 3×4 lope. In the essay "Lessons from a Fisher," I discuss watching a fisher up close, and though he switched from a 3×4 to a 2×2 lope right before my eyes, it wasn't apparent until I looked at the trail. The same fluid arcing motion is used for both gaits. What is unique about the 2×2 lope is that the front feet pick up and the rear feet land exactly where the fronts had been, creating a trail of

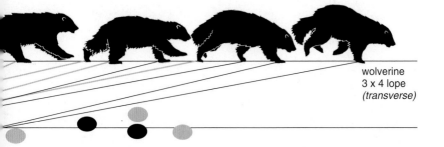

wolverine
3 x 4 lope
(transverse)

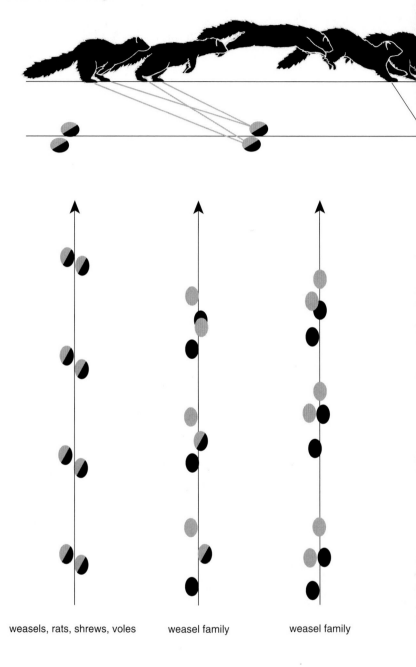

weasels, rats, shrews, voles

weasel family

weasel family

2 x 2 Lope *(Transverse)*   **3 x 4 Lope** *(Rotary)*   **3 x 4 Lope** *(Transverse)*

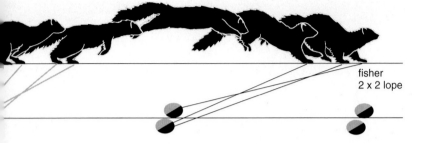

fisher
2 x 2 lope

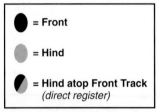

● = **Front**

● = **Hind**

◗ = **Hind atop Front Track**
(direct register)

An otter lopes across the expanse along a receding lake surface. (MT)

paired tracks in which each set of two is actually a set of four—the front feet registering first, and the rear feet registering directly on top of them. Meadow voles and smaller shrews use this gait in deep snow. Based on Hildebrand's research on the 3×4 lope, I am assuming that a front foot is still in contact with the ground when the first rear foot touches down. If not, then technically, this gait would be a gallop.

Hopping and Bounding

The hopping and bounding gaits of rabbits and many rodents are differentiated from lopes and gallops, in that the rear feet land and push off simultaneously, or nearly so. This is evident in the trail, as the rear tracks appear parallel to each other. Any local park should present ample opportunities to study squirrels using these gaits. Hops are similar to lopes, in that there is one moment when the animal is airborne during each cycle of footfalls, just after the rear feet push off. Bounds parallel gallops, in that

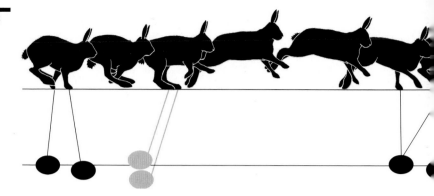

= Front

= Hind

there are two times when the animal is airborne during each cycle of footfalls, first after the front feet push off, and again after the rear feet push off.

The difference between hop and bound track patterns is the relationship between the rear and front tracks. When hopping, the front feet of an animal land either together or one after the other, followed by the rear feet touching down together behind the front feet. Then the front feet pick up, followed by a push and liftoff from the rear feet. The animal is airborne until the front feet touch down again, and the cycle repeats. Hopping is less common than bounding, but it can be observed in short-tailed shrews, large voles, muskrats, and southern flying squirrels.

Hopping and bounding begin in the same way, with the front feet landing either as a pair or one after the other, but in bounds, the rear feet move forward, beyond, and to either side of the front feet. The front feet pick up as the rear feet pass to the outside, and there is a moment when the animal loses contact with the ground before the rears come down and push off again. This push-off is followed by a second moment in the air, before the front feet touch down and the cycle begins again. Numerous species bound, including squirrels, chipmunks, and cottontails.

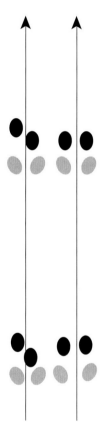

large voles, short-tailed shrews, muskrats

southern flying squirrels, other squirrels

Hop Variations

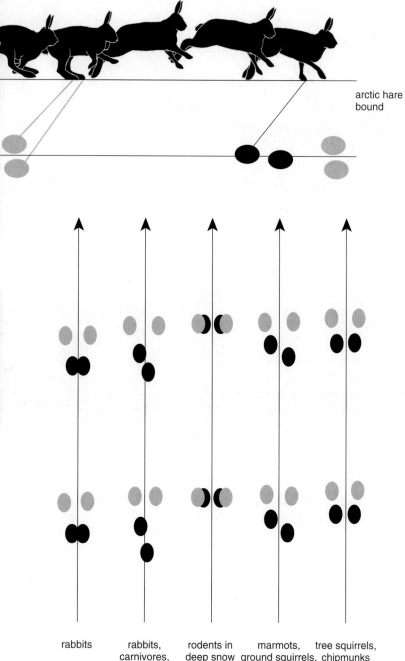

arctic hare
bound

rabbits

rabbits,
carnivores,
ungulates

rodents in
deep snow

marmots,
ground squirrels,
chipmunks, red
squirrels

tree squirrels,
chipmunks

Bound Variations

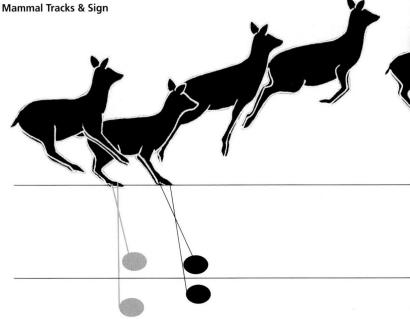

Pronk

An unusual gait used by mule deer, pronghorn, elk and occasionally other mammals is the *pronk*. In this bouncing gait, an
animal pushes off with all four feet at the same time and then
lands on all four feet simultaneously. Mammals moving in this

● = Front

● = Hind

way appear to be using pogo sticks. Leonard Lee Rue writes that a possible benefit of this gait may be that the animal can radically change direction whenever touching down, responding to external stimuli quickly.

Bipedal Motion

Kangaroo rats, and occasionally other species, require us to include several gaits usually used to describe bird movements: the bipedal hop and
the bipedal skip. These gaits are used when mammals move on their
hind legs only and do not touch down with the front feet at all.

Bipedal Hopping

Both hopping and skipping involve trails in which the hind tracks are
paired, rather than falling independently at regular intervals, as in the
previously described gaits. In hopping trails, paired hind tracks appear
right next to each other, or nearly so. This pattern is possible because
both hind feet hit the ground simultaneously. Technically, the feet would
truly hit simultaneously only if they were placed exactly next to each
other or the animal were coming straight down. However, for our purposes, *simultaneously* means at the same time or nearly so.

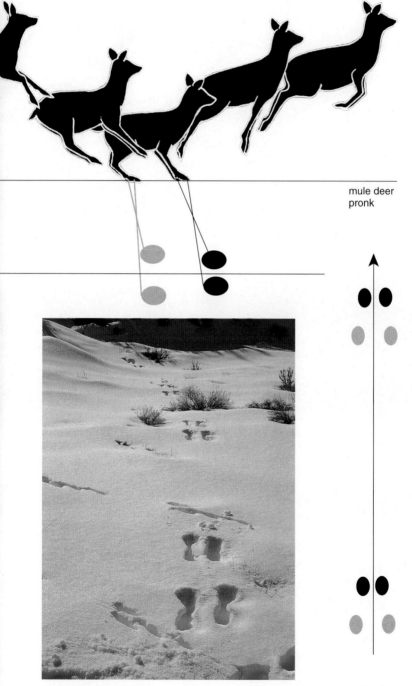

mule deer
pronk

A mule deer's pronk. (ID)

Pronk

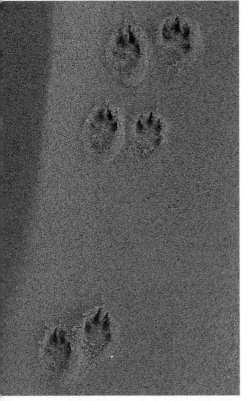

= Hind

Bipedal Skipping

In skipping trails, tracks are also paired, but each hind foot lands completely independently of the other. Looking at the trail pattern, a hop becomes a skip when one hind track registers completely in front of the other hind track. When a kangaroo rat moves in this way, it stays very low to the ground and takes very long strides. Hind feet rotate forward, one foot strikes down, and as the body moves forward over this foot, the second foot touches down. The momentum continues, propelling the body forward over the second foot while the first foot lifts up behind the animal. Continuing forward, the second foot joins the first behind the animal and lifts off, and together they rotate forward for another cycle. Momentum is more horizontal, and very little energy is wasted with vertical rise.

Bipedal hopping trail of a Gulf Coast kangaroo rat. (TX)

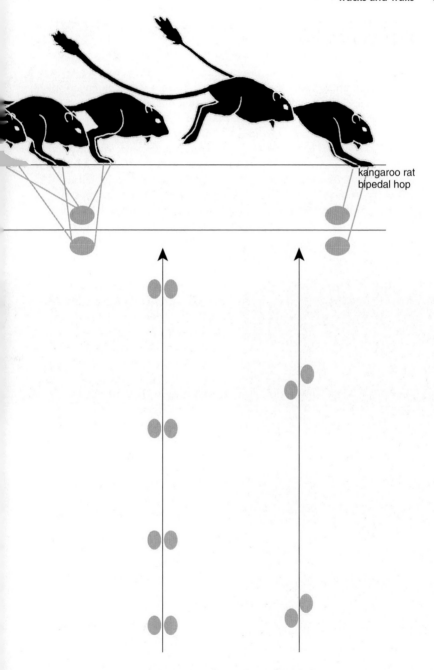

kangaroo rat
bipedal hop

Bipedal Hop   **Bipedal Skip**

Interpretation

Each time an animal shifts from its natural rhythm, there is a reason, and thus an opportunity for us to ask why. Certain gaits can be associated with specific moods, behaviors, or intentions. This is why journaling the three perspectives is so important. You begin to associate certain gaits and track patterns with specific environmental conditions. You'll know if the animal is out in the open, and potentially uncomfortable, or in deep cover, possibly hunting. And if you really get to know an area and its inhabitants, you may be able to determine whether an animal is out of its usual territory or you've discovered a transient or trespasser.

Successful interpretation of track patterns comes with experience and patience. I suggest that you journal every gait for a species and begin to assign possible interpretations or behaviors to each track pattern. Be flexible in your thinking, and remember that you are bound to be wrong as often as you are right, at least in the beginning. The more natural history information you have about a species and the more time you spend trailing that particular animal, the better prepared you are for this process. Regardless of experience, there will always be trails that perplex and confound you. Accept the fact that tracking is not a perfect science but a lifetime of learning.

Use yourself as an example to better grasp the approach to trail interpretation. You have your typical walking gait and speed and resulting track pattern. Should you be late for work or focused on a specific destination, your pace and track pattern would change. If you were hungry and stood in the midst of five great restaurants, you'd likely wander a bit and then move with determination once you'd decided where to dine. You'd jump if you were scared and run if your life were threatened. The list of possibilities

Typical overstep walking trail of a coyote. Note that the hind tracks wander from the median line of travel far more than the front tracks do. (AK)

Coyote Trails and Possible Interpretations

Understep walk. *Extreme rest:* I have found this pattern around dens, especially when a coyote shifts from one bedding spot to another. *Extreme attention/fear:* This is also the gait used when stalking prey very slowly—like a cat. It could also be used to sneak away if the coyote felt at great risk and wanted to avoid detection. *Exhaustion.*

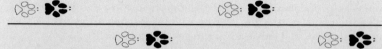

Direct register walk. This gait is more often a reflection of substrate or grade rather than mood or behavior. In deep substrates, coyotes direct register walk when traveling. However, Jon Young points out that in specific locales, coyotes use this gait to travel about. He explains that the potential dangers in an environment, such as a high density of cougars, influence when, where, and how coyotes move.

Overstep walk. This is the typical walking gait for canines. *Exploration:* Often coyotes shift from a trot to a walk when investigating and pinpointing an odor they cross in the woods. They'll walk around scenting out apples buried in early snow, investigating squirrel activity, and checking another coyote's scent post. *Ease:* Coyotes walk when they feel relatively safe, often in the company of others or in areas with good visibility and where scents carry far and well. They feel most at ease in the heart of their own territory. *Scenting and communication:* Coyotes may shift to a walk in order to scent, before moving on. A great deal of social exchange is done while walking, but many gaits are used. Movement in the immediate area of dens is usually done in a walk. *Well fed:* A coyote who is not actively hunting may walk. *Caution:* A cautious coyote walks.

Understep trot. This is a rare gait. I have seen this pattern as a result of playing with others—like a slow prance.

Direct register trot. This is the natural rhythm of the coyote. *Hunting and patrolling:* Coyotes move through their range in a trot. *Awareness:* Coyotes are actively investigating their surroundings in this gait. *Comfort:*

(continued on page 72)

Although the animal is keenly aware, this gait shows little stress or discomfort. This is the usual gait for moving about the home range.

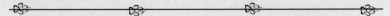

Overstep trot. This is an uncommon gait for coyotes. *Dominance:* I have seen this gait used in pack communication on several occasions. I believe that the vertical "hop" of this gait may be involved in a visual communication of dominance. *Stress:* Dan Gardogui noted this gait and track pattern in females trying to keep up with the insatiable appetites of their maturing pups, and in coyotes skirting wolf territories.

Straddle trot. In coyotes, this is a transition gait found only in short sections of trail. However, it shows that the animal is not alarmed or reacting to something in its environment, in which case a transition gait would be skipped altogether.

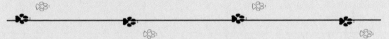

Side trot. *Travel mode:* This gait may indicate that a coyote has a destination in mind and has picked up the pace slightly. It is often seen on easier travel routes, such as beaches, roads, and trail systems. *Increased awareness:* This gait is often used when coyotes are exposed and away from cover, or between areas of cover, but not yet in full alarm. Trespassing coyotes might also pick up their pace when moving through another pack's territory.

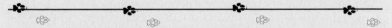

Extended direct register trot. *Eager/excited:* John McCarter reported finding this gait when coyotes had just found a carcass or a moose dying of brain worm, or some other bonanza. The extended trot pattern looks very much like the standard direct register trot, but the strides are nearly twice as long, often around 40 inches.

Slow lope. *Play and communication:* The "rocking horse" lope uses tremendous energy and is often found in coyote interactions. Sticks are sometimes picked up and carried for short distances in this gait. Motion is often erratic and circular. *Hunting in tall grass:* Jon Young has watched coyotes use this gait while hunting cottontails in high grass. *Safety:* A coyote using the gait is not alarmed.

Lope. *Discomfort and fear:* The coyote has picked up the pace to move out of the area for some reason. A coyote may lope when it is exposed between areas of cover or when it is trespassing. *Transition:* A coyote that is not in immediate peril but still alarmed may transition from a trot to a lope to a gallop. *Play/excitement:* Often, faster gaits in mammal species show fear, but the same gaits can be interpreted in the opposite way. Playing coyotes lope, as do coyotes that are eager and excited—a similar interpretation to the extended trot. *Hunting:* Coyotes sometimes run prey to exhaustion, although this is more likely done at a gallop.

Bound. *Alarm and fear:* Frightened coyotes use this gait to move from stationary or a slow gait to full speed. *Chasing:* This coyote has just taken up pursuit of prey, a trespasser, or a playmate. *Deep substrates:* Bounds are also used to increase the speed of travel in deep snow—in this case, all four tracks are made in the same hole.

Gallop. *Fear:* Coyotes run from what they fear most. *Hunting:* Coyotes run down their prey, twisting and turning in pursuit. There is less time between footfalls than in the stretch gallop, allowing the coyote to react quickly to changes in direction.

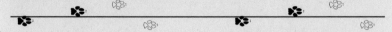

Stretch gallop. *Extreme fear:* This coyote has lowered its awareness of the area in exchange for putting distance between itself and a sound, predator, or location as fast as possible. *Hunting:* A coyote stretches fully and invests everything to capture prey, which in turn replenishes its energy supply. Most often, prey twist and turn when closely pursued, so it is difficult to maintain the highest speed through turns; look for regular gallops as the coyote closes in.

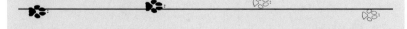

Patterns created by rolling, lunging, attacking, holding onto prey, or other specific behaviors, as well as the various interpretations of coyotes in varied habitats and conditions across North America must be learned in the field and with experience.

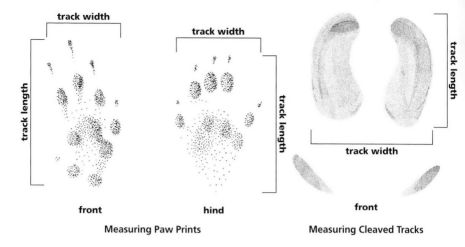

track width

track length

front

track width

track length

hind

Measuring Paw Prints

track length

track width

front

Measuring Cleaved Tracks

goes on and on. Why wouldn't all these changes be apparent in wild animal trails? The answer, of course, is that they are.

Base your initial journals on the coyote trails provided below, assuming that the natural rhythm for your animal would be interpreted in the same way as the natural rhythm of the coyote, regardless of whether they are different gaits. Then work your way from there. These interpretations are only a starting point; add your own, and change what feels wrong for your area. Before you know it, you'll be interpreting behaviors from track patterns, in addition to identifying the animal.

There are also specific track patterns that are easily interpreted. Deer "point" to food, many mammals "t-up" when they pause (see page 147), and animals often sit down during

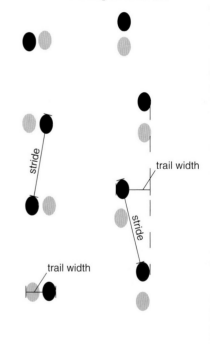

stride

trail width

stride

trail width

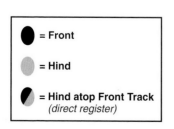

● = Front

● = Hind

◗ = Hind atop Front Track
(direct register)

2 x 2 Walks   **Understep Walks**

the day. You'll find essays on specific track patterns and behaviors throughout the Species Accounts portion of this chapter, as well as other helpful hints.

Measuring Tracks and Trails

A ruler is a wonderful tool to help you build confidence in your perceptive and intuitive skills. Measurements aid in identification and are useful for scientific documentation of species in your area; they can also be shared in research or used to compare species characteristics. Tape

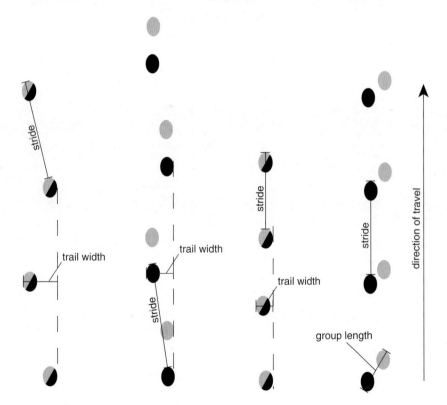

Direct Register Walks   **Overstep Walks**   **Direct Register Trots**   **Overstep Trots**

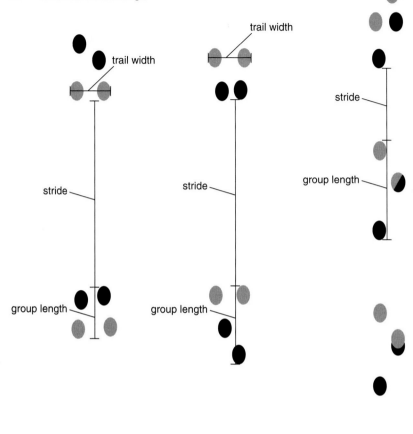

Hop   **Bounds**   **Lopes**

measures will likely be a necessary component of species identification in the beginning, but as your visual and intuitive skills improve, you may move your tape measure from your pocket to your pack and bring it out only on special occasions.

Like Rezendes (1999) and others, I measure tracks in their entirety, including nails and posterior pads. Many trackers do not include the nails, but because certain mammal species (e.g., porcupines and pocket mice) rarely register digital pads, measurements would be impossible without them. Avoid measuring drag marks or the impressions made by the foot as it entered and left a particular substrate—measure the floor of the actual track, not the walls. Refer to the illustrations on page 74.

All hooves are measured without the dewclaws. They register inconsistently in many species, and I wanted a measurement system that

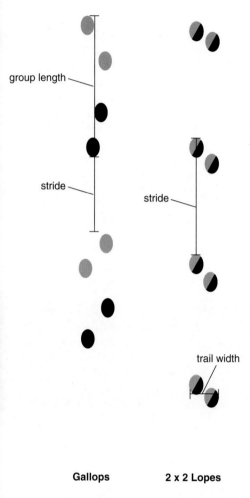

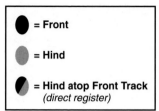

= Front

= Hind

= Hind atop Front Track
(direct register)

group length

stride

stride

trail width

Gallops   **2 x 2 Lopes**

allows cross-species comparison. Carpal pads, which lie high on the legs of canines and felines, are not included in measurements because they register only at high speeds or in deep substrates.

Always measure several front and rear tracks of the species you encounter. An individual animal can show incredible variation in track size, and within a given mammal species, there is even greater variation. For this reason, this book provides track ranges rather than averages, for easier identification.

Walks and trots are measured from the tip of the front track to the tip of the next front track. Direct registering trails are measured from the tip of the rear track to the tip of the next rear track. Straddle and side trots are also measured from front track to front track. When I compared parameters in walking trails measured from rear to rear with those measured from front to front, rear-to-rear parameters were very similar but always larger. The trail widths of walks and trots are taken at their widest points. Additional measurements can be useful for comparing species, such as the group length of paired tracks in a side trot trail.

Lopes, gallops, bounds, and hops are measured in the same way, with the exception of the 2×2 lope used by weasels. In all these gaits, the length of each group of four tracks is measured. The stride is the distance between groups of four tracks. The 2×2 lope is unique. Although it is inconsistent with the other lopes and gallops, I was reluctant to throw out

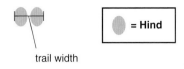

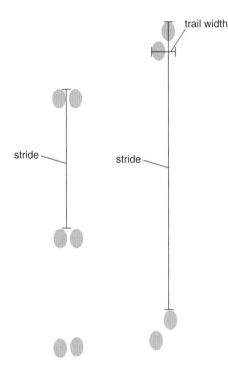

trail width

= Hind

trail width

trail width

stride

stride

Bipedal Hops   **Bipedal Skips**

years of data just for consistency's sake. Measurements are taken from the tip of the lead track in a pair to the tip of the lead track in the next pair. The trail width is also measured straight across—not at an angle—and is helpful for species comparisons.

The trail width is also a useful measurement in bounds and hops. It is taken at the widest point of the trail—the distance between and including the two hind tracks.

Species Accounts

What follows are species accounts of track and trail information. The illustrations should aid you in quick track identification in the field. All drawings are made from slides taken in natural settings across North America and were drawn with painstaking accuracy to convey real tracks in real substrates. Remember that track pattern recognition is a tremendous tool in species identification and is sometimes far more useful than studying the individual tracks.

A quick note about parameters: Some authors prefer to provide track and stride averages rather than ranges. There is some concern about making such ranges too large and thus less useful. I am a supporter of ranges, and I have included both splayed and tight tracks in the numbers. I would rather have beginners consider more possible options when faced with overlapping parameters than ignore the correct interpretation because they happen to be tracking in wet snow and all the tracks are splayed.

Species are arranged phylogenetically, which is the method preferred by professional mammalogists. Species are ordered in evolutionary terms from oldest to youngest. However, this evolution is not a linear event; it occurs on many fronts as species split and continue to branch over time into other species. For this reason, I follow the example of *The Smithsonian's Book of North American Mammals* and place only orders and families in phylogenetic order.

One benefit of keeping mammals in family groups is training the mind to see how species are related to one another and how some behaviors and characteristics are shared across a family and not just a species. The "Family Notes" at the start of most new family sections provide shared track, trail, and behavior information.

Range maps are an incredible tool for naturalists and trackers in the field. Yet even the best range maps are merely guesses of where mammals move and live and should be used only as a guide. Be flexible in your field interpretations.

Front track of a gray fox. (NH)

Tracks

Cinereus or masked
shrew (*Sorex* sp.),
pages 120–24, 126

Northern short-tailed
shrew *(Blarina
brevicauda)*, pages 124–25

Western harvest mouse
(*Reithrodontomys* sp.),
pages 312–13

Least weasel
(Mustela nivalis),
pages 175–76

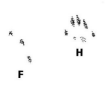

Oldfield mouse
(Peromyscus polionotus),
pages 318–19

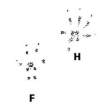

Woodland vole
(*Microtus* sp.),
page 331

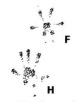

Hairy-tailed mole
(Parascalops breweri),
pages 127–28

White-footed mouse
(*Peromyscus* sp.),
pages 314–18

Southern red-backed vole
(Clethrionomys gapperi),
pages 326–27

Meadow vole
(*Microtus* sp.), pages 327–31
Similar to Lemmings,
pages 334–35

Little pocket mouse
(*Perognathus* and
Chaetodipus spp.),
pages 296–98

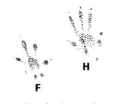

Painted-spiny pocket
mouse *(Liomys pictus)*,
pages 307–8

F= Front   H= Hind   All tracks actual size

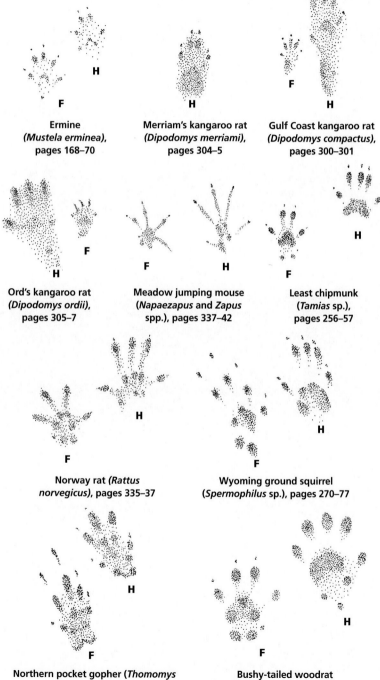

Ermine
(Mustela erminea),
pages 168–70

H F

Merriam's kangaroo rat
(Dipodomys merriami),
pages 304–5

H

Gulf Coast kangaroo rat
(Dipodomys compactus),
pages 300–301

F H

Ord's kangaroo rat
(Dipodomys ordii),
pages 305–7

F H

Meadow jumping mouse
(Napaezapus and Zapus
spp.), pages 337–42

F H

Least chipmunk
(Tamias sp.),
pages 256–57

F H

Norway rat (Rattus
norvegicus), pages 335–37

F H

Wyoming ground squirrel
(Spermophilus sp.), pages 270–77

F H

Northern pocket gopher (Thomomys
and Geomyes sp.), pages 292–94

F H

Bushy-tailed woodrat
(Neotoma cinerea), pages 321–22

F H

Actual Size Tracks

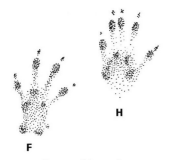

Eastern chipmunk
(Tamias striatus),
pages 257–59

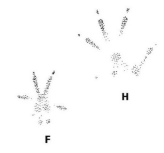

Marsh rice rat
(Oryzomys palustris),
pages 311–12
Similar to *Sigmodon* sp., page 319

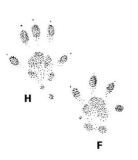

White-throated woodrat
(Neotoma sp.)*,
pages 320–26

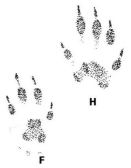

White-tailed antelope squirrel
(Ammospermophilus leucurus),
pages 264–66

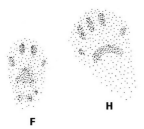

Southern flying squirrel
(Glaucomys volans),
pages 290–91

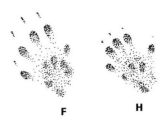

Pygmy skunk
(Spilogale pygmaea),
pages 189–90

F= Front   H= Hind   All tracks actual size

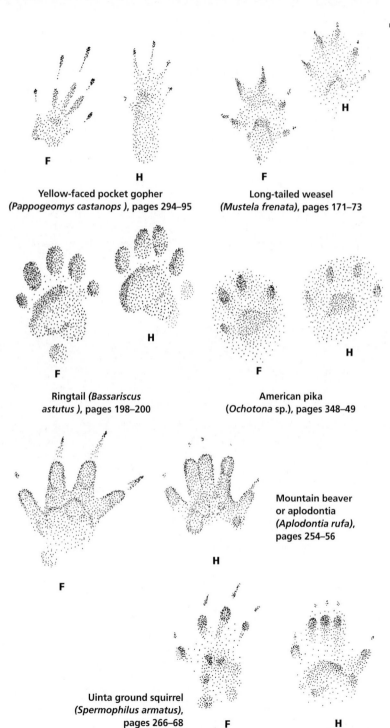

Yellow-faced pocket gopher
(Pappogeomys castanops), pages 294–95

Long-tailed weasel
(Mustela frenata), pages 171–73

Ringtail *(Bassariscus
astutus)*, pages 198–200

American pika
(Ochotona sp.), pages 348–49

Mountain beaver
or aplodontia
(Aplodontia rufa),
pages 254–56

Uinta ground squirrel
(Spermophilus armatus),
pages 266–68

F

H

Actual Size Tracks

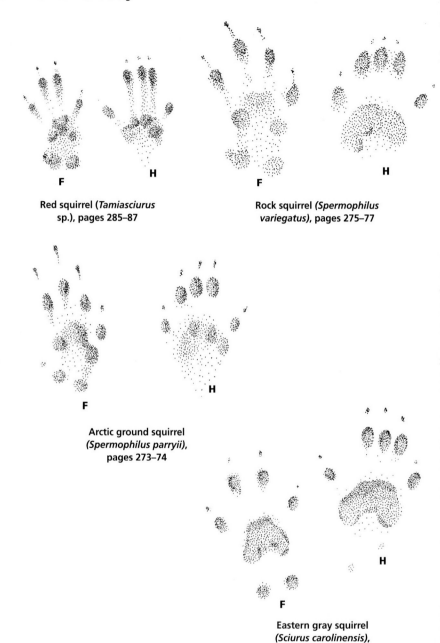

F   **H**

Red squirrel (*Tamiasciurus* sp.), pages 285–87

F   **H**

Rock squirrel (*Spermophilus variegatus*), pages 275–77

F   **H**

Arctic ground squirrel (*Spermophilus parryii*), pages 273–74

F   **H**

Eastern gray squirrel (*Sciurus carolinensis*), pages 281–83

F= Front   H= Hind   All tracks actual size

Actual Size Tracks

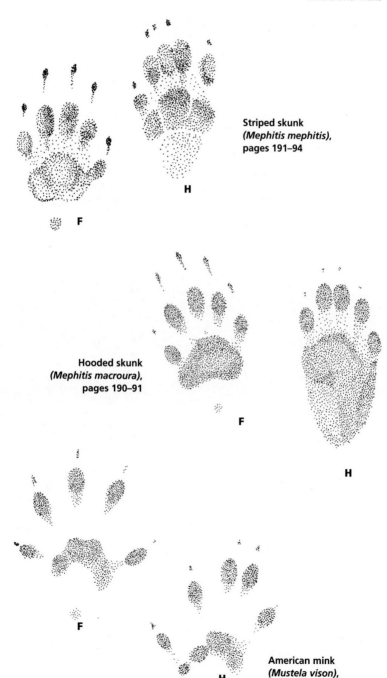

Striped skunk
(Mephitis mephitis),
pages 191–94

H

F

Hooded skunk
(Mephitis macroura),
pages 190–91

F

H

F

H

American mink
(Mustela vison),
pages 176–79

Actual Size Tracks

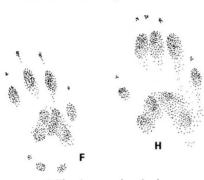

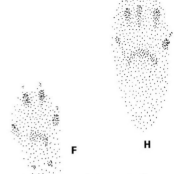

California ground squirrel
(*Spermophilus beecheyi*), pages 268–70

Northern flying squirrel
(*Glaucomys sabrinus*), pages 288–90

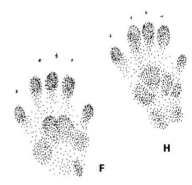

Desert kangaroo rat (large
Dipodomys sp.), pages 302–4

Western spotted skunk
(*Spilogale* sp.), pages 187–90

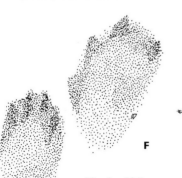

Marsh rabbit
(*Sylvilagus palustris*),
pages 355–56

Black-footed ferret
(*Mustela nigripes*),
pages 173–75

F= Front   H= Hind   All tracks actual size

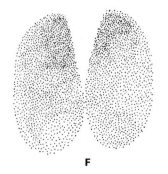

Collared peccary or javelina
(Pecari tajacu), pages 229–31

F

H

**Western hognose
skunk *(Conepatus*
sp.), pages 194–96**

F

H

F

Black-tailed prairie dog
(Cynomys sp.), pages 277–80

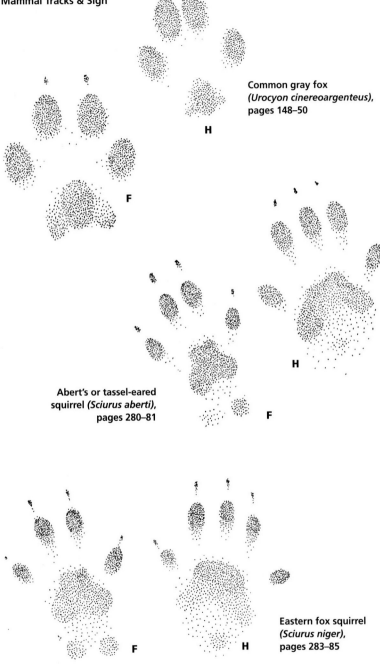

Common gray fox
(Urocyon cinereoargenteus),
pages 148–50

H

F

Abert's or tassel-eared
squirrel *(Sciurus aberti)*,
pages 280–81

H

F

Eastern fox squirrel
(Sciurus niger),
pages 283–85

F

H

F= Front   H= Hind   All tracks actual size

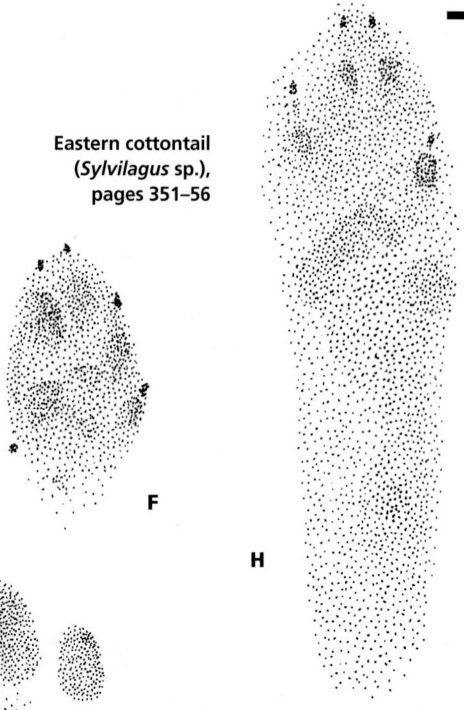

Eastern cottontail
(*Sylvilagus* sp.),
pages 351–56

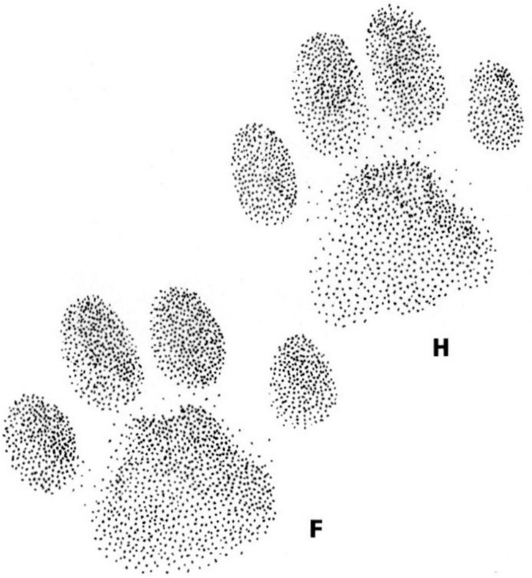

F

H

House cat
(Felis domesticus),
pages 211–12

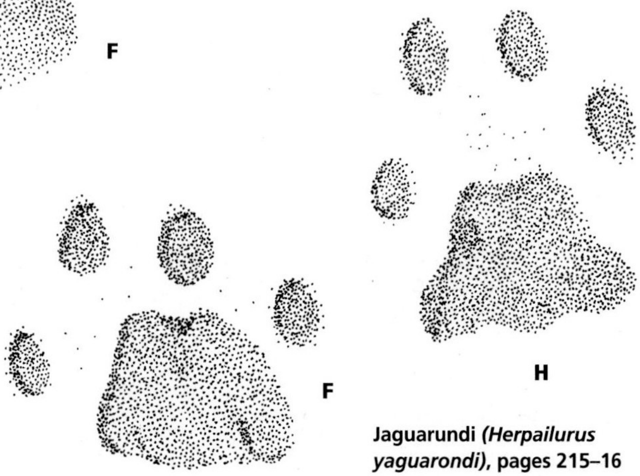

H

F

Jaguarundi *(Herpailurus
yaguarondi)*, pages 215–16

F

H

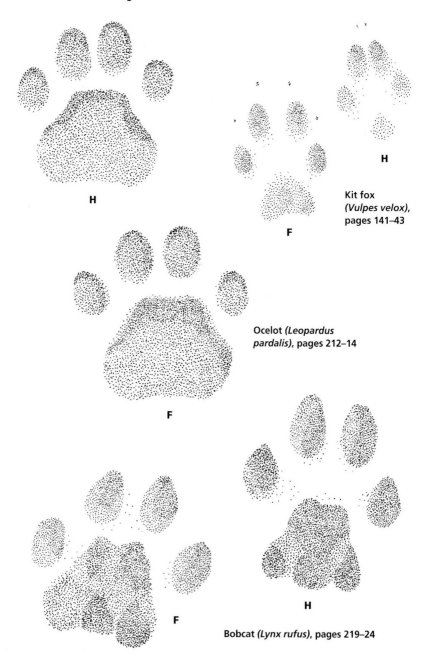

H

H

Kit fox
(Vulpes velox),
pages 141–43

F

Ocelot *(Leopardus
pardalis)*, pages 212–14

F

F

H

Bobcat *(Lynx rufus)*, pages 219–24

F= Front   H= Hind   All tracks actual size

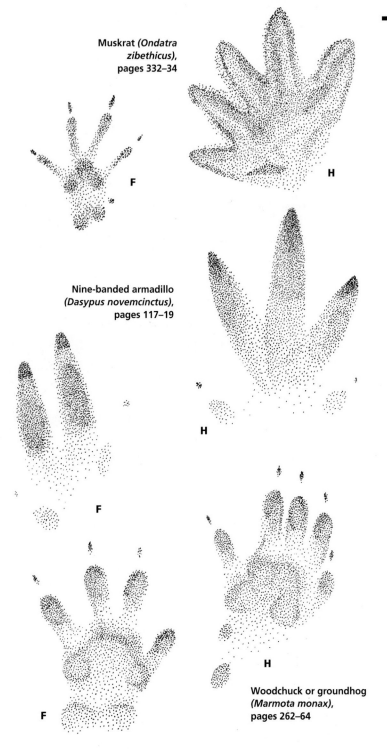

Muskrat *(Ondatra zibethicus),* pages 332–34

F

H

Nine-banded armadillo *(Dasypus novemcinctus),* pages 117–19

H

F

F

H

Woodchuck or groundhog *(Marmota monax),* pages 262–64

Actual Size Tracks

Arctic fox
(*Alopex lagopus*),
pages 138–40

H

F

Hoary marmot
(*Marmota* sp.),
pages 259–62

H

F

F= Front   H= Hind   All tracks actual size

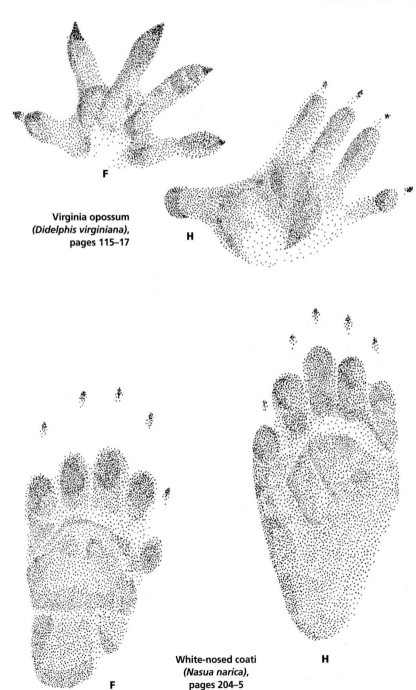

F

Virginia opossum
(Didelphis virginiana),
pages 115–17

H

White-nosed coati
(Nasua narica),
pages 204–5

F

H

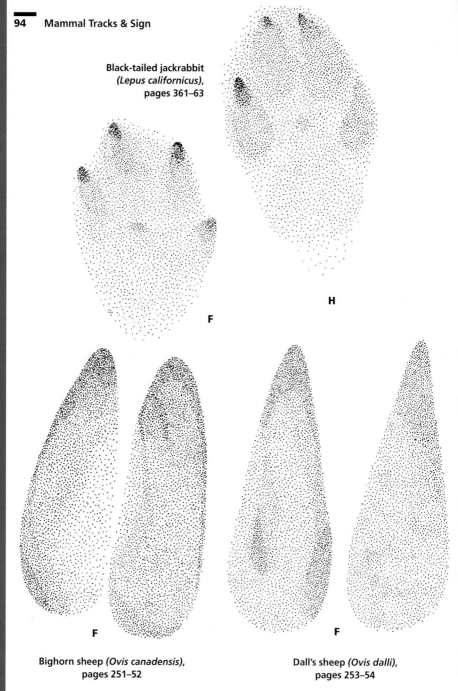

Black-tailed jackrabbit
(Lepus californicus),
pages 361–63

H

F

F

Bighorn sheep *(Ovis canadensis),*
pages 251–52

F

Dall's sheep *(Ovis dalli),*
pages 253–54

F= Front   H= Hind   All tracks actual size

Mule deer
(Odocoileus hemionus),
pages 233–35

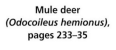

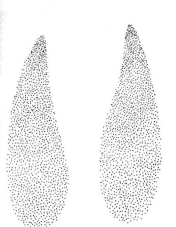

F

F
Smaller subspecies

White-tailed deer
(Odocoileus virginianus),
pages 235–38

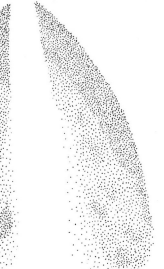

F
Larger subspecies

Actual Size Tracks

Actual Size Tracks

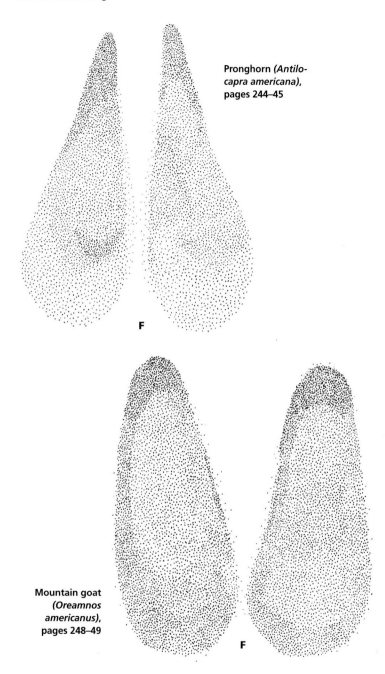

Pronghorn *(Antilo-capra americana)*, pages 244–45

F

Mountain goat *(Oreamnos americanus)*, pages 248–49

F

F= Front   H= Hind   All tracks actual size

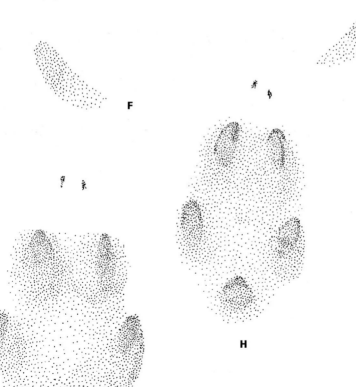

Wild boar or feral hog
(Sus scrofa), pages 226–28

F

H

F

Red fox
(Vulpes vulpes),
pages 143–46

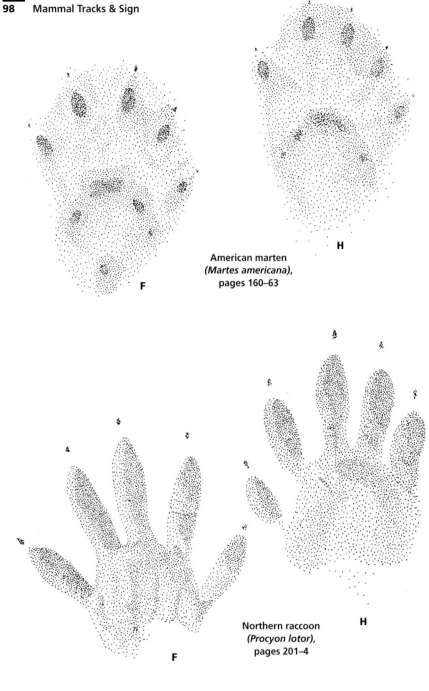

American marten
(Martes americana),
pages 160–63

H

F

Northern raccoon
(Procyon lotor),
pages 201–4

H

F

F= Front   H= Hind   All tracks actual size

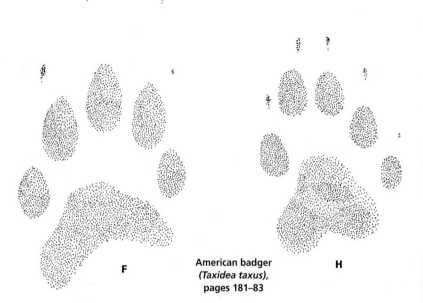

F   American badger   H
(Taxidea taxus),
pages 181–83

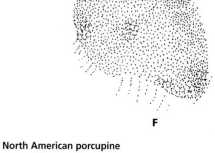

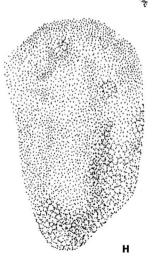

H   North American porcupine   F
(Erethizon dorsatum),
pages 342–45

Western coyote
(Canis latrans),
pages 129–33

H

F

Eastern coyote
(Canis latrans),
pages 129–33

H

F

F= Front   H= Hind   All tracks actual size

Tracks at 50 Percent

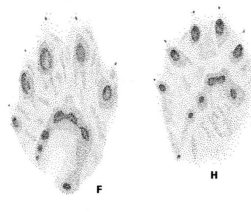

Fisher *(Martes pennanti)*, pages 163–67

F

H

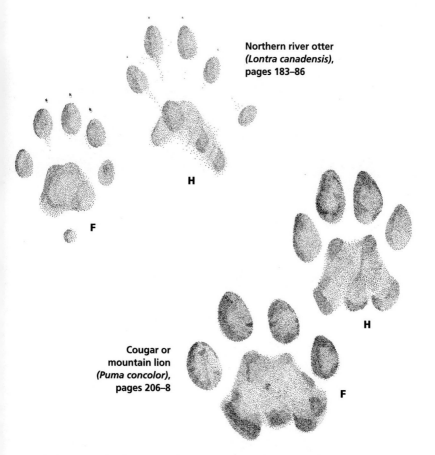

Northern river otter *(Lontra canadensis)*, pages 183–86

H

F

H

Cougar or mountain lion *(Puma concolor)*, pages 206–8

F

F= Front   H= Hind   All tracks 50 percent of actual size

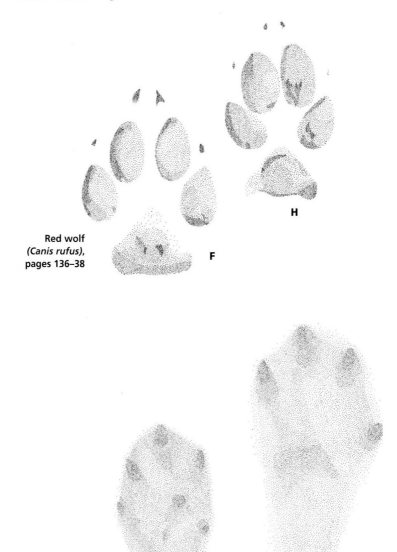

Red wolf
(Canis rufus),
pages 136–38

H

F

White-tailed jackrabbit
(Lepus townsendii),
pages 363–64

F

H

F= Front   H= Hind   All tracks 50 percent of actual size

Canada lynx
(Lynx canadensis),
pages 216–19

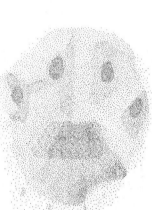

H

F

Snowshoe hare
(Lepus americanus),
pages 357–59

H

F

Tracks at 50 Percent

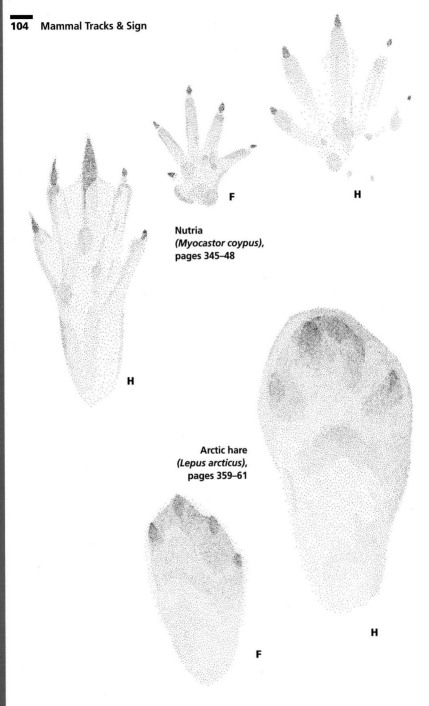

F

H

**Nutria
(*Myocastor coypus*),
pages 345–48**

H

**Arctic hare
(*Lepus arcticus*),
pages 359–61**

H

F

F= Front   H= Hind   All tracks 50 percent of actual size

H

Jaguar
(Panthera onca),
pages 224–25

F

H

Wolverine
(Gulo gulo),
pages 179–81

F

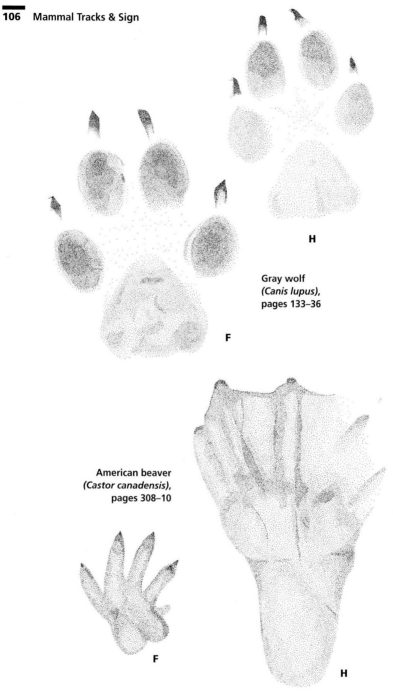

Tracks at 50 Percent

Gray wolf
(Canis lupus),
pages 133–36

H

F

American beaver
(Castor canadensis),
pages 308–10

F

H

F= Front   H= Hind   All tracks 50 percent of actual size

F

**American black bear
(*Ursus americanus*),
pages 151–53**

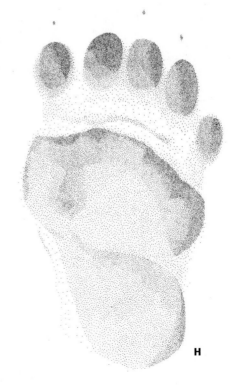

H

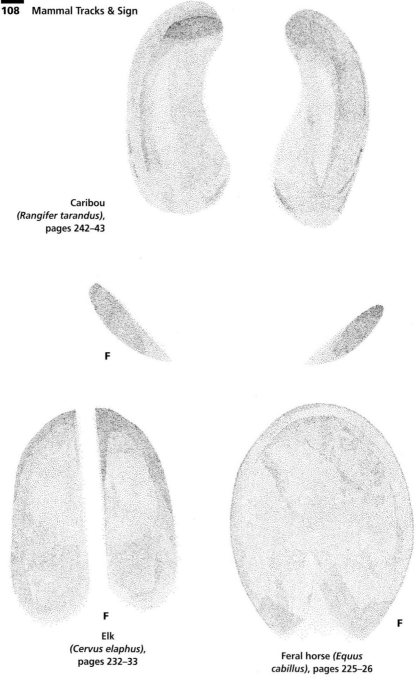

Tracks at 50 Percent

Caribou
(Rangifer tarandus),
pages 242–43

F

F

Elk
(Cervus elaphus),
pages 232–33

F

Feral horse *(Equus
cabillus)*, pages 225–26

F= Front   H= Hind   All tracks 50 percent of actual size

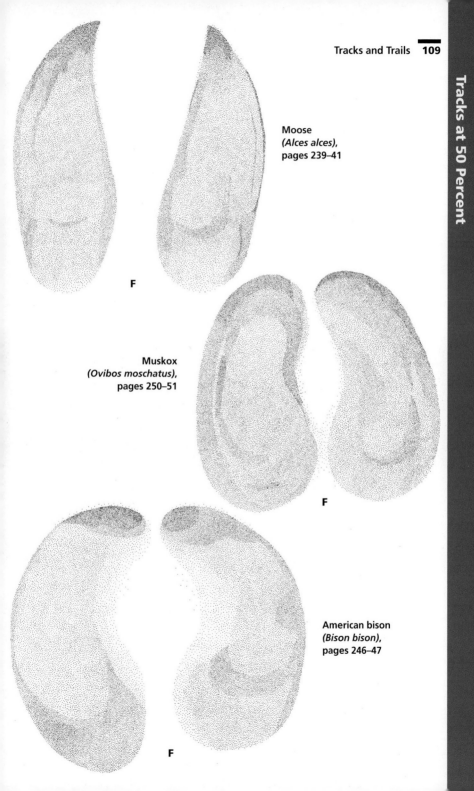

Moose
(Alces alces),
pages 239–41

F

Muskox
(Ovibos moschatus),
pages 250–51

F

American bison
(Bison bison),
pages 246–47

F

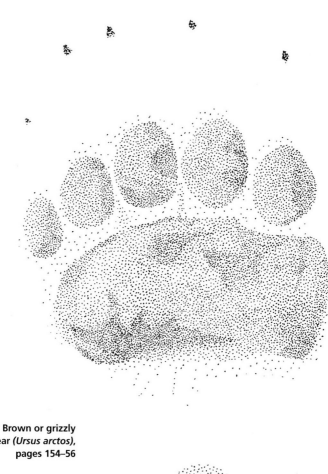

**Brown or grizzly
bear *(Ursus arctos)*,
pages 154–56**

F

F= Front   H= Hind   All tracks 50 percent of actual size

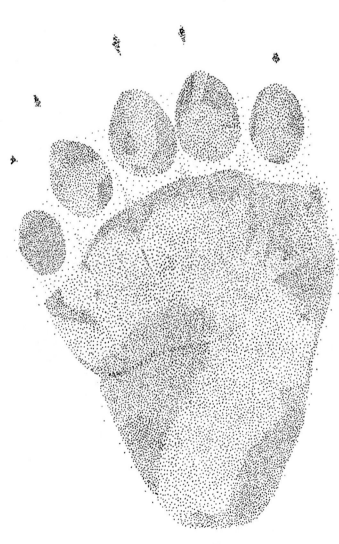

H

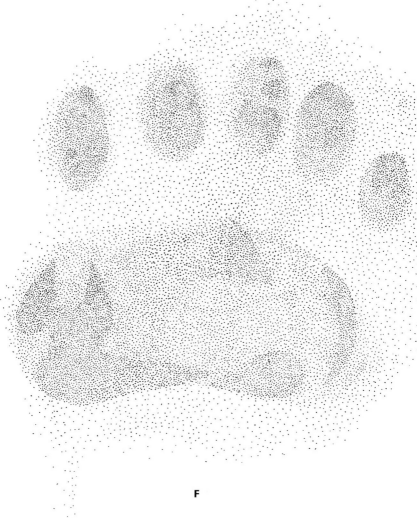

F

Polar bear
(Ursus maritimus),
pages 157–59

F= Front   H= Hind   All tracks 50 percent of actual size

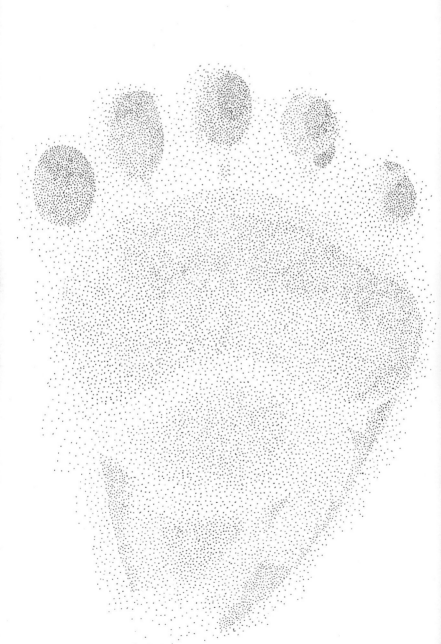

H

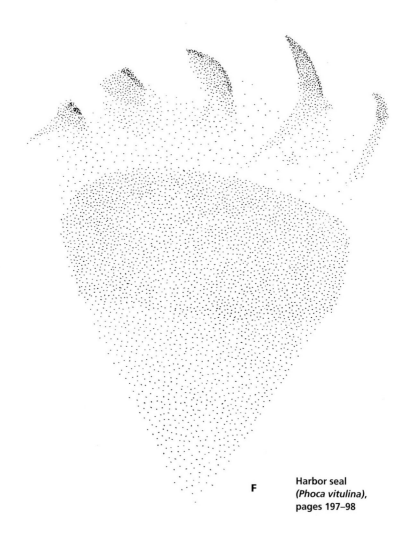

F

Harbor seal
(Phoca vitulina),
pages 197–98

F= Front   H= Hind   All tracks 50 percent of actual size

Order Didelphimorphia

Opossums: Family Didelphidae

In southern Mexico, you may encounter signs of two additional opossum species about the same size as the Virginia opossum, one of which has webbed feet. There are also several very small, arboreal species found in Mexico.

Virginia Opossum *(Didelphis virginiana)*

Track: Front 1–2⁵/₁₆ in. (2.5–7.5 cm) L x 1¹/₄–2¹/₂ in. (3.2–6.3 cm) W

Small to medium. Digitigrade. Symmetrical. Five toes, radiating from the metacarpal region like a rising sun. Six metacarpal pads; the posterior two might be considered a heel. Nails may or may not register. Appearance is very splayed and starlike.

Rear 1³/₁₆–2³/₄ in. (3–7 cm) L x 1¹/₂–3 in. (3.8–7.6 cm) W

Small to medium. Digitigrade. Very asymmetrical. Five toes: Toe 1, the thumb, sits opposite and separate from the remaining digits, pointing into the center of the trail. Toes 2, 3, and 4 tend to register together, close to digit 5. Six metacarpal pads. Toe 1 has no claw, and the remaining nails may or may not register.

Trail: Walk   Stride: 4¹/₂–9 in. (11.4–22.9 cm)

Trail width: 3³/₄–5 in. (9.5–12.7 cm)

Trot   Stride: 10–15 in. (25.4–38.1 cm)

Trail width: 2¹/₂–4 in. (6.3–10.2 cm)

Bound   Stride: 13–19 in. (33–48.3 cm)

Trail width: 5–7¹/₂ in. (12.7–19.1 cm)

Group length: 9–11¹/₂ in. (22.9–29.2 cm)

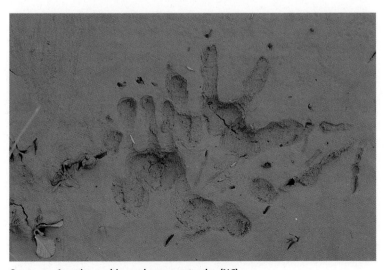

Opossum, American robin, and sparrow tracks. (NC)

Notes:

- Tend to walk during exploration and while in suitable cover but often switch to a trot to cross open ground or travel beaches and trails more quickly. These two gaits leave very similar trail patterns and may be confused.

- Use a bound to escape or chase prey, although in encounters with predators they may "play dead" rather than attempting to run away.

- Occasionally drag their tails while walking, but trotting animals (or those moving faster) hold their tails straight out behind them, keeping them well clear of the ground.

- Often use roads and trails for travel purposes.

- Found in a variety of habitats in warmer climates but are more restricted to coastlines, cities, and other developed areas in the far north of their range. Opossums were introduced widely along the west coast of the United States.

- Capable climbers and swimmers.

- Use holes and cavities, including drains, culverts, and basements, to rest and escape from extreme cold.

Opossum walk.

Opossum trot.

Left: Opossum tracks; the front track sits above the hind. (WA) *Right:* An opossum trots across an open expanse of beach. (Mexico)

- Do not venture out much in deep snow, as their feet and tails are prone to frostbite. When they do, they walk and leave continuous drag marks between tracks; the tail may or may not be evident.
- Generally a solitary animal.

Order Xenarthra

Armadillos: Family Dasypodidae

Nine-banded Armadillo *(Dasypus novemcinctus)*

Track: Front 1½–2 in. (3.8–5.1 cm) L x 1³/₈–1⁵/₈ in. (3.5–4.1 cm) W

Small. Asymmetrical. Four toes: The inner two toes (digits 3 and 4) are significantly longer than the outer toes and are often the only ones that register clearly; outer toes sit at a higher plane on the foot. The metacarpal region is unique and appears to be tough skin; if "pads" are present, they are fused. Large nails reliably register.

Rear 2–3¹/₄ in. (5.1–8.3 cm) L x 1¹/₂–2³/₈ in. (3.8–6 cm) W

Medium. Symmetrical. Five toes: Toes 2, 3, and 4 are significantly larger than the others and are often the only ones that clearly register in tracks. As in the front, the metacarpal region appears to be tough skin; if "pads" are present, they are fused. Large nails reliably register. Both front and rear tracks are somewhat birdlike in appearance.

Trail: Direct register walk   Stride: 4¹/₂–7 in. (11.4–17.8 cm)
                               Trail width: 3¹/₂–4 in. (8.9–10.2 cm)
       Overstep walk   Stride: 5–9 in. (12.7–22.9 cm)
                               Trail width: 3–4 in. (7.6–10.2 cm)
       Lope   Stride: 3–8 in. (7.6–20.3 cm)
                               Group length: 9–14 in. (22.9–35.6 cm)

Notes:
• Lope while exploring and moving in exposed areas; slow to walking gaits when foraging and working an area over for insects. Also known to leap straight up into the air when startled.

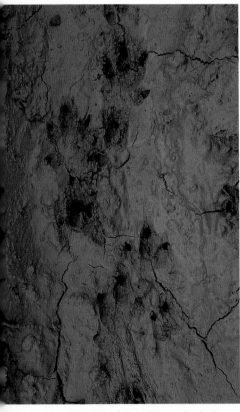

A jumble of armadillo tracks. (TX)

Armadillo lope.

Armadillo overstep walk.

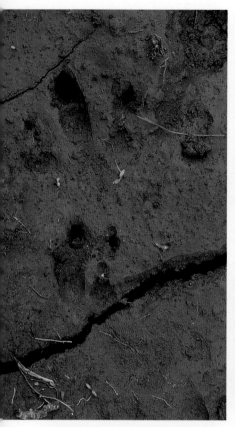

Left: This is the most consistent armadillo track registration I've found in the field—two toes for the smaller front tracks, and three toes for the hind tracks. (TX) *Right:* Typical armadillo lope pattern. From bottom to top, the tracks are front-hind-front-hind. (FL)

- Will move in open areas.
- Readily use existing roads and trails.
- Dig frequently, so look for associated signs.
- Do not climb but are capable swimmers and may even walk across the bottoms of streams and ponds.
- Dig their own burrows and also use those of others.
- Generally solitary animals.

Order Insectivora
Shrews: Family Soricidae

- Shrews dig their own burrows and create tunnel networks for hunting but also use burrows and runs created by other small mammals.

- The climbing ability of many shrew species is little documented.

- Many shrews are capable swimmers.

- The larger and harder a road surface, the greater the potential that the road will limit shrew movements. Narrow trails and dirt roads will be crossed but generally not followed.

- We do not typically see shrew trails in deep snow, as they prefer to tunnel beneath the snow layer and stay close to the debris and earth surface, where they continue to hunt.

- Shrews tend to be solitary animals.

Cinereus or Masked Shrew
(Sorex cinereus)

Track: Front 3/16–1/4 in. (.5–.6 cm) L
x 3/16–1/4 in. (.5–.6 cm) W

Very small. Slightly asymmetrical. Five toes: Toe 3 is longer than toes 2 and 4, so the tips of the three toes form an arch or curve. The metacarpal region has six pads: four "palm" and two posterior "heel" pads. Not all pads register reliably. Nails register more often than not.

Cinereus shrew bound.

Cinereus shrew trot into straddle trot.

Rear 3/16–3/8 in. (.5–1 cm) L x 3/16–1/4 in. (.5–.6 cm) W
Very small. Symmetrical toes, asymmetrical metacarpal pads. Five toes: Toe 3 is equal in length to toes 2 and 4, so the tips of the three toes form a straight line. The metacarpal region has six pads: four "palm" and two posterior "heel" pads. Not all pads register reliably. Nails register more often than not. Tracks and trails of smaller shrew species are easily confused.

Trail: Walk/trot   Stride: 1–1 1/2 in. (2.5–3.8 cm)
Trail width: 3/4–1 in. (1.9–2.5 cm)

Straddle trot   Stride: 1 3/16–1 3/8 in. (3–3.5 cm)
Trail width: 3/4–7/8 in. (1.9–2.2 cm)

Bound   Stride: 1–3 1/2 in. (2.5–8.9 cm)
Trail width: 3/4–1 in. (1.9–2.5 cm)
Group length: 5/8–1 11/16 in. (1.6–4.3 cm)

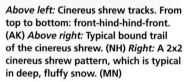

Above left: Cinereus shrew tracks. From top to bottom: front-hind-hind-front. (AK) *Above right:* Typical bound trail of the cinereus shrew. (NH) *Right:* A 2x2 cinereus shrew pattern, which is typical in deep, fluffy snow. (MN)

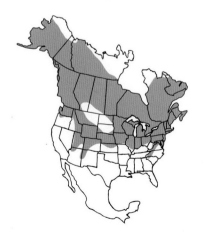

Notes:

- Use the trot and straddle trot to cover ground quickly while continuously hunting; slow to a walk only when something needs further attention. Bound to cross an open area or when they feel exposed.
- Move in the open, especially along water systems, but generally speed up when completely exposed.
- Capable swimmers.
- In deep snow, use a 2x2 bound or 2x2 lope.

Smoky Shrew *(Sorex fumeus)*

Track: Front ¼–5/16 in. (.6–.8 cm) L x ¼–5/16 in. (.6–.8 cm) W

Very small. Slightly asymmetrical. Five toes: Toe 3 is longer than toes 2 and 4, so the three toes form an arch or curve. The metacarpal region has six pads: four "palm" and two posterior "heel" pads. Not all pads register reliably. Nails register more often than not.

Rear ¼–7/16 in. (.6–1.1 cm) L x ¼–5/16 in. (.6–.8 cm) W

Very small. Symmetrical toes, asymmetrical metacarpal pads. Five toes: Toe 3 is equal in length to toes 2 and 4, so the tips of the three toes form a straight line. The metacarpal region has six pads: four "palm" and two posterior "heel" pads. Not all pads register reliably. Nails register more often than not. Tracks and trails of smaller shrew species are easily confused.

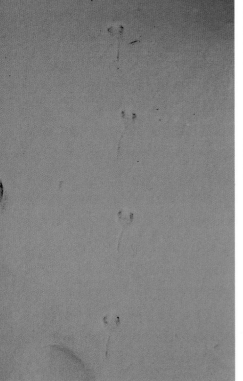

Trail: Bound   Stride: 1–7 in. (2.5–17.8 cm)

Trail width: 7/8–15/16 in. (2.2–3.3 cm)

Group length: 7/8–21/8 in. (2.2–5.4 cm)

Note: In deep snow, this species uses a 2x2 bound or 2x2 lope, generally taking longer strides than the smaller cinereus shrews.

A smoky shrew trail. Note the long strides and tail drag. (NH)

Merriam's Shrew *(Sorex merriami)*

Track: Front ³/₁₆–¹/₄ in. (.5–.6 cm) L x ³/₁₆–¹/₄ in.
(.5–.6 cm) W

Very small. Slightly asymmetrical. Five
toes: Toe 3 is longer than toes 2 and 4,
so the three toes form an arch or curve.
The metacarpal region has six pads:
four "palm" and two posterior "heel"
pads. Not all pads register reliably. Nails
register more often than not.

Rear ³/₁₆–³/₈ in. (.5–1 cm) L x ³/₁₆–¹/₄ in.
(.5–.6 cm) W

Very small. Symmetrical toes,
asymmetrical metacarpal pads. Five
toes: Toe 3 is equal in length to toes 2
and 4, so the tips of the three toes form
a straight line. The metacarpal region
has six pads: four "palm" and two
posterior "heel" pads.

Merriam's shrew
straddle trot.

A loping track pattern of a Merriam's shrew;
from bottom to top, tracks are front-hind-front-
hind. (CO)

Not all pads register reliably. Nails register more often than not. Tracks and trails of smaller shrew species are easily confused.

Trail: Bound   Stride: 1–3 in. (2.5–7.6 cm)

Trail width: 11/16–1 in. (1.7–2.5 cm)

Group length: 7/8–13/4 in. (2.2–4.4 cm)

Note: I've found Merriam's shrews in trots and loping gaits and walking when investigating something.

Northern Short-tailed Shrew *(Blarina brevicauda)*
Southern Short-tailed Shrew *(Blarina carolinensis)*

Track: Front 1/4–3/8 in. (.6–1 cm) L x 7/32–11/32 in. (.6–.9 cm) W

Very small. Slightly asymmetrical. Five toes: Toe 3 is longer than toes 2 and 4, so the three toes form an arch or curve. The metacarpal region has six pads: four "palm" and two posterior "heel" pads. Not all pads register reliably. Nails register more often than not and can be quite long.

Rear 1/4–3/8 in. (.6–1 cm) L x 3/16–11/32 in. (.5–.9 cm) W

Very small. Symmetrical toes, asymmetrical metacarpal pads. Five toes: Toe 3 is equal in length to toes 2 and 4, so the tips of the three toes form a straight line. The metacarpal region has six pads: four "palm" and two

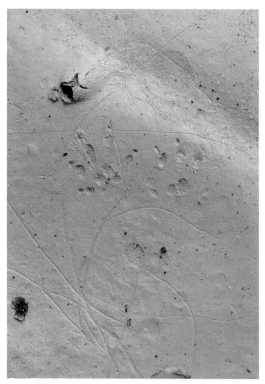

Hind (at left) and front tracks of a northern short-tailed shrew. (NH)

Northern short-tailed shrew trot.

Left: Classic direct register trot trail of short-tailed shrews. (NH) *Right:* Two additional short-tailed shrew trot trails, and an exit-entrance into the snow layer. (NH)

posterior "heel" pads. Not all pads register reliably. Nails register more often than not. Tracks larger than those of *Sorex* species.

Trail: Walk   Stride: 1–1¼ in. (2.5–3.2 cm)
               Trail width: 1¼–1⅝ in. (3.2–4.1 cm)
        Trot   Stride: 1⅝–2⅛ in. (4.1–5.4 cm)
               Trail width: 1–1⅜ in. (2.5–3.5 cm)

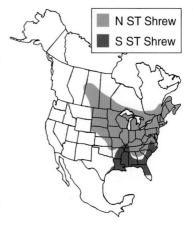

Notes:

• Trot when traveling and exploring and understep walk when investigating something. Occasionally speed up into a bound when completely exposed or crossing trails and roads, and I've also found them hopping, with rear feet registering behind the front.

• Widespread and found in varied habitats.

• In deep snow, tend to stay in a direct register trot but may also use a 2x2 lope.

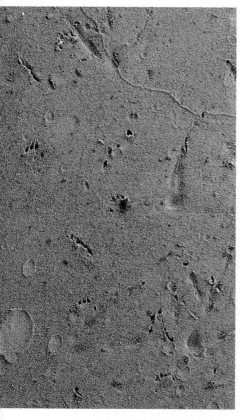

Order Carnivora

Dogs: Family Canidae

- Canines have five toes on each front foot and four toes on each rear foot. Toe 1 on the front foot is smaller and raised up high on the inside of the leg; it does not typically register in tracks unless the animal is moving at speed or stepping in deep substrate. (Note: Some domestic breeds have five toes on all feet.)

- The metacarpal pads of canines are fused and are a much smaller portion of the overall track dimensions compared with cat tracks. Canines shift their weight forward as well, and the toes register more reliably than the metacarpal pads.

- Canines are generally comfortable in the open, and you will find trails crossing open pastures and meadows.

A hairy-tailed mole trail in wet silt. (MA)

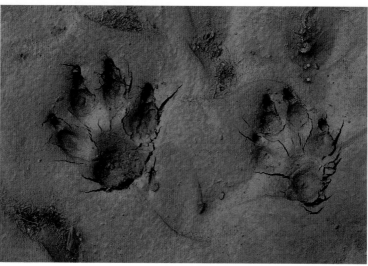

Perfect domestic dog tracks. The larger track is the front, and the smaller the hind. (AK)

- Canines use trails and roads readily, and they often choose places along trails to scent mark.

- They are capable swimmers, although most foxes use natural bridges to cross streams and other water systems and avoid swimming when possible.

Coyote *(Canis latrans)*

Eastern track: Front 2⅝–3½ in. (6.7–8.9 cm) L x 1⅝–2⅞ in. (4.1–7.3 cm) W
Western track: Front 2¼–3¼ in. (5.7–8.3 cm) L x 1½–2½ in. (3.8–6.4 cm) W

Medium. Digitigrade. Symmetrical. Five toes: Toe 1 is greatly reduced and raised up on the inner leg. Four toes reliably register in tracks. The metacarpal pads are fused and create one triangular pad; the posterior edge may register "wings," two lobes pointing backward. The negative space between toes and metacarpals forms an *X*. An additional carpal pad sits high on the leg and registers only at high speeds or in deep substrates. Nails register reliably, although the nails on toes 2 and 5 do so less reliably and are often so close to toes 3 and 4 that they are overlooked. All nails are very fine and thin. Nails on toes 3 and 4 often point inward and register very close together. Front track larger than rear track.

 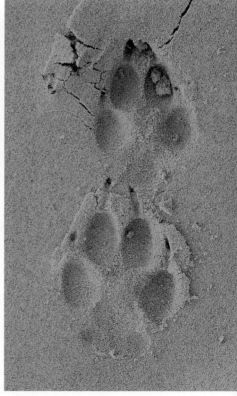

Left: Coyote tracks. The larger is the front track; the smaller, the hind. (CA) *Right:* Front and hind (above) tracks of a western coyote. (TX)

Eastern track: Rear 2³/₈–3¹/₄ in. (6–8.3 cm) L x 1⁵/₈–2³/₈ in. (4.1–6 cm) W
Western track: Rear 2¹/₈–3 in. (5.4–7.6 cm) L x 1¹/₈–2 in. (2.9–5.1 cm) W

Medium. Digitigrade. Symmetrical. Four toes. The metacarpal pads are fused and create one triangular pad; the metacarpal pads may register lightly and look like a dot, no larger than one of the digits. The negative space between toes and metacarpals forms an X. Nails register reliably, although the

| Coyote overstep walk. | Coyote gallop. | Coyote side trot. | Coyote direct register trot. |

Front and hind (leading) tracks of an eastern coyote. (NH)

nails on toes 2 and 5 do so less reliably and are often so close to toes 3 and 4 that they are overlooked. All nails are very fine and thin. Nails on toes 3 and 4 often point inward and register very close together.

A perfect eastern coyote front track. (NH)

Trail: Trot   East   Stride: 16¹/₂–26 in. (42–66 cm)
                               Trail width: 2³/₁₆–5¹/₄ in. (5.6–13.3 cm)
                      West   Stride: 15–21 in. (38.1–53.3 cm)
                               Trail width: 2¹/₄–4 in. (5.7–10.2 cm)
         Walk   East   Stride: 13¹/₂–17 in. (34.3–43.2 cm)
                               Trail width: 4³/₄–6 in. (12.1–15.2 cm)
                      West   Stride: 11–17 in. (27.9–43.2 cm)
                               Trail width: 4–5¹/₂ in. (10.2–14 cm)
         Side trot   East   Stride: 20¹/₂–30¹/₂ in. (52–77.4 cm)
                               Group length: 6–13 in. (15.2–33 cm)
                      West   Stride: 19–27 in. (48.3–68.6 cm)
                               Group length: 4¹/₂–11¹/₂ in. (11.4–29.2 cm)
         Extended trot   Stride: Up to 40 in. (1.02 m)
                               (Data compliments of John McCarter)
         Lope   Stride: 5–20 in. (12.7–50.8 cm)
                               Group length: 26–33 in. (66–83.8 cm)
         Gallop   Stride: 12–90 in. (30.5–228.6 cm)
                               Group length: 35–101 in. (88.9–256.5 cm)

Notes:

• Trot when traveling and exploring but walk when stalking small prey, investigating a smell, and for numerous other reasons. (Coyote gaits are discussed at length earlier in the chapter.)

• Do not climb.

• Walk in deep snow, often establishing runs between hunting and bedding areas. Occasionally bound, but for shorter distances.

• Social animals. Although single animals may be found occasionally, pairs and packs can be found at any time of year. Packs function much like wolf packs and may have stragglers, or orbit animals, as well.

A coyote glides across this frozen lake surface in a direct register trot. (MA)

Coyote vs. Dog

Distinguishing dog from coyote tracks is tricky business. Numerous dogs can leave convincing coyote tracks, some can leave coyote-like trails, and a few can do both, as well as mimic coyote behaviors. Follow confusing trails, looking at behaviors.

Many dog tracks can be differentiated from those of coyotes by looking for certain characteristics. Coyotes tend to leave tighter tracks than dogs: The palm pads register on a much higher plane than the digital pads (tracks are angled), the claws are sharp and pointy, the side claws may be absent or register so close to toes 3 and 4 that they are overlooked, and the lead claws often point toward each other and register close together. Coyotes are also more aerodynamic, in that toes 2 and 5 are farther back in the track and partially tucked behind toes 3 and 4. Dog tracks are often splayed, with thick, blunt claws and toes pointing in four different directions. Their tracks are flatter, and a greater portion of their palm pads more reliably registers in both front and hind tracks.

Coyote trails are "cleaner," in a general sense. They direct register far more often than dogs and leave narrower trails. Coyote trails are straighter, and there's less wasted energy. Yet coyotes also play and chase each other. The way a coyote moves in the woods must be experienced firsthand.

Gray Wolf *(Canis lupus)*

Track: Front 3³/₄–5³/₄ in. (9.5–14.6 cm) L x 2⁷/₈–5 in. (7.3–12.7 cm) W
(reports of 6-inch [15.2–cm] tracks)

Large. Digitigrade. Symmetrical. Five toes: Toe 1 is greatly reduced and raised up on the inner leg. Four toes reliably register in tracks. The metacarpal pads are fused and create one triangular pad. The negative space between toes and metacarpals forms an *H* more often than an *X*. There is an additional carpal pad higher on the leg. Nails register reliably. Front track larger and rounder than rear track.

Rear 3³/₄–5¹/₄ in. (9.5–13.3 cm) L x 2⁵/₈–4¹/₂ in. (6.7–11.4 cm) W

Large. Digitigrade. Symmetrical. Four toes. The metacarpal pads are fused and create one triangular pad; the metacarpal pads may register only partially. The negative space between toes and metacarpals forms an *X*. Nails register reliably. Rear track far more elongated than front track.

Trail: Direct register trot   Stride: 22–34 in. (55.9–86.4 cm)

Trail width: 4–9¹/₄ in. (10.2–23.5 cm)

Side trot   Stride: 26–39 in. (66–99.1 cm)

Group length: 7–15¹/₂ in. (17.8–39.4 cm)

Walk   Stride: 13–24 in. (33–61 cm)

Trail width: 6–10 in. (15.2–25.4 cm)

Lope   Stride: 20–23 in. (50.8–58.4 cm)

Group length: 40–49 in. (1.02–1.25 m)

Gallop   Stride: 6–68 in. (15.2–172.7 cm)

Group length: 55–99 in. (1.4–2.52 m)

Gray wolf
overstep
walk.

Gray wolf
side trot.

Gray wolf
direct
register trot.

Gray wolf
lope track
group.

Gray wolf
gallop track
group.

Front and hind (leading) tracks of the gray wolf. (AK)

Notes:

- Trot incredible distances while exploring and patrolling home ranges. Like coyotes, use numerous gaits, depending on mood and behaviors.
- Do not climb.
- Trot may be duck-toed, with tracks pointing outward.
- Walk in deep snow (although they have the strength to continue to trot to impressive depths). Occasionally bound, but for shorter distances.
- Social animals. Although single animals may be found occasionally, pairs or packs can be found at any time of year. Pack size varies across their range and is dependent on prey species and a host of other variables—numbers range from 4 to more than 30 animals.

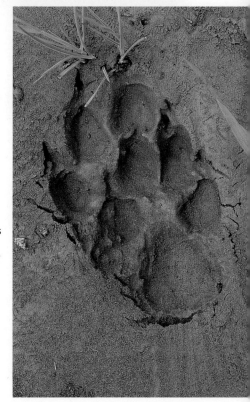

Here is an indirect register, in which a rear track sits on top of a front track. (WY)

Front and hind gray wolf tracks in dust. (ID)

Red Wolf *(Canis rufus)*

Track: Front 3–4¹/₈ in. (7.6–10.5 cm) L x 2¹/₈–3 in. (5.4–7.6 cm) W
Medium to large. Digitigrade. Symmetrical. Five toes: Toe 1 is greatly reduced and raised up on the inner leg. Four toes reliably register in tracks. The metacarpal pads are fused and create one triangular pad. The negative space between toes and metacarpals forms an *X*. There is an additional carpal pad higher on the leg. Nails register reliably. Front track larger than rear track.

Red wolf tracks in sand. The larger track is the front. (NC)

**Red wolf
overstep walk.**

**Red wolf
direct register trot.**

Red wolf tracks in shallow mud;
the front track sits below the hind
track. (NC)

Rear 2³/₄–3³/₄ in. (7–9.5 cm) L x 1¹⁵/₁₆–2³/₄ in. (4.9–7 cm) W

Medium to large. Digitigrade. Symmetrical. Four toes. The metacarpal pads are fused and create one triangular pad; the metacarpal pads may register only partially. The negative space between toes and metacarpals forms an *X*. Nails register reliably. Rear track far more elongated than front track. Overall tracks and individual digital pads more robust than those of coyotes.

(All data gathered in North Carolina.)

Trail:	Direct register trot	Stride: 20–28 in. (50.8–71.1 cm)
		Trail width: 5–9¹/₄ in. (12.7–23.5 cm)
	Side trot	Stride: 24–34¹/₂ in. (61–87.7 cm)
		Group length: 7–15 in. (17.8–38.1 cm)
	Walk	Stride: 14–22 in. (35.6–55.9 cm)
		Trail width: 6–8 in. (15.2–20.3 cm)

Notes:

- Move like coyotes and gray wolves.
- Do not climb.
- Social animals. May be found singly on occasion or in pairs or small family packs at any time of year.
- There is debate about the ancestry and origin of the red wolf. Some believe that it is only a southeastern animal, but others are working to prove that the

wolves of eastern Canada are also red wolves. Research is made difficult by the fact that wolves in the Northeast and Southeast readily interbreed with coyotes, therefore diluting their gene pool. Wildlife officials maintain a coyote-free zone near the coast of North Carolina, at the heart of one of the largest remaining wild red wolf populations.

Arctic Fox *(Alopex lagopus)*

Track: Front 2¹/₄–2³/₄ in. (5.7–7 cm) L x 1³/₄–2¹/₈ in. (4.4–5.4 cm) W

Medium. Digitigrade. Symmetrical. Five toes: Toe 1 is greatly reduced and raised up on the inner leg. Four toes reliably register in tracks. The metacarpal pads are fused and create one triangular pad. Digital and metacarpal pads register very small during summer, as fur grows thick in between the toes and pads, as well as covering the pads on the foot. In winter, no distinct pads may register due

A red wolf side trots while traveling back roads on a coastal reserve. (NC)

to the increased amount of fur covering the feet. The negative space between the toes and metacarpals forms an *X*. There is an additional carpal pad higher on the leg. Nails may or may not register. Front track larger than rear track.

Rear 2–2³/₈ in. (5.1–6 cm) L x 1⁵/₈–1⁷/₈ in. (4.1–4.8 cm) W

Medium. Digitigrade. Symmetrical. Four toes. The metacarpal pads are fused and create one triangular pad; the metacarpal pads may register only partially. Digital and metacarpal pads register very small during summer, as fur grows thick in between the toes and pads, as well as covering the pads on the foot. In winter, no distinct pads may register due to the increased amount of fur covering the feet. The negative space between the toes and metacarpals forms an *X*. Nails may or may not register. Rear track more elongated than front track.

Arctic fox direct register trot.

Arctic fox classic lope used for exploration.

Trail: Direct register trot   Stride: 9–14¹/₂ in. (22.9–36.8 cm)
Trail width: 2¹/₄–4 in. (5.7–10.2 cm)

Walk   Stride: 6–8 in. (15.2–20.3 cm)
Trail width: 3³/₄–4¹/₂ in. (9.5–11.4 cm)

Lope   Stride: 6–10 in. (15.2–25.4 cm)
Group length: 22–32 in. (55.9–80.2 cm)

Notes:
- Explore their range in a lope and use direct register trots and side trots for short trails. The walk is used to investigate—tracking a scent to the source.
- The track is large in proportion to the size of the animal, especially when compared with other canines.

- Follow polar bears during the winter months, feeding off the remains at successful seal kills.
- Live on the open tundra in the far north of Canada and Alaska.
- Can be seen with others, as well as alone.

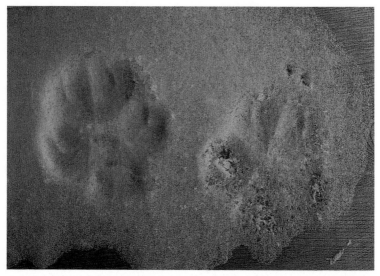

Arctic fox tracks. The front is the larger track, with clear nail registration. (Canada)

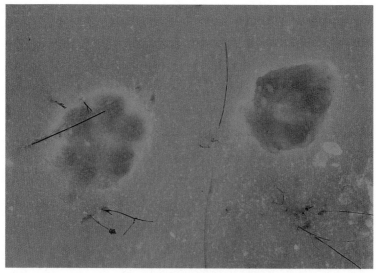

Front and hind (leading) arctic fox tracks in deeper conditions. Toe impressions are faint due to the dense fur covering the feet in winter. (Canada)

Kit or Swift Fox *(Vulpes velox)*

Track: Front 1–1¹¹/₁₆ in. (2.5–4.3 cm) L x ¹⁵/₁₆–1¹/₂ in. (2.4–3.8 cm) W

> Small. Digitigrade. Symmetrical. Five toes: Toe 1 is greatly reduced and raised up on the inner leg. Four toes reliably register in tracks. The metacarpal pads are fused and create one triangular pad. The registration of digital and metacarpal pads may or may not be reduced by additional fur growing on the feet; some kit and swift foxes have furred soles, but others do not. The negative space between toes and metacarpals forms an *H*. There is an additional carpal pad higher on the leg. Nails may or may not register. Front track larger than rear.

Rear 1¹/₈–1⁵/₈ in. (2.9–4.1 cm) L x ⁷/₈–1¹/₄ in. (2.2–3.2 cm) W

> Small. Digitigrade. Symmetrical. Four toes. The metacarpal pads are fused and create one triangular pad; the metacarpal pads may register only partially. The registration of digital and metacarpal pads may or may not be reduced by additional fur growing on the soles; some kit and swift foxes have furred feet, but others do not. The negative space between toes and metacarpals forms an *X*. Nails may or may not register. Rear track more elongated than front track. Tracks in loose sand are splayed and larger.

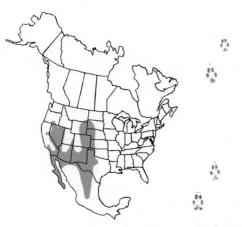

Kit fox side trot.   Kit fox direct register trot.   Kit fox gallop.

Trail: Walk   Stride: 5–7 in. (12.7–17.8 cm)
         Trot   Stride: 8–13 in. (20.3–33 cm)
                         Trail width: 1¼–2⅜ in. (3.2–6 cm)
         Side trot   Stride: 10–14 in. (25.4–35.6 cm)
                         Group length: 3–4¾ in. (7.6–12.1 cm)
         Straddle trot   Stride: 14–16 in. (35.6–40.6 cm)
         Lope   Stride: 5–9 in. (12.7–22.9 cm)
                         Group length: 15–19¾ in. (38.1–50.2 cm)
         Gallop   Stride: 8–36 in. (20.3–91.4 cm)
                         Group length: 25–45 in. (63.5–114.3 cm)

Notes:

- There is still debate whether the kit and swift foxes are individual species or subspecies of the same animal. Measurements provided here involve both animals.
- Often explore in a lope and use side trots and direct register trots. Use walks to investigate more thoroughly.
- Only fox found in extreme desert conditions.
- In some parts of its range, such as Bakersfield, California, the kit fox is doing quite well in urban environments. The swift fox is being introduced in grasslands in the north-central United States and south-central Canada, where foxes once roamed.

Left: Front and hind (behind) swift fox tracks. Note the "bar" on the front foot, similar to that found in larger red fox tracks. (CO) *Right:* Dainty tracks of a kit fox in mud. Note the fur covering the toe pads. (CA)

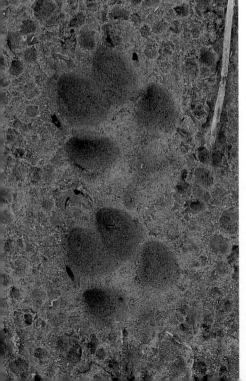

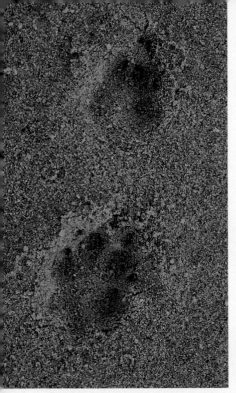

Left: **Perfect front and hind (above) tracks of a kit fox in sand dune habitat. (CA)**
Right: **A kit fox's side trot. (CA)**

- Tend to be solitary, but may crisscross trails of other foxes.
- Den and lay up in underground dens and burrows.

Red Fox *(Vulpes vulpes)*

Track: Front 1⁷/₈–2⁷/₈ in. (4.8–7.3 cm) L x 1³/₈–2¹/₈ in. (3.5–5.4 cm) W
(young: 1³/₈ x 1³/₈ in. [3.5 x 3.5 cm])

Small to medium. Digitigrade. Symmetrical. Five toes: Toe 1 is greatly reduced and raised up on the inner leg. Four toes reliably register in tracks. The metacarpal pads are fused and create one triangular pad. The registration of digital and metacarpal pads is greatly reduced by fur growing on the feet, although less so during summer. The negative space between the toes and pads is exaggerated by the excess fur and reduced exposure of the toe pads. The metacarpal pad often appears in the track as a chevron-shaped or flat line and is a key feature for quick identification. The negative space between toes and metacarpals forms an *X*. There is an additional carpal pad higher on the leg, which registers when the fox is pouncing or traveling at high speeds. Nails are semiretractable and may or may not register. Front track larger and often rounder than rear.

Rear 1⁵/₈–2¹/₂ in. (4.1–6.4 cm) L x 1¹/₄–1⁷/₈ in. (3.2–4.8 cm) W
(young: 1³/₈ x 1³/₁₆ in. [3.5 x 3 cm])

Small to medium. Digitigrade. Symmetrical. Four toes. The metacarpal pads are fused and create one triangular pad; the metacarpal pads may register only partially. The registration of digital and metacarpal pads is

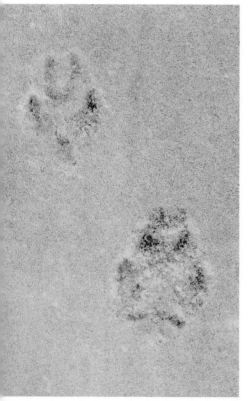

Front and hind (above) red fox tracks in a dusting of snow. The heavy fur on the foot surface blurs the tracks considerably. (NH)

Red fox direct register trot.

Red fox side trot.

greatly reduced by fur growing on the feet, although less so during summer. The negative space between the toes and pads is exaggerated by the excess fur and reduced exposure of the toe pads. The negative space between toes and metacarpals forms an *X*. Nails are semiretractable and may or may not register.

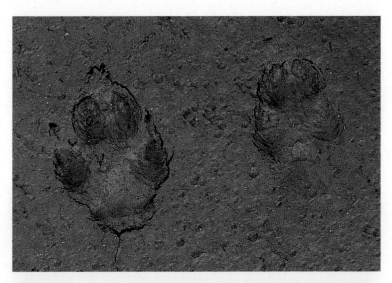

Top: The front and hind tracks of a red fox, and a mouse trail. The front is the larger track. (ID) *Bottom:* Red fox tracks in sand. Hair does not register, as in mud, but the large space between the toes and palm hints at a furry sole. The front track is larger than the hind track. (MA)

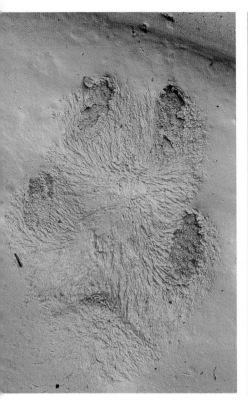

Left: A beautiful close-up of a red fox hind track in wet clay. There is lots of fur. Look closely for the sharp nails, which registered near the edge of the picture. (NH) *Right:* Walking trail of a red fox. (NH)

Trail:	Walk	Stride: 8–12 in. (20.3–30.5 cm)
	Trot	Stride: 13–20 in. (33–50.8 cm)
		Trail width: 2–3¾ in. (5.1–9.5 cm)
	Side trot:	Stride: 14–22¾ in. (35.6–57.8 cm)
		Group length: 4½–8 in. (11.4–20.3 cm)
	Lope	Stride: 9–15 in. (22.9–38.1 cm)
		Group length: 20–29 in. (50.8–73.7 cm)
	Gallop	Stride: 8–55 in. (20.3–139.7 cm); occasionally up to 109 in. (2.77 m)
		Group length: 25–60 in. (63.5 –152.4 cm)

Notes:

- Natural rhythm is the trot; most often found moving in a direct register. Regularly use the side trot as well and occasionally use a straddle trot, but never for sustained distances. Walk to explore, and use lopes and gallops at speed.
- In deep snow, most often walk but may also bound; each hole in the snow would then be all four feet and body.
- Comfortable among human habitations and live in our largest cities.
- Do not climb but easily move up angled trunks and can cruise along the tops of stone walls, logs, and the like with a catlike agility.
- Generally solitary, except from breeding season into the denning season.

t-Trails and Box Stops

When walking and trotting animals pause momentarily, there is often a **t** in the trail. The vertical line of the **t** is the regular trail pattern, and the horizontal slash is created by the two front tracks lying next to each other.

This pattern is often seen before crossing a road, at a trail junction, or when something is heard a distance away.

A variation of the **t**-trail is the box stop, where two corners are the front tracks and the other two corners are the hind tracks. The additional hind track that has been set down midstride is often very light.

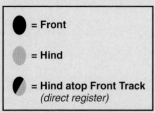

● = Front

● = Hind

◗ = Hind atop Front Track
(direct register)

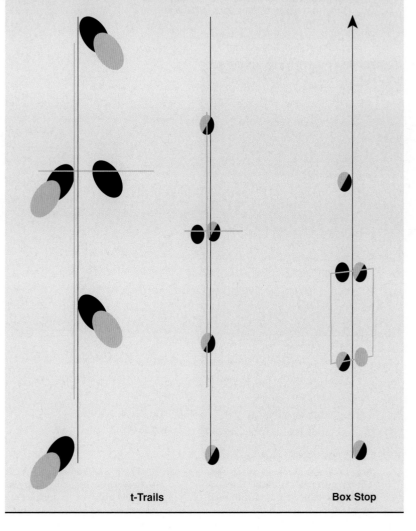

t-Trails   Box Stop

Common Gray Fox
(Urocyon cinereoargenteus)

Track: Front 1³/₈–1⁷/₈ in. (3.5–4.8 cm) L
x 1³/₁₆–1³/₄ in. (3–4.4 cm) W

Small. Digitigrade. Symmetrical. Five toes: Toe 1 is greatly reduced and raised up on the inner leg. Four toes reliably register in tracks. The metacarpal pads are fused and create one rounded but triangular pad. The negative space between the toes and metacarpals forms an *H*. There is an additional carpal pad higher on the leg. Nails are semiretractable and may or may not register. Front track larger and rounder than rear.

Rear 1¹/₄–1³/₄ in. (3.2–4.4 cm) L
x ¹⁵/₁₆–1¹/₂ in. (2.4–3.8 cm) W

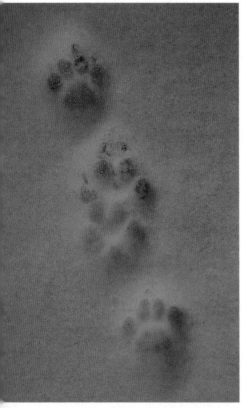

Gray fox tracks bordered on top and bottom by house cat tracks. The two species are often confused with each other. (NH)

Gray fox
straddle trot.

Gray fox
indirect register
trot.

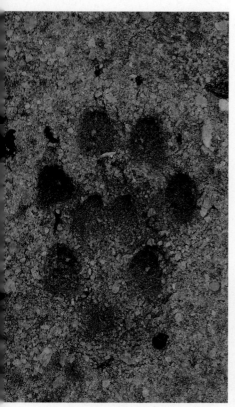 

Left: Gray fox tracks. (FL) *Right:* Beautiful gray fox front and hind (above) tracks. (TX)

Small. Digitigrade. Symmetrical. Four toes. The metacarpal pads are fused and create one rounded but triangular pad; the metacarpal pads may register only partially. The negative space between the toes and metacarpals forms an *X*. Nails are semiretractable and may or may not register. Rear track more elongated than front track.

Trail:	Walk	Stride: 6–10 in. (15.2–25.4 cm)
		Trail width: 3–4½ in. (7.6–11.4 cm)
	Trot	Stride: 9–18 in. (22.9–45.7 cm)
		Trail width: 1⅞–4 in. (4.8–10.2 cm)
	Straddle trot	Stride: 13–16 in. (33–40.6 cm)
		Group length: 3½–4½ in. (8.9–11.4 cm)
	Lope	Stride: 15–22 in. (38.1–55.9 cm)
		Group length: 16–20 in. (40.6–50.8 cm)
	Gallop	Stride: 13–68 in. (33–172.7 cm)
		Group length: 15–51 in. (38.1–129.5 cm)

Notes:

• Move about their range in a trot, but also travel roads and cross open areas in a straddle trot. I have seen a gray fox in a side trot only once; they almost exclusively speed up into a straddle trot.

Left: A round front track and a small hind track of a gray fox. (NH) *Right:* Gray fox (left) and house cat trails sharing a frozen inlet. (NH)

- Capable climbers, although they generally climb angled trunks and saplings, as well as trees with ample lower limbs. May bed in trees and shrubs. Trails often found along the tops of logs, walls, fences, and other raised surfaces, evidence of their catlike agility.

- Often use holes, slash piles, or other cover for bedding purposes and rarely lay out in the open. (Most of my experience with gray foxes has been in the Northeast. They may bed in different areas in warmer and drier climates.)

- Tend to struggle in deep snow and will hole up for long periods when conditions are poor (I had one hole up for 10 days near an old apartment, deep in a slash pile). When snowmobile or cross-country trails are available, they use these as their primary travel routes, taking short excursions off to either side to hunt and forage.

- Generally solitary, except from breeding season into denning season.

Bears: Family Ursidae

- Bears are large, wide-bodied mammals with five toes on each foot.
- Bears fear little except other bears and humans, and their fear of people can be overcome with food reinforcements.
- They use trails and road systems readily.
- Bears are solitary, except for mating season and family groups, which are composed of a female and her most recent offspring. Food abundance may create scenarios in which bears congregate and interact.

American Black Bear *(Ursus americanus)*

Track: Front 3³/₄–8 in. (9.5–20.3 cm) L x 3¹/₄–6 in. (8.3–15.2 cm) W (cub: 3¹/₄ x 2³/₄ in. [8.3 x 7 cm])

Large to very large. Plantigrade. Asymmetrical. Five toes: Toe 1 is the smallest, located on the inside of the track, and does not register reliably. The metacarpal pads are fused and create one large, curved pad that is much wider than long; the curve of the anterior edge is useful when differentiating between brown and black bears. There is an additional circular pad (the heel) at the posterior edge of the track, which may or may not show. The negative space between the toes and metacarpals is filled with fur, which may blur the overall track appearance. Nails may or may not register, and they vary in length from bear to bear; nails on the front feet are longer than on hinds.

Rear 5³/₈–8⁷/₈ in. (13.7–22.5 cm) L x 3¹/₂–6 in. (8.9–15.2 cm) W (cub: 3¹/₄ x 2³/₄ in. [8.3 x 7 cm])

Large to very large. Plantigrade. Asymmetrical. Five toes: Toe 1 is the smallest. The metacarpal pads are fused and create one large pad. The "palm" and "heel" are covered in tough skin

Black bear over-step walk.   Black bear lope into gallop.

Above: Black bear tracks. (CT) *Below left:* Black bear. Note that the heel of the rear track (above) did not register. (AK) *Below right:* A perfect black bear front track. Note the additional round heel pad at the posterior edge of the track. (WY)

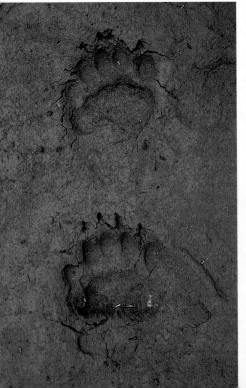

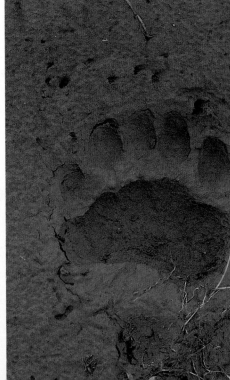

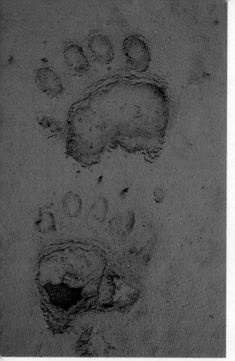

Left: Black bear front and hind (above) tracks in glacial silt. (AK) *Right:* A black bear explores a river edge in an overstep walk, which is a typical gait and trail pattern. (AK)

and are all connected; look for a *V* cut into the pad, filled with fur at the place where the palm and heel meet in the track (useful to differentiate from brown bears, as is the curvature of the anterior edge). The negative space between the toes and metacarpals is filled with fur, which may blur the overall track appearance. Nails may or may not register, and they vary in length from bear to bear.

Trail:		
	Direct register walk	Stride: 17–25 in. (43.2–63.5 cm)
		Trail width: 8–14 in. (20.3–35.6 cm)
	Overstep walk	Stride: 19–28 in. (48.3–71.1 cm)
		Trail width: 8–14 in. (20.3–35.6 cm)
	Trot	Stride: 27–37 in. (68.6–94 cm)
		Trail width: 6–10 in. (15.2–25.4 cm)
	3x lope	Stride: 25–30 in. (63.5–76.2 cm)
		Group length: 38–50 in. (96.5–127 cm)
	Gallop	Stride: 24–60 in. (61–152.4 cm)
		Group length: 49–75 in. (124.5–190.5 cm)

Notes:
- Tend to walk about the landscape, but trot to cover open ground or when they feel threatened or exposed. Lope when startled or to leave an area, and gallop in extreme circumstances or when afraid.
- Incredibly widespread, and increasing in numbers in many areas of North America.
- Play in isolation as well as with other bears.
- Competent climbers; can also walk along logs and porch railings, balancing on narrow surfaces at various heights off the ground.
- Direct register walk in deep snow and sometimes use a 2x2 lope, much like weasels.

Brown or Grizzly Bear *(Ursus arctos)*

Track: Front 7–13½ in. (17.8–34.3 cm) L x 5–8¾ in. (12.7–22.2 cm) W

Very large. Plantigrade. Asymmetrical. Five toes: Toe 1 is the smallest, located on the inside of the track, and does not register reliably. The metacarpal pads are fused and create one large pad that is much wider than long; the curvature of the anterior edge is useful when differentiating between brown and black bears. There is an additional circular pad (the heel) at the posterior edge of the track, which may or may not show. There is far less fur in the track than in those of either black or polar bears. Nails almost always register and can be incredibly long. Claws vary in length from bear to bear and are useful when differentiating other bear species, but do not rely on claw length alone, as there are both brown bears with short claws and black bears with long claws.

Rear 8¼–14 in. (21–35.6 cm) L x 4⅝–8½ in. (11.7–21.6 cm) W (There are records of 16-inch [40.6–cm] tracks.)

Very large. Plantigrade. Asymmetrical. Five toes: Toe 1 is the smallest. The metacarpal pads are fused and create one large pad. The "palm" and "heel" are covered in tough skin and are connected. Far less fur registers in the tracks of grizzly bears than in those of either black or polar bears. Nails tend to register and vary in length from bear to bear.

Brown bear
slow 2x2 walk.

Brown bear
overstep walk.

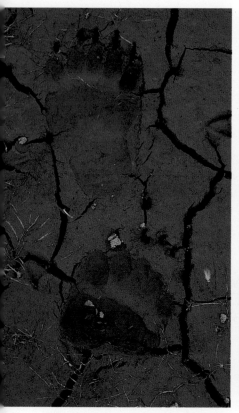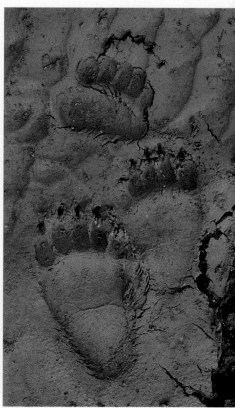

Left: Grizzly bear tracks. (MT) *Right:* A grizzly sow's front and hind (below) tracks, and the track of a second-year cub. (AK)

Trail:	Pacelike walk	Stride: 25–33 in. (63.5–83.8 cm)
		Trail width: 10–16 in. (25.4–40.6 cm)
	Direct register walk	Stride: 19–29 in. (48.3–73.7 cm)
		Trail width: 13–20 in. (33–50.8 cm)
	Overstep walk	Stride: 25–42 in. (63.5–106.7 cm)
		Trail width: 10–19 in. (25.4–48.3 cm)
	3x lope	Stride: 18–33 in. (45.7–83.8 cm)
		Group length 59–87 in. (1.5–2.21 m)
	Gallop	Stride: 30–35 in. (76.2–88.9 cm)
		Group length: 85–95 in. (2.16–2.41 m)

Notes:

• Brown bears and grizzlies were once considered separate species, but no longer. Coastal bears along the Pacific in Canada and Alaska are generally referred to as brown bears, while inland bears and southern populations in the lower 48 states tend to be called grizzly bears.

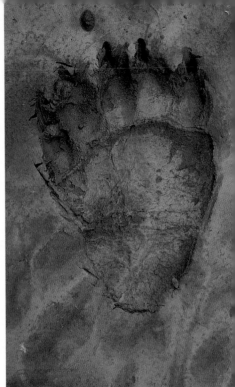

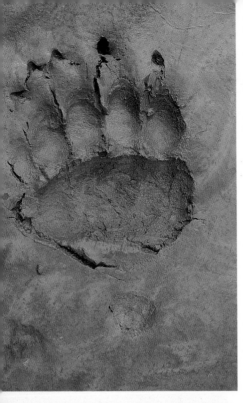

Above left: **Perfect front track of a large brown bear. (AK)** *Above right:* **The accompanying perfect hind track. (AK)** *Left:* **A grizzly's overstep walk. (MT)**

- Tend to walk about the landscape. Lope when startled or to leave an area, and gallop in extreme circumstances or when afraid.
- Use a slow walk in which front and hind limbs on one side move nearly simultaneously—much like a raccoon.
- Found only in northwest North America.
- Known to play in isolation as well as with other bears.
- Can climb, but generally stay on the ground, especially the larger animals.
- Direct register walk in deep snow.

The Head

The position of the head as an animal moves can often be determined by looking for the deepest part of an individual front track. Significant head movements are often more easily determined by studying the overall track pattern. This method of determining an animal's head placement, and potentially where it was looking, is most effective with slower gaits. Walking is best, but it also applies to trotting.

There has been discussion in the field about interpreting where a canine is looking by noting which side is kicked out during a side trot. I pursued this subject in my own research, but unfortunately, I found that a canine can look wherever it wants, regardless of which way the rear end is angled.

= Front

= Hind

In this polar bear trail, the bear looked backwards over his right shoulder. Both the third and fourth paired tracks are influenced in this case, as the bear twisted substantially to look behind itself. An animal looking to either side will leave subtle track pattern variations.

Polar Bear *(Ursus maritimus)*

Track: Front 6–14 in. (15.2–35.6 cm) L x 6–10 in. (15.2–25.4 cm) W

Very large. Plantigrade. Asymmetrical. Five toes: Toe 1 is the smallest, located on the inside of the track, and does not register reliably. The metacarpal pads are fused and create one large, curved pad that is much wider than long (more similar to black than brown bears); the curvature of the anterior edge is useful when differentiating between brown and polar bears. There is an additional pad (the heel) at the posterior edge of the track, which may or may not show. The negative space between the toes

and metacarpals is filled with fur, which may blur the overall track appearance. Nails may or may not register, and they vary in length from bear to bear. The width of polar bear tracks is significantly greater than that of other bears; this is especially apparent in the tracks of mature animals.

Rear 8$\frac{1}{2}$–15 in. (21.6–38.1 cm) L x 6–9$\frac{3}{4}$ in. (15.2–24.8 cm) W

Very large. Plantigrade. Asymmetrical. Five toes: Toe 1 is the smallest. The metacarpal pads are fused and create one large pad. The "palm" and "heel" are covered in tough skin and are connected. The negative space between the toes and metacarpals is filled with fur, which may blur the overall track appearance. Nails may or may not register, and they vary in length from bear to bear. The width of polar

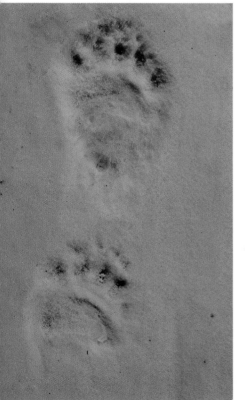

Polar bear slow walk.

Front and hind (above) tracks of a subadult polar bear under the illumination of streetlights at night. (Canada)

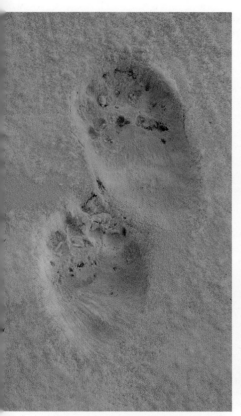

Left: Furry front and hind (behind) tracks of a mature polar bear. (Canada) *Right:* Typical walking track pattern of an adult polar bear. (Canada)

bear tracks is significantly greater than that of other bears; this is especially apparent in the tracks of mature animals.

Trail: Direct register walk   Stride: 22–35 in. (55.9–88.9 cm)

Trail width: 13–26 in. (33–66 cm)

Notes:

• Tend to walk about the landscape. Lope when startled or to leave an area, and gallop in extreme circumstances or when afraid.

• Arctic animals, found only in the far north.

• Direct register walk in deep snow.

• The Hudson Bay population gathers in great numbers to wait for the bay to freeze. During this time, males are often seen wandering, resting, and engaging in short, intense wrestling bouts.

Weasels: Family Mustelidae

- Weasels have five toes on each foot, and each front foot has an arcing pattern of fused and separate metacarpal pads, as well as an additional pad or two at the rear of the track.

- Weasels tend to be crepuscular and nocturnal in areas where people are active but may be found moving at any time of day or night.

- Small weasels explore and hunt in a lope or modified bound, but slow to a walk to explore potential resources. When very exposed or in pursuit, small weasels use a rabbitlike bound.

- The track and trail parameters of least weasels, ermines, and long-tailed weasels involve some overlap. Large ermines can easily be mistaken for smaller long-tailed weasels, and large least weasels can be mistaken for smaller ermines.

- The bounding and loping trails of all three small weasels can be quite erratic, in that they are a mix of long and short strides. Weasels can also make incredibly sharp turns; from one set of four tracks to the next, a turn up to 360 degrees is possible.

American Marten *(Martes americana)*

Track: Front 1⅝–2¾ in. (4.1–7 cm) L x 1⁵⁄₁₆–2⅝ in. (3.3–6.7 cm) W
Small to medium. Plantigrade. Asymmetrical. Five toes: Toe 1 is the smallest, located on the inside of the track, and does not register reliably. Several metacarpal pads are fused, and others register individually; there are two additional pads (the heel) at the posterior edge of the track, one of which may or may not show. The negative space between the toes and metacarpals is filled with fur, which often blurs the overall track appearance. Nails may or may not register. Front track more symmetrical than rear track.
Rear 1½–2¾ in. (3.8–7 cm) L x 1³⁄₁₆–2¼ in. (3–5.7 cm) W
Small to medium. Plantigrade. Asymmetrical. Five toes: Toe 1 is the smallest. Some of the metacarpal pads are fused, and others register separately. The furred "heel" often registers, as well. The negative space between the toes and metacarpals is filled with fur, which often blurs the overall track appearance. Nails may or may not register. Because toe 1 sits farther back in rear tracks than front tracks, rear tracks are far more asymmetrical than fronts. There is some overlap in track dimensions with fishers and mink.

Trail: 3x4 lope   Stride: 8–32 in. (20.3–81.3 cm)
Group length: 7½–20 in. (19.1–50.8 cm)
2x2 lope   Stride: 10–34 in. (25.4–86.4 cm); occasionally up to 6 ft. (1.83 m)
Trail width: 2½–4½ in. (6.4–11.4 cm)
Group length: 3½–7½ in. (8.9–19.1 cm)
Walk   Stride: 5–9 in. (12.7–22.9 cm)
Trail width: 3¼–5½ in. (8.3–13.3 cm)
Body print (without tail): 9–14 in. (22.9–35.6 cm) L x 4–8 in. (10.2–20.3 cm) W

Notes:
- Roam their home range in a 3x4 lope (more often a 2x2 in deep snow). Walk when exploring and investigating.
- Move in the open, but generally do not cross completely open fields.

- Use trails readily and mark them more than fishers do. Will cross roads, but often seek culverts to do so.
- Inhabit the mountain regions of Colorado, the Northwest, California, and the extreme northeastern United States, and more varied terrain in Canada and Alaska.
- Competent climbers; spend much of their time hunting in trees. Rear feet may turn 180 degrees, allowing them to move head-first down trunks, as well as up.

American marten
3x4 gallop into
3x4 lope.

American marten
walk.

American marten
2x2 lope.

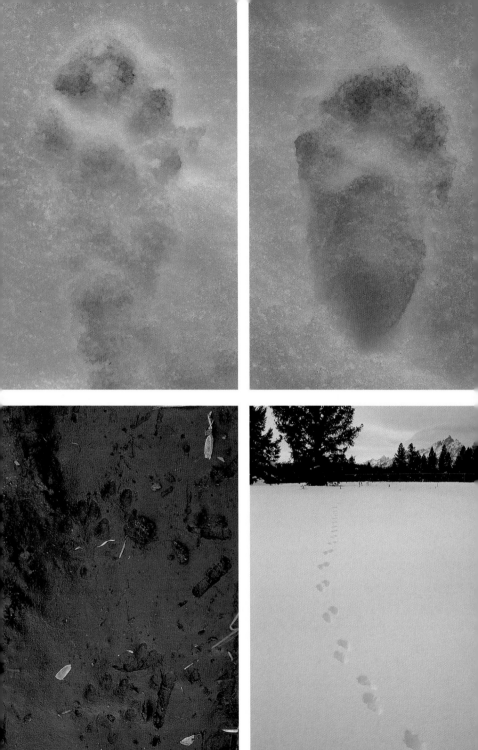

Facing page, top left: Front track of a marten. (ID) *Top right:* The accompanying hind track. (ID) *Bottom left:* Marten tracks in a mud puddle along with grouse and western jumping mouse tracks. (ID) *Bottom right:* A marten's 2x2 lope. (WY)

Look for body prints—where they have jumped from a tree rather than climbed down—up to 18 ft. 10 in. from trees; body prints are found more often along marten trails than fisher trails.
- Trails explore holes and nooks within root wads and boulder jumbles. Use culverts to cross under roads and may be found holing up underground.
- In deep snow, tend to use a 2x2 lope or walk.
- Solitary animals, except for mating and rearing of young.

Fisher *(Martes pennanti)*

Track: Front 2¹/₈–3⁷/₈ in. (5.4–9.8 cm) L x 1⁷/₈–4¹/₄ in. (4.8–10.8 cm) W

Medium. Plantigrade. Asymmetrical. Five toes: Toe 1 is the smallest, located on the inside of the track, and does not register reliably. Several metacarpal pads are fused, and others register individually; there are two additional pads (the heel) at the posterior edge of the track, one of which may or may not show. The negative space between the toes and metacarpals is filled with fur, which may blur the overall track appearance; compare this feature with the relatively naked feet of otters. Nails may or may not register. Front track is larger and more symmetrical than rear track.

Rear 2–3¹/₈ in. (5.1–7.9 cm) L x 1¹/₂–3¹/₂ in. (3.8–8.9 cm) W

Medium. Plantigrade. Asymmetrical. Five toes: Toe 1 is the smallest. Some of the metacarpal pads are fused, and others register separately. The furred "heel" often registers as well. The negative space between the toes and metacarpals is filled with fur, which may blur the overall track appearance. Nails may or may not register. Because toe 1 sits farther back in rear tracks than front tracks, rear tracks are far more asymmetrical than fronts. There is some overlap in track dimensions with martens and otters.

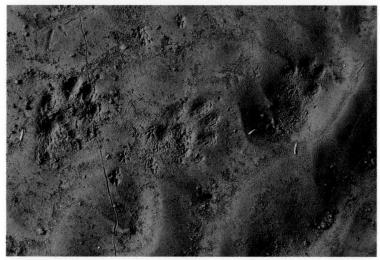

Large front tracks and smaller hind tracks along a muddy riverbank. A chipmunk passes between the two front tracks. (MA)

Fisher
walk.

Fisher
3x4 lope.

Fisher
2x2 lope.

Facing page, top left: Fisher tracks in wet snow register toes and claws clearly.
Compare these tracks with those in the next photo. (NH) *Top right:* These fisher
tracks are in drier, shallow snow. (NH) *Bottom left:* A fisher's walk in deep snow.
Note the prominent claws. (NH) *Bottom right:* Body print where a fisher landed
after jumping from a tree. Often the tail registers as well, but the snow was quite
shallow here. (NH)

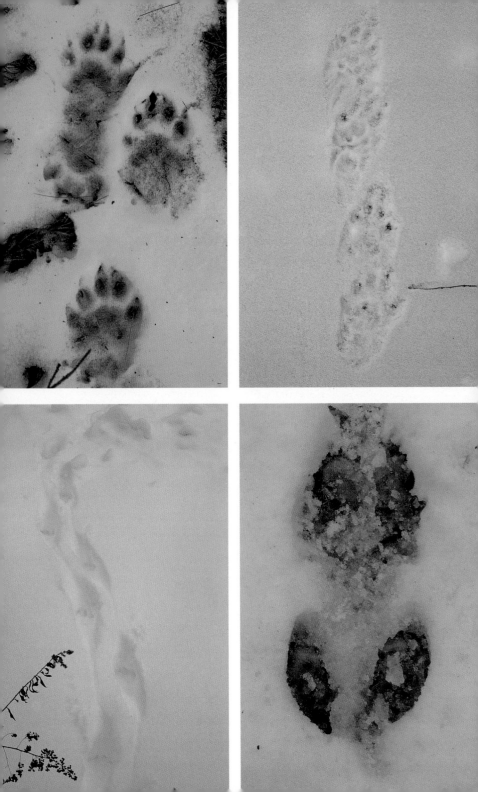

Lessons from a Fisher

It was a fine sunny morning when I left home for one of my favorite local tracking spots. The snow had stopped the evening before, leaving a white carpet between 1 and 2 inches thick—perfect tracking conditions. With so little snow, animals would remain in their most natural gaits and glide effortlessly through the forest.

I soon encountered a long-tailed weasel trail on a closed road, and not 10 feet beyond, that of a short-tailed weasel. It was great to see these two animal trails so close together. I stood staring at the trails, wishing that they'd move a bit closer together for photography purposes, when I heard something.

Moving toward me from upslope was the muffled sound of feet on leaf litter. He came into view, and I watched him glide from snag to rock outcrop to log, pausing to check every nook and cranny. As he moved closer, I was thrilled to realize that on his present course, he'd come out on the road right before me.

The fisher mounted the road easily and paused not 8 feet from where I stood, completely exposed on the shoulder. Standing 2½ feet tall, he raised up on his hind feet to study me further. He was beautiful. His dark chocolate coat was streaked with milk chocolate, and the tips of his fur seemed frosted, glistening in the mid-morning sun. His eyes were filled with curiosity, intelligence, and mischief. Satisfied, he dropped down and moved downhill along the road. It was the perfect opportunity to watch a fisher move in its natural rhythm. His lope was effortless, like a dolphin surfacing for air. He glided in arcing motions with fluid elasticity.

About 30 feet down the road he stopped and reared up on his hind feet to study me again. This was the most fascinating part. I watched his eyes as he moved his attention slowly down my body to my feet and then backward along my boot prints to where my trail passed several feet from him. He dropped down, walked over to the nearest boot print, and stuffed his nose in it for confirma-

Trail:	3x4 lope	Stride: 5³/₄–30 in. (14.6–76.2 cm)
		Group length: 12–26 in. (30.5–66 cm)
	Full gallop	Stride: 15–31 in. (38.1–78.7 cm)
		Group length: 31–40 in. (78.7–101.6 cm)
	2x2 lope	Stride: 17–45 in. (43.2–114.3 cm); have seen up to 78 in. (1.98 m)
		Trail width: 3–5½ in. (7.6–14 cm)
		Group length: 6–13 in. (15.2–33 cm)
	Walk	Stride: 7–11½ in. (17.8–29.2 cm)
		Trail width: 5–6½ in. (12.7–16.5 cm)
	Trot	Stride: 13½–19 in. (34.3–48.3 cm)
		Trail width: 3–4⅞ in. (7.6–12.4 cm)
	Body print (without tail) : 10–18 in. (25.4–45.7 cm) L	

tion of his suspicions. His head jerked up, and his eyes looked surprised. Then he was off! He glided in much the same way as before, but took longer strides and was clearly moving faster.

I had the perfect opportunity to study and correlate track patterns with body mechanics. I expected the patterns to be similar, but they were not. He had switched his order of footfalls from a rotary lope (3×4) to a transverse lope (2×2), in addition to taking longer strides to increase speed.

Fishers also use the 2×2 lope to maintain energy efficiency in deep snow. I have watched fishers gliding through deep snow in a natural rhythm without alarm or awareness of me. They use the 2×2 lope, and the strides are fairly short. It makes sense to reuse the holes and packed surface created by the front feet rather than punch new holes for the rear feet. The size and weight of the animal influence what is meant by "deep" substrate. In 3 inches of light snow, a marten may move mostly in a 2×2 lope, while a large fisher may still be able to move efficiently in a 3×4 lope.

A fisher moving in a 3x4 lope. (NH)

Notes:
- Use a 3x4 lope for much of the time, exploring and investigating in a walk.
- Avoid moving in open areas.
- Generally ignore trails and roads made by other species, crossing them and preferring to move where they choose.
- Although sporadically found in the wilder portions of the West, they are common in the Northeast and successfully expanding their range south.
- Competent climbers; spend time hunting in trees as well as on the ground. Rear feet may turn 180 degrees, allowing them to move head-first down trunks, as well as up. Look for body prints, where they have jumped from a tree rather than climbed down.
- Trails explore holes and nooks within root wads and boulder jumbles, as well as cavities in trees and snags. Occasionally, I have found them holing up in underground burrows—which they did not dig.
- In deep snow, tend to use a 2x2 lope or walk.
- Solitary animals, except for mating and rearing of young.

Ermine or Short-tailed Weasel *(Mustela erminea)*

Track: Front $^7/_{16}$–$^5/_8$ in. (1.1–1.6 cm) L x $^7/_{16}$–$^5/_8$ in. (1.1–1.6 cm) W

Alaska front $^3/_4$–1$^1/_8$ in. (1.9–2.9 cm) L x $^7/_{16}$–$^7/_8$ in. (1.1–2.2 cm) W

Very small to small. Plantigrade. Asymmetrical. Five toes: Toe 1 is the smallest, located on the inside of the track, and does not register reliably. Several metacarpal pads are fused but individually lobed, and others register individually; there is an additional pad (the heel) at the posterior edge of the track, which may or may not show. The negative space between the toes and metacarpals is furry, which influences the track appearance. Nails may or may not register. Front track often larger and more symmetrical than rear track; occasionally the rear registers larger than the front.

Rear $^7/_{16}$–$^9/_{16}$ in. (1.1–1.4 cm) L x $^3/_8$–$^3/_4$ in. (1–1.9 cm) W

Alaska rear $^5/_8$–1 in. (1.6–2.5 cm) L x $^7/_{16}$–$^7/_8$ in. (1.1–2.2 cm) W

Very small to small. Plantigrade. Asymmetrical. Five toes: Toe 1 is the smallest. Some of the metacarpal pads are fused, and others register separately. The furred "heel" may register. The negative space between the toes and metacarpals is furry, which influences the track appearance. Nails may or may not register. Because toe 1 sits farther back in rear tracks than front tracks, rear tracks are far more asymmetrical than fronts. Track and trail parameters overlap with those of other small weasels.

Ermine lope in
shallow substrate.

Ermine 2x2 lope
in deep snow.

Trail: 2x2 gallop   Stride: 4–40 in. (10.2–101.6 cm)
                           Trail width: $^7/_8$–1$^7/_8$ in. (2.2–4.8 cm)
         Bound (Alaska)   Stride: 14–22 in. (35.6–55.9 cm)
                           Trail width: 1$^3/_4$–2$^1/_2$ in. (4.4–6.4 cm)
                           Group length: 2$^5/_8$–4 in. (6.7–10.2 cm)

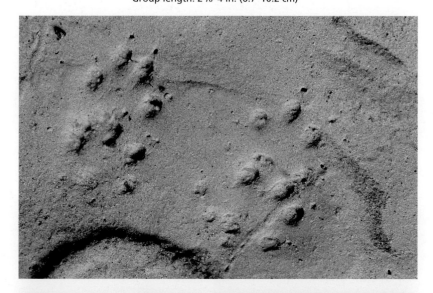

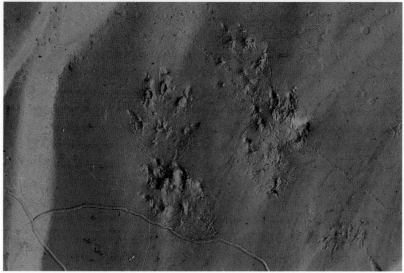

Top: Ermine tracks. (WA) *Bottom:* Large ermine tracks. The uppermost and lower-most tracks are the hind tracks; the two in line with each other are the front tracks. (AK)

Left: **Small ermine tracks. The penny is ³/₄ inch (1.9 cm) in diameter. (WY)** *Right:* **An ermine explores an old burn site in a 2x2 lope. (MT)**

Notes:
- Ermines in the far northern portion of their range are notably larger than their southern counterparts. For this reason, I lumped my data into two chunks—those I collected in the lower 48 states, and those I collected in central Alaska.
- Quite comfortable moving out in the open.
- Roads and trails do not generally influence their movements.
- Widespread in habitat and across the country; inhabit the far north but do not inhabit the desert Southwest or Mexico.
- Can climb.
- Trails explore holes, nooks, and crannies in rock walls, in root systems, under buildings, in trees, and under snow.
- In deep snow, tend to stick to a 2x2 lope, but occasionally investigate in a walk. Tunnel in deep snow as well.
- Solitary animals, except for mating and rearing of young; however, pairs are occasionally seen traveling together outside the mating season.

Long-tailed Weasel *(Mustela frenata)*

Track: Front ⁵/₈–1⁷/₁₆ in. (1.6–3.7 cm) L x ³/₄–1³/₁₆ in. (1.9–3 cm) W

Very small to small. Plantigrade. Asymmetrical. Five toes: Toe 1 is the smallest, located on the inside of the track, and does not register reliably. Several metacarpal pads are fused but individually lobed, and others register individually; there is an additional pad (the heel) at the posterior edge of the track, which may or may not show. The negative space between the toes and metacarpals is furry, which influences track appearance. Nails may or may not register. Front track larger and more symmetrical than rear track; occasionally, rear registers larger than front.

Rear ³/₄–1¹/₂ in. (1.9–3.8 cm) L x ⁹/₁₆–1 in. (1.4–2.5 cm) W

Very small to small. Plantigrade. Asymmetrical. Five toes: Toe 1 is the smallest. Some of the metacarpal pads are

Long-tailed weasel bound.

Long-tailed weasel 2x2 lope in deep snow.

Long-tailed weasel tracks in a bound pattern. The two smaller rear tracks register beyond the fronts. The penny is ³/₄ inch (1.9 cm) in diameter. (MA)

Often, weasel tracks consist only of claws. (MA)

fused, and others register separately. The furred "heel" may register. The negative space between the toes and metacarpals is furry, which influences track appearance. Nails may or may not register. Because toe 1 sits farther back in rear tracks than front tracks, rear tracks are far more asymmetrical than fronts. Track and trail parameters overlap with those of other small weasels.

Trail: 2x2 lope   Stride: 10–45 in. (25.4–114.3 cm)
                   Trail width: $1^5/_8$–$2^7/_8$ in. (3.5–7.3 cm)
       Bound   Stride: 15–25 in. (38.1–63.5 cm)
                   Trail width: $1^7/_8$–$2^7/_8$ in. (4.8–7.3 cm)
                   Group length: 6–11 in. (15.2–27.9 cm)

Notes:
- Quite comfortable moving out in the open.
- Roads and trails generally do not influence their movements.
- Widespread in habitat and across the country; limited to the southern portions of Canada.
- Can climb and swim; it is not uncommon to find trails entering and exiting water.
- Trails explore holes, nooks, and crannies in rock walls, in root systems, under buildings, in trees, and under snow.
- In deep snow, tend to stick to a 2x2 lope, but occasionally investigate in a walk. Tunnel in deep snow as well.
- Solitary animals, except for mating and rearing of young.

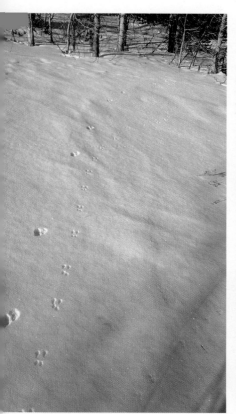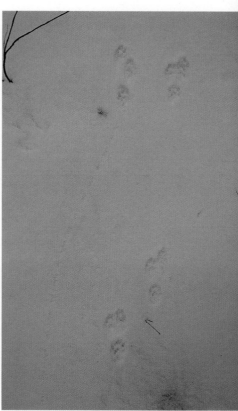

Left: A long-tailed weasel follows the bounding trail of a white-footed mouse species in a 2x2 lope. (MT) *Right:* Two 3x4 long-tailed weasel lope trails in shallow snow. (NH)

Black-footed Ferret
(Mustela nigripes)

Track: Front 1¹/₈–1⁵/₈ in. (2.9–4.1 cm) L
x ⁷/₈–1⁵/₈ in. (2.2–4.1 cm) W

Small. Plantigrade. Asymmetrical. Five toes: Toe 1 is the smallest, located on the inside of the track, and does not register reliably. Several metacarpal pads are fused but individually lobed, and others register individually; there is an additional pad (the heel) at the posterior edge of the track, which may or may not show. The negative space between the toes and metacarpals is furry, which

influences track appearance. Nails may or may not register. Front track larger and more symmetrical than rear track; occasionally, rear registers larger than front.

Rear ³/₄–1³/₈ in. (1.9–3.5 cm) L x ⁷/₈–1³/₈ in. (2.2–3.5 cm) W

Small. Plantigrade. Asymmetrical. Five toes: Toe 1 is the smallest. Some of the metacarpal pads are fused, and others register separately. The furred "heel" may register. The negative space between the toes and metacarpals is furry, which influences track appearance. Nails may or may not register. Because toe 1 sits farther back in rear tracks than front tracks, rear tracks are far more asymmetrical than fronts.

(Parameters created from a limited data pool).

Trail: 2x2 lope   Stride: 8–35 in. (20.3–88.9 cm)

Trail width: 2–4 in. (5.1–10.2 cm)

Walk   Stride: 4–7 in. (10.2–17.8 cm)

Notes:

• Travel and explore in a lope and even speed up to a bound to cross wide expanses and when feeling threatened. Slow to a walk when investigating scents and other stimuli.

• Creatures of open country and grasslands; almost always found in association with prairie dog towns.

Black-footed ferret 2x2 lope in shallow snow.

Black-footed ferret trail. (SD) Photo courtesy of Black-footed Ferret Program, Badlands National Park.

A black-footed ferret's 2x2 lope trail. (SD) Photo courtesy of Black-footed Ferret Program, Badlands National Park.

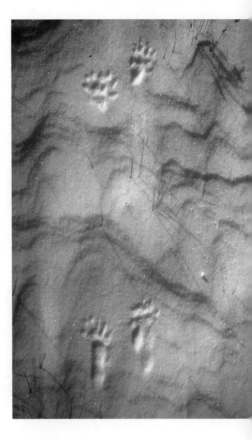

- Endangered; remain in only a tiny fraction of their original range. Reintroduction efforts have created populations in western South Dakota, southeastern Wyoming, and north-eastern Montana.
- Excavate burrows in a very different manner from rodents.
- In deep snow, tend toward a 2x2 lope.
- Solitary animals for most of the year.

Least Weasel (*Mustela nivalis*)

Track: Front $^5/_{16}$–$^5/_8$ in. (.8–1.6 cm) L x $^3/_8$–$^9/_{16}$ in. (1–1.4 cm) W

Very small. Plantigrade. Asymmetrical. Five toes: Toe 1 is the smallest, located on the inside of the track, and does not register reliably. Several metacarpal pads are fused but individually lobed, and others register individually; there is an additional pad (the heel) at the posterior edge of the track, which may or may not show. The negative space between the toes and metacarpals is furry, which influences track appearance. Nails may or may not register. Front track often larger and more symmetrical than rear track; occasionally, rear registers larger than front.

Rear $^5/_{16}$–$^7/_8$ in. (.8–2.2 cm) L x $^5/_{16}$–$^9/_{16}$ in. (.8–1.4 cm) W

Very small. Plantigrade. Asymmetrical. Five toes: Toe 1 is the smallest. Some of the metacarpal pads are fused, and others register separately. The furred "heel" may register. The negative space between the toes and metacarpals is furry, which influences track appearance. Nails may or may not register. Because toe 1 sits farther back in rear tracks than front tracks, rear tracks are far more asymmetrical than fronts. Track and trail parameters overlap with those of other small weasels.

A least weasel in a 2x2 lope. (MN)

Trail: 2x2 lope   Stride: 4–30 in.
                                      (10.2–76.2 cm)
                                      Trail width: ¹¹/₁₆–1³/₈
                                      in. (1.7–3.5 cm)

Notes:

• Creatures of open country, preferring marsh and field to woodland.

• Trails explore holes, nooks, and crannies in rock walls, in root systems, under buildings, in trees, and under snow.

• In deep snow, tend to stick to a 2x2 lope, but occasionally investigate in a walk. Tunnel in deep snow as well.

• Solitary animals, except for mating and rearing of young.

American Mink *(Mustela vison)*

Track: Front 1¹/₈–1⁷/₈ in. (2.9–7.3 cm)
             L x ⁷/₈–1³/₄ in. (2.2–4.4 cm) W
             Small. Plantigrade. Asymmetrical. Five toes: Toe 1 is the smallest, located on the inside of the track. Proximal webbing may or may not show. Several metacarpal pads are fused but lobed, and others register individually; there is an additional pad (the heel) at the posterior edge of the track, which may or may not show. The negative space between the toes and metacarpals is less furry than in other weasels, and mink have larger metacarpal pads than other smaller weasels. Nails may or may not register. Track dimensions overlap with those of black-footed and domestic ferrets. Front track larger and more symmetrical than rear track.

Rear ¹³/₁₆–1³/₄ in. (2.1–4.4 cm) L x ¹⁵/₁₆–1⁵/₈ in. (2.4–4.1 cm) W

Very small to small. Plantigrade. Asymmetrical. Five toes: Toe 1 is the smallest and does not register reliably. Some of the metacarpal pads are fused, and others register separately. Proximal webbing may or may not show. The negative space between the toes and metacarpals is less furry than in other small weasels. Nails may or may not register. Because toe 1 sits farther back in rear tracks than front tracks, rear tracks are more asymmetrical.

Trail: 2x2 lope   Stride: 9–38 in. (22.9–96.5 cm); up to 50 in. (1.27 m)
                                      Trail width: 2–3³/₄ in. (5.1–9.5 cm)
             3x4 lope   Stride: 6–36 in. (15.2–91.4 cm)
                                      Group length: 5–14 in. (12.7–35.6 cm)
             Bound   Stride: 11–26 in. (27.9–66 cm)
                                      Group length: 5–16 in. (12.7–40.6 cm)

Walk	Stride: 3½–7¾ in. (8.9–19.7 cm)
Slide	Trail width: 3–5 in. (7.6–12.7 cm)

Notes:

- Explore and hunt in a lope or modified bound, but slow to a walk to explore potential resources. When very exposed or in pursuit, use a rabbitlike bound.

- Stride of the 2x2 lope pattern more consistent than that of smaller weasels; smaller weasel trails tend to be created from numerous short strides mixed with long ones.

American mink understep walk.

American mink 2x2 lope.

American mink 3x4 lope.

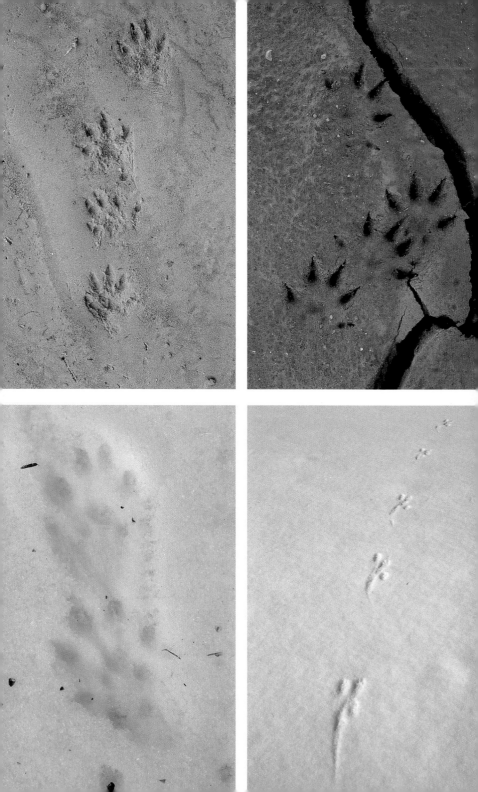

Facing page, top left: Mink tracks. From bottom to top: front-hind-front-hind. (MA) *Top right:* Front and hind (above) mink tracks. Toes often appear pointy and sharp. (CT) *Bottom left:* Perfect front and hind (above) tracks of a mink. (NH) *Bottom right:* A bound trail. Minks often cross open areas at high speed. (NH)

- Slide downhill in snow conditions. I have not found a slide on flat surfaces or uphill, as is often observed when trailing otters.
- Associated with wetland systems and water bodies, but may be found traveling across large land expanses when hunting or moving between water sources.
- Capable swimmers; do much foraging in the water. Also capable climbers.
- Often found exploring nooks and crannies in stream banks, root systems, stone walls, and the like.
- In deep snow, tend toward the 2x2 lope.
- Generally solitary animals.

Wolverine *(Gulo gulo)*

Track: Front 3⁵/₈–6¹/₄ in. (9.2–15.9 cm) L x 3¹/₂–5¹/₄ in. (8.9–13.3 cm) W

Medium to very large. Plantigrade. Asymmetrical. Five toes: Toe 1 is the smallest, located on the inside of the track. The metacarpal pads are fused but strongly lobed; there are additional pads (the heel) at the posterior edge of the track, which may or may not show. The negative space between the toes and metacarpals is especially furry in winter and influences track appearance. Nails may or may not register. Front track more symmetrical than rear track, but front and rear track parameters similar.

Rear 3⁵/₈–6 in. (9.2–15.2 cm) L x 3¹/₄–5¹/₄ in. (8.3–13.3 cm) W

Medium to large. Plantigrade. Asymmetrical. Five toes: Toe 1 is the smallest and does not register reliably. The metacarpal pads are fused but strongly lobed. The furred "heel" often registers as well. The negative space between the toes and metacarpals is furry and may influence track appearance. Nails may or may not register. At a glance, tracks can easily be confused with those of domestic dogs.

**Wolverine
3x4 lope.**

Left: Front track of a wolverine. (AK) Right: A wolverine and coyote share a dusted snowmobile trail. (ID) Photo by Jeff Copeland.

Front and hind (behind) tracks of a wolverine. They could easily be mistaken for dog tracks at a glance. (AK)

Trail: 3x4 lope   Stride: 7–45 in. (17.8–114.3 cm)
                         Group length: 27–45 in. (68.6–114.3 cm)
        Walk   Stride: 8–15 in. (20.3–38.1 cm)
        2x2 lope   Stride: 12–40 in. (30.5–101.6 cm)
                         Trail width: 7–10 in. (17.8–25.4 cm)

Notes:

- Explore and hunt in a lope, traveling great distances. Slow down to a walk to investigate potential food sources and to engage in scenting and other behaviors.
- Comfortable in the open; often seen moving at high altitudes above the tree line, as well as inhabiting the treeless tundra in the far north.
- Inhabit only a portion of their previous range. Found in the far north across Canada and Alaska and in the northern Rockies and Cascades; a few follow the mountains south into California.
- Competent climbers.
- In deep snow, either walk or use a 2x2 lope. Feet are covered in more fur in winter.
- Solitary animals.

American Badger
(Taxidea taxus)

Track: Front 2$^7/_8$–3$^7/_8$ in. (7.3–9.8 cm) L x 1 $^9/_{16}$–2$^5/_8$ in. (4–6.7 cm) W

Medium. Plantigrade. Asymmetrical. Five toes: Toe 1 is the smallest, located on the inside of the track, and does not register reliably. Track rarely splays. The metacarpal pads are fused and form a large pad that is wider than long. The foot is not furred like that of other weasels. Nails are large and long and reliably register. Front track significantly larger than rear track.

American badger walk.   **American badger trot.**

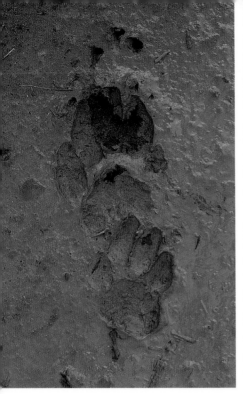

Above left: Front and rear (behind) tracks of a badger. (CO) *Above right:* A walking trail. (CO) *Left:* A long walking trail in snow. (UT)

Rear 1⁷/₈–2³/₄ in. (4.8–7 cm) L x 1³/₈–2 in. (3.5–5.1 cm) W

Small to medium. Plantigrade. Asymmetrical. Five toes: Toe 1 is smallest and often does not register. The metacarpals are fused to form one large pad. Nails may or may not register. Rear tracks much smaller than fronts.

Trail:	Walk	Stride: 5¹/₂–9³/₄ in. (14–24.8 cm)
		Trail width: 5–7¹/₂ in. (12.7–19.1 cm)
	Trot	Stride: 10–15 in. (25.4–38.1 cm)
		Trail width: 3–6 in. (7.6–15.2 cm)
	Lope	Stride: 10–12 in. (25.4–30.5 cm)
		Group length: 17–20 in. (43.2–50.8 cm)

Notes:
- Walk while foraging, often travel in a trot, and lope when alarmed or exposed.
- American badgers, as opposed to their European relatives, are creatures of grasslands, desert, and open country.
- Cross roads and trails but do not tend to follow them.
- Do not climb.
- Trail inevitably begins and ends with a burrow.
- Walk in deep snow; tracks connected by contiguous drag marks.
- Solitary animals.

Northern River Otter
(Lontra canadensis)

Track: Front 2¹/₈–3¹/₄ in. (5.4–8.3 cm) L
x 1⁷/₈–3 in. (4.8–7.6 cm) W

Medium. Plantigrade. Asymmetrical. Five toes: Toe 1 is the smallest. Mesial webbing may or may not show. The metacarpal pads are fused and strongly lobed; there is an additional pad (the heel) at the posterior edge of the track, which may or may not show. The negative space between the toes and metacarpals has little to no fur. Nails may or may not register. Front track more symmetrical than rear track, but smaller; size comparison between fronts and rears helps to differentiate from fisher tracks.

Rear 2¹/₈–4 in. (5.4–10.2 cm) L
x 2¹/₈–3³/₄ in. (5.4–9.5 cm) W

Medium. Plantigrade. Asymmetrical. Five toes: Toe 1 is well developed and long. Mesial webbing. The metacarpals are fused to form one large pad. Nails may or may not register. Rear tracks are larger than fronts. Because toe 1 sits farther back in rear tracks than front tracks, rear tracks are more asymmetrical.

Trail: Walk Stride: 5³/₄–14 in. (14.6–35.6 cm)

Trail width: 4¹/₂–7 in. (11.4–17.8 cm)

3x4 lope Stride: 6–28 in. (15.2–71.1 cm)

Group length: 10–20¹/₂ in. (25.4–52.1 cm)

Northern river otter walk.

Northern river otter 3x4 lope.

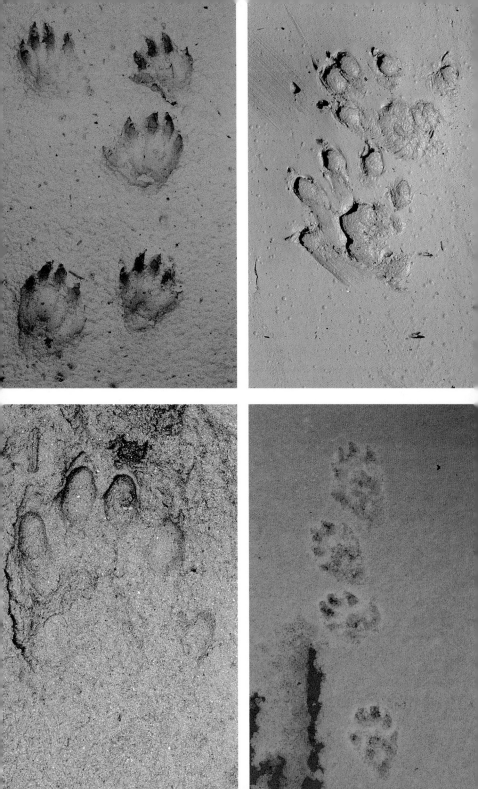

Otter vs. Fisher

Differentiating between otter and fisher tracks can be done if you slow down and look for specific features and characteristics. Habitat features are a useful clue, but they can be misleading. Almost every fisher trail I've followed has found some way to cross a stream or river without swimming, but on occasion fishers do enter water. Otters may cross great tracts of land far from water while moving from one water source to another.

Otters are gregarious animals, whereas fishers are fiercely territorial. Should you be following a pair of animals or a group, you've likely discovered otter trails, or possibly mating fishers.

Otters' rear tracks are larger than their fronts and are more obviously webbed, whereas the front feet of fisher are larger than their rears (also webbed). Also consider the amount of fur on the sole of the foot, which is quite dense on fisher feet and sparse on otter. For this reason, the digital pads tend to be much smaller in fisher tracks in proportion to the overall size of the tracks. Also study the size of toe 1 on each hind foot. This toe is well developed on otters, and the digital pad is equal to the other toes; toe 1 is very long and sticks out quite far. On fishers, toe 1 is reduced, being the smallest digital pad by far, and it is often absent in tracks altogether.

Last, consider the track patterns. Fishers create a long, aerodynamic track pattern when in a 3×4 lope, whereas otter patterns tend to be boxier and squatter. Also, look for sliding. I've seen fishers slide only twice in my life, and both times I was sliding too, due to the slope of the terrain. Otters, in contrast, almost always slide downhill, slide as often as possible on flats, and occasionally slide when moving uphill.

2x2 lope	Stride: 15–40 in. (25.4–101.6 cm)
	Trail width: 4¹/₂–7 in. (11.4–17.8 cm)
	Group length: 6–12¹/₂ in. (15.2–31.8 cm)
Slide	Trail width: 6–10 in. (15.2–25.4 cm)

Facing page, top left: Three larger hind tracks and two smaller front tracks of a river otter. (NC) *Top right:* Perfect otter tracks. Study the shape of the hind track—four toes clustered together and the fifth, toe 1, set back and long. (NH) *Bottom left:* A hind track of an otter. (WA) *Bottom right:* Otter tracks in shallow snow. From bottom to top: front-hind-front-hind. (MA)

Left: The boxy gallop–modified bound of an otter. (MD) *Right:* A pair of otters, loping and sliding across a frozen lake surface. (MA)

Notes:

- When on land, travel distance in a 3x4 lope and explore in a walking gait.
- Use all sorts of wetland and water habitats, including saltwater marshes, open beaches, and tidal pools.
- Slide in various substrates, from leaf litter to snow. Downhills or flat ground are always traversed with lopes and slides in snow, and on a number of occasions, I've followed otters sliding short distances uphill.
- Most often found close to wetland systems, water bodies, and tidal pools; however, often cross large land masses—even mountains—when moving between water systems.
- I've watched otters climbing in shrubs but I've never followed an otter trail up a tree.
- Use culverts and drains; investigate and rest in burrows and cavities in root systems of all kinds.
- Deep snow is covered in 2x2 lopes, with walks and plenty of sliding.
- Form runs between water systems, especially evident at the narrowest point between two water sources.
- Often found in pairs and family groups.

Skunks: Family Mephitidae

- Skunks explore and rest in all sorts of holes and cavities, from those dug by armadillos and woodchucks to culverts and basements. They may also dig their own burrows.

- Skunks generally do not climb. (There are records of spotted skunks climbing.)

- Skunks are solitary creatures, except during the breeding season and females raising young.

- Skunk tracks do not splay like those of other mammals, and in several species, toes are partially fused to create tight, clean tracks.

Western Spotted Skunk *(Spilogale gracilis)*
Eastern Spotted Skunk *(Spilogale putorius)*

Track: Front 1–1⅝ in. (2.5–4.1 cm) L x ¾–1¹¹/₁₆ in. (1.9–2.7 cm) W

Small. Plantigrade. Asymmetrical. Five toes: Toe 1 is the smallest, located on the inside of the track. Toes 2, 3, and 4 form a curved line, helping to differentiate fronts from rears. Track rarely splays. The metacarpal pads are partially fused but register more separately than *Mephitis* species. There are two additional pads (the heel), which may or may not register; one registers more often than the other. Digital, palm, and heel pads are naked. Nails are large and long and reliably register. Measurements comparing fronts and rears are very similar.

Rear ⅞–1⅜ in. (2.2–3.5 cm) L x ¾–1 in. (1.9–2.5 cm) W

Small. Plantigrade. Asymmetrical. Five toes: Toe 1 is smallest and is distinctly

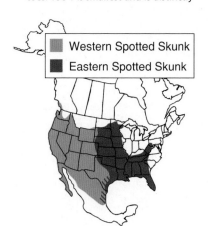

Western Spotted Skunk
Eastern Spotted Skunk

Western spotted skunk bound.

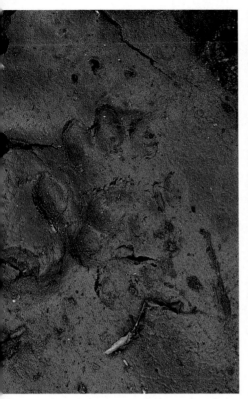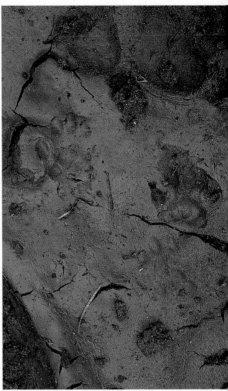

Left: Front track of a western spotted skunk. (WA) *Right:* Bound pattern of a spotted skunk. (WA)

farther back in the track than toe 5 (a feature that helps differentiate tracks from those of *Mephitis* species). Toes 2, 3, and 4 form a straight line and register as a unit, helping to differentiate fronts from rears. The metacarpals are fused to form one large pad. Two heel pads often register and are distinctly separate, as opposed to tracks of larger skunks. Digital, palm, and heel pads are naked. Nails may or may not register.

Trail:

Walk	Stride: 2–4 in. (5.1–10.2 cm)	
Overstep walk	Stride: 5½–6½ in. (14–16.5 cm)	
	Trail width: 3–4 in. (7.6–10.2 cm)	
Bound	Stride: 6–30 in. (15.2–76.2 cm)	
	Trail width: 2¼–4 in. (5.7–10.2 cm)	
Lope	Group length: 9–11 in. (22.9–27.9 cm)	

Notes:

- Travel in lopes and bounds and explore and move in greater cover in walking gaits.
- Widespread, but many believe their numbers are declining in many portions of their range.
- Far more carnivorous than larger skunks, engaging in pursuit of small mammals and birds more often.
- Use existing trail systems; sometimes found among human habitations.
- Can climb trees.

Pygmy Spotted Skunk *(Spilogale pygmaea)*

Track: Front ³/₄–1¹/₈ in. (1.9–2.9 cm) L x ¹/₂–¹¹/₁₆ in.
(1.3–1.7 cm) W

Very small to small. Plantigrade. Asymmetrical. Five toes: Toe 1 is the smallest, located on the inside of the track, and does not register reliably. Toes 2, 3, and 4 form a curved line, helping to differentiate fronts from rears. Track rarely splays. There are two additional pads (the heel), which may or may not register; one registers more often than the other. Digital, palm, and heel pads are naked. Nails are large and long and reliably register. Measurements comparing fronts and rears are very similar. This species inhabits a separate range from the slightly larger western spotted skunk.

Rear ¹/₂–⁷/₈ in. (1.3–2.2 cm) L x ¹/₂–³/₄ in.
(1.3–1.9 cm) W

**Pygmy skunk
bound.**

Very small to small. Plantigrade. Asymmetrical. Five toes: Toe 1 is smallest and is distinctly farther back in the track than toe 5 (a feature that helps differentiate tracks from those of *Mephitis* species). Toes 2, 3, and 4 form a straight line and register as a unit, helping to differentiate fronts from rears. The metacarpals are fused to form one large pad. Two heel pads often register and are distinctly separate. Digital, palm, and heel pads are naked. Nails may or may not register.

Trail: Walk Stride: 2–3 in. (5.1–7.6 cm)
Trail width: 2–2¹/₄ in. (5.1–5.7 cm)

Bound Stride: 5–25 in. (12.7–63.5 cm)
Trail width: 2–3 in. (5.1–7.6 cm)

Front and hind tracks of a pygmy spotted skunk. (Mexico)

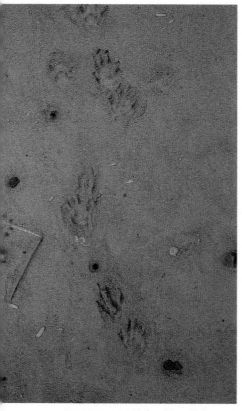

Notes:
- Travel in lopes and bounds and explore and move in greater cover in walking gaits.
- Found only along the Pacific coast of Mexico; the smallest of the skunks.
- Although I have found trails on beaches, these skunks seem to avoid exposed areas.
- Use a variety of habitats but are especially linked to dry tropical forests.
- Can climb and are active hunters; in some ways, they may fill the niche usually held by smaller weasels, which do not share their habitat.

A pygmy spotted skunk's walking trail. (Mexico)

Hooded Skunk *(Mephitis macroura)*

Track: Front 1⁵/₈–1¹⁵/₁₆ in. (4.1–4.9 cm) L x ¹⁵/₁₆–1¹/₈ in. (2.4–2.9 cm) W

Small. Plantigrade. Asymmetrical. Five toes: Toe 1 is the smallest, located on the inside of the track. Toes are partially fused; track does not splay. Metacarpal pads are fused to form a larger pad. There is an additional pad (the heel) which may or may not register. Digital, palm, and heel pads are naked. Nails are large and long and reliably register.

Rear 1⁵/₁₆–2¹/₈ in. (3.3–5.4 cm) L x ¹⁵/₁₆–1¹/₈ in. (2.4–2.9 cm) W

Small. Plantigrade. Asymmetrical. Five toes: Toe 1 is smallest and often does not register. Toes are partially fused. The metacarpals are fused to form one large pad, but palm and heel are clearly separate in track. Digital, palm, and heel pads are naked. Nails may or may not register. Track and trail parameters are difficult to distinguish from those of the striped skunk.

Trail: Walk   Stride: 5–7¹/₂ in. (12.7–19.1 cm)

Trail width: 3–4¹/₄ in. (7.6–10.8 cm)

Hooded skunk tracks. The larger is the rear foot. (Mexico)

Notes:

- Often explore and cover open areas in a lope; slow down to investigate and search areas more intensively in a walk.
- Trails are often found crossing open areas, such as beaches or agricultural lands, and marching straight down the middle of trails and roads. When exposed, they tend to speed up into a lope.
- Seem to be more abundant in forests than their striped counterpart, which is more abundant in edge and open habitats.
- Use existing trail systems when foraging.
- I have tracked hooded skunks far less than striped skunks, but behaviors and trail patterns seem very similar. In areas where the two species overlap, striped skunks tend to be far more common. Their tracks and trails are difficult to differentiate.

Striped Skunk *(Mephitis mephitis)*

Track: Front 1⁵/₈–2¹/₁₆ in. (4.1–5.2 cm) L x 1–1³/₁₆ in. (2.5–3 cm) W

Small. Plantigrade. Asymmetrical. Five toes: Toe 1 is the smallest, located on the inside of the track. Toes are partially fused; track does not splay. Metacarpal pads are fused to form a larger pad. There is an additional pad (the heel), which may or may not register. Digital, palm, and heel pads are naked. Nails are large and long and reliably register.

Rear 1⁵/₁₆–2 in. (3.3–5.1 cm) L x ¹⁵/₁₆–1³/₁₆ in. (2.4–3 cm) W

Small. Plantigrade. Asymmetrical. Five toes: Toe 1 is smallest and often does not register. Toes are partially fused. The metacarpals are fused to form one large pad, but palm and heel are clearly separate in track. Digital, palm, and heel pads are naked. Nails may or may not register. Track and trail parameters are difficult to distinguish from those of the hooded skunk.

Trail: Direct register walk   Stride: 4–8 in. (10.2–20.3 cm)
                                Trail width: 3–4½ in. (7.6–11.4 cm)
         Overstep walk   Stride: 5¾–9 in. (14.6–22.9 cm)

Striped skunk overstep walk.

Striped skunk direct register walk in snow.

Striped skunk lope.

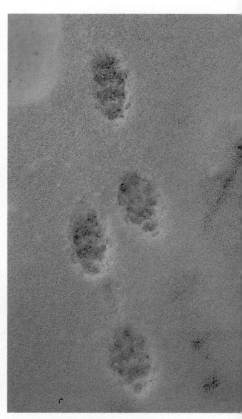

Left: Front and hind (behind) tracks of a striped skunk. Note that the heel portion of the rear track did not register. (NH) *Right:* Classic lope pattern of the striped skunk. From bottom to top: front-hind-front-hind. (NH)

Direct register trot	Stride: 8–11 in. (20.3–27.9 cm)
	Trail width: 2³/₈–4¹/₂ in. (6–11.4 cm)
Lope	Stride: 3–7¹/₂ in. (7.6–19.1 cm)
	Group length: 8–16¹/₂ in. (20.3–42 cm)
Gallop	Stride: 3³/₄–7³/₄ in. (9.5–19.7 cm)
	Group length: 10–18 in. (25.4–45.7 cm)

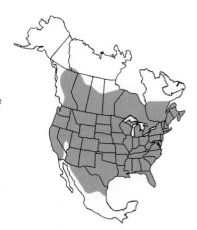

Notes:

• Often explore and cover open areas in a lope; slow down to investigate and search areas more intensively in a walk.

Left: A walking gait of a striped skunk. (WY) *Right:* A striped skunk's direct register walk in deep snow. (ID)

- Trails often found crossing wide open areas and marching straight down the middle of trails and roads. When exposed, tend to speed up into a lope.
- Found in a variety of habitats, including the largest cities.
- Differentiating trots and walks can usually be done by measurements, but note that when trotting, drag marks will be straight rather than curved, and tracks will be less pigeon-toed.
- In deep snow, use a direct register walk, which appears very pigeon-toed, and can be confused with the trails of house cats.

Western Hognose Skunk *(Conepatus mesoleucus)*
Eastern Hognose Skunk *(Conepatus leuconotus)*

Track: Front 1⅞–2¾ in. (4.8–7 cm) L x 1⅜–1⅝ in. (3.5–4.1 cm) W

Small to medium. Plantigrade. Asymmetrical. Five toes: Toe 1 is the smallest, located on the inside of the track. Toes are partially fused; track does not splay. Metacarpal pads are fused to form a larger pad. There is an additional pad (the heel), which may or may not register. Digital, palm, and heel pads are naked. Nails are large and long and reliably register. Tracks

Western hognose skunk overstep walk.

Western hognose skunk lope.

Western hognose skunk tracks in deep dust. The hind track has a larger metacarpal region and smaller claws; also note the squared posterior edge. (Mexico)

are significantly larger and more robust than those of *Mephitis* species.

Rear 1⁵/₈–2¹/₂ in. (4.1–6.4 cm) L x 1¹/₈–1⁵/₈ in. (2.9–4.1 cm) W

Small to medium. Plantigrade. Asymmetrical. Five toes: Toe 1 is smallest and often does not register. Toes are partially fused. The metacarpals are fused to form one large pad, but palm and heel are clearly separate in track. Posterior edge squared. Digital, palm, and heel pads are naked. Nails may or may not register.

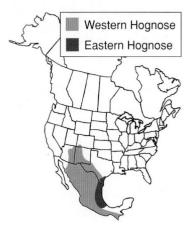

Western Hognose
Eastern Hognose

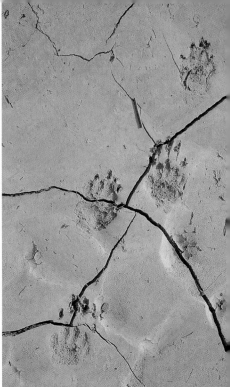

Left: **Hognose skunk front and hind (above) tracks in mud. (TX)** *Right:* **Loping gait of a hognose skunk. (TX)**

Trail:	Lope	Stride: 6³/₄–10 in. (17.1–25.4 cm)
		Group length: 11¹/₄–16 in. (28.6–40.6 cm)
	Overstep walk	Stride: 5¹/₂–8¹/₂ in. (14–21.6 cm)
		Trail width: 3¹/₂–5 in. (8.9–12.7 cm)

Notes:
- Move about the landscape exploring in a walk, but speed up to a lope or even a gallop when exposed or threatened.
- Commonly found in open areas, such as cultivated areas and riparian zones.
- Tracks are significantly larger than those of *Mephitis* species and spotted skunks.
- Eastern hognose skunks overlap in size with western species, but they also outgrow the western hognose skunk and are the largest skunk species in North America.

Seals: Family Phocidae

- Seal trails are associated with oceans and beaches and are generally found below the high-water mark.
- Seals are gregarious; although you may find the trail of a single animal, the trails of many are likely to be in close proximity.
- Seals do not walk or lope but move on land in their own fashion. Both front flippers move together, lifting and propelling the animal forward. It lands on its chest and belly; then the flippers rotate forward to lift the animal again. Body drag is continuous in the trail.

Harbor Seal *(Phoca vitulina)*

Track: Front 8–12 in. (20.3–30.5 cm) L
x 7–10 in. (17.8–25.4 cm) W

Very large. Asymmetrical. Five
toes, although not all toes
reliably register in tracks. Palm
is unique to aquatic lifestyle.
Body drag is a significant
characteristic of trails. Claws
help differentiate from trails
of sea turtles.

Notes:

- Ocean mammals, but often seen
following estuaries and even
upstream in freshwater rivers that
empty into the sea.

- Gregarious, where you find one,
you'll often find others.

Left: Classic trail of a harbor seal. (OR) *Right:* A trail in deeper, softer sand. Note
the claw marks, which help differentiate seal trails from those of sea turtles. (OR)

Northern Elephant Seal
(*Mirounga angustirostris*)

Very large. Asymmetrical. Five toes, although not all toes reliably register in tracks. Palm is unique to aquatic lifestyle. Body drag is a significant characteristic of trails.

Trail width: up to 6 feet (1.8 m) across

Trail of a massive elephant seal. (CA)

Ringtails, Raccoons, and Coatis: Family Procyonidae

- Members of this family are competent climbers. All three species rest on tree limbs and in cavities and tend to bear young in tree hollows.

- These species also balance on logs and walk leaning trunks and rock walls just as easily as they move on the ground.

- These animals are all omnivorous and have varied palates.

Ringtail (*Bassariscus astutus*)

Track: Front 1 1/8–1 7/16 in. (2.9–3.7 cm) L x 15/16–1 1/4 in. (2.4–3.2 cm) W

Small. Plantigrade. Symmetrical. Five toes: Toe 1 is the smallest, located on the inside of the track, and does not register reliably. Metacarpal pads are fused to form a larger pad. There is an additional pad (the heel) which registers more often than not. Digital, palm, and heel pads are naked. Nails are semiretractable and do not register in most tracks.

Rear 1–1 3/8 in. (2.5–3.5 cm) L x 7/8–1 1/16 in. (2.2–2.7 cm) W

Small. Plantigrade. Asymmetrical. Five toes: Toe 1 is smallest and rarely registers well in tracks when using slower gaits. The metacarpals are fused

Ringtail tracks in dust. Note that the rear track tends to register four rather than five toes. (TX)

to form one large pad that is much longer than wide. Digital, palm, and heel pads are naked. Nails are semiretractable and do not register in most tracks. Because toe 1 is often absent, the rear track can be confused with that of a small cat; note the unusually large palm pad, which takes up a large portion of the track.

Ringtail tracks in mud. (TX)

Trail: Direct register walk Stride: 3–8 in. (7.6–20.3 cm)
Trail width: 1¼–3½ in. (3.2–8.9 cm)
Bound Stride: 1–4 ft. (.3–1.2 m)
Trail width: 3–4½ in. (7.6–11.4 cm)

Notes:
- Walk during explorations and hunting forays, but speed up into bounds and lopes when exposed, threatened, or chasing prey.
- Tend to stay near cover, whether boulders, brush, trees, or rocky cliffs.
- Use existing trail systems.
- Often explore cavities, under overhangs, and burrows.
- Tend to be solitary animals, but paired trails may be encountered throughout the year.

A ringtail pauses, briefly setting down its front and hind feet to create a box stop, before walking off in a new direction. (CA) Photo by Jim Lowery.

Ringtail bound into lope.

Ringtail walk.

Northern Raccoon *(Procyon lotor)*

Track: Front 1³/₄–3¹/₈ in. (4.4–7.9 cm) L x 1¹/₂–3¹/₄ in. (3.8–8.3 cm) W

Medium. Plantigrade. Symmetrical. Five toes. Digital pads connect to palm in most tracks. Metacarpal pads are fused to form a larger pad, which appears distinctly curved in tracks. There is an additional pad (the heel), which occasionally registers. Digital, palm, and heel pads are naked. Nails may or may not register. Tracks are often confused with coati, otter, and fisher tracks.

Northern raccoon 2x2 walk.

Northern raccoon fast 2x2 walk.

Northern raccoon slow 2x2 walk.

Northern raccoon bound into gallop.

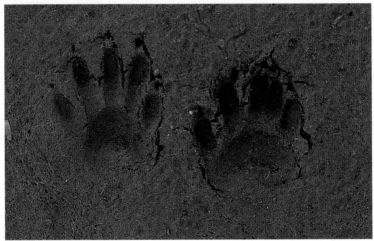

Top: **Perfect front and hind (behind) raccoon tracks. (WY)** *Bottom:* **Raccoon tracks. Note that the heel portion of the hind track (slightly behind) did not register. (CO)**

Rear 2$^{1}/_{8}$–3$^{7}/_{8}$ in. (5.4–10.2 cm) L x 1$^{1}/_{2}$–2$^{5}/_{8}$ in. (3.8–6.7 cm) W

Medium. Plantigrade. Asymmetrical. Five toes: Toe 1 is smallest and sits farther back in the track than the other four toes. Digital pads connect to the palm. The metacarpals are fused to form one large pad that is much longer than wide. Heel may or may not register. Digital, palm, and heel pads are naked. Nails may or may not register in tracks. When toe 1 is absent, the rear track is often mistaken for a bobcat track.

Trail:		
2x2 walk	Stride: 8–19 in. (20.3–48.3 cm)	
	Trail width: 3$^{1}/_{2}$–7 in. (8.9–17.8 cm)	
Direct register walk	Stride: 8–14 in. (20.3–35.6 cm)	
	Trail width: 3$^{1}/_{2}$–6 in. (8.9–15.2 cm); trots down to 2$^{1}/_{2}$ in. (6.4 cm)	
Fast 2x2 walk	Stride: 18–25 in. (45.7–63.5 cm)	
	Trail width: 3$^{1}/_{2}$–6 in. (8.9–15.2 cm)	
Bound	Stride: 10–30 in. (25.4–76.2 cm)	
	Group length: 15–27 in. (38.1–68.6 cm)	

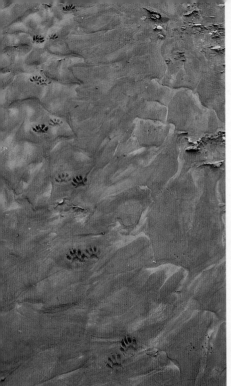

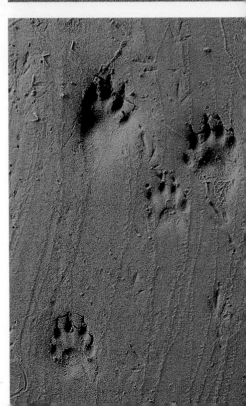

Top left: A 2x2 walking gait of a raccoon. This gait is common in raccoons; only occasionally do a few other species leave a similar track pattern. (CO) *Top right:* Fast walking gait of a raccoon— trot speed. The limbs on the same side of the body move nearly simultaneously. (OR) *Right:* Raccoon bounding track pattern. (WY)

Notes:
- Walk in their travels and while foraging, leaving track patterns shared by few other North American mammals. Lopes and gallops used when alarmed or threatened.
- Use existing roads and trail systems.
- Trails often lead straight from dens or holes to good feeding areas, with little wandering until within an area good for harvesting. Trails can be quite long and straight.
- Although raccoon trails may be encountered in many environments, they are often seen near wetland systems and following waterways.
- Inhabit cities.

- Explore and use abandoned burrows, culverts, basements, and other available hollows.
- In deep snow, use a direct register walk, which might be confused with a walking fisher or even a bobcat.
- Solitary animals, except during mating season and females with young. However, winter holes may hold numerous individuals.

Raccoon range

White-nosed Coati
(*Nasua narica*)

Track: Front 2¼–3¼ in. (5.7–8.3 cm) L x 1¼–1⅞ in. (3.2–4.8 cm) W

Medium. Plantigrade. Slightly asymmetrical. Five toes. Digital pads may or may not connect to palm and are more bulbous than those of raccoon. Metacarpal pads are fused to form a larger pad. There are two additional large pads (the heel), which register more often than not and help differentiate coati from raccoon tracks. Digital, palm, and heel pads are naked. Nails are much longer than those of raccoons and reliably register.

Rear 2⅝–3⅝ in. (6.7–9.2 cm) L x 1⅜–2¹⁄₁₆ in. (3.5–5.2 cm) W

Tracks of young are as little as 1¾ in. (4.4 cm) L and can be confused with those of hognose skunks.

Left: Front track of a coati. Note the short claws, which could lead the tracker astray. (AZ) *Right:* Front and rear tracks (behind) of a coati. (Mexico)

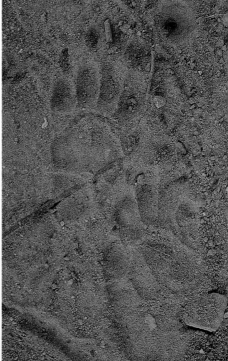

Medium. Plantigrade. Asymmetrical. Five toes: Toe 1 is smallest and sits farther back in the track than the other four toes. Digital pads may or may not connect to palm in tracks. The metacarpals are fused to form one large pad that is much longer than wide. Heel almost always registers. Digital, palm, and heel pads are naked. Nails may or may not register in tracks. Rear tracks often confused with those of raccoons.

Trail:		
2x2 walk	Stride: 8–10½ in. (20.3–26.7 cm)	
	Trail width: 3¼–4¼ in. (8.3–10.8 cm)	
Direct register walk	Stride: 7–10½ in. (17.8–26.7 cm)	
	Trail width: 3½–3¾ in. (8.9–9.5 cm)	
Overstep walk	Stride: 8–11 in. (20.3–27.9 cm)	
	Trail width: 3½–5¾ in. (8.9–14.6 cm)	
Lope	Stride: 4–8 in. (10.2–20.3 cm)	
	Group length: 21–28 in. (53.3–71.1 cm)	

Notes:

• Generally walk in their travels, but speed up to a lope when startled or threatened.

• Diurnal; may be encountered anytime during the day.

• Prefer to stay near cover but move in the open as well; often seen in plantations, along beaches, and in riparian areas.

• Use existing trails and roads.

• Rest in trees, and raise young in tree cavities and occasionally burrows. Rear feet may turn 180 degrees, allowing them to move headfirst down trunks, as well as up.

• Often found in groups throughout the year, but from December through March, these "troops" may be exceptionally large. One man I met in Arizona saw a troop of 75 animals in January 1999 on the Muleshoe Ranch Cooperative lands.

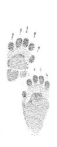

White-nosed coati lope track group.

White-nosed coati overstep walk.

Cats: Family Felidae

- Cats are solitary animals, except during breeding season and when raising young. Lynx often stay with their young through their first winter, and cougars may be found with kittens at any time of year.
- Cats are capable climbers; they often rest in trees and may even climb to wait in ambush for prey.
- Cats walk about the landscape, speeding up to a trot when exposed or a threat comes nearer. They move in lopes, bounds, or gallops when startled, chasing prey, feeling exposed, or playing.
- Cats have tremendous control over the flex of their toes and therefore the size of their tracks. It is not uncommon to find splayed rear tracks larger than tight front tracks.

Cougar or Mountain Lion *(Puma concolor)*

Track: Front 2³/₄–3⁷/₈ in. (7–9.8 cm) L x 2⁷/₈–4⁷/₈ in. (7.3–12.4 cm) W
Medium to large. Asymmetrical. Five toes: Toe 1 is greatly reduced and raised up on the inner leg. Four toes reliably register in tracks. The metacarpal pads are fused and create one large trapezoidal pad; the

Left: **Perfect front and hind tracks of a cougar. The front tracks are larger, rounder, and more asymmetrical than the hind tracks. (MT)** *Right:* **Cougar tracks in the dust, where the hind track has registered beyond the front. (ID)**

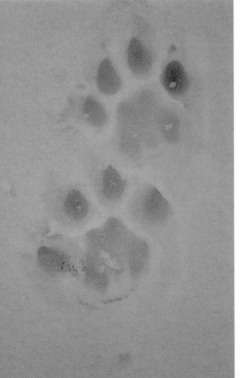

Cougar bound.   Cougar overstep walk.

A cougar's direct register walk, which is the typical track pattern seen in snow conditions other than dustings. (ID)

Heel Pad Measurements

Trackers and researchers have long used metacarpal pad width measurements, the palm pad, to help differentiate cougars from large bobcats. Here are the parameters for each:

Cougar: 1⁹/₁₆–2⁷/₈ in. (4–7.3 cm)
Bobcat: 1–1⁹/₁₆ in. (2.5–4 cm)

leading edge is bilobate, and the posterior edge has three lobes, all of which are more pronounced than in jaguar tracks. The metacarpal pads form a much larger proportion of the track surface than do similar pads in canine tracks. The negative space between the toes and metacarpals forms a *C*. An additional carpal pad sits high on the leg and registers only at high speeds or in deep substrates. Nails are retractable and seldom register; exceptions are on slippery surfaces, when climbing, and while chasing prey. Nails are very thin and decurved. Front track larger and rounder than rear.

Rear 3–4¹/₈ in. (7.6–10.5 cm) L x 2⁹/₁₆–4⁷/₈ in. (6.5–12.4 cm) W

Medium to large. Slightly asymmetrical. Four toes. The metacarpal pads are fused and create one large trapezoidal pad. The negative space between the toes and metacarpals forms a *C* or *H*. Nails are retractable and seldom register. Rear track more elongated and symmetrical than front.

Trail:	Overstep walk	Stride: 19–32 in. (48.3–81.3 cm)
		Trail width: 5–9 in. (12.7–22.9 cm)
	Direct register walk	Stride: 15–28 in. (38.1–71.1 cm)
		Trail width: 4–11 in. (10.2–27.9 cm)
	Trot	Stride: 29–38 in. (73.7–96.5 cm)
		Trail width: 3–5¹/₂ in. (7.6–14 cm)
	3x lope	Stride: 45–55 in. (1.14–1.4 m)
		Group length: 40–50 in. (1.02–1.27 m)
	Gallop	Stride: 36–120 in. (91.4–304.8 cm); occasionally modified bounds up to 25 feet (762 cm)
		Group length: 50–75 in. (1.27–1.9 m)

Notes:

• Walk most of the time, twisting and turning often when hunting, but moving in straighter lines when traveling between hunting areas and lays or between feeding areas.

• Range is in constant dispute. Cougar sightings and sign have been recorded throughout New England, along the Appalachian Mountains down the eastern seaboard, and in Minnesota. Yet there is ongoing debate whether these cats were released pets, relocated by wildlife fanatics, or actually wild cougars that had been secretly inhabiting the area or had dispersed from known populations. Regardless, cougar sign crops up in eastern states from time to time, and wildlife officials should be notified immediately.

• Tend to stay near cover or steep terrain, but may cross exposed ridges, and alpine meadows and are occasionally found in exposed valley fields and cultivated areas.

• Exposed ridges are especially important for resting and laying.

• When roads and trails are encountered, they are crossed more than followed.

• Live in a wide range of habitats.

• Direct register walk in deep snow.

Snow Tracking

Snow tracking can be a simple exercise in perfect track identification or an incredibly difficult interpretation of deep, windblown trails. You must be aware of the gait changes animals make when moving about in snow. Animals that do not typically direct register will suddenly begin to do so. For example, consider the raccoon, which is notorious for its unique 2×2 walking gaits. But in snow, raccoons use a direct register walk, which looks similar to those created by walking fishers. Mammals that tend to trot or lope in shallow substrates will walk more frequently. Be flexible in your interpretations and remember that the depth of substrate is one of the key variables in determining how an animal moves. Following are some of the techniques I use when interpreting tracks and trails in snow.

• The direction of travel is the direction pointed to by the deepest part of a track. Check several tracks to be sure. I stick my hand into completely blown-in trails to feel the direction of travel. This is best done without gloves.

• The mound in the center of snowed-in canine tracks can often be clearly felt, or the ridge between palm and toe pads in a cat track, or the shape of hooves. You'll also be able to tell the approximate size of the track. The area compressed by the animal is always firmer than the snow that has blown in. I use the body heat of my hands to melt out tracks, allowing me to not only feel the track but also re-create it visually. Don't force your fingers into spots; carefully and slowly melt out the existing track floor.

• Light snow can sometimes be blown out of the track, keeping it intact. This is an especially useful technique when temperatures are cold and a fresh, light layer of snow has covered tracks.

• Consider the angle of the floor of the track. In deep snow, most mammals' tracks are angled quite steeply, although there is some variation across species. Canine tracks tend to be far more steeply angled than cat tracks. Check several tracks in succession before making a judgment.

• Look for the placement of claws in snow tracks. In deep snow, only the pinprick claw marks of toes 3 and 4 may be visible in coyote tracks; you may have to squat to see them. This may allow you to differentiate a deer from a coyote trail in deep conditions. Bobcats and other cats can be differentiated from canine tracks by looking for claws that register on a higher plane than the floor of the track. The claws appear to be above the toes, because this is where they sit when sheathed.

• The walls of the track created as the foot enters and exits snow are filled with clues for species identification. The back wall may hold a metacarpal pad or dewclaws on a higher plane than the track. The shape of the front wall is especially important for interpretation. Is the track pointed or rounded? Refer to the illustrations for examples.

(continued on page 210)

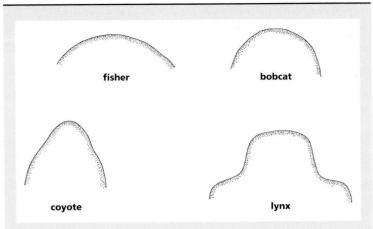

Front wall shape of tracks in deep snow.

• The drag marks between tracks are also useful. Gray squirrel and cottontail trails can be differentiated by studying the drag marks between sets of four tracks; squirrels tend to drag on the outside edges of the track pattern, while cottontails tend to drag along the median line. The shapes of the drag marks and the entrance and exit holes along the surface of the snow are also worthy of study. For example, cats walking in snow create perfect triangles. Or look for the paired lines made by dragging hooves in deer trails.

Note the placement of the drag marks in this cottontail trail. (MA)

House Cat *(Felis domesticus)*

Track: Front 1–1⁵/₈ in. (2.5–4.1 cm) L x ⁷/₈–1³/₄ in. (2.2–4.4 cm) W

Small. Asymmetrical. Five toes: Toe 1 is greatly reduced and raised up on the inner leg. Four toes reliably register in tracks. The metacarpal pads are fused and create one large trapezoidal pad; the leading edge is bilobate, and the posterior edge has three lobes. The metacarpal pads cover the majority of the overall track surface. The negative space between the toes and metacarpals forms a *C*. An additional carpal pad sits high on the leg and registers only at high speeds or in deep substrates. Nails are retractable and often do not register; exceptions are on slippery surfaces, when climbing, and while chasing prey. Nails are very thin and decurved. Front track larger and rounder than rear, yet has shorter toes than hind feet.

Rear 1¹/₈–1¹/₂ in. (2.9–3.8 cm) L x ⁷/₈–1⁵/₈ in. (2.2–4.1 cm) W

Small. Slightly asymmetrical. Four toes. The metacarpal pads are fused and create one large trapezoidal pad. The negative space between the toes and metacarpals forms a *C* or *H*. Nails are retractable and often do

House cat
walk in mud.

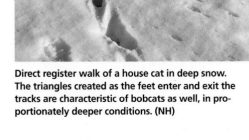

Direct register walk of a house cat in deep snow. The triangles created as the feet enter and exit the tracks are characteristic of bobcats as well, in pro-portionately deeper conditions. (NH)

House cat tracks. Note that in this case, the front tracks are smaller than the hind tracks. (NH)

not register. Rear track more elongated and symmetrical than front, although this is often less pronounced than in wild felines.

Trail:	Walk	Stride: 6–12¹/₂ in. (15.2–31.8 cm)
		Trail width: 2–4³/₄ in. (5.1–12.1 cm)
	Trot	Stride: 10–16 in. (25.4–40.6 cm)
	Gallops	Stride: 14–40 in. (35.6–101.6 cm)
		Group length: 10–33 in. (25.4–83.8 cm)

Notes:
- Widespread; commonly found in national parks and other areas that might be considered too remote.
- Direct register walk in deep snow.

Ocelot *(Leopardus pardalis)*

Track: Front 1⁵/₈–2¹/₄ in. (4.1–5.7 cm) L x 1⁵/₈–2¹/₈ in. (4.1–5.4 cm) W

Small to medium. Asymmetrical. Five toes: Toe 1 is greatly reduced and raised up on the inner leg. Four toes reliably register in tracks. The metacarpal pads are fused and create one large trapezoidal pad; the leading edge is bilobate, and the posterior edge has three lobes, although this is far less pronounced than in bobcat tracks. The metacarpal pads cover the majority of the overall track surface. The negative space between the toes and metacarpals forms a C. An additional carpal pad

Ocelot overstep walk.

Ocelot front and hind (above) tracks in deep dust. (Mexico)

sits high on the leg and registers only at high speeds or in deep substrates. Nails are retractable and often do not register; exceptions are on slippery surfaces, when climbing, and while chasing prey. Nails are very thin and decurved. Front track larger and rounder than rear.

Rear 1³/₄–2¹/₄ in. (4.4–5.7 cm) L x 1¹/₂–2¹/₈ in. (3.8–5.4 cm) W

Small to medium. Slightly asymmetrical. Four toes. The metacarpal pads are fused and create one large trapezoidal pad. The negative space between the toes and metacarpals forms a *C* or *H*. Nails are retractable and often do not register. Rear track more elongated and symmetrical than front. Ocelot tracks are far more robust and meaty and less curvaceous than bobcat tracks. As jaguar tracks are to cougar tracks (relative to shape and robustness), so ocelot tracks are to bobcat tracks. Refer to the illustrations.

Trail: Direct register walk   Stride: 10–13 in. (25.4–33 cm)
                              Trail width: 3³/₄–5 in. (9.5–12.7 cm)
       Overstep walk   Stride: 12 –14¹/₂ in. (30.5–36.8 cm)
                              Trail width: 3³/₄–5¹/₂ in. (9.5–14 cm)

Top: **Perfect front track of an ocelot in dust. (Mexico)** *Bottom:* **Front and hind (ahead) ocelot tracks in shallow substrate. (Mexico)**

Notes:
- Walk when hunting and traveling.
- Prefer to stay in cover, but will hunt open beaches and edge environments, including cultivated areas.
- Use existing trail systems and small roads when traveling.
- Within their range, use varied habitats.
- Tracks can easily be confused with those of a bobcat, especially when splayed. Clear tracks can be differentiated with confidence (refer to the illustrations).

Jaguarundi *(Herpailurus yaguarondi)*

Track: Front 1¹/₁₆–1³/₄ in. (2.7–4.4 cm) L x 1³/₁₆–1³/₄ in. (3–4.4 cm) W

Small. Asymmetrical. Five toes: Toe 1 is greatly reduced and raised up on the inner leg. Four toes reliably register in tracks. The metacarpal pads are fused and create one large trapezoidal pad; the leading edge is bilobate, and the posterior edge has three lobes. The negative space between the toes and metacarpals forms a *C*. An additional carpal pad sits high on the leg and registers only at high speeds or in deep substrates. Nails are retractable and often do not register; exceptions are on slippery surfaces, when climbing, and while chasing prey. Nails are very thin and decurved. Front track larger and rounder than rear.

Top: Front track of a captive jaguarundi. *Bottom:* Front and hind tracks of a captive jaguarundi. In this case, the rear is larger than the front track.

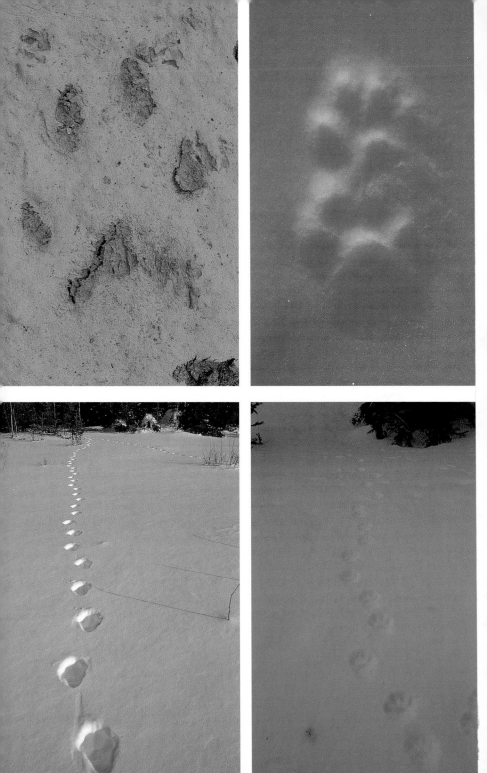

Facing page, top left: The rear track of a lynx. (AK) *Top right:* Lynx tracks in snow. (MT) *Bottom left:* A direct register walk of a lynx in deep snow conditions. (ME) *Bottom right:* An overstep walk of a lynx, except for the third track from the bottom, which is a direct register. (MT)

Straddle trot:	Stride: 20–24 in. (50.8–61 cm)
	Group length: 6–8 in. (15.2–20.3 cm)
Gallop	Stride: 45–65 in. (1.14–1.65 m); 4–10½ ft. (1.22–3.2 m) leaps when chasing hare
	Group length: 36–60 in. (91.4–152.4 cm)

Notes:

- Walk about the landscape, searching every possible cover where a hare might be hiding. When one is found, the chase begins.
- Move across open areas, but often speed up to a trot to do so.
- Often killed on roads, but readily take to old logging roads, especially when not maintained or used during the winter months.
- Canada lynx is considerably smaller and lighter than its European cousin *(Lynx lynx),* so track and sign parameters for this animal should not be applied in North America.
- Snow-belt cats, living in the far north as well as in the Rockies and the mountains of the Northeast and West.
- Ample snowshoe hare sign almost always accompanies lynx sign.
- Direct register walk in deep snow; toes splay in such a way as to create a cross shape, which is unique to this species.
- Sue Morse discovered that the toes on the hind feet are longer than on the front, so when toes are splayed, hind foot impressions are larger than front foot impressions.
- Solitary, but females often keep their young through their first winter; family groups, composed of female and young, are common in winter months.

Bobcat *(Lynx rufus)*

Track: Front 1⅝–2½ in. (4.1–6.4 cm) L
x 1⅜–2⅝ in. (3.5–6.7 cm) W
(can splay over 3 in. [7.6 cm] W)

Small to medium. Asymmetrical. Five toes: Toe 1 is greatly reduced and raised up on the inner leg. Four toes reliably register in tracks. The metacarpal pads are fused and create one large trapezoidal pad; the leading edge is bilobate, and the posterior edge has three lobes (more pronounced than in ocelot tracks). The metacarpal pads cover the majority of the overall track surface. The negative space between the toes and metacarpals forms a *C.* An additional carpal pad sits high on the leg and registers only at high speeds or in deep substrates. Nails are retractable and often do not register; exceptions are on slippery surfaces, when climbing, and while chasing prey. Nails are very thin and decurved. Front track larger and rounder than rear.

Sit-downs

Learn the shape of patterns created by sitting mammals. Sit-downs are a feature of hunting bobcat and lynx trails; these cats often pause where views of prey are good or in prey-abundant areas. If they wait for a longer period, they are more likely to create a hunting lay.

I have also found canines sitting in areas with wonderful views or when something has piqued their curiosity and they paused to watch. Sitting is also common at den and rendezvous sites and near kill sites of larger prey.

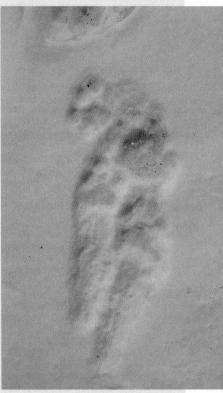

Left: The hunting sit of a lynx in an area with abundant hares and a commanding view. (MT) *Right:* The sit spot of a cougar kitten near a kill site. (ID)

Rear 1⁹/₁₆–2¹/₂ in. (4–6.4 cm) L x 1³/₁₆–2⁵/₈ in. (3–6.7 cm) W

Small to medium. Slightly asymmetrical. Four toes. The metacarpal pads are fused and create one large trapezoidal pad. The negative space between the toes and metacarpals forms a *C* or *H*. Nails are retractable and often do not register. Rear track more elongated and symmetrical than front. Tracks can be confused with those of an ocelot.

Trail: Direct register walk   Stride: 6–14 in. (15.2–35.6 cm)

                                     Trail width: 5–9¹/₂ in. (12.7–24.1 cm)

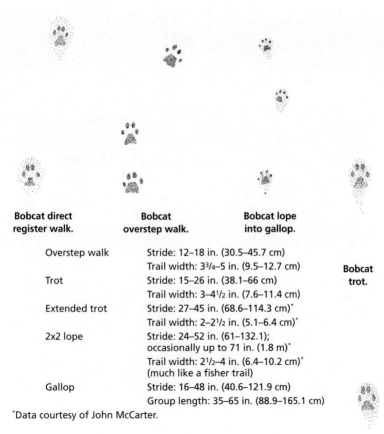

Bobcat direct register walk.

Bobcat overstep walk.

Bobcat lope into gallop.

Bobcat trot.

Overstep walk	Stride: 12–18 in. (30.5–45.7 cm)
	Trail width: 3¾–5 in. (9.5–12.7 cm)
Trot	Stride: 15–26 in. (38.1–66 cm)
	Trail width: 3–4½ in. (7.6–11.4 cm)
Extended trot	Stride: 27–45 in. (68.6–114.3 cm)*
	Trail width: 2–2½ in. (5.1–6.4 cm)*
2x2 lope	Stride: 24–52 in. (61–132.1); occasionally up to 71 in. (1.8 m)*
	Trail width: 2½–4 in. (6.4–10.2 cm)* (much like a fisher trail)
Gallop	Stride: 16–48 in. (40.6–121.9 cm)
	Group length: 35–65 in. (88.9–165.1 cm)

*Data courtesy of John McCarter.

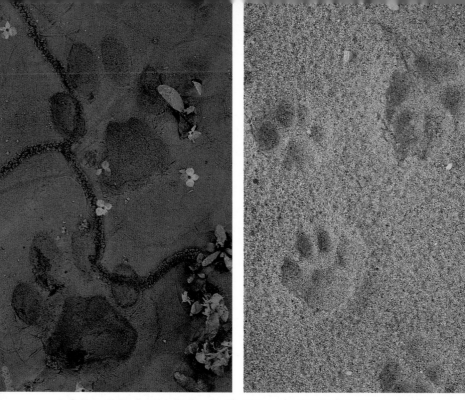

Left: Beautiful bobcat tracks showing the strong curvature in the metacarpal pads. Note the bilobate anterior edges. (CA) *Right:* Front and rear tracks of a bobcat, and front track of a domestic dog in loose sand. (MA)

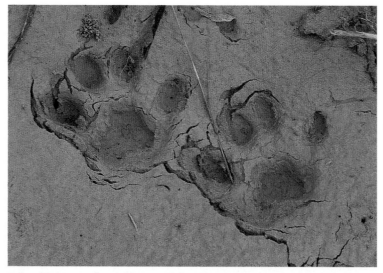

Splayed bobcat tracks. The front track has a larger metacarpal region than the hind track. (TX)

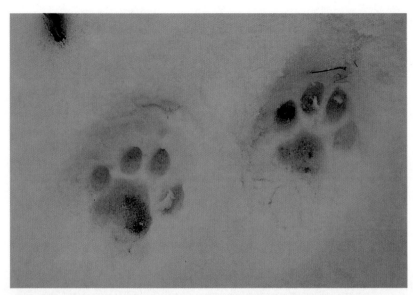

Above: Bobcat front and hind tracks in shallow snow. (MA) *Below left:* An overstep walk, which is the typical gait for bobcats when traveling in shallow substrates. (MA) *Below right:* A bobcat's direct register walk in deep snow conditions. (ID)

Notes:
- Move in the open, but prefer to stay within cover. Yet bobcats in different regions of the country move comfortably in various habitat conditions.
- Use logging roads and trails.
- Incredibly widespread and use a variety of habitats; especially connected to wetlands in the East.
- Direct register walk in deep snow; drag in such a way as to create a beautiful pattern of triangles.

Jaguar *(Panthera onca)*

Track: Front $2^{7}/_8$–$3^{7}/_8$ in. (7.3–9.8 cm) L x 3–$4^{7}/_8$ in. (7.6–12.4 cm) W

Medium to large. Asymmetrical. Five toes: Toe 1 is greatly reduced and raised up on the inner leg. Four toes reliably register in tracks. The metacarpal pads are fused and create one large trapezoidal pad; the leading edge is bilobate, and the posterior edge has three lobes, although these features rarely show as clearly as in cougar tracks. The metacarpal pads cover the majority of the overall track surface. The negative space between the toes and metacarpals forms a C. An additional carpal pad sits high on the leg and registers only at high speeds or in deep substrates.

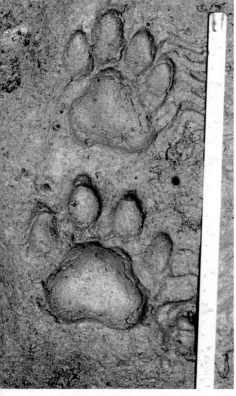

Left: Perfect jaguar tracks. (Mexico) Photo by Marcelo Aranda. *Right:* An overstep walk of a jaguar. (Mexico) Photo by Marcelo Aranda.

Nails are retractable and seldom register; exceptions are on slippery surfaces, when climbing, and while chasing prey. Nails are very thin and decurved. Front track larger and rounder than rear.

Rear 2³/₄–4 in. (7–10.2 cm) L x 2¹/₂–4¹/₂ in. (6.4–11.4 cm) W

Medium to large. Slightly asymmetrical. Four toes. The metacarpal pads are fused and create one large trapezoidal pad. The negative space between the toes and metacarpals forms a *C* or *H*. Nails are retractable and often do not register. Rear track more elongated and symmetrical than front. Tracks can easily be confused with those of cougars, but clear tracks are more robust and meaty than the smaller cougar tracks; they also lack the strongly lobed and curved palm pad shapes of the cougar.

Trail: Direct register/overstep walk   Stride: 16–30 in. (40.6–76.2 cm)

Note: Found in a variety of habitats, but particularly associated with wetland systems and large bodies of water.

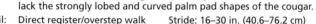

Order Perissodactyla

Feral Horses: Family Equidae

Feral Horse or Wild Pony *(Equus cabillus)*

Track: Front 4¹/₂–5¹/₂ in. (11.4–14 cm) L x 4–5¹/₄ in. (10.2–13.3 cm) W

Large. Symmetrical. Three toes: Toes 2 and 4 are raised up on the backside of the leg and do not register. Toe 3 forms the entire round hoof. Front track larger and rounder than rear track.

Rear 4¹/₄–5¹/₄ in. (10.8–13.3 cm) L x 3³/₄–4³/₄ in. (9.5–12.1 cm) W

Large. Symmetrical. Three toes: Toes 2 and 4 are raised up on the backside of the leg and do not register. Toe 3 forms the entire round hoof.

Trail: Walk   Stride: 23–38 in. (58.4–96.5 cm)

     Trail width: 7–16 in. (17.8–40.6 cm)

Front and hind (below) feral horse tracks. (MD)

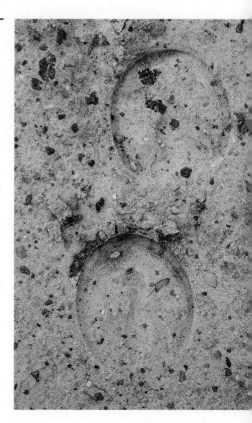

Notes:
- Walk about when foraging, but frolic in lopes and gallops.
- Populations are sprinkled across the United States and Mexico. Known populations include those found on the barrier islands of Maryland and Virginia, in central Florida, and several in the Southwest.

Feral horse walk.

Order Artiodactyla

Wild Boars: Family Suidae

Wild Boar or Feral Hog *(Sus scrofa)*

Track: Front 2¹/₈–2⁵/₈ in. (5.4–6.7 cm) L x 2¹/₄–3 in. (5.7–7.6 cm) W

Medium. Slightly asymmetrical. Four toes: Toes 2 and 5 are dewclaws, raised up on the backside of the leg. Toes 3 and 4 register in tracks; toe 3 is slightly smaller than toe 4. Dewclaws are common in tracks and register just behind and to the outside of the cleaves. Hooves are blunt and rounded, although in young, they may be pointed; inner walls are slightly concave. Front track larger than rear track. Do not include dewclaws in measurements.

Rear 1⁷/₈–2¹/₂ in. (4.8–6.4 cm) L x 2–2³/₄ in. (5.1–7 cm) W

Medium. Slightly asymmetrical. Four toes: Toes 2 and 5 are dewclaws, raised up on the backside of the leg. Toes 3 and 4 register in tracks; toe 3 is slightly smaller than toe 4. Dewclaws are common in tracks and register just behind and to the outside of the cleaves. Hooves are blunt and rounded; inner walls are slightly concave. Do not include dewclaws in measurements.

Trail:
Walk	Stride: 13–17 in. (33–43.2 cm)	
	Trail width: 7–8¹/₂ in. (17.8–21.6 cm)	
Direct register trot	Stride: 26–32 in. (66–81.3 cm)	
	Trail width: 3–4¹/₂ in. (7.6–11.4 cm)	
Lope/gallop	Stride: 36–52 in. (91.4–132.1 cm)	
	Group length: 46–52 in. (1.17–1.32 m)	

Front and hind (right) wild boar tracks. (TN)

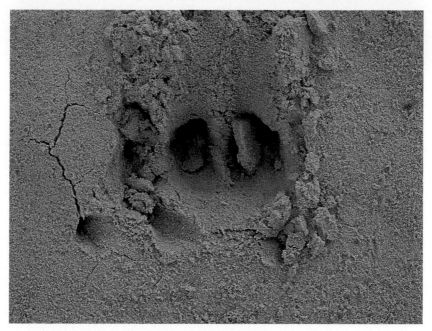

An indirect register: wild boar tracks in deep sand. (TX)

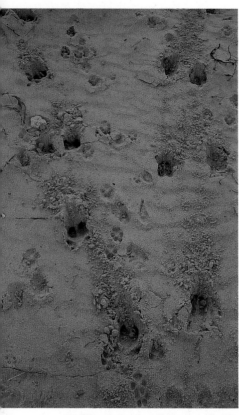

Walking trails of a wild boar and mule deer (right), and several track patterns of coyotes. (TX)

Wild boar walk.

Wild boar trot.

Notes:

- Walk about the landscape, feeding on the move. Trot to cover ground more quickly, and bound and gallop when alarmed.

- Introduced widely as a game species many years ago. Scattered populations still persist throughout many southeastern states, Texas, and California despite concerted efforts to remove them.

- Comfortable in the open; use established roads and trails readily.

- Look for obvious signs of rooting wherever hogs are moving.

- May be found moving alone or in groups.

Peccaries: Family Tayassuidae

Collared Peccary or Javelina *(Pecari tajacu)*

Track: Front 1–1⅞ in. (2.5–4.8 cm) L x ¾–2 in. (1.9–5.1 cm) W

Small. Slightly asymmetrical. Four toes: Toes 2 and 5 are dewclaws, raised up on the backside of the leg. Toes 3 and 4 register in tracks; toe 3 is slightly smaller than toe 4. Hooves are blunt and rounded, although in young, they may be pointed. Soles are flat. Front track larger than rear track.

Rear 1–1⅞ in. (2.5–4.8 cm) L x 1¹/₁₆–1¾ in. (2.7–4.4 cm) W

Small. Slightly asymmetrical. Three toes: Only one dewclaw, raised up on the backside of the leg. Toes 3 and 4 register in tracks; toe 3 is slightly smaller than toe 4. Hooves are blunt and rounded. Soles are flat.

Trail: Walk Stride: 8½–14 in. (21.6–35.6 cm)

Trail width: 2¾–7 in. (7–17.8 cm)

Collared peccary walk.

Collared peccary bound.

A peccary's walking trail in deep mud cuts across raccoon and human trails. (TX)

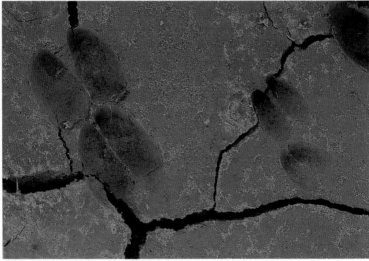

Top: Front and hind (behind) collared peccary tracks. (TX) *Bottom:* Tracks of an adult female and a young peccary. (TX)

Trot	Stride: 15–20 in. (38.1–50.8 cm)
	Trail width: 3–4³/₄ in. (7.6–12.1 cm)
Straddle trot	Stride: 14–20 in. (35.6–50.8 cm)
Bound	Stride: 1–5 ft. (.31–1.5 m)
	Trail width: 6–9 in. (15.2–22.9 cm)
	Group length: 10–32 in. (25.4–81.3 cm)

peccary
range

Notes:
- Walk about the landscape, feeding on the move. Trot to cover ground more quickly, and bound and gallop when alarmed.
- Comfortable in the open; use established trails and roads, as well as their own network of runs.
- Look for signs of feeding wherever peccaries travel to confirm tracks and trails.
- Often found in groups.

Deer and Relatives: Family Cervidae

- Members of the deer family walk when feeding and traveling. However, speed increases in proportion to the level of fear or discomfort an animal feels—from trot to lope to gallop.

- Deer have four toes on each foot. Toes 3 and 4 form the cloven hoof; toes 2 and 5 are on the back of the foot and higher on the "leg" (technically still the foot). These "dewclaws" are lower on the front feet than they are on the back feet. Digit 1 was lost with evolution.

- Members of the deer family create some of the most obvious runs you will find.

Pointing

Follow a deer trail in good substrate for a short distance, and you will likely find a spot where one track sticks off to the side of the rest. This is the front track on one side, positioned to hold the weight of the head as the deer reached out and browsed passing vegetation. The anterior edges of tracks are pointed and point directly to the vegetation browsed by the deer.

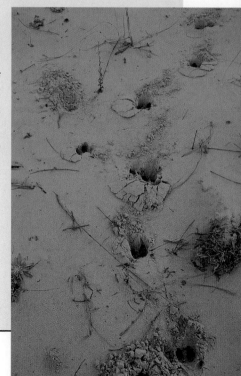

A feral hog illustrates pointing and a t-stop perfectly. Follow the trail, and note where a single track sits off to the left. Just beyond the track is a muzzle mark in the ground where a root was retrieved and eaten—a pause to forage before moving on. (TX)

Elk *(Cervus elaphus)*

Track: Front 3–4⅞ in. (7.6–12.4 cm) L
x 2⅝–4⅝ in. (6.7–11.7 cm) W

Medium to large. Unguligrade.
Slightly asymmetrical. Four toes: Toes
2 and 5 are dewclaws, raised up on
the backside of the leg. Toes 3 and 4
register in tracks; toe 3 is slightly smaller
than toe 4. Hooves are rounded,
sometimes pointed with wider tips;
interior hoof walls are slightly concave.
Soft pads at the posterior edge form
approximately one-quarter of overall track
length; the subunguinis fills the remainder of
the track. Front track larger than rear track. Splay
often due to substrate and/or speed.

Rear 2½–4½ in. (6.4–11.4 cm) L x 2⅜–4 in. (6–10.2 cm) W

Medium to large. Unguligrade. Slightly asymmetrical. Four toes: Toes 2 and
5 are dewclaws, raised up on the backside of the leg. Toes 3 and 4 register
in tracks; toe 3 is slightly smaller than toe 4. Hooves are rounded, sometimes
pointed with wider tips; interior hoof walls are slightly concave. Soft pads

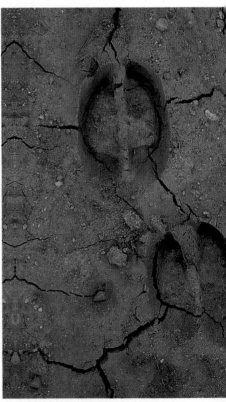

Left: **Front and hind (above) elk tracks. (WY)** *Right:* **Elk tracks in deep mud. (CO)**

form approximately one-third of overall track length; the subunguinis fills the remainder of the track.

Trail: Walk   Stride: 18–35 in. (45.7–88.9 cm)
                     Trail width: 6³/₄–13 in. (17.1–33 cm)
        Trot   Stride: 32–45 in. (81.3–114.3 cm)
                     Trail width: 3¹/₂–6 in. (8.9–15.2 cm)
        Straddle trot   Stride: 37–49 in. (94–124.5 cm)

Notes:

• Walk, but speed up into lopes and gallops when alarmed or threatened.

• Areas with resident elk populations are filled with obvious signs of browsing and feeding on bark. Look for these signs to confirm tracks and trails.

• Direct register walk in deep snow, leaving contiguous drag marks between tracks.

• Often found in groups during the winter months; herds may number in the hundreds or even thousands.

Mule Deer (Including Black-tailed Deer) (*Odocoileus hemionus*)

Track: Front 2¹/₄–4 in. (5.7–10.2 cm) L x 1⁵/₈–2³/₄ in. (4.1–7 cm) W

Medium. Unguligrade. Slightly asymmetrical. Four toes: Toes 2 and 5 are dewclaws, raised up on the backside of the leg. Toes 3 and 4 register in tracks; toe 3 is slightly smaller than toe 4. Hooves are heart-shaped, pointing in the direction of travel; interior hoof walls are concave for the forward half of the track. Soft pads fill tracks almost completely, and the subunguinis is only a thin strip before the hoof walls. Front track larger than rear track. Splay often due to substrate and/or speed.

Elk walk.

Rear 2–3¹/₂ in. (5.1–8.9 cm) L x 1¹/₂–2³/₈ in. (3.8–6 cm) W

Medium. Unguligrade. Slightly asymmetrical. Four toes: Toes 2 and 5 are dewclaws, raised up on the backside of the leg. Toes 3 and 4 register in tracks; toe 3 is slightly smaller than toe 4. Hooves are heart-shaped, pointing in the direction of travel; interior hoof walls are concave for the forward half of the track. Pads in track are distinctly separated from subunguinis and hoof walls.

Trail: Walk   Stride: 15–25¹/₂ in. (38.1–64.8 cm)
                     Trail width: 5–10 in. (12.7–25.4 cm)
        Straddle trot   Stride: 33–50 in. (83.8–127 cm)
                     Group length: 7–16 in. (17.8–40.6 cm)
        Pronk   Stride: 8–15 ft (2.44–4.57 m); occasionally longer
                     Group length: 30–42 in. (76.2–106.7 cm)

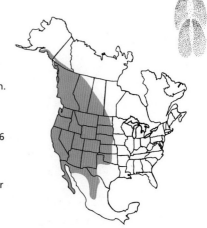

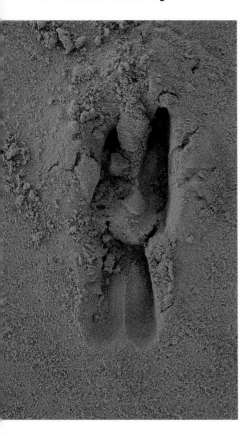

Mule deer
pronk in snow.

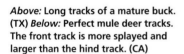

Above: Long tracks of a mature buck.
(TX) *Below:* Perfect mule deer tracks.
The front track is more splayed and
larger than the hind track. (CA)

Mule deer
walk.

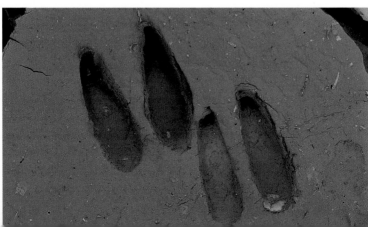

Left: Tracks of the black-tailed subspecies. (WA) *Right:* A straddle trot. The front tracks are the larger and deeper holes. (TX)

Notes:
- Walk, but speed up into lopes and gallops when alarmed or threatened.
- Often found in much drier conditions when overlapping with white-tailed deer in a given area. In the northern Rockies, the drier areas are at higher elevations; in the desert Southwest, such as in Big Bend National Park, mule deer inhabit the desert lowlands, while white-tailed deer stay in the moister mountains.
- Walk in deep snow, dragging their feet with almost every step; as snow deepens, they form runs used by many deer moving from feeding area to feeding area.
- May be found in isolation, but are found in small groups throughout much of the year.

White-tailed Deer *(Odocoileus virginianus)*

Track: Front $1^{3}/_{8}$–4 in. (3.5–10.2 cm) L x $^{7}/_{8}$–$2^{7}/_{8}$ in. (2.2–7.3 cm) W (fawns: $^{1}/_{2}$ in. [1.3 cm] L)

Medium. Unguligrade. Slightly asymmetrical. Four toes: Toes 2 and 5 are dewclaws, raised up on the backside of the leg. Toes 3 and 4 register in tracks; toe 3 is slightly smaller than toe 4. Hooves are heart-shaped,

pointing in the direction of travel; interior hoof walls are concave for the forward half of the track. Pads in track are distinctly separated from narrow band of subunguinis and hoof walls. Front track larger than rear track. Splay often due to substrate and/or speed.

Rear 1¼–3½ in. (3.2–8.9 cm) L x ¾–2⅜ in. (1.9–6 cm) W

Medium. Unguligrade. Slightly asymmetrical. Four toes: Toes 2 and 5 are dewclaws, raised up on the backside of the leg. Toes 3 and 4 register in tracks; toe 3 is slightly smaller than toe 4. Hooves are heart-shaped, pointing in the direction of travel; interior hoof walls are concave for the forward half of the track. Pads in track are distinctly separated from narrow band of subunguinis and hoof walls. Track sizes are highly variable across the continent, depending on region and subspecies.

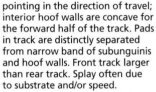

Trail:	Walk	Stride: 13–26 in. (33–66 cm)
		Trail width: 4–10 in. (10.2–25.4 cm)
	Trot	Stride: 29–56 in. (73.7–142.2 cm)
		Trail width: 2–4 in. (5.1–10.2 cm)
	Bound/gallop	Stride: 6–20 ft. (1.52–6.07 m)
		Group lengths: 10–60 in. (25.4–152.4 cm)

White-tailed deer trot.

White-tailed deer walk.

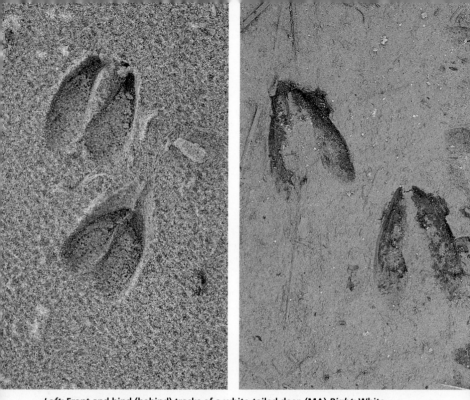

Left: Front and hind (behind) tracks of a white-tailed deer. (MA) *Right:* White-tailed deer tracks. (NC)

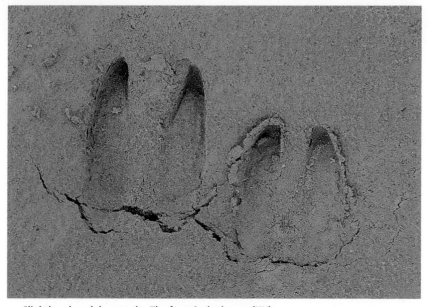

Slightly splayed deer tracks. The front is the larger. (NH)

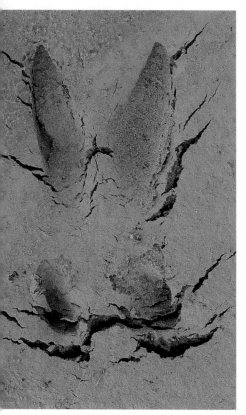 

Left: Splayed front track of bounding white-tailed deer. Note the deep and clear registration of toes 2 and 5, the dewclaws. (NH) *Right:* Bounding trails of white-tailed deer. Each hole in the snow holds four tracks. (MT)

Notes:
- Walk, but speed up into lopes and gallops when alarmed or threatened.
- Vary in size considerably, depending on location and subspecies. Tracks in New England can be twice the size of those in Mexico.
- Use trails and small roads, but are more likely to use their own well-established runs and paths.
- Walk in deep snow, dragging their feet with almost every step; as snow deepens, they form runs used by many deer moving from feeding area to feeding area. If the snow is very deep, they "yard up," or stay in a confined area; browse lines and runs quickly form and persist long after the snow has receded.
- Often found with other deer. From the end of the rut until antlers begin to sprout, males form bachelor groups. Females stay together, accompanied by fawns and yearlings.

Moose (*Alces alces*)

Track: Front 4³⁄₈–7 in. (11.1–17.8 cm) L
x 3³⁄₄–6 in. (9.5–15.2 cm) W
(young: 3¹⁄₄ x 2³⁄₄ in. [8.3 x 7 cm])

Large to very large. Unguligrade.
Slightly asymmetrical. Four toes:
Toes 2 and 5 are dewclaws, raised
up on the backside of the leg.
Toes 3 and 4 register in tracks;
toe 3 is slightly smaller than toe
4. Hooves are more heart-shaped
than elk tracks, as well as larger;
interior hoof walls are concave
for the forward half of the track.
Tips of hooves round out with
age and use. Pads in track are
distinctly separated from narrow
band of subunguinis and hoof
walls. Front track larger than
rear track. Splay often due to
substrate and/or speed.

Rear 4¹⁄₈–6¹⁄₂ in. (10.5–16.5 cm) L
x 3¹⁄₂–4⁵⁄₈ in. (8.9–11.7 cm) W
(young: 3 x 3 in. [7.6 x 7.6 cm])

Large to very large. Unguligrade.
Slightly asymmetrical. Four toes:
Toes 2 and 5 are dewclaws, raised
up on the backside of the leg.
Toes 3 and 4 register in tracks;
toe 3 is slightly smaller than toe
4. Hooves are heart-shaped,
pointing in the direction of
travel; interior hoof walls are
concave for the forward half
of the track. Pads in track are
distinctly separated from
narrow band of subunguinis
and hoof walls.

**Moose
walk.**

**Moose
straddle trot.**

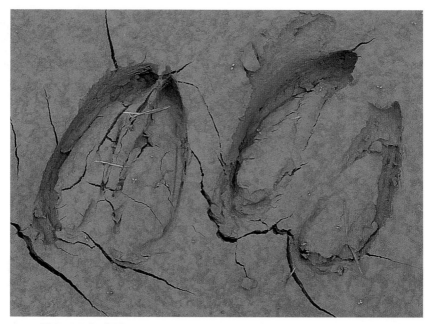

Moose tracks. (AK)

Moose tracks. The front (left) is larger and rounder. (MA)

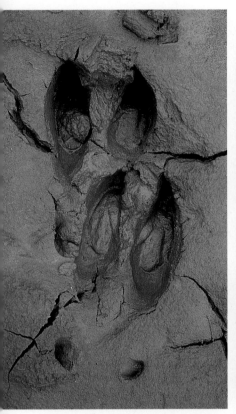 

Left: Deep moose tracks, with dewclaw registration. (AK) *Right:* Walking trails of a female and a calf moose. (AK)

Trail:	Walk	Stride: 28–44 in. (71.1–111.8 cm)
		Trail width: 8½–20 in. (21.6–50.8 cm)
	Trot	Stride: to 55 in. (1.4 m)
	Straddle trot	Stride: 52–72 in. (132.1–182.9 cm)
		Group length: 10–19 in. (25.4–48.3 cm)
	Gallop	Stride: 4–15 ft. (1.22–4.57 m)
		Group lengths: 5–10 ft. (1.52–3.05 m)

Notes:

- Walk, but speed up into lopes and gallops when alarmed or threatened.
- Often associated with wetland systems, moist woods, and willow thickets in high sagebrush habitat and tundra.
- Vary in size depending on location. Largest animals found in Alaska, then New England; smallest moose inhabit the Rocky Mountains.
- Deep snow hinders moose far less than other ungulates. Look for them to move in a direct register walk.
- Solitary animals, except for females with young. However, groups form during the rut in the fall, and pairs are occasionally found together at other times of year.

Caribou *(Rangifer tarandus)*

Track: Front 3¹/₄–5 in. (8.3–12.7 cm) L x 4–6 in. (10.2–15.2 cm) W

Medium to large. Unguligrade. Slightly asymmetrical. Four toes: Toes 2 and 5 are dewclaws, raised up on the backside of the leg. Toes 3 and 4 register in tracks; toe 3 is slightly smaller than toe 4. Hooves are very rounded, and tracks are round; interior hoof walls are very concave for the entire length of the track, and the negative space between cleaves is large. Dewclaws often register, and become more perpendicular to the line of travel with increased speed. Front track of larger than rear track. Splay often due to substrate and/or speed. Do not include dewclaws in measurements.

Rear 3–4¹/₂ in. (7.6–11.4 cm) L x 3⁵/₈–4³/₄ in. (9.2–12.1 cm) W

Medium to large. Unguligrade. Slightly asymmetrical. Four toes: Toes 2 and 5 are dewclaws, raised up on the backside of the leg. Toes 3 and 4 register in tracks; toe 3 is slightly smaller than toe 4. Hooves are very rounded, and tracks are round; interior hoof walls are very concave for the entire length of the track, and the negative space between cleaves is large. Dewclaws often register and become more perpendicular to the line of travel with increased speed. Do not include dewclaws in measurements.

Trail: Walk — Stride: 23–33 in. (58.4–83.8 cm)

Trail width: 10–17 in. (25.4–43.2 cm)

Straddle trot — Stride: 49–57 in. (1.25–1.45 m)

Caribou walk.

Caribou straddle trot.

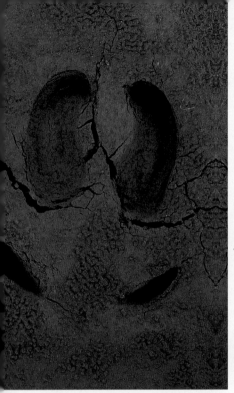

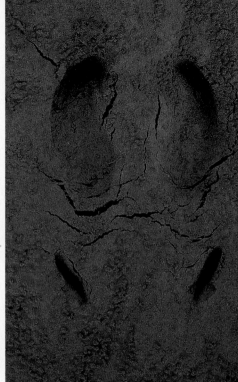

Above left: Perfect front track of a caribou in a straddle trot. (AK) *Above right:* The accompanying perfect rear track. (AK) *Right:* Front and rear (above) caribou tracks. Dewclaws do not always register. (AK)

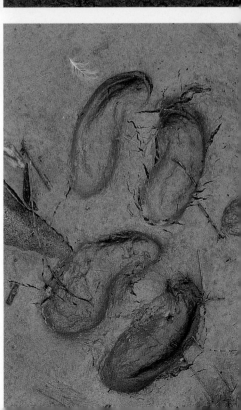

Notes:
- Walk, but speed up into lopes and gallops when alarmed or threatened.
- When caribou straddle trot, the rear tracks register nearly directly beyond the front tracks rather than off to the side, as is more common in other mammals.
- Creatures of the northern woods and open tundra.
- Walk in deep snow and drag their feet like other members of the deer family.
- Often found in the company of other caribou; form great herds during the winter months.

Pronghorn: Family Antilocapridae

Pronghorn *(Antilocapra americana)*

Track: Front 2¹/₈–3¹/₂ in. (5.4–8.9 cm) L x 1¹/₂–2¹/₄ in. (3.8–5.7 cm) W

Medium. Unguligrade. Slightly asymmetrical. Two toes: Pronghorns lack dewclaws (although an impression may register in deep substrate), and toes 3 and 4 register in tracks; toe 3 is slightly smaller than toe 4. Hooves are heart-shaped; interior hoof walls are concave for the forward half of the track, and outside walls are concave at about the center point or straight. Soft pads at the posterior edge of tracks are distinctly bulbous. Front and rear tracks have very similar dimensions. Splay often due to substrate and/or speed.

Rear 2¹/₄–3¹/₄ in. (5.7–8.3 cm) L x 1¹/₂–2¹/₈ in. (3.8–5.4 cm) W

Medium. Unguligrade. Slightly asymmetrical. Two toes: Pronghorns lack dewclaws, and toes 3 and 4 register in tracks; toe 3 is slightly smaller than toe 4. Hooves are heart-shaped; interior hoof walls are concave for the forward half of the track, and outside walls are concave at about the center point or straight. Soft pads at the posterior edge of tracks are distinctly bulbous.

Trail: Direct register walk   Stride: 17–26 in. (43.2–66 cm)

Trail width: 4³/₈–10 in. (11.1–25.4 cm)

Overstep walk   Stride: 19–29 in. (48.3–73.7 cm)

Bound/gallop   Stride: 29–61 in. (73.7–154.9 cm)

Group length: 36–82 in. (91.4–208.3 cm)

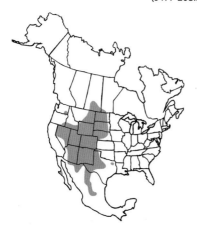

Pronghorn walk.

Pronghorn overstep walk, or amble.

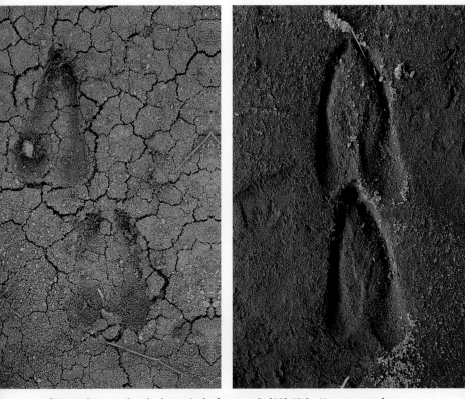

Left: **Pronghorn tracks. The larger is the front track. (CO)** *Right:* **Narrow pronghorn tracks. (WY)**

Notes:
- Direct register and overstep walk (unique among ungulates), and speed up into lopes and gallops when alarmed or threatened.
- Inhabit open grasslands and sagebrush deserts, relying on speed and sight to keep them safe while exposed.
- Direct register walk in deep snow.
- Often found with others, but single animals are also common.

Bison, Goats, Muskox, and Sheep: Family Bovidae

- Members of this family walk when feeding and traveling. However, speed increases in proportion to the level of fear or discomfort an animal feels—from trot to lope to gallop.

- These animals have four toes on each foot; toes 3 and 4 form the cloven hoof, and toes 2 and 5 are on the back of the foot and higher on the "leg" (technically still the foot). These "dewclaws" are lower on the front feet than they are on the back feet.

- Bison, cattle, sheep, and goats create some of the most obvious runs you will find.

American Bison *(Bison bison)*

Track: Front 4¹/₂–6¹/₂ in. (11.4–16.5 cm) L x 4¹/₂–6 in. (11.4–15.2 cm) W

Large to very large. Unguligrade. Slightly asymmetrical. Four toes: Toes 2 and 5 are dewclaws, raised up on the backside of the leg. Toes 3 and 4 register in tracks; toe 3 is slightly smaller than toe 4. Hooves are very rounded, and tracks are round; interior hoof walls are concave for the entire length of the track, and the negative space between cleaves is significant midtrack. Soft pad in track distinctly V-shaped at the posterior edge. Front track larger than rear track. Splay often due to substrate and/or speed. Tracks easily confused with those of domestic cows.

Rear 4¹/₄–6 in. (10.8–15.2 cm) L x 4–5¹/₂ in. (10.2–14 cm) W

Large to very large. Unguligrade. Slightly asymmetrical. Four toes: Toes 2 and 5 are dewclaws, raised up on the backside of the

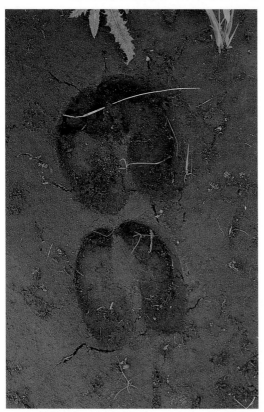

Bison tracks. The more robust is the front track. (WY)

American Bison walk.

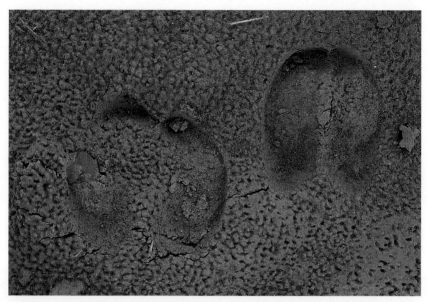

Bison tracks in shallow substrate. The front is rounder and larger than the hind. (WY)

leg. Toes 3 and 4 register in tracks; toe 3 is slightly smaller than toe 4. Hooves are very rounded; interior hoof walls are slightly concave for the entire length of the track, but the negative space between cleaves is very small. Soft pad in track distinctly V-shaped at the posterior edge.

Trail: Walk   Stride: 22–38 in.
(55.9–96.5 cm)

Trail width: 10–22 in.
(25.4–55.9 cm)

Trot   Stride: 40–44 in.
(1.02–1.12 m)

Trail width: 10–15 in.
(25.4–38.1 cm)

Notes:

• Walk, speeding up only when alarmed, threatened, or playing.

• Creatures of open grasslands, but can be found in nearby woodlands as well.

• Use existing trails and road systems.

• Plow through deep snow. You'll often find trails where they swing their heads from side to side, which I believe is a form of digging to prepare an area for further hoofing to gain access to grasses and other vegetation.

• Tend to be found in groups, but solitary animals are not uncommon.

Sexual Dimorphism

Many mammal species show sexual dimorphism, meaning that one sex is significantly larger and heavier than the other. In the case of mammals, the male is likely to be larger. Sexual dimorphism is especially prevalent and obvious in carnivore species and can often be interpreted from track and trail parameters; there are times when you should be able to differentiate mature males from smaller females and immature males, or males from females in mating pairs. In many species, track morphology also differs between the sexes and is often a more reliable clue to sex than measurements.

Mountain Goat *(Oreamnos americanus)*

Track: Front 2¹/₂–3¹/₂ in. (6.4–8.9 cm) L x 2¹/₂–3¹/₂ in. (6.4–8.9 cm) W

Medium. Unguligrade. Slightly asymmetrical. Four toes: Toes 2 and 5 are dewclaws, raised up on the backside of the leg. Toes 3 and 4 register in tracks; toe 3 is slightly smaller than toe 4. Hooves are pointed, but track shape is blocky; interior hoof walls are concave, and the negative space between cleaves is often significant. The points of the cleaves are in the middle of the hoof rather than on the inside, as in other wild ungulates. Track includes a large subunguinis area, which provides for better footing. Front track larger than rear track. Parameters overlap with those of bighorn sheep.

Rear 2¹/₂–3¹/₄ in. (6.4–8.3 cm) L x 2¹/₄–3 in. (5.7–7.6 cm) W

Medium. Unguligrade. Slightly asymmetrical. Four toes: Toes 2 and 5 are dewclaws, raised up on the backside of the leg. Toes 3 and 4 register in tracks; toe 3 is slightly smaller than toe 4. Hooves are pointed, but track shape is blocky; interior hoof walls are concave, and the negative space

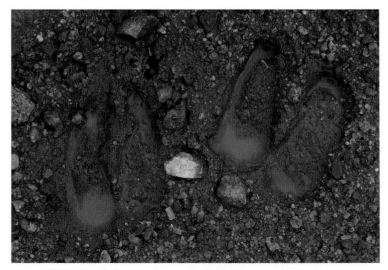

Front and hind (smaller) mountain goat tracks. (CO)

Mountain goat walk.

Walking trails. (CO)

between cleaves is often significant. The points of the cleaves are in the middle of the hoof rather than on the inside, as in other wild ungulates. Track includes a large subunguinis area, which provides for better footing.

Trail: Walk   Stride: 15–30 in. (38.1–76.2 cm)
              Trail width: 8–13 in. (20.3–33 cm)

Notes:

• Walk when moving about; occasionally bound up steep faces when threatened.

• Alpine animals, most comfortable near or on rocky crags and in the steepest terrain.

• Seem to be able to ascend nearly vertical walls of rock; tremendous climbers.

• Tend to stay in terrain where wind keeps snow levels down, but expect them to direct register walk and show lots of drag in deep snow conditions.

• Both single animals and groups are common.

Muskox *(Ovibos moschatus)*

Track: Front 4¹/₄–5¹/₂ in. (10.8–14 cm) L x 4³/₈–6 in. (11.1–15.2 cm) W

Large. Unguligrade. Slightly asymmetrical. Four toes: Toes 2 and 5 are dewclaws, raised up on the backside of the leg. Toes 3 and 4 register in tracks; toe 3 is slightly smaller than toe 4. Hooves are very rounded, and tracks are round; interior hoof walls are concave for the entire length of the track, and the negative space between cleaves is smaller than in caribou and reindeer. Front track larger than rear track. Splay often due to substrate and/or speed.

Rear 3³/₄–4¹/₂ in. (9.5–11.4 cm) L x 4–4¹/₂ in. (10.2–11.4 cm) W

Large. Unguligrade. Slightly asymmetrical. Four toes: Toes 2 and 5 are dewclaws, raised up on the backside of the leg. Toes 3 and 4 register in tracks; toe 3 is slightly smaller than toe 4. Hooves are very rounded, and tracks are round; interior hoof walls are concave for the entire length of the track, but the negative space between cleaves is smaller than in front tracks. Dewclaws often register and become more perpendicular to the line of travel with increases in speed.

Trail: Walk   Stride: 15–28 in. (38.1–71.1 cm)

           Trail width: 10–18 in. (25.4–45.7 cm)

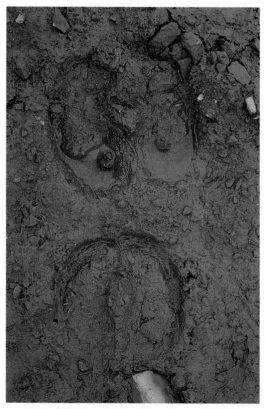

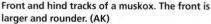

Front and hind tracks of a muskox. The front is larger and rounder. (AK)

Muskox walk.

Overlapping front and hind muskox tracks. (AK)

Notes:
- Generally move at a walk; lope and gallop when alarmed.
- Creatures of the open tundra and far north.
- Reintroductions have been successful in several areas of Alaska.
- Sedentary—conserving energy through the winter and avoiding overheating during the warmer months.
- Often found in groups.

Bighorn Sheep
(Ovis canadensis)

Track: Front 2¹/₈–3³/₈ in. (5.4–8.6 cm) L x 1¹/₂–3 in. (3.8–7.6 cm) W

Medium. Unguligrade. Slightly asymmetrical. Four toes: Toes 2 and 5 are dewclaws, raised up on the backside of the leg. Toes 3 and 4 register in tracks; toe 3 is slightly smaller than toe 4. Hooves are pointed and more heart-shaped than those of mountain goats. Front track larger than rear track.

Rear 2¹/₁₆–3¹/₄ in. (5.2–8.3 cm) L x 1¹/₂–2³/₈ in. (3.8–6 cm) W

Medium. Unguligrade. Slightly asymmetrical. Four toes: Toes 2 and 5 are dewclaws, raised up on the backside of the leg. Toes 3 and 4 register in tracks; toe 3 is slightly smaller than toe 4. Hooves are pointed and more heart-shaped than those of mountain goats. Parameters overlap with those of mountain goats.

Trail: Walk   Stride: 12–25 in. (30.5–63.5 cm)
                        Trail width: 4–11 in. (10.2–27.9 cm)
       Trot   Stride: 23–35 in. (58.4–88.9 cm)
                        Trail width: 3–6 in. (7.6–15.2 cm)
       Lope/gallop Group length 50–60 in. (1.27–1.52 m)

Notes:

- Walk in steep and rocky terrain, but more often trot when traveling on flat ground or feeling exposed.
- Move comfortably in steep, rocky terrain and can be found at a range of altitudes; tremendous climbers.
- Subspecies inhabit desert canyons, sagebrush mountains, and high peaks in the Rockies and Sierras.
- Direct register walk in deep snow.
- Often found with others. Males form groups and move separately from females with young for much of the year.

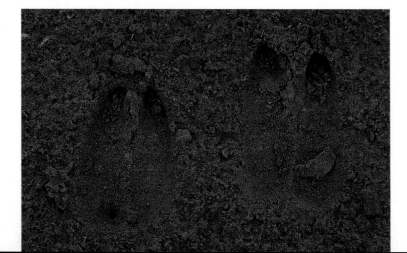

Bighorn sheep walk.

Front and hind (smaller) bighorn sheep tracks. (UT)

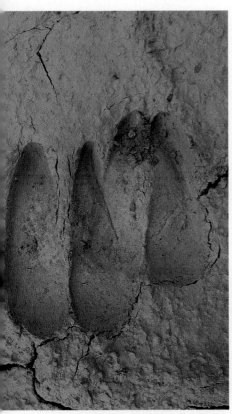

Left: Perfect bighorn sheep tracks. (CO) *Right:* Tracks of a mature bighorn ram. (MT)

Dall's Sheep *(Ovis dalli)*

Track: Front 2¼–3½ in. (5.7–8.9 cm) L x 2–2½ in. (5.1–6.4 cm) W (young: 1⅞ x 1½ in. [4.8 x 3.8 cm])

Medium. Unguligrade. Slightly asymmetrical. Four toes: Toes 2 and 5 are dewclaws, raised up on the backside of the leg. Toes 3 and 4 register in tracks; toe 3 is slightly smaller than toe 4. Hooves are pointed and more heart-shaped than those of mountain goats. Front track larger than rear track.

Rear 2¼–3¼ in. (5.7–8.3 cm) L x 2–2½ in. (5.1–6.4 cm) W

Medium. Unguligrade. Slightly asymmetrical. Four toes: Toes 2 and 5 are dewclaws, raised up on the backside of the leg. Toes 3 and 4 register in tracks; toe 3 is slightly smaller than toe 4.

Dall's sheep tracks. (AK)

Hooves are pointed and more heart-shaped than those of mountain goats. Parameters overlap with those of mountain goats.

Notes:

- Primarily walk, but speed up when threatened or alarmed.
- Move comfortably in steep, rocky terrain and can be found at a range of altitudes; tremendous climbers.
- Found only in the northwest portion of this continent—nowhere in the lower 48 states.
- Direct register walk in deep snow.
- Often found with others. Males form groups and move separately from females with young for much of the year.

Order Rodentia

Mountain Beavers: Family Aplodontidae

Mountain Beaver or Aplodontia *(Aplodontia rufa)*

Track: Front $^{15}/_{16}$–$1^{9}/_{16}$ in. (2.4–4 cm) L x 1–$1^{9}/_{16}$ in. (2.5–4 cm) W

Small. Plantigrade. Asymmetrical. Five toes: Toe 1 is reduced, lacks a claw, and rarely registers in tracks. The metacarpal pads are fused and lobed; there is an additional pad (the heel) at the posterior edge of the track, which may or may not show. The negative space between the toes and metacarpals has little to no fur. Nails are long and prominent in tracks. Front and rear tracks have similar dimensions. Hand outline is very clear in tracks.

Rear $^{7}/_{8}$–$1^{5}/_{8}$ in. (2.2–4.1 cm) L x $^{15}/_{16}$–$1^{1}/_{2}$ in. (2.4–3.8 cm) W

Small. Plantigrade. Slightly asymmetrical. Five toes: Toe 1 is smallest and often appears very pointed in tracks. Track is a classic rodent rear foot: Toes 1 and 5 point out to either side, and toes 2, 3, and 4 register close

Mountain beaver walk.

Aplodontia tracks. The front track has massive claws, and the hind tracks look like small hand-prints. (WA)

together, pointing forward. The metacarpals are fused to form a larger pad. Nails may or may not register and are much smaller than those of the front feet. The heel portion of the foot may or may not register.

Trail: Walk   Stride: 3³/₄–7 in. (9.5–17.8 cm)
                      Trail width: 3–6³/₄ in. (7.6–17.1 cm)

Notes:

- Understep walk when traveling and foraging, but bound and gallop when alarmed.
- Tend to live under significant cover—often a forest canopy and a thick understory.
- Found only in moist habitats along the Pacific coast in the northwestern United States and southwestern Canada.
- Competent climbers; spend a great deal of time harvesting cambium, buds, and leaves from trees and shrubs.
- Trail inevitably starts and ends at a burrow entrance.
- Walk in deep snow, which is rare in the areas they inhabit.
- Solitary animals.

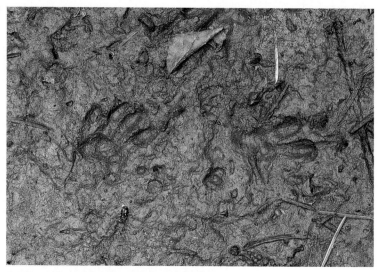

Front and hind tracks of an aplodontia. (WA)

Squirrels: Family Sciuridae

Least Chipmunk
(Tamias minimus)

Track: Front $^3/_8$–$^{11}/_{16}$ in. (1–1.7 cm) L
x $^5/_{16}$–$^9/_{16}$ in. (.8–1.4 cm) W

Very small. Plantigrade. Asymmetrical. Five toes in classic rodent structure: Toe 1 is a vestigial thumb and rarely registers in tracks. Toes 2 and 5 point toward the sides, and toes 3 and 4 point forward. Central metacarpal pads have fused, so look for three distinct palm pads; there are two additional pads (the heel) at the posterior edge of the track, which may or may not show. The negative space between the toes and metacarpals has little to no fur. Nails often prominent in tracks. Front and rear tracks have similar dimensions.

Rear $^1/_2$–$^{11}/_{16}$ in. (1.3–1.7 cm) L x $^1/_2$–$^{11}/_{16}$ in. (1.3–1.7 cm) W

Very small. Plantigrade. Slightly asymmetrical. Five toes in a classic rodent structure: Toes 1 and 5 point out to either side, and toes 2, 3, and 4 register close together, pointing forward. Some metacarpals are fused to form larger pads, but four distinct pads show in tracks. Nails often prominent. The heel portion of the foot is furred and may or may not register. Tracks of least chipmunks are difficult to differentiate from those of other small chipmunk species.

Trail: Bound Stride: 3–20 in. (7.6–50.8 cm)
Trail width: 1$^1/_2$–2$^3/_4$ in. (3.8–7 cm)
Group length: 1$^3/_4$–5 in. (4.4–12.7 cm)

Notes:
- Move about in bounds, with occasional hops. Walks may be used when foraging or tracking down an odor.
- Although not true hibernators, chipmunks stay underground for much of the snow season. However, it is not unusual to find them out and about during warm spells or as daylight hours increase near the end of winter.
- Inhabit varied forested habitats and are often found in close proximity to humans; common in parks and suburbs.
- Competent climbers; can be found harvesting fruits and nuts aboveground in trees and shrubs.
- Trails begin and end with a burrow or rock crevice or disappear into thick cover, such as a slash pile.
- In deep fluffy snow, use a modified 2x2 bound in which the front and rear tracks are found in the same holes.
- Solitary animals, but may be in close proximity to others.

Eastern Chipmunk *(Tamias striatus)*

Track: Front 3/4–1 in. (1.9–2.5 cm) L x 7/16–7/8 in. (1.1–2.2 cm) W

Very small to small. Plantigrade. Asymmetrical. Five toes in classic rodent structure: Toe 1 is a vestigial thumb and rarely registers in tracks. Toes 2 and 5 point toward the sides, and toes 3 and 4 point forward. Central metacarpal pads have fused, so look for three distinct palm pads; there are two additional pads (the heel) at the posterior edge of the track, which may or may not show. The negative space between the toes and metacarpals has little to no fur. Nails often prominent in tracks.

Eastern chipmunk bound.

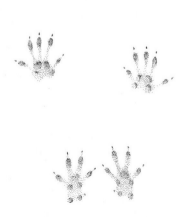

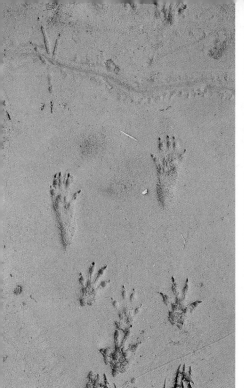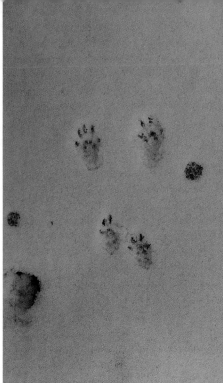

Left: **Eastern chipmunk tracks. Note the furred heel portions of the hind tracks. The trail at the top of the image is that of a dragonfly nymph emerging from the river. (MA)** *Right:* **Chipmunk tracks in snow. (NH)**

Front and rear tracks have similar dimensions and overlap with parameters of southern flying squirrels.

Rear 1/2–7/8 in. (1.3–2.2 cm) L x 5/8–15/16 in. (1.6–2.4 cm) W

Very small to small. Plantigrade. Slightly asymmetrical. Five toes in a classic rodent structure: Toes 1 and 5 point out to either side, and toes 2, 3, and 4 register close together, pointing forward. Some metacarpals are fused to form larger pads, but four distinct pads show in tracks. Nails often register. The heel portion of the foot is furred and may or may not register.

Trail: Bound   Stride: 4–23 in. (10.2–58.4 cm)

Trail width: 1 3/4–2 7/8 in. (4.4–7.3 cm); occasionally up to 3 in. (7.6 cm)

Group length: 2–5 in. (5.1–12.7 cm)

Notes:

- Move about in bounds, with occasional hops. Walks may be used when foraging or tracking down an odor.
- Although not true hibernators, chipmunks stay underground for much of the snow season. However, it is not unusual to find them out and about during warm spells or as daylight hours increase near the end of winter.
- Inhabit varied forested habitats and are often found in close proximity to humans; common in parks and suburbs.
- Competent climbers; can be found harvesting fruits and nuts aboveground in trees and shrubs.

- Trails begin and end with a burrow or rock crevice or disappear into thick cover, such as a slash pile.
- In deep fluffy snow, use a modified 2x2 bound in which the front and rear tracks are found in the same holes.
- Solitary animals, but may be in close proximity to others.

Hoary Marmot *(Marmota caligata)*

Track: Front 2$\frac{1}{8}$–3$\frac{1}{8}$ in. (5.4–7.9 cm) L
x 1$\frac{1}{4}$–2$\frac{5}{8}$ in. (3.2–6.7 cm) W

Medium. Plantigrade. Asymmetrical. Five toes in classic rodent structure: Toe 1 is a vestigial thumb and rarely registers in tracks. Toes 2 and 5 point toward the sides, and toes 3 and 4 point forward. The center metacarpal pads have fused but are still strongly lobed; tracks are composed of three distinct palm pads, although it may look like four; there are two additional pads (the heel) at the posterior edge of the track, which may or may not show. Pads of the foot are naked and exposed. Nails often prominent in tracks. Front and rear tracks have similar dimensions.

Rear 2–3$\frac{3}{8}$ in. (5.1–8.6 cm) L
x 1$\frac{3}{4}$–2$\frac{1}{2}$ in. (4.4–6.4 cm) W

Medium. Plantigrade. Slightly asymmetrical. Five toes in a classic rodent structure: Toes 1 and 5 point out to either side, and toes 2, 3, and 4 register close together, pointing forward. Some metacarpals are fused to form larger pads, but four distinct pads show in tracks. There are two additional pads in the

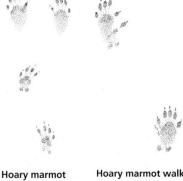

Hoary marmot bound.

Hoary marmot walk.

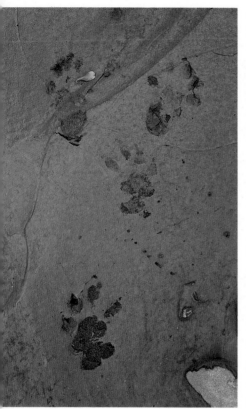

Left: Bound of a hoary marmot. (AK) *Right:* **A hoary marmot's hind track. (AK)**

posterior part of the track (the heel); the heel is hairless and may or may not register. Nails often register.

Trail:	Walk	Stride: 8–11 in. (20.3–27.9 cm)
		Trail width: 5–7 in. (12.7–17.8 cm)
	Bound	Stride: 8–32 in. (20.3–81.3 cm)
		Trail width: 4³/₄–7¹/₂ in. (12.1–19.1 cm)
		Group length: 4–16 in. (10.2–40.6 cm)

Notes:

- Walk much of the time, switching to a bound when retreating to a burrow for safety. Trots and lopes are also used when crossing exposed areas but there is no imminent danger.
- Thought to be more social than yellow-bellied marmots, so tracks and trails may mingle with those of others.
- Alpine animals found at high elevations and often in rocky terrain that offers cover. In the far north of their range, they are also found at lower elevations.
- Trails begin and end in rock crevices or burrows. Runs are often apparent at burrow entrances.
- Hibernate for much of the year, slumbering through the harsh winter season. Reappear while snow still lingers, surviving on stores created the previous summer and fall.

Yellow-bellied Marmot *(Marmota flaviventris)*

Track: Front 1³/₄–3 in. (4.4–7.6 cm) L x 1¹/₂–2³/₈ in. (3.8–6 cm) W

Small to medium. Plantigrade. Asymmetrical. Five toes in classic rodent structure: Toe 1 is a vestigial thumb and rarely registers in tracks. Toes 2 and 5 point toward the sides, and toes 3 and 4 point forward. The center metacarpal pads have fused but are still strongly lobed; tracks are composed of three distinct palm pads, although it may look like four; there are two additional pads (the heel) at the posterior edge of the track, which may or may not show. Pads of the foot are naked and exposed. Nails often prominent in tracks. Front and rear tracks have similar dimensions.

Rear 1³/₄–3¹/₄ in. (4.4–8.3 cm) L x 1⁵/₈–2¹/₂ in. (4.1–6.4 cm) W

Small to medium. Plantigrade. Slightly asymmetrical. Five toes in classic rodent structure: Toes 1 and 5 point out to either side, and toes 2, 3, and 4 register close together, pointing forward. Some metacarpals are fused to form larger pads, but four distinct pads show in tracks. There are two additional pads in the posterior part of the track (the heel); the heel is hairless and may or may not register. Nails often register.

Trail: Walk Stride: 3¹/₂–10 in. (8.9–25.4 cm)

Trail width: 4¹/₄–7 in. (10.8–17.8 cm)

Bound Stride: 9–31 in. (22.9–78.7 cm)

Trail width: 4³/₄–7³/₄ in. (12.1–19.7 cm)

Group length: 6–14 in. (15.2–35.6 cm)

Notes:

- Walk much of the time, switching to a bound when retreating to a burrow for safety. Trots and lopes are also used when crossing exposed areas but there is no imminent danger.

- Alpine animals associated with rocky terrain, but also found in high-elevation forests, living under boulders and in burrows.

The front track of this yellow-bellied marmot sits beyond the hind. (WY)

- Trails begin and end in rock crevices or burrows. Runs are often apparent at burrow entrances.
- Hibernate for much of the year, slumbering through the harsh winter season. Reappear while snow still lingers, surviving on stores created the previous summer and fall.

Woodchuck or Groundhog (*Marmota monax*)

Track: Front 1⁷⁄₈–2³⁄₄ in. (4.8–7 cm) L x 1–2¹⁄₈ in. (2.5–5.4 cm) W

Small to medium. Plantigrade. Asymmetrical. Five toes in classic rodent structure: Toe 1 is a vestigial thumb and rarely registers in tracks. Toes 2 and 5 point toward the sides, and toes 3 and 4 point forward. The center metacarpal pads have fused but are still strongly lobed; tracks are composed of three distinct palm pads, although it may look like four; there are two additional pads (the heel) at the posterior edge of the track, which may or may not show. Pads of the foot are naked and exposed. Nails

Walking trail of a yellow-bellied marmot. (CO)

Perfect front and hind (right) woodchuck tracks. (VT)

often prominent in tracks. Front and rear tracks have similar dimensions.

Rear 1⁵/₈–3¹/₈ in. (4.1–7.9 cm) L x 1³/₈–2 in. (3.5–5.1 cm) W

Small to medium. Plantigrade. Slightly asymmetrical. Five toes in a classic rodent structure: Toes 1 and 5 point out to either side, and toes 2, 3, and 4 register close together, pointing forward. Some metacarpals are fused to form larger pads, but four distinct pads show in tracks. There are two additional pads in the posterior part of the track (the heel); the heel is hairless and may or may not register. Nails often register.

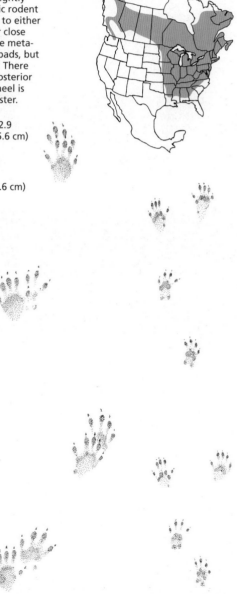

Trail: Walk   Stride: 4¹/₄–9 in. (10.8–22.9 cm); trot up to 14 in. (35.6 cm)

Trail width: 4³/₈–5¹/₂ in. (11.1–14 cm); trot down to 3¹/₄ in. (8.3 cm)

Bound   Stride: 7–27 in. (17.8–68.6 cm)

Trail width: 4³/₄–7³/₄ in. (12.1–19.7 cm)

Group length: 4³/₄–15 in. (12.1–38.1 cm)

Notes:

• Walk much of the time, switching to a bound when retreating to a burrow for safety. Trots and lopes are also used when crossing exposed areas but there is no imminent danger.

• Widespread creatures of open fields, valleys, and low elevations; also inhabit open woodlands near fields and substantial forest openings.

• Trails begin and end in rock crevices or burrows. Runs are often apparent at burrow entrances.

• Climb shrubs and trees.

• Hibernate for much of the year, slumbering through the harsh winter season. Reappear while snow still lingers in the northern part of their range, surviving on stores created the previous summer and fall.

• Solitary animals, but often found living in close proximity to others.

Woodchuck walk.   Woodchuck bound.

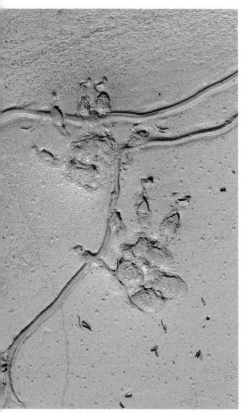

Left: Front and hind woodchuck tracks in wet mud. (NH) *Right:* A walking trail. Compare the larger woodchuck tracks with eastern chipmunk and deer mouse trails, as well as those of robins and other birds. (MA)

White-tailed Antelope Squirrel
(Ammospermophilus leucurus)

Track: Front ⁵/₈–¹⁵/₁₆ in. (1.6–2.4 cm) L
x ³/₈–⁵/₈ in. (1–1.6 cm) W

Very small to small. Plantigrade. Asymmetrical. Five toes in classic rodent structure: Toe 1 is a vestigial thumb and rarely registers in tracks. Toes 2 and 5 point toward the sides, and toes 3 and 4 point forward. Central metacarpal pads have fused, so look for three distinct palm pads; there are two additional pads (the heel) at the posterior edge of the track, which register less than in chipmunk tracks. The negative space between the toes and metacarpals has little to no fur. Claws are well developed and prominent in tracks.

White-tailed antelope squirrel bound.

White-tailed antelope squirrel tracks. (CA)

Rear $^{11}/_{16}$–1 in. (1.7–2.5 cm) L x $^9/_{16}$–$^{13}/_{16}$ in. (1.4–2.1 cm) W

Very small to small. Plantigrade. Slightly asymmetrical. Five toes in a classic rodent structure: Toes 1 and 5 point out to either side, and toes 2, 3, and 4 register close together, pointing forward. Some metacarpals are fused to form larger pads, but four distinct pads show in tracks. Nails are prominent in tracks. The heel portion of the foot may or may not register. Front and rear tracks have similar dimensions and overlap with chipmunk parameters, yet their morphology is much more similar to tracks of ground squirrels.

Trail: Bound Stride: 5–15 in. (12.7–38.1 cm)

Trail width: 2$^1/_8$–3$^1/_2$ in. (5.4–8.9 cm)

Group length: 2–4$^1/_2$ in. (5.1–11.4 cm)

Notes:

• Move in bounds and occasional hops; walk when foraging or sunning themselves at burrow entrances.

• Associated with and adapted for dry habitats.

• Competent climbers.

• Do not hibernate; remain active throughout the year.

• Often found near others and may share burrow systems with several animals and other species during winter.

Left: Two white-tailed antelope squirrel hind tracks (above) and a single front track. (UT) *Right:* A bounding trail pattern of a white-tailed antelope squirrel. (UT)

Uinta Ground Squirrel *(Spermophilus armatus)*

Track: Front $^{15}/_{16}$–1$^{1}/_{2}$ in. (2.4–3.8 cm) L x $^{1}/_{2}$–$^{13}/_{16}$ in. (1.3–2.1 cm) W

Small. Plantigrade. Asymmetrical—more so than chipmunks and tree squirrels. Five toes in classic rodent structure: Toe 1 is a vestigial thumb. Toes 2 and 5 point toward the sides, and toes 3 and 4 point forward. Some of the metacarpal pads have fused, but the track is composed of three distinct palm pads; there are two additional pads (the heel) at the posterior edge of the track, which may or may not show. The negative space between the toes and metacarpals has little to no fur. Nails are long and prominent in tracks. Front and rear tracks have similar dimensions.

Rear 1$^{1}/_{16}$–1$^{9}/_{16}$ in. (2.7–4 cm) L x $^{11}/_{16}$–1$^{1}/_{16}$ in. (1.7–2.7 cm) W

Small. Plantigrade. Slightly asymmetrical. Five toes in classic rodent structure: Toes 1 and 5 point out to either side, and toes 2, 3, and 4 register close together, pointing forward. Some metacarpals are fused to form larger pads, but four distinct pads show in tracks. Nails prominent in tracks, but smaller than those of the front feet. The heel portion of

**Uinta ground squirrel
2x2 lope.**

Front and hind (below) tracks of a Uinta ground squirrel. (WY)

the foot, which is naked and composed of several distinct pads, may or may not register.

Trail: Bound   Stride: 4^1/$_2$–15 in. (11.4–38.1 cm)
                     Trail width: 2^5/$_8$–3^1/$_2$ in. (6.7–8.9 cm)
                     Group length: 3–5 in. (7.6–12.7 cm)
      2x2 lope/bound   Stride: 3–9 in. (7.6–22.9 cm)
                     Trail width: 2^1/$_2$–4^1/$_4$ in. (6.4–10.8 cm)

Notes:
- Bound when traveling aboveground; slow to a walk when foraging, and occasionally use lopes to cross open areas at a medium pace.
- Diurnal. Associated with open habitats—ideal for sightings. May live close to human settlements.
- Trails begin and end with a burrow entrance.
- Hibernate for much of the year.
- Often found living in close proximity to other squirrels and may even share burrows.

Uinta ground squirrel tracks in a 2x2 lope. (WY)

California Ground Squirrel *(Spermophilus beecheyi)*

Track: Front $^{15}/_{16}$–1$^3/_8$ in. (2.4–3.5 cm) L x $^5/_8$–1$^3/_8$ in. (1.6–3.5 cm) W

Small. Plantigrade. Asymmetrical—more so than chipmunks and tree squirrels. Five toes in classic rodent structure: Toe 1 is a vestigial thumb. Toes 2 and 5 point toward the sides, and toes 3 and 4 point forward. Some of the metacarpal pads have fused, but the track is composed of three distinct palm pads; there are two additional pads (the heel) at the posterior edge of the track, which may or may not show. The negative space between the toes and metacarpals has little to no fur. Nails are long and prominent in tracks. Front and rear tracks have similar dimensions.

Rear 1–1$^{13}/_{16}$ in. (2.5–4.6 cm) L x $^5/_8$–1$^1/_2$ in. (1.6–3.8 cm) W

Small. Plantigrade. Slightly asymmetrical. Five toes in classic rodent structure: Toes 1 and 5 point out to either side, and toes 2, 3, and 4 register close together, pointing forward. Some metacarpals are fused

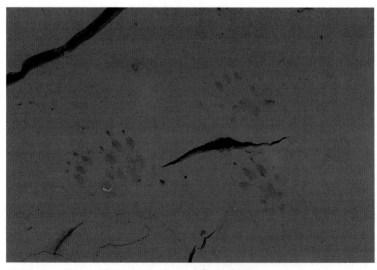

A variation of the California ground squirrel bound. (CA)

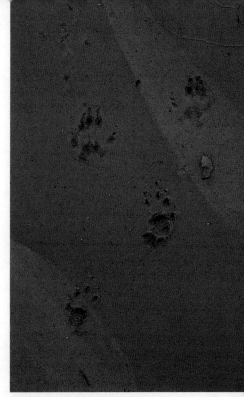

California ground squirrel tracks in a bounding gait. (CA)

California ground squirrel bound.

California ground squirrel walk.

to form larger pads, but four distinct pads show in tracks. Nails prominent, but smaller than those of the front feet. The heel portion of the foot, which is naked and composed of several distinct pads, may or may not register. Tracks of this species are similar in dimension to those of the tree-dwelling gray squirrel.

Trail: Walk Stride: 3³/₄–5³/₄ in. (9.5–14.6 cm)
Trail width: 2¹/₄–3¹/₂ in. (5.7–8.9 cm)

Bound   Stride: 5–25 in. (12.7–63.5 cm)
         Trail width: 2⁷/₈–4¹/₂ in. (7.3–11.4 cm)
         Group length: 2³/₄–8 in. (7–20.3 cm)

Notes:

• Bound when traveling aboveground; walk when foraging and exploring.
• Diurnal; associated with open habitats, especially agricultural lands.
• Trails begin and end with a burrow entrance.
• Hibernate for much of the year.
• Are often found living in close proximity to other squirrels and may even share burrows.

Wyoming Ground Squirrel *(Spermophilus elegans)*

Track: Front ⁷/₈–1⁵/₁₆ in. (2.2–3.3 cm) L x ¹/₂–¹⁵/₁₆ in. (1.3–2.4 cm) W

Small. Plantigrade. Asymmetrical—more so than chipmunks and tree squirrels. Five toes in classic rodent structure: Toe 1 is a vestigial thumb. Toes 2 and 5 point toward the sides, and toes 3 and 4 point forward. Some of the metacarpal pads have fused, but the track is composed of three distinct palm pads; there are two additional pads (the heel) at the posterior edge of the track, which may or may not show. The negative space between the toes and metacarpals has little to no fur. Nails are long and prominent in tracks. Front and rear tracks have similar dimensions.

Rear ¹³/₁₆–1³/₈ in. (2.1–3.5 cm) L x ¹/₂–¹³/₁₆ in. (1.3–2.1 cm) W

Small. Plantigrade. Slightly asymmetrical. Five toes in classic rodent structure: Toes 1 and 5 point out to either side, and toes 2, 3, and 4 register close together, pointing forward. Some metacarpals are fused to form larger pads, but four distinct pads show in tracks. Nails prominent, but smaller than those of the front feet. The heel portion of the foot, which is naked and composed of several distinct pads, may or may not register.

Wyoming ground squirrel bound.

 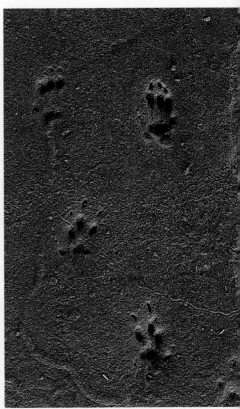

Left: **Wyoming ground squirrel tracks. (WY)** *Right:* **A Wyoming ground squirrel's bounding track pattern. (WY)**

Trail: Bound Stride: 5–16 in. (12.7–40.6 cm)
Trail width: 2¼–3¼ in. (5.7–8.3 cm)
Group length: 1¾–5½ in. (4.4–14 cm)

Notes:

- Bound when traveling aboveground; slow to a walk when foraging, and occasionally use lopes to cross open areas at a medium pace.
- Diurnal. Associated with open habitats—ideal for sightings. May live close to human settlements.
- Trails begin and end with a burrow entrance.
- Hibernate for much of the year.
- Often found living in close proximity to other squirrels; will share burrows with prairie dogs.

Golden-mantled Ground Squirrel *(Spermophilus lateralis)*

Track: Front ⅞–1 in. (2.2–2.5 cm) L x ½–⁹⁄₁₆ in. (1.3–1.4 cm) W

Small. Plantigrade. Asymmetrical—more so than chipmunks and tree squirrels. Five toes in classic rodent structure: Toe 1 is a vestigial thumb. Toes 2 and 5 point toward the sides, and toes 3 and 4 point forward. Some of the metacarpal pads have fused, but the track is composed of three distinct palm pads; there are two additional pads (the heel) at the

Golden-mantled ground squirrel tracks. (UT)

posterior edge of the track, which may or may not show. The negative space between the toes and metacarpals has little to no fur. Nails are long and prominent in tracks. Front and rear tracks have similar dimensions.

Rear 7/8 in. (2.2 cm) L x 5/8–11/16 in. (1.6–1.7 cm) W

Small. Plantigrade. Slightly asymmetrical. Five toes in classic rodent structure: Toes 1 and 5 point out to either side, and toes 2, 3, and 4 register close together, pointing forward. Some metacarpals are fused to form larger pads, but four distinct pads show in tracks. Nails prominent, but smaller than those of the front feet. The heel portion of the foot, which is naked and composed of several distinct pads, may or may not register.

(Data created from two animals.)

Trail: Bound   Trail width: 2¾ in.
                (7 cm)

Notes:

- Bound when traveling aboveground; slow to a walk when foraging, and occasionally use lopes to cross open areas at a medium pace.
- Diurnal. Unlike other ground squirrels, associated with forested habitats. Live close to human settlements; common in parks and campgrounds.
- Often found alongside chipmunks, which resemble them in many ways.
- Trails begin and end with a burrow entrance.
- Hibernate for much of the year.
- Solitary.

Arctic Ground Squirrel *(Spermophilus parryii)*

Track: Front 1¹/₁₆–1¹¹/₁₆ in. (2.7–4.3 cm) L x ½–1⁷/₁₆ in. (1.3–3.7 cm) W

Small. Plantigrade. Asymmetrical—more so than chipmunks and tree squirrels. Five toes in classic rodent structure: Toe 1 is a vestigial thumb. Toes 2 and 5 point toward the sides, and toes 3 and 4 point forward. Some of the metacarpal pads have fused, but the track is composed of three distinct palm pads; there are two additional pads (the heel) at the posterior edge of the track, which may or may not show. The negative space between the toes and metacarpals has little to no fur. Nails are long and prominent in tracks. Front and rear tracks have similar dimensions.

Rear ¹⁵/₁₆–1¹³/₁₆ in. (2.4–4.6 cm) L x ⁵/₈–1¹/₈ in. (1.6–2.9 cm) W

Small. Plantigrade. Slightly asymmetrical. Five toes in classic rodent structure: Toes 1 and 5 point out to either side, and toes 2, 3, and 4 register close together, pointing forward. Some metacarpals are fused to form larger pads, but four distinct pads show in tracks. Nails prominent, but smaller than those of the front feet. The heel portion of the foot, which is naked and composed of several distinct pads, may or may not register.

Front track of an arctic ground squirrel. (AK)

Arctic ground squirrel bound.

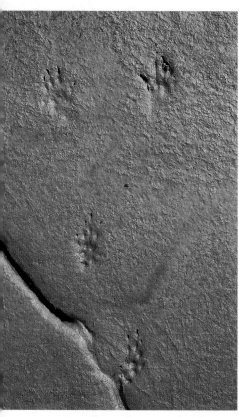

Bounding track pattern of arctic ground squirrel. (AK)

Trail:	Bound	Stride: 8–22 in. (20.3–55.9 cm)
		Trail width: 2³/₄–4¹/₂ in. (7–11.4 cm)
		Group length: 4–11¹/₂ in. (10.2–29.2 cm)

Notes:

• Bound when traveling aboveground; walk when foraging.

• Diurnal; associated with open tundra and alpine meadow habitats.

• Trails begin and end with a burrow entrance.

• Hibernate for seven months of the year.

• Colonial, living in close proximity to other squirrels.

Thirteen-lined Ground Squirrel *(Spermophilus tridecemlineatus)*

Track: Front ¹³/₁₆–1³/₈ in. (2.1–3.5 cm) L x ¹¹/₁₆–1³/₁₆ in. (1.7–3 cm) W

> Small. Plantigrade. Asymmetrical—more so than chipmunks and tree squirrels. Five toes in classic rodent structure: Toe 1 is a vestigial thumb. Toes 2 and 5 point toward the sides, and toes 3 and 4 point forward. Some of the metacarpal pads have fused, but the track is composed of three distinct palm pads; there are two additional pads (the heel) at the posterior edge of the track, which may or may not show. The negative space between the toes and metacarpals has little to no fur. Nails are long and prominent in tracks. Front and rear tracks have similar dimensions.

> Rear ⁷/₈–1⁵/₁₆ in. (2.2–3.3 cm) L x ¹¹/₁₆–1³/₁₆ in. (1.7–3 cm) W

> Small. Plantigrade. Slightly asymmetrical. Five toes in classic rodent structure: Toes 1 and 5 point out to either side, and toes 2, 3, and 4 register close together, pointing forward. Some metacarpals are fused to form larger pads, but four distinct pads show in tracks. Nails prominent, but smaller than those of the front feet. The heel portion of the

foot, which is naked and composed
of several distinct pads, may or may
not register.

(Data taken from two individuals.)

Trail: Bound   Stride: 4–18 in. (10.2–45.7 cm)

                  Trail width: 2¹/₂–4 in. (6.4–10.2 cm)

                  Group length: 2³/₄–5 in. (7–12.7 cm)

Notes:

• Bound when traveling aboveground; slow to a walk
when foraging, and occasionally use lopes to cross
open areas at a medium pace.

• Diurnal; associated with open habitats.

• Trails begin and end with a burrow entrance.

• Hibernate for much of the year.

• Often found living in close proximity to other squirrels
and may even share burrows.

Rock Squirrel *(Spermophilus variegatus)*

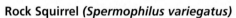

Track: Front 1–1¹³/₁₆ in. (2.5–4.6 cm) L x ⁷/₈–1³/₈ in. (2.2–3.5 cm) W

          Small. Plantigrade. Asymmetrical—more so than
chipmunks and tree squirrels. Five toes in classic rodent
structure: Toe 1 is a vestigial thumb. Toes 2 and 5 point
toward the sides, and toes 3 and 4, which are different
lengths, point forward. Some of the metacarpal pads
have fused, but the track is composed of three distinct
palm pads; there are two additional pads (the heel) at the
posterior edge of the track, which may or may not show.
The negative space between the toes and metacarpals
has little to no fur. Nails are long and prominent in tracks.
Front and rear tracks have similar dimensions.

          Rear 1¹/₈–1⁵/₈ in. (2.9–4.1 cm) L x ⁷/₈–1¹/₂ in. (2.2–3.8 cm) W

          Small. Plantigrade. Slightly asymmetrical. Five toes
in classic rodent structure: Toes 1 and 5 point out to
either side, and toes 2, 3, and 4 register close together,
pointing forward. Some metacarpals are fused to form

**Rock squirrel
bound.**

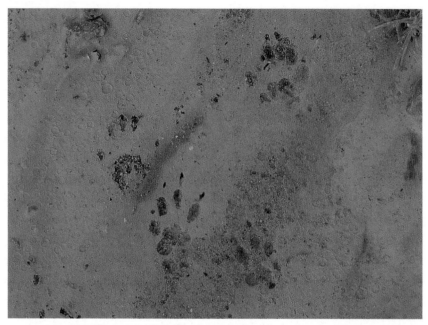

Rock squirrel tracks in a bounding pattern. (UT)

A rock squirrel's modified bound. (UT)

larger pads, but four distinct pads show in tracks. Nails prominent, but smaller than those of the front feet. The heel portion of the foot, which is naked and composed of several distinct pads, may or may not register. Tracks of this species are similar in dimension to those of the tree-dwelling gray squirrel.

Trail: Walk   Stride: 4–5¹/₂ in.
                (10.2–14 cm)

                Trail width: 2⁵/₈–3 in.
                (6.7–7.6 cm)

        Bound   Stride: 5–26 in.
                (12.7–66 cm)

                Trail width: 3–5 in.
                (7.6–12.7 cm)

                Group length: 5–9¹/₄ in.
                (12.7–23.5 cm)

Notes:

- Bound when traveling aboveground; walk when foraging or exploring.
- Diurnal; associated with dry habitats.
- Trails begin and end with a burrow entrance, a rock crevice, or occasionally a tree nest.
- Hibernate for much of the year.
- Colonial, living in close proximity to other squirrels.

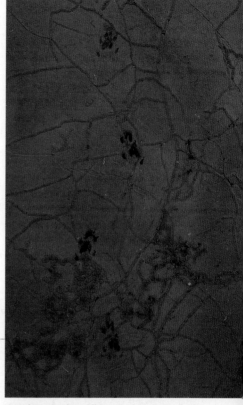

A rock squirrel's walking track pattern. (UT)

Black-tailed Prairie Dog *(Cynomys ludovicianus)*
White-tailed Prairie Dog *(Cynomys leucurus)*

Track: Front 1¹/₄–1 ⁷/₈ in. (3.2–4.8 cm) L
        x 1–1¹/₂ in. (2.5–3.8 cm) W

        Small. Plantigrade. Asymmetrical. Five toes in classic rodent structure: Toe 1 is a vestigial thumb. Toes 2 and 5 point toward the sides, and toes 3 and 4 point forward. Some of the metacarpal pads have fused, but the track is composed of three distinct palm pads; there are two additional pads (the heel) at the posterior edge of the track, which may or may not show. The negative space between the toes and metacarpals has little to no fur. Nails are long and prominent in tracks. Front and rear tracks have similar dimensions.

        Rear 1³/₈–2¹/₄ in. (3.5–5.7 cm) L
        x 1–1⁷/₁₆ in. (2.5–3.7 cm) W

        Small to medium. Plantigrade. Slightly asymmetrical. Five toes in classic rodent

**Black-tailed prairie
dog walk.**

**Black-tailed prairie
dog lope.**

**Black-tailed prairie
dog 2x2 lope.**

structure: Toes 1 and 5 point out to either side, and toes 2, 3, and 4 register close together, pointing forward. Some metacarpals are fused to form larger pads, but four distinct pads show in tracks. Nails prominent, but smaller than those of the front feet. The heel portion of the foot, which is furred, may or may not register. Tracks are significantly larger than those of ground squirrels.

Trail: Walk   Stride: 4–6 in. (10.2–15.2 cm)

                   Trail width: 3–4½ in. (7.6–11.4 cm)

       3x4 lope   Stride: 5–6 in. (12.7–15.2 cm)

                   Trail width: 3½–4¼ in. (8.9–10.8 cm)

                   Group length: 8–10 in. (20.3–25.4 cm)

       Bound   Stride: 9–20 in. (22.9–50.8 cm)

                   Trail width: 3¼–4¼ in. (8.3–10.8 cm)

                   Group length: 10–17½ in. (25.4–44.5 cm)

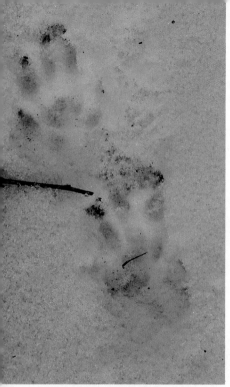

Top left: Front and hind (above) tracks of a black-tailed prairie dog. (CO) *Top right:* A black-tailed prairie dog walking track pattern, showing characteristic drag marks. (CO) *Right:* Loping trails come and go between burrow entrances in a black-tailed prairie dog colony. (CO)

Notes:
- Walk much of the time, but speed up to lopes when feeling exposed and to faster bounds when alarmed or threatened.
- Use range maps and habitat clues to differentiate the tracks and trails of other prairie dogs, some of which may be slightly larger and just outside the parameters provided for this species. When white-tailed and black-tailed prairie dogs overlap in range, the white-tailed variety is found at higher elevations.
- Live in massive colonies, called towns, that may cover vast amounts of open ground. Trails inevitably begin and end with a burrow entrance and are close to those of other prairie dogs. Other mammal species also use prairie dog burrows for shelter.

- Do not hibernate; intermittent activity is seen during snowy months in the northern part of their range. In deep snow, they walk and use a 2x2 lope for faster travel.

Abert's or Tassel-eared Squirrel (*Sciurus aberti*)

Track: Front 1 1/4–1 15/16 in. (3.2–4.9 cm) L x 1 1/8–1 1/4 in. (2.9–3.2 cm) W

Small. Plantigrade. Asymmetrical. Five toes in classic rodent structure: Toe 1 is a vestigial thumb and rarely registers in tracks. Toes 2 and 5 point toward the sides, and toes 3 and 4 point forward. Some of the metacarpal pads have fused, but the track is composed of three distinct palm pads; there are two additional pads (the heel) at the posterior edge of the track, which may or may not show. The negative space between the toes and metacarpals has little to no fur. Nails may or may not register in tracks. Front and rear tracks have similar dimensions.

Rear 1 1/4–2 7/8 in. (3.2–7.3 cm) L x 1 1/8–1 1/2 in. (2.9–3.8 cm) W

Small to medium. Plantigrade. Slightly asymmetrical. Five toes in classic rodent structure: Toes 1 and 5 point out to either side, and toes 2, 3, and 4 register close together, pointing forward. Some metacarpals are fused to form larger pads, but four distinct pads show in tracks. Nails may or

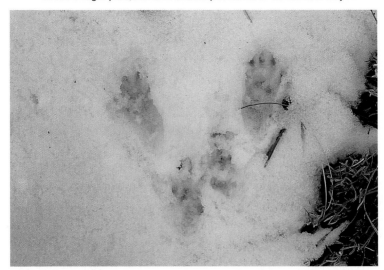

Abert's squirrel tracks. (AZ)

may not register. The heel portion of the foot may or may not register. Tracks overlap with parameters of other *Sciurus* species.

Trail: Bound   Stride: 6–30 in. (15.2–76.2 cm); occasionally longer

Trail width: 4–7 in. (10.2–17.8 cm)

Group length: 4–8½ in. (10.2–21.6 cm)

Notes:

• Large and arboreal. Bound when traveling on the ground; walk when foraging or investigating.

• Most often found in ponderosa pine woodlands, but also in areas mixed with pinyon pines.

• In deep fluffy snow, the group length for bounds is reduced, and rear feet register next to or very close to the front tracks; the impression is that each group is composed of only two tracks rather than four.

• Solitary, although others live close by.

Eastern Gray Squirrel *(Sciurus carolinensis)*
Western Gray Squirrel *(Sciurus griseus)*

Track: Front 1¼–1¾ in. (3.2–4.4 cm) L x ⅝–1⅛ in. (1.6–2.9 cm) W

Small. Plantigrade. Asymmetrical. Five toes in classic rodent structure: Toe 1 is a vestigial thumb and rarely registers in tracks. Toes 2 and 5 point toward the sides, and toes 3 and 4 point forward. Some of the metacarpal pads have fused, but the track is composed of three distinct palm pads; there are two additional pads (the heel) at the posterior edge of the track, which may or may not show. The negative space between the toes and metacarpals has little to no fur. Nails may or may not register in tracks. Front and rear tracks have similar dimensions.

Rear 1¼–3¼ in. (3.2–8.3 cm) L x 1–1½ in. (2.5–3.8 cm) W

Small to medium. Plantigrade. Slightly asymmetrical. Five toes in classic rodent structure: Toes 1 and 5 point out to either side, and toes 2, 3, and 4 register close together, pointing forward. Some metacarpals are fused to form larger pads, but four distinct pads show in tracks. Two additional pads are found in the heel portion of the track,

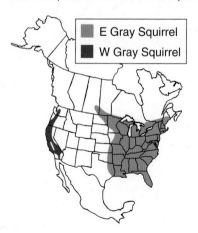

Eastern gray squirrel bound.

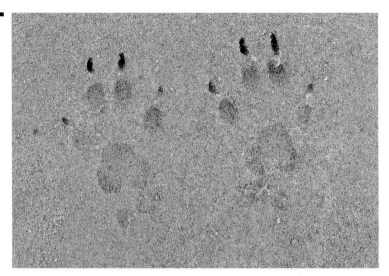

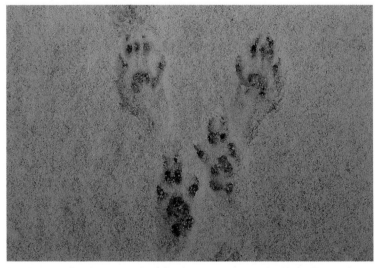

Top: Front tracks of a gray squirrel. (MA) *Bottom:* Gray squirrel bounding track pattern. (VT)

which is naked during summer months. The heel may or may not register. Nails may or may not register. Tracks overlap with parameters of other *Sciurus* species.

Trail: Bound Stride: 6–30 in. (15.2–76.2 cm); occasionally longer

Trail width: 3³/₄–6 in. (9.5–15.2 cm)

Group length: 2–9 in. (5.1–22.9 cm)

Notes:

• Large and arboreal. Bound when traveling on the ground; walk when foraging or investigating. I've also seen grays stalk, or slow walk, away from me on the ground if they think they haven't been spotted.

Gray squirrel tracks in mud. (NY)

- Inhabit mixed and deciduous forests throughout the East; common in urban and suburban settings. Widely introduced in urban areas of California, Oregon, and Washington.
- In deep fluffy snow, the group length for bounds is reduced, and rear feet register next to or very close to the front tracks; the impression is that each group is composed of only two tracks rather than four.
- Unlike the fiercely territorial red squirrels, grays are much more tolerant of other gray squirrels. In winter, several may even share cavity space to maintain warmth.

Eastern Fox Squirrel *(Sciurus niger)*

Track: Front 1¼–2 in. (3.2–5.1 cm) L x 1–1⅜ in. (2.5–3.5 cm) W

Small. Plantigrade. Asymmetrical. Five toes in classic rodent structure: Toe 1 is a vestigial thumb and rarely registers in tracks. Toes 2 and 5 point toward the sides, and toes 3 and 4 point forward. Some of the metacarpal pads have fused, but the track is composed of three distinct palm pads; there are two additional pads (the heel) at the posterior edge of the track, which may or may not show. The negative space between the toes and metacarpals has little to no fur. Nails may or may not register in tracks. Front and rear tracks have similar dimensions.

Rear 1¼–3½ in. (3.2–8.9 cm) L x ⅞–1¾ in. (2.2–4.4 cm) W

Small to medium. Plantigrade. Slightly asymmetrical. Five toes in classic rodent structure: Toes 1 and 5 point out to either side, and toes 2, 3, and 4 register

Left: Front and hind (below) tracks of a fox squirrel. (ND) *Right:* Fox squirrel bounding track patterns. (CO)

close together, pointing forward. Some metacarpals are fused to form larger pads, but four distinct pads show in tracks. Additional pads are found in the heel portion of the track, which is naked during warmer months. The heel may or may not register. Nails may or may not register. Track parameters in the field are often the same as for gray squirrels. Large fox squirrels that create tracks larger than gray squirrel parameters are not common but occur more often in the Southeast than in the Midwest. Tracks overlap with parameters of other *Sciurus* species.

Trail: Walk   Stride: 4–6 in. (10.2–15.2 cm)
                 Trail width: 3³/₄–4¹/₄ in. (9.5–10.8 cm)
         Bound   Stride: 6–30 in. (15.2–76.2 cm); occasionally longer
                 Trail width: 4–7 in. (10.2–17.8 cm)
                 Group length: 3³/₄–9 in. (9.5–22.9 cm)

Notes:
• Large and arboreal. Bound when traveling on the ground; walk when foraging or investigating. Diurnal.

- Although researchers believe that fox squirrel populations are declining in the Southeast, they are expanding in the Midwest. Common in urban settings throughout the Midwest.
- Wander far from trees into open areas—much farther than gray squirrels under normal circumstances. Prefer more open habitat than grays overall.
- In deep fluffy snow, the group length for bounds is reduced, and rear feet register next to or very close to the front tracks; the impression is that each group is composed of only two tracks rather than four.
- Often found with others; territories overlap, as with gray squirrels.

Eastern fox squirrel walk.

Eastern fox squirrel bound.

Douglas Squirrel *(Tamiasciurus douglasii)*
Red Squirrel *(Tamiasciurus hudsonicus)*

Track: Front 1–1¼ in. (2.5–3.2 cm) L x ⁹⁄₁₆–1 in. (1.4–2.5 cm) W

Small. Plantigrade. Asymmetrical. Five toes in classic rodent structure: Toe 1 is a vestigial thumb and rarely registers in tracks. Toes 2 and 5 point toward the sides, and toes 3 and 4 point forward. Some of the metacarpal pads have fused, but the track is composed of three distinct palm pads; there are two additional pads (the heel) at the posterior edge of the track, which may or may not show. The negative space between the toes and metacarpals has little to no fur. Nails may or may not register in tracks. Front and rear tracks have similar dimensions.

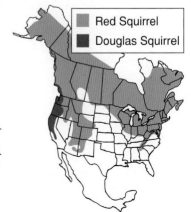

Red Squirrel

Douglas Squirrel

Rear ⁷⁄₈–2¼ in. (2.2–5.7 cm) L x ⁵⁄₈–1⅛ in. (1.6–2.9 cm) W

Small. Plantigrade. Slightly asymmetrical. Five toes in classic rodent structure: Toes 1 and 5 point out to either side, and toes 2, 3, and 4 register close together, pointing forward. Some metacarpals are fused to form larger pads, but four

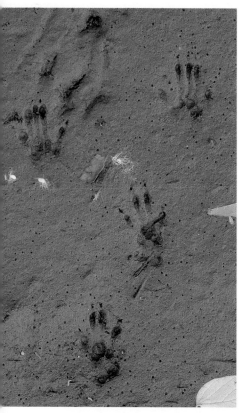

Red squirrel tracks. (MA)

Red squirrel bound.

Compare the larger red squirrel tracks with those of a smaller eastern chipmunk. (MA)

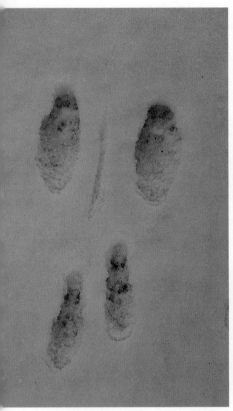

Left: Red squirrel tracks in snow. (MN) *Right:* A red squirrel's bounding trail in deep snow. (NM)

distinct pads show in tracks. Nails may or may not register. The heel, which is furred, may or may not register.

Trail: Bound   Stride: 4–25 in. (10.2–63.5 cm); occasionally longer
Trail width: $2^{7}/_{8}$–$4^{3}/_{8}$ in. (7.3–11.1 cm)
Group length: 2–11 in. (5.1–27.9 cm)

Walk   Stride: $3^{1}/_{2}$–$5^{1}/_{4}$ in. (8.9–13.3 cm)
Trail width: $2^{3}/_{8}$–$2^{3}/_{4}$ in. (6–7 cm)

Notes:
• Medium-sized and arboreal. Diurnal. Bound when traveling on the ground.
• Red and Douglas squirrels are presented together because track and trail parameters are essentially identical, and they share many behaviors and characteristics.
• Associated with coniferous forests, but also found in mixed woodlands.
• In deep fluffy snow, the group length for bounds is reduced, and rear feet register next to or very close to the front tracks; the impression is that each group is composed of only two tracks, rather than four. Form tunnels in deep snow.
• Fiercely territorial, yet ranges are small; therefore, other squirrels are close by.

Northern Flying Squirrel *(Glaucomys sabrinus)*

Track: Front $^{11}/_{16}$–$1^{1}/_{4}$ in. (1.7–3.2 cm) L x $^{1}/_{2}$–$^{3}/_{4}$ in. (1.3–1.9 cm) W

Small. Plantigrade. Asymmetrical. Five toes in classic rodent structure: Toe 1 is a vestigial thumb and rarely registers in tracks. Toes 2 and 5 point toward the sides, and toes 3 and 4 point forward. Some of the metacarpal pads have fused, but the track is composed of three distinct palm pads; there are two additional pads (the heel) at the posterior edge of the track, which may or may not show. The negative space between the toes and metacarpals has more fur than in red squirrels. Nails may or may not register in tracks. Front track smaller than rear track, and parameters overlap with those of red squirrels.

Rear $1^{1}/_{4}$–$1^{7}/_{8}$ in. (3.2–4.8 cm) L x $^{5}/_{8}$–$^{15}/_{16}$ in. (1.6–2.4 cm) W

Small. Plantigrade. Slightly asymmetrical. Five toes in classic rodent structure: Toes 1 and 5 point out to either side, and toes 2, 3, and 4 register close together, pointing forward. Metacarpals are fused to form a larger, curved pad, but lobes may be apparent. There is significantly more hair filling the negative space than in red squirrel tracks, contributing to a blurry appearance. Nails may or may not register. The heel, which is furred, may or may not register. Track and trail parameters are similar to those of red squirrels.

This landing sitzmark of a northern flying squirrel measured over 2 feet (61 cm) long. (MT)

Northern flying squirrel bound.

Northern flying squirrel variation of the bound.

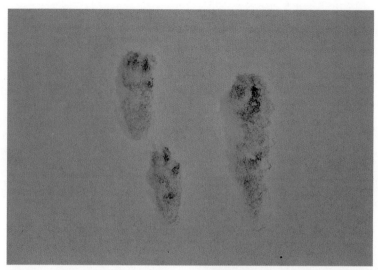

Northern flying squirrel tracks. (MN)

Trail: Bound   Stride: 6–34 in.
(15.2–86.4 cm);
occasionally longer

Trail width: 2³/₄–4¹/₄ in.
(7–10.8 cm)

Group length: 2–7 in.
(5.1–17.8 cm)

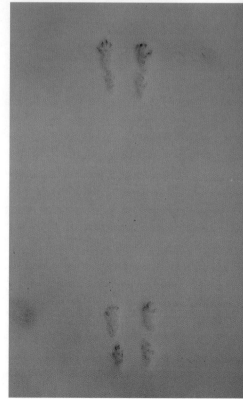

**Boxy trail of a bounding flying squirrel.
(MN)**

Notes:

• Generally bound when traveling on the ground, but the front feet are often wide apart, giving groups of tracks a boxy appearance. Occasionally hop, but far less often than southern flying squirrels.

• Nocturnal. In areas where northern and southern flying squirrels overlap, the southern tends to be more common and to inhabit the lowlands and valleys; the northerns stay at higher elevations.

• Trails may originate far from trees, where an animal glided and landed. This landing spot is referred to as a *sitzmark*. With practice, you'll be able to differentiate flying squirrel trails from those of other squirrels and chipmunks. This is important because flying squirrels usually climb down trees, rather than gliding down. Do not rely on an obvious sitzmark to identify the trails of flying squirrels.

Southern Flying Squirrel *(Glaucomys volans)*

Track: Front $^5/_{16}$–$^3/_4$ in. (.8–1.9 cm) L x $^5/_{16}$–$^3/_4$ in. (.8–1.9 cm) W

Small. Plantigrade. Asymmetrical. Five toes in classic rodent structure: Toe 1 is a vestigial thumb and rarely registers in tracks. Toes 2 and 5 point toward the sides, and toes 3 and 4 point forward. Some of the metacarpal pads have fused but the track is composed of three distinct palm pads; there are two additional pads (the heel) at the posterior edge of the track, which may or may not show. The negative space between the toes and metacarpals has more fur than found in chipmunk species. Nails may or may not register in tracks. Front and rear tracks have similar dimensions, and parameters overlap with those of eastern chipmunks.

Rear $^1/_2$–$1^3/_8$ in. (1.3–3.5 cm) L x $^3/_8$–$^7/_8$ in. (1–2.2 cm) W

Small. Plantigrade. Slightly asymmetrical. Five toes in classic rodent structure: Toes 1 and 5 point out to either side, and toes 2, 3, and 4 register close together, pointing forward. Metacarpals are fused to form a larger, curved pad, but lobes may be apparent. There is significantly more hair filling the negative space than in chipmunk tracks, which contributes to a blurrier appearance. Nails may or may not register. The heel, which is furred, may or may not register.

Trail: Hop/bound Stride: 6–21 in. (15.2–53.3 cm)

Trail width: $1^5/_8$–3 in. (4.1–7.6 cm); occasionally up to $3^1/_4$ in. (8.3 cm)

Group length: $1^1/_2$–4 in. (3.8–10.2 cm)

Notes:

• May bound, but more often hop; front tracks register in front of hind tracks in a given set of four.

• Small and nocturnal. May carry a specific roundworm that has no negative effects on it but may be fatal if transmitted to northern flying squirrels. Researchers believe that this is one of the reasons northern flying squirrels are becoming rare in areas where their ranges overlap. Northerns tend to stay at high elevations, surrounded by larger populations of southerns inhabiting the lower elevations.

• Use varied forested habitat; may be found in suburbs and parks as well. Seem particularly associated with spruce stands.

Southern flying squirrel hop.

Left: A southern flying squirrel's landing and trail. The tracks just above the landing are those of a weasel moving in the opposite direction. (MA) *Right:* Characteristic hopping trail of a southern flying squirrel, moving away from the camera. (MA)

- Studies of this species in New Hampshire showed that populations in a given woodland tended to congregate around the largest mast-producing trees.
- Trails may originate far from trees, where an animal glided and landed. This landing spot is referred to as a *sitzmark*. With practice, you'll be able to differentiate flying squirrel trails from those of other squirrels and chipmunks. This is important, because flying squirrels usually climb down trees rather than gliding down. Do not rely on an obvious sitzmark to identify the trails of flying squirrels.
- During winter months, may be found sharing the same cavity with others—which may be in a tree or an attic.

Pocket Gophers: Family Geomyidae

• Pocket gophers may be found moving aboveground at any time of year, but spring is the season in which I've found nearly all my tracks and trails. In my experience, their tracks and trails are far more common than previous literature suggests.

• Few pocket gopher species overlap in range, but when they do, they often have distinct habitat preferences.

Northern Pocket Gopher *(Thomomys talpoides)*

Track: Front ⁷/₈–1⁵/₁₆ in. (2.2–3.3 cm) L x ⁷/₁₆–¹/₂ in. (1.1–1.3 cm) W

Small. Plantigrade. Asymmetrical. Five toes: Toe 1 is reduced but clawed, and it registers. Like toe 5, 1 is located farther back in the track. Toes 2, 3, and 4 point forward. Some of the metacarpal pads are fused, but the track is composed of three distinct palm pads; there are two additional pads (the heel)

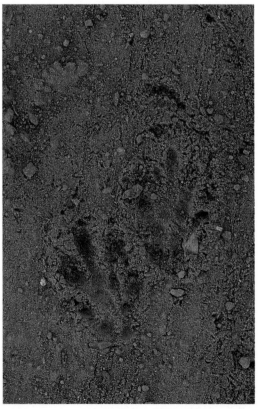

Perfect northern pocket gopher front
and hind (behind) tracks in dust. (CO)

Northern pocket
gopher walk.

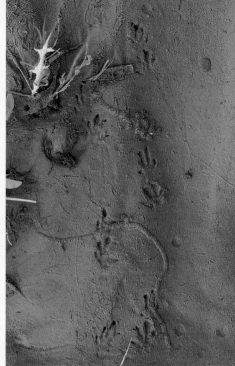

Left: Front and hind (beyond) Northern pocket gopher tracks in mud. (WY) *Right:* A Northern pocket gopher walking trail. (WY)

at the posterior edge of the track, which may or may not show. Nails are long and a significant feature of tracks.

Rear 5/8–7/8 in. (1.6–2.2 cm) L x 7/16–11/16 in. (1.1–1.7 cm) W

Small. Plantigrade. Slightly asymmetrical. Five toes in classic rodent structure: Toes 1 and 5 are small, farther back in the track, and point out to either side. Toes 2, 3, and 4 register close together, pointing forward. Some metacarpals are fused, but distinct pads are often apparent. Nails register well in tracks. The heel may or may not register.

Trail: Walk   Stride: 1 3/8–3 in. (3.5–7.6 cm)
               Trail width: 1 1/8–2 in.
               (2.9–5.1 cm)
       Trot   Stride: 3 1/2–4 1/8 in. (8.9–10.5 cm)
               Trail width: 1 3/8–1 1/2 in.
               (3.5–3.8 cm)

Notes:

- Walk aboveground and trot when feeling exposed. I once found a pocket gopher in a bound.
- Widespread species found in various open habitats, elevations, and vegetative covers.
- Burrows, dirt mounds, and "eskers" should be apparent where pocket gophers are active.
- In deep snow, they move along the surface within the snow layer—especially evident when dirt cores cover the landscape after the snow recedes.
- Solitary animals.

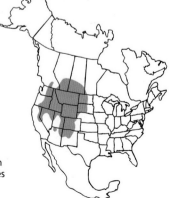

Plains Pocket Gopher *(Geomys bursarius)*

Track: Front 1½–1⅝ in. (3.8–4.1 cm) L
x 1 in. (2.5 cm) W

Small. Plantigrade. Asymmetrical. Five toes: Toe 1 is reduced but clawed, and it registers. Like toe 5, toe 1 is located farther back in the track. Toes 2, 3, and 4 point forward. Some of the metacarpal pads are fused, but the track is composed of three distinct palm pads; there are two additional pads (the heel) at the posterior edge of the track, which may or may not show. Nails are long and a significant feature of tracks.

Rear 1⅛–1¼ in. (2.9–3.2 cm) L x 1⅛–1¼ in. (2.9–3.2 cm) W

Small. Plantigrade. Slightly asymmetrical. Five toes in classic rodent structure: Toes 1 and 5 point out to either side, and toes 2, 3, and 4 register close together, pointing forward. Some metacarpals are fused, but distinct pads are often apparent. Nails register well in tracks. The heel may or may not register.

Trail: Walk   Stride: 4¾–5¼ in. (12.1–13.3 cm)
Trail width: 2⅞–3¼ in. (7.3–8.3 cm)

Notes:
- Walk aboveground and trot when feeling exposed. I once found a pocket gopher in a bound.
- Associated with sandy soils.
- Burrows, dirt mounds, and "eskers" should be apparent where pocket gophers are active.
- In deep snow, they move along the surface within the snow layer—especially evident when dirt cores cover the landscape after the snow recedes.
- Solitary animals.

Yellow-faced Pocket Gopher *(Pappogeomys castanops)*

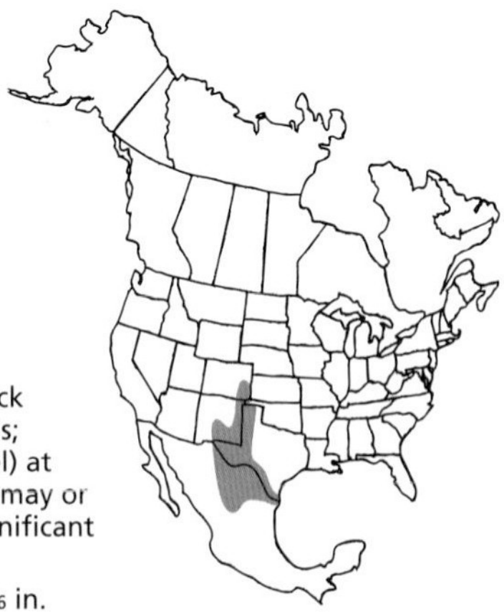

Track: Front 1⅛–1¼ in. (2.9–3.2 cm) L
x ⅜–11/16 in. (1–1.7 cm) W

Small. Plantigrade. Asymmetrical. Five toes: Toe 1 is reduced but clawed, and it registers. Like toe 5, 1 is located farther back in the track. Toes 2, 3, and 4 point forward. Some of the metacarpal pads are fused, but the track is composed of three distinct palm pads; there are two additional pads (the heel) at the posterior edge of the track, which may or may not show. Nails are long and a significant feature of tracks.

Rear ⅞–1¼ in. (2.2–3.2 cm) L x 9/16–11/16 in. (1.4–1.7 cm) W

Small. Plantigrade. Slightly asymmetrical. Five toes in classic rodent structure: Toes 1 and 5 point out to either side, and toes 2, 3, and 4

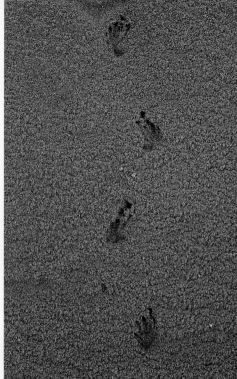

Left: Yellow-faced pocket gopher tracks. The front track is below. (TX) *Right:* Trotting trail of a yellow-faced pocket gopher. (TX)

register close together, pointing forward. Some metacarpals are fused, but distinct pads are often apparent. Nails register well in tracks. The heel may or may not register.

Trail: Walk/trot   Stride: 2–4¹/₂ in. (5.1–11.4 cm)
Trail width: 1⁵/₈–2¹/₈ in. (4.1–5.4 cm)

Notes:

- Walk aboveground and trot when feeling exposed. I once found a pocket gopher in a bound.
- Associated with sandy soils and able to tolerate very arid conditions.
- Burrows and dirt mounds should be apparent where pocket gophers are active.
- Solitary animals.

Pocket Mice: Family Heteromyidae

- Members of this family are good swimmers but avoid water when possible.
- Pocket mice and kangaroo rats are well adapted for extremely dry habitats and are able to survive without access to standing water.
- Members of this family are nocturnal and are often seen in headlights on late-night drives.
- Kangaroo rat species use bipedal gaits for much of their travel aboveground.

Little Pocket Mouse *(Perognathus longimembris)*

Track: Front ³/₈ in. (1 cm) L x ¼ in. (.6 cm) W

Very small. Plantigrade. Asymmetrical. Five toes in classic rodent structure: Toe 1 is a vestigial thumb and rarely registers in tracks. Toes 2 and 5 point toward the sides, and toes 3 and 4 point forward. The metacarpal region is furred, but pads are often evident. Nails are long and a significant feature of tracks. Front tracks smaller than rear tracks.

Rear ⁵/₁₆–¹/₂ in. (.8–1.3 cm) L x ¼ in. (.6 cm) W

Very small. Plantigrade. Asymmetrical. Five toes: Toe 1 is greatly reduced and easily overlooked in the track; toes 2, 3, 4, and 5 are of similar proportions. The metacarpal region is furred and often indistinct. Nails are often apparent. The heel may or may not register. Tracks may be confused with those of other pocket mice species.

Trail: Bound Stride: 3–6 in. (7.6–15.2 cm)

Trail width: ³/₄–1¹/₈ in. (1.9–2.9 cm)

Group length: 1–1⁵/₈ in. (2.5–4.1 cm)

Little pocket mouse bound.

Complete tracks of a Great Basin pocket mouse, the largest of the pocket mice. (ID)

Notes:
- Bound for travel purposes when foraging and exploring. Tail drags when moving slowly.
- Remain dormant in burrows for as much as nine months of the year, surviving on seed caches between long naps at reduced body temperatures.

Desert Pocket Mouse (*Chaetodipus penicillatus*)

Track: Front ¹/₄–³/₈ in. (.6–1 cm) L x ⁵/₁₆–³/₈ in. (.8–1 cm) W

Very small. Plantigrade. Asymmetrical. Five toes in classic rodent structure: Toe 1 is a vestigial thumb and rarely registers in tracks. Toes 2 and 5 point toward the sides, and toes 3 and 4 point forward. The metacarpal region is furred, but pads are often evident. Nails are long and a significant feature of tracks. Front tracks smaller than rear tracks.

Rear ⁵/₁₆–⁷/₁₆ in. (.8–1.1 cm) L x ⁵/₁₆–³/₈ in. (.8–1 cm) W

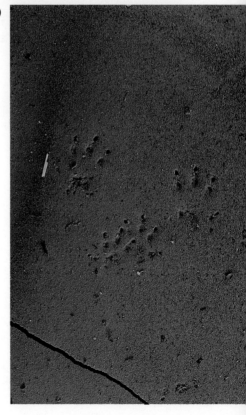

Little pocket mouse tracks in a bounding gait. (CA)

Very small. Plantigrade. Asymmetrical. Five toes: Toe 1 is greatly reduced and easily overlooked in the track; toes 2, 3, 4, and 5 are of similar proportions. The metacarpal region is furred and often indistinct. Nails are often apparent. The heel may or may not register. Tracks may be confused with those of other pocket mice species.

Trail: Bound Stride: 2¹/₄–6 in. (5.7–15.2 cm)

Trail width: ³/₄–1¹/₄ in. (1.9–3.2 cm)

Group length: 1¹/₄–3¹/₄ in. (3.2–8.3 cm)

Bounding trail of a desert pocket mouse. (CA)

Notes:

• Bound for travel purposes when foraging and exploring. Tail drags when moving slowly.

• Remain dormant in burrows for much of the year, surviving on seed caches between long naps at reduced body temperatures.

Agile Kangaroo Rat *(Dipodomys agilis)*

Track: Front ³/₈–⁹/₁₆ in. (1–1.4 cm) L x ³/₁₆–¹/₄ in. (.5–.6 cm) W

Very small. Plantigrade. Asymmetrical. Five toes: Toe 1 is a vestigial thumb. Toes 2 and 5 point toward the sides, and toes 3 and 4 point forward. Central metacarpal pads are fused; there are two additional pads (the heel) at the posterior edge of the track, which may or may not show. Nails are long and an important feature of tracks. Front tracks significantly smaller than rear tracks.

Rear ¹¹/₁₆–⁷/₈ in. (1.7–2.2 cm) L x ³/₈–¹/₂ in. (1–1.3 cm) W

Very small to small. Plantigrade. Asymmetrical. Five toes: Toe 1 is a vestigial thumb, and the remaining long toes register close together. The metacarpal region is furred and often indistinct. Nails are often apparent but are smaller than those of the front feet. The heel may or may not register.

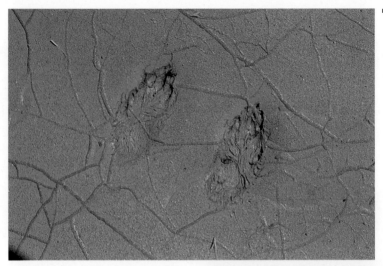

Perfect hind tracks of an agile kangaroo rat. (CA)

Trail: Bipedal hop Stride: 4–20 in.
(10.2–50.8 cm)
Trail width: 3/4–13/4
in. (1.9–4.4 cm)

Notes:

• Bipedal hop when traveling and exploring. When threatened or alarmed, strides of the bipedal hop increase significantly, and animals may switch to a skip. When foraging and investigating small areas, they use a slow bipedal hop or bound on all four feet. There is apparent tail drag when bounding.

• Burrows are conspicuous in areas they inhabit.

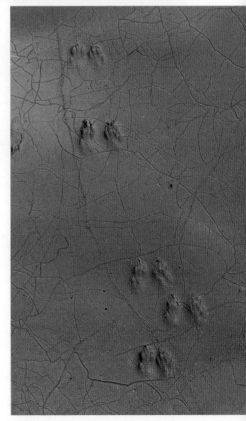

Bipedal hopping trails of agile kangaroo rats. (CA)

Gulf Coast Kangaroo Rat *(Dipodomys compactus)*

Track: Front $^3/_8$–$^1/_2$ in. (1–1.3 cm) L x $^5/_{16}$–$^3/_8$ in. (.8–1 cm) W

Very small. Plantigrade. Asymmetrical. Five toes: Toe 1 is but a vestigial thumb. Toes 2 and 5 point toward the sides, and toes 3 and 4 point forward. Central metacarpal pads are fused; there are two additional pads (the heel) at the posterior edge of the track, which may or may not show. Nails are long and an important feature of tracks. Front tracks significantly smaller than rear tracks.

Rear $^3/_8$–1$^1/_4$ in. (1–3.2 cm) L x $^3/_8$–$^3/_4$ in. (1–1.9 cm) W

Very small to small. Plantigrade. Asymmetrical. Five toes: Toe 1 is a vestigial thumb, and the remaining long toes register close together. The metacarpal region is furred and often indistinct. Nails are often apparent but are smaller than those of the front feet. The heel may or may not register.

Trail: Bipedal hop Stride: 2–20 in. (5.1–50.8 cm); up to 6 ft. (1.8 m) at full speed

Trail width: 1–2 in. (2.5–5.1 cm)

Notes:

• Bipedal hop when traveling and exploring. When threatened or alarmed, strides of the bipedal hop increase significantly, and animals may switch to a skip.

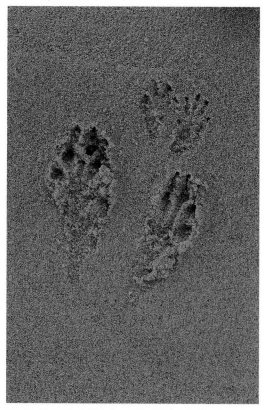

Hind and much smaller front tracks of a Gulf Coast kangaroo rat. (TX)

Gulf Coast kangaroo rat bipedal hop.

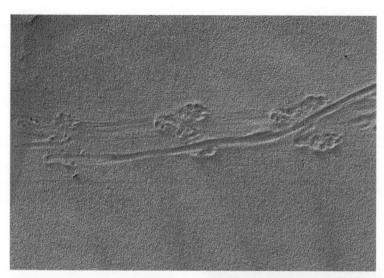

Gulf Coast kangaroo rat slow bounding trail with continuous tail drag. (TX)

When foraging and investigating small areas, they use a slow bipedal hop or bound on all four feet. There is apparent tail drag when bounding.

- Considered a subspecies of Ord's kangaroo rat in the past; they are now separated by range and habitat.
- Burrows are conspicuous in areas they inhabit.

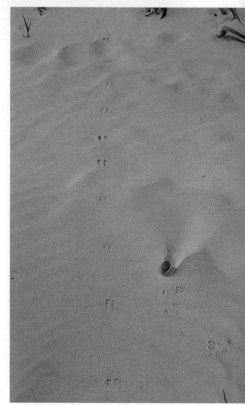

Typical Gulf Coast kangaroo rat bipedal hopping trail. (TX)

Hopping trails of desert kangaroo rats. (CA)

Desert Kangaroo Rat
(Dipodomys deserti)

Track: Front ⁵/₈–³/₄ in. (1.6–1.9 cm) L x ³/₈–¹/₂ in. (1–1.3 cm) W

Very small. Plantigrade. Asymmetrical. Five toes: Toe 1 is a vestigial thumb. Toes 2 and 5 point toward the sides, and toes 3 and 4 point forward. Central metacarpal pads are fused; there are two additional pads (the heel) at the posterior edge of the track, which may or may not show. Nails are long and an important feature of tracks. Front tracks are significantly smaller than rear tracks.

Rear 1³/₈–2³/₁₆ in. (3.5–5.6 cm) L x ¹¹/₁₆–1 in. (1.7–2.5 cm) W

Small. Plantigrade. Asymmetrical. Four toes: Toe 1 is absent, and the remaining long toes register close together. The metacarpal region is furred and often indistinct. Nails are often apparent but are smaller

Bounding trails of slowly moving desert kangaroo rats. (CA)

than those of the front feet. The heel portion of the foot, which is furred, may or may not register.

Trail: Slow bipedal hop   Stride: 2–10 in. (5.1–25.4 cm)

Trail width: 2½–3 in. (6.4–7.6 cm)

Bipedal hop/skip   Stride: 6–54 in. (15.2–137.2 cm); occasionally longer

Trail width: 1³⁄₈–2⁵⁄₈ in. (3.5–6.7 cm)

Notes:

- Bipedal hop when traveling and exploring. When threatened or alarmed, strides of the bipedal hop increase significantly, and this species favors the skip when moving at top speeds. When foraging and investigating small areas, they use a slow bipedal hop or bound on all four feet. There is apparent tail drag when bounding.

Desert kangaroo rat bipedal hop.

Desert kangaroo rat skip.

- Signs of this very large kangaroo rat species are common in sand dunes in the extreme desert conditions of the Southwest.
- Burrows are conspicuous in areas they inhabit.

Giant Kangaroo Rat (Dipodomys ingens)

Track: Front: Very small. Plantigrade. Asymmetrical. Five toes: Toe 1 is a vestigial thumb. Toes 2 and 5 point toward the sides, and toes 3 and 4 point forward. Central metacarpal pads are fused; there are two additional pads (the heel) at the posterior edge of the track, which may or may not show. Nails are long and an important feature of tracks. Front tracks significantly smaller than rear tracks.

Rear 1–1⅛ in. (2.5–2.9 cm) L x 1 in. (2.5 cm) W

Small. Plantigrade. Asymmetrical. Five toes: Toe 1 is a vestigial thumb, and the remaining long toes register close together. The metacarpal region is furred and often indistinct. Nails are often apparent but are smaller than those of the front feet. The heel may or may not register.

(Data collected from a small data pool.)

Trail: Bipedal hop   Trail width: 2¼–2¾ in. (5.7–7 cm)

Notes:

• Bipedal hop when traveling and exploring. When threatened or alarmed, strides of the bipedal hop increase significantly, and this species favors the skip when moving at top speeds. When foraging and investigating small areas, they use a slow bipedal hop or bound on all four feet. There is apparent tail drag when bounding.

• The endangered giant kangaroo rat inhabits only a very small area in southern California.

• Burrows are conspicuous in areas they inhabit.

Merriam's Kangaroo Rat (*Dipodomys merriami*)

Track: Front ⁷⁄₁₆ in. (1.1 cm) L x ¼ in. (.6 cm) W

Very small. Plantigrade. Asymmetrical. Five toes: Toe 1 is a vestigial thumb. Toes 2 and 5 point toward the sides, and toes 3 and 4 point forward. Central metacarpal pads are fused; there are two additional pads (the heel) at the posterior edge of the track, which may or may not show. Nails are long and an important feature of tracks. Front tracks significantly smaller than rear tracks.

Rear ³⁄₈–⁷⁄₈ in. (1–2.2 cm) L x ³⁄₈–½ in. (1–1.3 cm) W

Very small. Plantigrade. Asymmetrical. Four toes: Toe 1 is absent, and the remaining long toes register close together. The metacarpal region is furred and often indistinct. Nails are often apparent but are smaller than those of the front feet. The heel portion of the foot, which is furred, may or may not register.

The bipedal hopping trail of a Merriam's kangaroo rat parallels some white-footed mouse species traffic. (TX)

Trail: Bipedal hop   Stride: 2–15 in.
                        (5.1–38.1 cm)

                        Trail width:
                        $^9/_{16}$–1$^1/_2$ in.
                        (1.4–3.8 cm)

Notes:

- Bipedal hop when traveling and exploring. When threatened or alarmed, strides of the bipedal hop increase significantly, and this species favors the skip when moving at top speeds. When foraging and investigating small areas, they use a slow bipedal hop or bound on all four feet. There is apparent tail drag when bounding.
- A small kangaroo rat species.
- Burrows are conspicuous in areas they inhabit.

Ord's Kangaroo Rat
(Dipodomys ordii)

Track: Front $^3/_8$–$^9/_{16}$ in. (1–1.4 cm) L
         x $^5/_{16}$–$^3/_8$ in. (.8–1 cm) W

         Very small. Plantigrade. Asymmetrical. Five toes: Toe 1 is a vestigial thumb. Toes 2 and 5 point toward the sides, and toes 3 and 4 point forward. Central metacarpal pads are fused; there are two additional pads (the heel) at the posterior edge of the track, which may or may not show. Nails are long and an important feature of tracks. Front tracks significantly smaller than rear tracks.

Merriam's kangaroo rat bipedal hop.

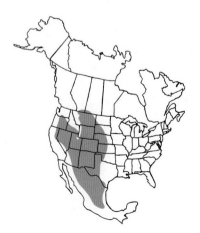

Ord's kangaroo rat bipedal hop.

Tight Ord's kangaroo rat hind tracks in mud. (CO)

Splayed Ord's kangaroo rat tracks in deep dust. (ID)

Rear ³/₈–1¹/₂ in. (1–3.8 cm) L
x ³/₈–¹⁵/₁₆ in. (1–2.4 cm) W

Very small to small. Plantigrade.
Asymmetrical. Five toes: Toe 1
is a vestigial thumb, and the
remaining long toes register
close together. The metacarpal
region is furred and often
indistinct. Nails are often
apparent but are smaller than
those of the front feet. The
heel may or may not register.

Trail: Bipedal hop Stride: 2–38 in.
(5.1–96.5 cm); up
to 8 ft. (2.4 m)
at top speed

Trail width: 1–2 in.
(2.5–5.1 cm)

Notes:

• Bipedal hop when traveling and
exploring. When threatened or alarmed,
strides of the bipedal hop increase
significantly, and animals may switch to
a skip. When foraging and investigating
small areas, they use a slow bipedal hop
or bound on all four feet. There is
apparent tail drag when bounding.

• The most widespread kangaroo rat.

• Burrows are conspicuous in areas they
inhabit.

• More solitary than other kangaroo rats
but in close proximity to others.

Painted-Spiny Pocket Mouse
(Liomys pictus)

Track: Front ⁵/₁₆–¹/₂ in. (.8–1.3 cm) L
x ³/₈–⁷/₁₆ in. (1–1.1 cm) W

Very small. Plantigrade.
Asymmetrical. Five toes in
classic rodent structure: Toe 1
is a vestigial thumb and rarely
registers in tracks. Four long
and slender toes in tracks: Toes
2 and 5 point toward the sides,
and toes 3 and 4 point forward.
Some of the metacarpal pads are
fused, but the track is composed
of three distinct palm pads; there
are two additional pads (the
heel) at the posterior edge of
the track, which may or may
not show. Nails may or may not
register. Front tracks smaller than
rears. Similar to the tracks of
jumping mice.

**Typical Ord's kangaroo rat bipedal
hopping gait in shallow snow. (UT)**

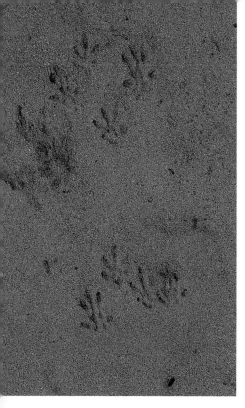

Tracks of a painted-spiny pocket mouse. (Mexico)

Rear $^7/_{16}$–$^1/_2$ in. (1.1–1.3 cm) L x $^5/_{16}$–$^7/_{16}$ in. (.8–1.1 cm) W

Very small. Plantigrade. Slightly asymmetrical. Five slender, long toes in a classic rodent structure: Toes 1 and 5 point out to either side, and toes 2, 3, and 4 register close together, pointing forward. Some metacarpals are fused to form larger pads, but distinct pads sometimes show in tracks. Nails may or may not register. The heel may or may not register.

Trail: Bound Stride: 2–10 in. (5.1–25.4 cm); occasionally longer

Trail width: 1$^1/_8$–1$^7/_{16}$ in. (2.9–3.7 cm)

Group length: 1$^1/_4$–1$^5/_8$ in. (3.2–4.1 cm)

Notes:
- Travels in a bound, and slows to a walk to forage.
- Common track in dry tropical forests in Mexico.

Beavers: Family Castoridae

American Beaver *(Castor canadensis)*

Track: Front 2$^1/_2$–3$^7/_8$ in. (6.4–9.8 cm) L x 2$^1/_4$–3$^1/_2$ in. (5.7–8.9 cm) W

Medium. Plantigrade. Asymmetrical. Five toes in classic rodent structure: Toe 1 is reduced, clawed, and occasionally obvious in tracks. Toes 2 and 5 point toward the sides, and toes 3 and 4 point forward. All toes are strongly curved. Some of the metacarpal pads are fused; there are two additional pads (the heel) at the posterior edge of the track, which may or may not show. Nails are long, blunt, and prominent in tracks. Front tracks significantly smaller than rears and often lost in the trail, crushed by the hind feet and tail that follow.

Rear 4$^3/_4$–7 in. (12.1–17.8 cm) L x 3$^1/_4$–5$^1/_4$ in. (8.3–13.3 cm) W

Large to very large. Plantigrade. Asymmetrical. 5 long toes: Toes 1 and 2 are not always obvious in tracks. Distal webbing may or may not register. Metacarpal pads are fused to form larger pads, but these may or may not be distinct, depending on substrate. Nails are large, short, and blunt. Heel almost always registers. Nutria tracks are more slender, have sharp claws, and tend not to register the heel portion of rear feet.

Trail:
Walk	Stride:	6–11½ in. (15.2–29.2 cm)
	Trail width:	5¾–11 in. (14.6–27.9 cm)
Bound	Stride:	10–32 in. (25.4–81.3 cm)
	Trail width:	6¾–13½ in. (17.1–34.3 cm)
	Group length:	7–14½ in. (17.8–36.8 cm)

Notes:

• Walk when traveling on the ground for the vast majority of time. When threatened or alarmed, bound to the safety of water.

• Although much of their time is spent in the water, beaver trails are commonly found leaving water sources to forage, scent mark, and occasionally travel to other water sources.

• Track and trail quality is tremendously dependent on how much the tail drag registers. Occasionally, tracks are almost completely cleaned by the tail, and front tracks are often lost when massive, heavy rears direct register on top of them.

American beaver walk.

American beaver bound.

Beaver tracks. (WY)

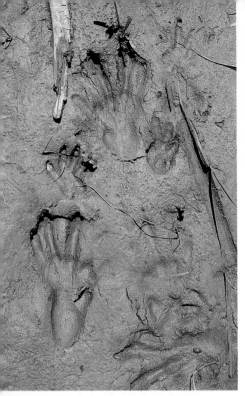

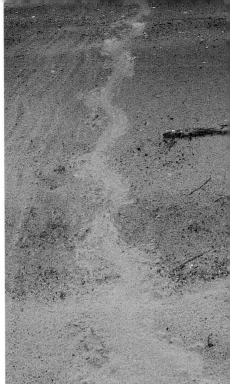

Top left: **Beautiful, clear hind beaver tracks and smaller front tracks. (WY)** *Top right:* **All that is evident in this beaver trail is the curvature of the tail drag. (MA)** *Left:* **A beaver bound. An otter lopes towards the camera. (AK)**

- Do not climb, but occasionally shuffle up leaning logs and branches.
- Tracks or trails may be seen in snow; expect them to use a direct register walk.
- Live in small family groups, and trails may mingle with those of other beavers.

Rats and Mice: Family Muridae

Marsh Rice Rat (*Oryzomys palustris*)

Track: Front 9/16–3/4 in. (1.4–1.9 cm) L x 1/2–5/8 in. (1.3–1.6 cm) W

Very small. Plantigrade. Asymmetrical. Five toes in classic rodent structure: Toe 1 is greatly reduced. Toes 2 and 5 point toward the sides, and toes 3 and 4 point forward. In the track, toes generally connect to the metacarpal region. Some of the metacarpal pads are fused, but there are three distinct palm pads; there are two additional pads (the heel) at the posterior edge of the track, which tend not to show. Front tracks smaller than rear tracks.

Rear 3/4–1 1/4 in. (1.9–3.2 cm) L x 5/8–13/16 in. (1.6–2.1 cm) W

Small. Plantigrade. Slightly asymmetrical. Five long toes in classic rodent structure: Toes 1 and 5 are to the sides, and toes 2, 3, and 4 all point forward together. Metacarpal pads are fused to form larger pads, but four palm pads should be distinct, with two additional heel pads at the posterior edge of the track. Nails are small and may or may not register. The heel often registers. Long, slender toes and a greater disproportion between front and rear tracks help separate all rats from chipmunks.

Trail: Bound   Stride: 3 1/2–6 in. (8.9–15.2 cm)

Trail width: 2–3 1/4 in. (5.1–8.3 cm)

Walk   Stride: 1 5/8–3 in. (4.1–7.6 cm)

Notes:

• Walk when foraging or exploring, and bound across open areas and when feeling threatened or exposed.

• Good swimmers and capable climbers; tend to nest aboveground in shrubs and trees.

• Associated with coastal marsh environments, and inland wetlands.

• Densities can be quite high under ideal conditions, and signs may be plentiful.

Marsh rice rat walk.

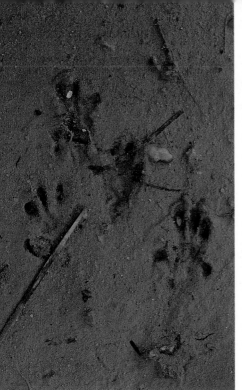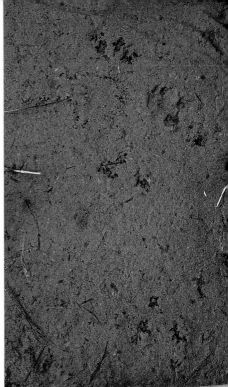

Left: Marsh rice rat tracks in a hopping gait. (NC) *Right:* Marsh rice rat bounding trail pattern. (FL)

Western Harvest Mouse *(Reithrodontomys megalotis)*
Eastern Harvest Mouse *(Reithrodontomys humulis)*

Track: Front ¼–⅜ in. (.6–1 cm) L x ¼–⁵/₁₆ in. (.6–.8 cm) W

Very small. Plantigrade. Asymmetrical. Five toes in classic rodent structure: Toe 1 is greatly reduced. Toes 2 and 5 point toward the sides, and toes 3 and 4 point forward. In the track, the digital pads are bulbous. Some of the metacarpal pads are fused, but there are three distinct palm pads; there are two additional pads (the heel) at the posterior edge of the track, which may or may not show. Nails may or may not register. Front tracks smaller than rear tracks.

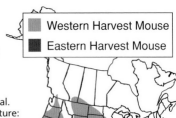

Rear ¼–½ in. (.6–1.3 cm) L x ⁷/₃₂–⁵/₁₆ in. (.6–.8 cm) W

Very small. Plantigrade. Asymmetrical. Five long toes in classic rodent structure: Toes 1 and 5 are to the sides, and toes 2, 3, and 4 all point forward together. However, toe 1 is slightly longer and farther back in the track than in other mouse species. Some metacarpal pads are fused to form larger pads, but four palm pads should be distinct, with two additional heel pads at the posterior edge of the track.

Western harvest mice tracks. Note the shape and placement of toe 1 on the rear feet, which is unique to this group of mice. (CA)

Nails and heel may or may not register. The position and shape of toe 1 in rear tracks help differentiate harvest mice from other mouse species.

Trail: Bound Stride: 2–9 in.
(5.1–22.9 cm)

Trail width: 7/8–13/8 in.
(2.2–3.5 cm)

Group length: 1–13/4 in.
(2.5–4.4 cm)

Notes:

• Move in a bound; walk only when foraging or under thick, protective cover.

• Quite adaptable, found in various habitats within their range.

• Competent climbers; may be found at any height in vegetative strata.

• Tracks and trails begin and end with suitable cover, which may be dense vegetation, holes in earth or root systems, or cavities in trees.

• Often share nests with others.

Western harvest mouse trail in dust. (CA)

Small Mammals on Track Plates

Track plates are a wonderful tool for wildlife inventories and research, especially to prove the presence of mustelids and skunk species where substrates make track identification difficult or impossible. I've also been experimenting with small mammal surveys using baited track plates, with some success. When live trapping is not an option, further development of this method might prove useful. Track plates are discussed further in chapter one.

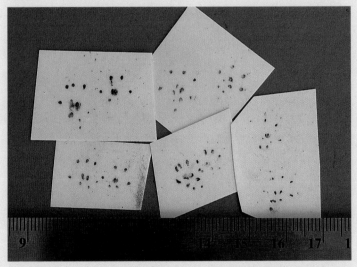

Small mammal tracks on track plates: upper left, meadow vole; upper middle, white-footed mouse; lower left, southern red-backed vole; lower middle, northern short-tailed shrew; far right, woodland vole. (NH, MA)

Brush Mouse *(Peromyscus boylii)*

Track: Front ³/₈ in. (1 cm) L x ³/₈ in. (1 cm) W

Very small. Plantigrade. Asymmetrical. Five toes in classic rodent structure: Toe 1 is greatly reduced. Toes 2 and 5 point toward the sides, and toes 3 and 4 point forward. In the track, the digital pads are bulbous and tend to be separate from the palm region. Some of the metacarpal pads are fused, but there are three distinct palm pads; there are two additional pads (the heel) at the posterior edge of the track, which may or may not show. Nails and heel may or may not register.

Rear ⁷/₁₆–¹/₂ in. (1.1–1.3 cm) L x ⁷/₁₆ in. (1.1 cm) W

Very small. Plantigrade. Asymmetrical. Five long toes in classic rodent structure: Toes 1 and 5 are to the sides, and toes 2, 3, and 4 all point forward together. Digital pads are bulbous. Some metacarpal pads are fused to form larger pads, but four palm pads should be distinct, with two additional heel pads at the posterior edge of the track. Nails and heel may or may not register. Front tracks smaller than rear tracks. Rely on habitat

clues to differentiate among
Peromyscus species of similar
sizes; where several species
overlap, tracks and trails are
difficult to separate.

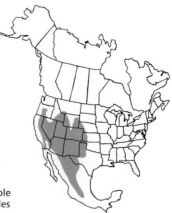

Trail: Bound   Trail width: 1³/₈–1³/₄ in.
                 (3.5–4.4 cm)

Notes:

• Move in a bound; walk only when
foraging or under thick, protective cover.

• Associated with high-elevation ledges,
boulders, and forests with lots of logs,
rocks, and other cover.

• Competent climbers; may be found at any
height in vegetative strata.

• Tracks and trails begin and end with suitable
cover, which may be dense vegetation, holes
in earth or root systems, or cavities in trees.

• In deep snow, *Peromyscus* species continue to move on top of the snow layer;
bounds are used to traverse such terrain, and in softer conditions, front and rear
tracks blend together, leaving a 2x2 bound. Tail drag may or may not be obvious.

White-footed Mouse *(Peromyscus leucopus)*
Deer Mouse *(Peromyscus maniculatus)*

Track: Front ¹/₄–⁷/₁₆ in. (.6–1.1 cm) L x ⁵/₁₆–¹/₂ in. (.8–1.3 cm) W

Very small. Plantigrade. Asymmetrical. Five toes in classic rodent structure:
Toe 1 is greatly reduced. Toes 2 and 5 point toward the sides, and toes 3
and 4 point forward. In the track, the digital pads are bulbous. Some of
the metacarpal pads are fused, but there are three distinct palm pads;
there are two additional pads (the heel) at the posterior edge of the track,

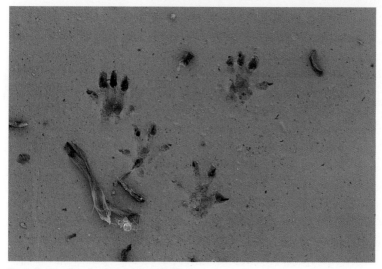

Bounding tracks of a deer mouse. (NH)

which may or may not show. Nails and heel may or may not register. Front tracks smaller than rear tracks.

Rear 1/4–9/16 in. (.6–1.4 cm) L x 5/16–1/2 in. (.8–1.3 cm) W

Very small. Plantigrade. Asymmetrical. 5 long toes in classic rodent structure: Toes 1 and 5 to the sides, and toes 2, 3, and 4 all point forward together. Digital pads are bulbous. Some metacarpal pads are fused to form larger pads, but four palm pads should be distinct, with two additional heel pads at the posterior edge of the track. Nails and heel may or may not register. Rely on habitat clues to differentiate among *Peromyscus* species of similar sizes; where several species overlap, tracks and trails are difficult to separate.

Trail: Walk   Stride: 1 3/8–2 1/8 in. (3.5–5.4 cm)

                  Trail width: 1–1 3/4 in. (2.5–4.4 cm)

        Bound   Stride: 4–20 in. (10.2–50.8 cm)

                  Trail width: 1 1/4–1 3/4 in. (3.2–4.4 cm)

                  Group length: 1 1/8–2 1/8 in. (2.9–5.4 cm)

Walking track pattern of a white-footed mouse species. (WY)

White-footed mouse bound.

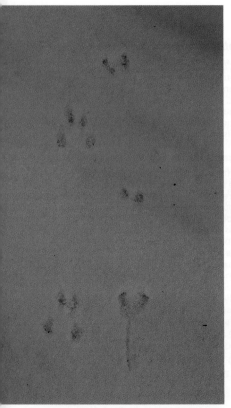 

Left: Bounding white-footed mouse and smoky shrew. The larger animal is the mouse. (NH) *Right:* Bounding trail of a white-footed mouse species. (WY)

Notes:

- Move in a bound; walk only when foraging or under thick, protective cover.
- The white-footed mouse is the most abundant mammal in much of the East's woodlands, and the deer mouse is the most widespread North American rodent.
- Capable swimmers and competent climbers; may be found at any height in vegetative strata.
- Tracks and trails begin and end with suitable cover, which may be dense vegetation, holes in earth or root systems, or cavities in trees.
- In deep snow, *Peromyscus* species will continue to move on top of the snow layer; bounds are used to traverse such terrain, and in softer conditions, front and rear tracks blend together, leaving a 2x2 bound. Tail drag may or may not be obvious.

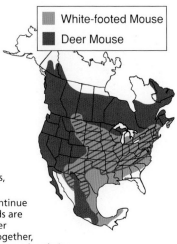

White-footed Mouse
Deer Mouse

White-throated Woodrat *(Neotoma albigula)*

Track: Front 3/8–5/8 in. (1–1.6 cm) L x 7/16–5/8 in. (1.1–1.6 cm) W

Very small. Plantigrade. Asymmetrical. Five toes in classic rodent structure: Toe 1 is greatly reduced. Toes 2 and 5 point toward the sides, and toes 3 and 4 point forward. In the track, the digital pads are bulbous and often separate from the palm. Some of the metacarpal pads are fused, but there are three distinct palm pads; there are two additional pads (the heel) at the posterior edge of the track, which may or may not show. Nails tend not to register. Front tracks smaller than rear tracks.

Rear 7/16–3/4 in. (1.1–1.9 cm) L x 7/16–11/16 in. (1.1–1.7 cm) W

Very small. Plantigrade. Slightly asymmetrical. Five long toes in classic rodent structure: Toes 1 and 5 are to the sides, and toes 2, 3, and 4 all point forward together. Digital pads are bulbous, but slender toes may also register. Partial fusing of some metacarpal pads, but four palm pads should be distinct; two additional heel pads at the posterior edge of the track may not show. Nails tend not to register. Rely on habitat clues and range to distinguish among woodrat species.

Trail: Bound   Stride: 3–8 in. (7.6–20.3 cm)
             Trail width: 2–2⁷/₈ in. (5.1–7.3 cm)

Notes:

- Bound across exposed areas or when threatened; tend to walk in or near cover.
- Inhabit varied arid terrain, but nests are particularly associated with prickly pear species.
- Form substantial runs leading from nests or burrows to regular harvesting areas; these runs inevitably hold scat.
- Competent climber; may live and harvest aboveground.

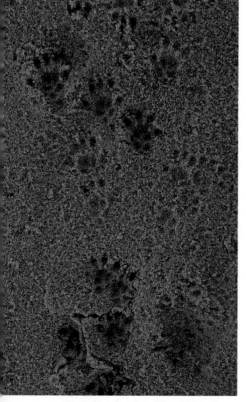

Myriad tracks of a white-throated woodrat in a run. (TX)

Bushy-tailed Woodrat *(Neotoma cinerea)*

Track: Front ½–1 in. (1.3–2.5 cm) L x ⁹/₁₆–¹⁵/₁₆ in. (1.4–2.4 cm) W

Very small. Plantigrade. Asymmetrical. Five toes in classic rodent structure: Toe 1 is greatly reduced. Toes 2 and 5 point toward the sides, and toes 3 and 4 point forward. In the track, the digital pads are bulbous and separate from the palm. Some of the metacarpal pads are fused, but there are three distinct palm pads; there are two additional pads (the heel) at the posterior edge of the track, which may or may not show. Nails tend not to register. Front tracks smaller than rear tracks.

Rear ⅝–1¼ in. (1.6–3.2 cm) L x ⁹/₁₆–1 in. (1.4–2.5 cm) W

Very small. Plantigrade. Slightly asymmetrical. 5 long toes in classic rodent structure: toes 1 and 5 are to the sides, and toes 2, 3, and 4 all point forward together. Digital pads are bulbous, but slender toes may also register. Partial fusing of some metacarpal pads, but four palm pads should be distinct; two additional heel pads at the posterior edge of the track. Nails tend not to register, and heel may or may not do so. Rely on habitat clues and range to distinguish among woodrat species.

Trail: Bound   Stride: 4–8 in. (10.2–20.3 cm)
Trail width: 2⅛–2¾ in. (5.4–7 cm)

Walk   Stride: 2–3½ in. (5.1–8.9 cm)

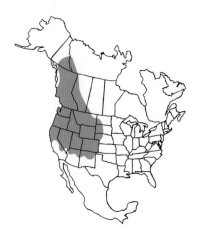

Bushy-tailed woodrat bound.

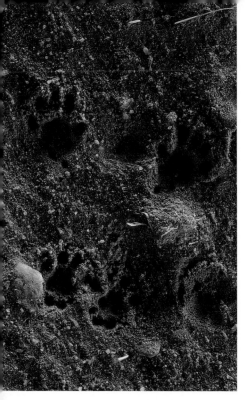

Bounding tracks of a bushy-tailed woodrat in the filtered light under a bridge. (MT)

Notes:

- Bound across exposed areas or when threatened; tend to walk in or near cover.
- Largest of the woodrat species, and parameters exceed those of smaller species.
- Form substantial runs leading from nests or burrows to regular harvesting areas; these runs inevitably hold scat.
- Competent climbers; may live and harvest aboveground.
- Use unadorned burrows, as well as construct nests.
- Very territorial; except for breeding and family groups, expect one animal per den site.

Dusky-footed Woodrat
(Neotoma fuscipes)

Track: Front $3/8$–$5/8$ in. (1–1.6 cm) L
x $7/16$–$5/8$ in. (1.1–1.6 cm) W

Very small. Plantigrade. Asymmetrical. Five toes in classic rodent structure: Toe 1 is greatly reduced. Toes 2 and 5 point toward the sides, and toes 3 and 4 point forward. In the track, the digital pads are bulbous and separate from the palm. Some of the metacarpal pads are fused, but there are three distinct palm pads; there are two additional pads (the heel) at the posterior edge of the track, which may or may not show. Nails tend not to register. Front tracks smaller than rear tracks.

Rear $7/16$–$3/4$ in. (1.1–1.9 cm) L
x $7/16$–$11/16$ in. (1.1–1.7 cm) W

Very small. Plantigrade. Slightly asymmetrical. Five long toes in classic rodent structure: Toes 1 and 5 are to the sides, and toes 2, 3, and 4 all point forward together. Digital pads are bulbous, but slender toes may also register. Partial fusing of some metacarpal pads, but four palm pads should be distinct; two additional heel

Dusky-footed woodrat bound.

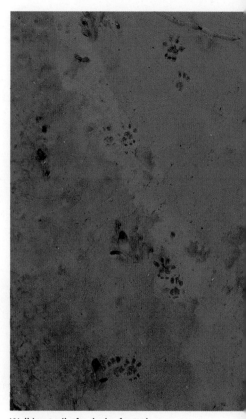

pads at the posterior edge of the
track. Nails tend not to register,
and heel may or may not do
so. Rely on habitat clues and
range to distinguish among
woodrat species.

Trail: Walk Stride: 1⁵⁄₈–3¹⁄₂ in.
(4.1–8.9 cm)

Trail width: 1⁵⁄₈–2¹⁄₄ in.
(4.1–5.7 cm)

Notes:

• Bound across exposed areas or when
threatened; tend to walk in or near
cover.

• Reach their highest densities in
habitats with full canopies and thick
understories. However, they inhabit
varied terrain, as long as there is a
vertical component to the vegetative
structure.

**Walking trail of a dusky-footed
woodrat. (CA)**

• Form substantial runs leading from nests
or burrows to regular harvesting areas;
these runs inevitably hold scat.

• Competent climbers; may live and
harvest aboveground.

Desert Woodrat *(Neotoma lepida)*

Track: Front ⁷⁄₁₆–¹¹⁄₁₆ in. (1.1–1.7 cm) L
x ⁷⁄₁₆–³⁄₄ in. (1.1–1.9 cm) W

Very small. Plantigrade.
Asymmetrical. Five toes in classic
rodent structure: Toe 1 is greatly
reduced. Toes 2 and 5 point toward
the sides, and toes 3 and 4 point
forward. In the track, the digital
pads are bulbous and separate
from the palm. Some of the

Front and hind (behind) desert woodrat tracks.
(CA)

Desert woodrat walk.

metacarpal pads are fused, but there are three distinct palm pads; there are two additional pads (the heel) at the posterior edge of the track, which may or may not show. Nails tend not to register. Front tracks smaller than rear tracks.

Rear 1/2–1 1/4 in. (1.3–3.2 cm) L x 1/2–7/8 in. (1.3–2.2 cm) W

Very small. Plantigrade. Slightly asymmetrical. Five long toes in classic rodent structure: Toes 1 and 5 are to the sides, and toes 2, 3, and 4 all point forward together. Digital pads are bulbous, but slender toes may also register. Partial fusing of some metacarpal pads, but four palm pads should be distinct; two additional heel pads at the posterior edge of the track. Nails tend not to register, and heel may or may not do so. Rely on habitat clues and range to distinguish among woodrat species.

Trail: Bound   Stride: 3–8 in. (7.6–20.3 cm)
                  Trail width: 2 3/8–3 1/8 in. (6–7.9 cm)
       Walk   Stride: 1 3/4–3 3/4 in. (4.4–9.5 cm)
                  Trail width: 1 3/4–2 1/2 in. (4.4–6.4 cm)

Desert woodrat tracks in dust. (UT)

Notes:
- Bound across exposed areas or when threatened; tend to walk in or near cover.
- Regardless of their name, desert woodrats inhabit tremendously varied terrain, in addition to the most arid habitats.
- Form substantial runs leading from nests or burrows to regular harvesting areas; these runs inevitably hold scat.
- Competent climbers; may live and harvest aboveground.

Southern Plains Woodrat (*Neotoma micropus*)

Track: Front ³/₈–⁵/₈ in. (1–1.6 cm) L x ⁷/₁₆–⁵/₈ in. (1.1–1.6 cm) W

Very small. Plantigrade. Asymmetrical. Five toes in classic rodent structure: Toe 1 is greatly reduced. Toes 2 and 5 point toward the sides, and toes 3 and 4 point forward. In the track, the digital pads are bulbous and separate from the palm. Some of the metacarpal pads are fused, but there are three distinct palm pads; there are two additional pads (the heel) at the posterior edge of the track, which may or may not show. Nails tend not to register. Front tracks smaller than rear tracks.

Rear ⁷/₁₆–³/₄ in. (1.1–1.9 cm) L x ⁷/₁₆–¹¹/₁₆ in. (1.1–1.7 cm) W

Very small. Plantigrade. Slightly asymmetrical. Five long toes in classic rodent structure: Toes 1 and 5 are to the sides, and toes 2, 3, and 4 all point forward together. Digital pads are bulbous, but slender toes may also register. Partial fusing of some metacarpal pads, but four palm pads should be distinct; two additional heel pads at the

Walking trail of a southern plains woodrat. (TX)

posterior edge of the track. Nails tend not to register, and heel may or may not do so. Rely on habitat clues and range to distinguish among woodrat species.

Trail: Walk   Stride: 1¾–4 in. (4.4–10.2 cm)
                Trail width: 1⅝–2¼ in. (4.1–5.7 cm)

Notes:

- Bound across exposed areas or when threatened; tend to walk in or near cover.
- Associated with flat, semiarid plains of grasses and cacti.
- Form substantial runs leading from nests or burrows to regular harvesting areas; these runs inevitably hold scat.
- Competent climbers; may live and harvest aboveground.

Southern Red-backed Vole (*Clethrionomys gapperi*)

Track: Front ¼–⁷⁄₁₆ in. (.6–1.1 cm) L x ⁵⁄₁₆–⅜ in. (.8–1 cm) W

Very small. Plantigrade. Asymmetrical. Five toes in classic rodent structure: Toe 1 is greatly reduced. Toes 2 and 5 point toward the sides, and toes 3 and 4 point forward. In the track, the digital pads are less bulbous than those of mice, and the ribbed toes are slender and often connected to the palm. Some of the metacarpal pads are fused, but there are three distinct palm pads; there are two additional pads (the heel) at the posterior edge of the track, which may or

A red-backed vole trail—lope into trot. (NH)

may not show. Nails may or may not register. Front tracks smaller than rear tracks.

Rear ¹/₄–¹/₂ in. (.6–1.3 cm) L x ¹/₄–⁷/₁₆ in. (.6–1.1 cm) W

Very small. Plantigrade. Slightly asymmetrical. Five long toes in classic rodent structure: Toes 1 and 5 are to the sides, and toes 2, 3, and 4 all point forward together. In the track, the slender, ribbed toes often connect to the palm. Partial fusing of some metacarpal pads, but four palm pads should be distinct; two additional heel pads at the posterior edge of the track. Nails and heel may or may not register. A small vole track.

Trail: Trot ␣␣␣␣␣ Stride: 2–2³/₄ in. (5.1–7 cm)
␣␣␣␣␣␣␣␣␣␣␣␣␣␣ Trail width: 1–1¹/₂ in. (2.5–3.8 cm)
␣␣␣␣␣␣ 3x4 lope ␣␣ Stride: 2–4 in. (5.1–10.2 cm)
␣␣␣␣␣␣␣␣␣␣␣␣␣␣ Group length: ³/₄–2³/₄ in. (1.9–7 cm)

Notes:

- Trot when moving in runs and traveling; speed up to lopes and bounds more often than larger voles do when threatened or exposed.
- Common creatures of woodlands, but cross more open habitats in dispersion, which generally occurs in autumn.
- Climb more than other voles do.
- Small holes in leaf litter, earth, or snow may be found when following voles.
- Tend to stay under snow when depths are significant, tunneling in search of sustenance.

Long-tailed Vole *(Microtus longicaudus)*

Track: Front ⁷/₁₆–¹/₂ in. (1.1–1.3 cm) L x ⁷/₁₆–¹/₂ in. (1.1–1.3 cm) W

Very small. Plantigrade. Asymmetrical. Five toes in classic rodent structure: Toe 1 is greatly reduced. Toes 2 and 5 point toward the sides, and toes 3 and 4 point forward. In the track, the digital pads are less bulbous than those of mice, and the ribbed toes are slender and often connected to the palm. Some of the metacarpal pads are fused, but there are three distinct palm pads; there are two additional pads (the heel) at the posterior edge of the track, which may or may not show. Nails may or may not register. Front tracks smaller than rear tracks.

Rear ³/₈–⁵/₈ in. (1–1.6 cm) L x ³/₈–¹/₂ in. (1–1.3 cm) W

Very small. Plantigrade. Slightly asymmetrical. Five long toes in classic rodent structure: Toes 1 and 5 are to the sides, and toes 2, 3, and 4 all point forward together. In the track, the slender, ribbed toes often connect to the palm. Partial fusing of some metacarpal pads, but four palm pads should be distinct; two additional heel pads at the posterior edge of the track. Nails and heel may or may not register. A medium to large vole track. Tracks and trails are nearly identical to those of meadow voles, which sometimes share the same habitat.

Long-tailed vole hop.

Trail: Trot Stride: 2–3 in. (5.1–7.6 cm)

Trail width: 1³/₁₆–1⁹/₁₆ in. (3–4 cm)

Hop Stride: 5¹/₂–7 in. (14–17.8 cm)

Trail width: 1³/₈–1¹/₂ in. (3.5–3.8 cm)

Group length: 1¹/₂–2 in. (3.8–5.1 cm)

Notes:

• Medium to large vole species almost always travel in a direct register trot, speeding up into hops, lopes, and bounds when exposed or threatened. They also forage in an understep walk.

• This vole species shares many characteristics and preferences with the meadow vole.

Meadow Vole or Field Mouse *(Microtus pennsylvanicus)*

Track: Front ¹/₄–⁷/₁₆ in. (.6–1.1 cm) L x ⁹/₃₂–⁹/₁₆ in. (.7–1.4 cm) W

Very small. Plantigrade. Asymmetrical. Five toes in classic rodent structure: Toe 1 is greatly reduced. Toes 2 and 5 point toward the sides, and toes 3 and 4 point forward. In the track, the digital pads are less bulbous than those of mice, and the ribbed toes are slender and often connected to the palm. Some of the metacarpal pads are fused, but there are three distinct palm pads; there are two additional pads (the heel) at the posterior edge of the track, which may or may not show. Nails may or may not register. Front tracks smaller than rear tracks.

Rear ³/₈–⁵/₈ in. (1–1.6 cm) L x ³/₈–⁹/₁₆ in. (1–1.4 cm) W

Very small. Plantigrade. Slightly asymmetrical. Five long toes in classic rodent structure: Toes 1 and 5 are to the sides, and toes 2, 3, and 4 all point forward together. In the track, the slender, ribbed toes often connect to the palm. Partial fusing of some metacarpal pads, but four palm pads should be distinct; two additional heel pads at the posterior edge of the track. Nails and heel may or may not register. A medium to large vole track.

Trail: Trot Stride: 2–3¹/₄ in. (5.1–8.3 cm)

Trail width: ⁷/₈–1¹¹/₁₆ in. (2.2–4.3 cm)

Walk Stride: 1¹/₄–1¹⁵/₁₆ in. (3.2–4.9 cm)

Trail width: 1¹/₄–2 in. (3.2–5.1 cm)

Bound Stride: 4–9¹/₄ in. (10.2–23.5 cm)

Trail width: 1³/₁₆–1¹/₂ in. (3–3.8 cm)

2x2 lope Stride: 3–7 in. (7.6–17.8 cm)

Trail width: 1–1³/₈ in. (2.5–3.5 cm)

Hop Stride: 5¹/₂–7 in. (14–17.8 cm)

Trail width: 1³/₈–1¹/₂ in. (3.5–3.8 cm)

Group length: 1¹/₂–2 in. (3.8–5.1 cm)

Notes:

• Medium to large vole species almost always travel in a direct register trot, speeding up into hops, lopes, and bounds when exposed or threatened. They also forage in an understep walk.

Front and hind (above) tracks of a
meadow vole. (NH)

Meadow vole trot.

A meadow vole in a slow trot parallels
a spotted sandpiper trail, and another
in a direct register trot cuts across in the
opposite direction. (NH)

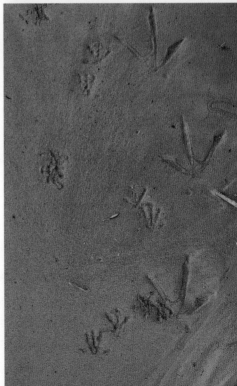

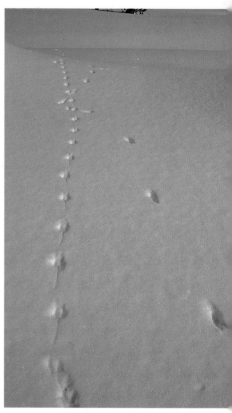

Left: A long trot trail in shallow snow, and a few spots where the vole attempted to tunnel beneath but was stopped by the frozen surface of the stream it was crossing. (NH) *Right:* A meadow vole followed by an ermine, which leaves the longer strides. (ID)

- Creatures of field and wetland, they tend to stay under the cover of long grasses, sedges, and shrubs when possible.
- In general, voles do not climb without the aid of deep snowpack.
- Small holes in leaf litter, earth, or snow may be found when following voles.
- Tend to stay under snow when depths are significant, tunneling in search of sustenance.
- Densities are cyclic in nature; number of animals in a given area may climb, crash, and climb again.

Woodland Vole *(Microtus pinetorum)*

Track: Front ¼–⁷/₁₆ in. (.6–1.1 cm) L x ⁵/₁₆–⁷/₁₆ in. (.8–1.1 cm) W

Very small. Plantigrade. Asymmetrical. Five toes in classic rodent structure: Toe 1 is greatly reduced. Toes 2 and 5 point toward the sides, and toes 3 and 4 point forward. In the track, the digital pads are less bulbous than those of mice, and the ribbed toes are slender and often connected to the palm. Some of the metacarpal pads are fused, but there are three distinct palm pads; there are two additional pads (the heel) at the posterior edge of the track, which may or may not show. Nails may or may not register. Front tracks smaller than rear tracks.

Rear ⁵/₁₆–½ in. (.8–1.3 cm) L x ⁵/₁₆–³/₈ in. (.8–1 cm) W

Very small. Plantigrade. Slightly asymmetrical. Five long toes in classic rodent structure: Toes 1 and 5 are to the sides, and toes 2, 3, and 4 all point forward together. In the track, the slender, ribbed toes often connect to the palm. Partial fusing of some metacarpal pads, but four palm pads should be distinct; two additional heel pads at the posterior edge of the track. Nails and heel may or may not register. A medium to large vole track.

(Data collected from one mature female during fall dispersion.)

Trail: Walk   Stride: 1–1³/₈ in. (2.5–3.5 cm)

Trail width: 1–1³/₈ in. (2.5–3.5 cm)

Notes:

- Medium to large vole species almost always travel in a direct register trot, speeding up into lopes and bounds when exposed or threatened. They also forage in an understep walk.

- Spend much of their time foraging in subsurface runs, venturing above-ground far less than other vole species.

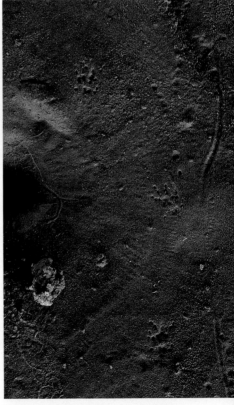

Trotting trail of a sagebrush vole. (WY)

Muskrat *(Ondatra zibethicus)*

Track: Front ⁷/₈–1¹/₂ in. (2.2–3.8 cm) L x 1–1¹/₂ in. (2.5–3.8 cm) W

Small. Plantigrade. Asymmetrical. Five toes in classic rodent structure: Toe 1 is greatly reduced but has a claw. Toes 2 and 5 point toward the sides, and toes 3 and 4 point forward. In the track, the digital pads are somewhat bulbous, but also have slender toes that often connect to the palm. Some of the metacarpal pads are fused, but there are three distinct palm pads; there are two additional pads (the heel) at the posterior edge of the track, which often show. Nails are long and prominent in tracks. Front tracks significantly smaller than rear tracks.

Rear 1¹/₂–2³/₄ in. (3.8–7 cm) L x 1¹/₂–2¹/₂ in. (3.8–6.4 cm) W

Small to medium. Plantigrade. Asymmetrical. Five long toes in a rodent structure: Toes 1 and 5 are to the sides, and toes 2, 3, and 4 register closer together and are of similar dimensions. In the track, the wide, ribbed toes connect to the palm and are surrounded by a "shelf" created by the stiff hairs surrounding the toes (which aid in swimming). Partial fusing of some metacarpal pads; although

Muskrat tracks. Note the "shelf" that surrounds the toes of the hind feet, which is created by stiff, long hairs that aid in swimming. (MA)

Muskrat overstep into indirect register walk.

individual pads are separate, they do not often appear so in tracks. There are two additional heel pads at the posterior edge the track, which rarely register. Nails tend to register. Rear tracks tend to register at a severe angle, pointing inward, contributing to their asymmetry.

Trail:	Direct register	
	walk/overstep	Stride: 3–7 in. (7.6–17.8 cm)
		Trail width: 3–5 in. (7.6–12.7 cm)
	Lope	Stride: 1⅝–4½ in. (4.1–11.4 cm)
		Group length: 7¼–9¾ in. (18.4–24.8 cm)
	Hop	Stride: 6–17 in. (15.2–43.2 cm)
		Group length: 3½–6½ in. (8.9–16.5 cm)

Notes:
- Walk when traveling and exploring, but speed up into hops and lopes when exposed or threatened.
- Muskrats are associated with riparian areas of every kind, including salt water marshes, tidal inlets, and even coastal islands.

Muskrat hop into lope.

Muskrat overstep walk. (NH)

A direct register muskrat walking trail in shallow snow. **(MN)**

- As far as I know, muskrats do not climb.
- In some areas, muskrats use burrow systems rather than building lodges, and regular runs will be seen connecting these to foraging areas.
- Although generally very territorial, muskrats will live close together, and in winter come together to huddle and warm the chilly air in their lodges and burrows.

Richardson's Collared Lemming *(Discrostonyx richardsoni)*
Brown Lemming *(Lemmus trimucronatus)*

Track: Front $7/16$–$5/8$ in. (1.1–1.6 cm) L
x $1/2$–$3/4$ in. (1.3–1.9 cm) W

Very small. Plantigrade. Asymmetrical. Five toes in classic rodent structure: Toe 1 is greatly reduced. Toes 2 and 5 point toward the sides, and toes 3 and 4 point forward. In the track, the digital pads are less bulbous than mice and ribbed toes are slender and often connected to palm. Some of the metacarpal pads are fused, but there are three distinct palm pads; there are two additional pads (the heel) at the posterior edge of the track, which may or may not show. Nails may or may not register. Front tracks smaller than rear tracks.

Richardson's collared lemming trail. (Canada)

Rear ⅝–¾ in. (1.6–1.9 cm) L
x 9/16–¾ in. (1.4–1.9 cm) W

Very small. Plantigrade. Slightly asymmetrical. Five long toes in classic rodent structure: Toes 1 and 5 are to the sides, and toes 2, 3, and 4 all point forward together. In the track, the slender, ribbed toes often connect to the palm. Partial fusing of some metacarpal pads, but four palm pads should be distinct; two additional heel pads at the posterior edge of the track. Nails and heel may or may not register. Tracks and trails are similar to those of large vole species.

(Data taken from a small data pool.)

Trail: Trot   Stride: 2½–3⅜ in. (6.4–8.6 cm)
                      Trail width: 1½–2¼ in. (3.8–5.7 cm)

Notes:

- Lemming species travel in a direct register trot, speeding up into hops, lopes, and bounds when exposed or threatened. They also forage in an understep walk.

- True lemmings are creatures of the far north and tundra.

- In deep snow, lemmings tend to tunnel, but may be seen using a direct register trot along the surface from time to time.

- At high densities, Norwegian lemmings are renowned for mass migrations. North American species do not engage in such behaviors.

Norway Rat *(Rattus norvegicus)*

Track: Front ½ in–⅞ in. (1.3–2.2 cm) L
            x ½–¾ in. (1.3–1.9 cm) W

Very small to small. Plantigrade. Asymmetrical. Five toes in classic rodent structure: Toe 1 is greatly reduced. Toes 2 and 5 point toward the sides, and toes 3 and 4 point forward. In the track, the toes generally connect to the metacarpal region. Some of the metacarpal pads are fused, but there are three distinct palm pads; there are two additional pads (the heel) at the posterior edge of the track, which may or may not show. Nails tend not to register. Front tracks smaller than rear tracks.

Rear ³/₄–1³/₈ in. (1.9–3.5 cm) L x ⁵/₈–1³/₁₆ in. (1.6–3 cm) W

Small. Plantigrade. Slightly asymmetrical. Five long toes in classic rodent structure: Toes 1 and 5 are to the sides, and toes 2, 3, and 4 all point forward together. Metacarpal pads are fused to form larger pads, but four palm pads should be distinct, with two additional heel pads at the posterior edge of the track. Nails may or may not register. Heel often registers. Long, slender toes and a greater disproportion between front and rear tracks help separate all rats from chipmunks.

Trail: Walk   Stride: 3–5 in. (7.6–12.7 cm)
                 Trail width: 1⁵/₈–2³/₄ in. (4.1–7 cm)

       Trot   Stride: 4–6 in. (10.2–15.2 cm)
                 Trail width: 2¹/₂–2⁵/₈ in. (6.4–6.7 cm)

       Bound Stride: 6–21 in. (15.2–53.3 cm)
                 Trail width: 1⁵/₈–3¹/₄ in. (4.1–8.3 cm)
                 Group length: 2³/₈–4 in. (6–10.2 cm)

       2x2 lope Stride: 7¹/₄–10 in. (18.4–25.4 cm)
                 Trail width: 1⁵/₈–2 in. (4.1–5.1 cm)
                 Group length: 1³/₈–2¹/₄ in. (3.5–5.7 cm)

A Norway rat bounds along a riverbank. (MA)

Norway rat walk.   Norway rat bound.

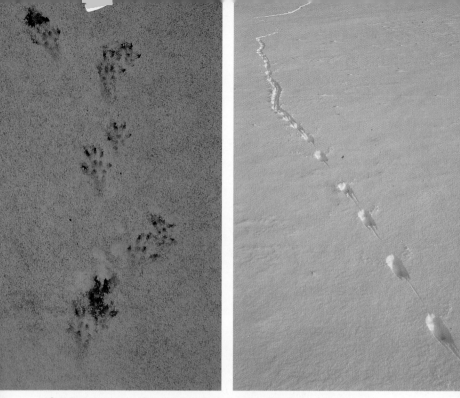

Left: A Norway rat's walking trail in shallow snow. (VT) *Right:* A Norway rat bounding in deep snow. Note the tail marks. (NH)

Notes:
- Walk when foraging and exploring; trot when speeding up. Bounds are used for traveling in exposed areas or when threatened.
- Norway rats, which were brought to the Americas long ago, have spread throughout the continent and are especially prevalent in urban areas and on farms.
- Competent swimmers and climbers.
- Look for their trails to start and end with burrows, holes, drains, culverts, or some other cover.
- In deep snow, they tend to use either a 2x2 lope or 2x2 bound. Tail drag is often obvious.
- Often gregarious, but signs of individuals are common outside urban centers.

Jumping Mice: Family Dipodidae

- All jumping mouse species are associated with woodland and riparian areas.
- They are capable swimmers and divers.
- In the north of their ranges, jumping mice hibernate for half the year, and only one-third of the population survives this period. They rely heavily on fat stores accumulated the previous summer.

Woodland Jumping Mouse *(Napaeozapus insignis)*
Meadow Jumping Mouse *(Zapus hudsonius)*

Track: Front 7/16–5/8 in. (1.1–1.6 cm) L
x 3/8–5/8 in. (1–1.6 cm) W

Very small. Plantigrade. Asymmetrical. Five toes in classic rodent structure: Toe 1 is a vestigial thumb and rarely registers in tracks. Four long and slender toes register in tracks. Toes 2 and 5 point toward the sides or curve backward, and toes 3 and 4 point forward. Some of the metacarpal pads are fused, but the track is composed of three distinct palm pads; there are two additional pads (the heel) at the posterior edge of the track, which may or may not show. Nails may or may not register. Front tracks smaller than rear tracks. Long, slender toes separate these from other mouse species.

Rear 7/16–7/8 in. (1.1–2.2 cm) L
x 3/8–11/16 in. (1–1.7 cm) W

Very small. Plantigrade. Slightly asymmetrical. Five slender, long toes in classic rodent structure: Toe 1, which is very small, and toe 5 point out to either side and are significantly shorter than toes 2, 3, and 4, which point forward. Toes 2 and 4 often curve outward. Toes are long, connected to the palm, and ribbed. Some metacarpals are fused to form larger pads, but distinct pads sometimes show in tracks. Nails

Meadow jumping
mouse bound.

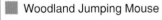

☐ Woodland Jumping Mouse
■ Meadow Jumping Mouse

are more prominent than in other mouse tracks. Contrary to previous literature, I have found that the heel portion of the feet rarely registers in jumping mouse tracks.

Trail: Bound   Stride: 6–48 in. (15.2–121.9 cm); Woodland
                  capable of bounding 12 ft. (3.66 m)
                  Trail width: 1½–2¼ in. (3.8–5.7 cm)
                  Group length: 1–2½ in. (2.5–6.4 cm)

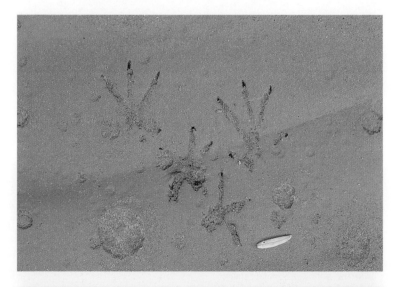

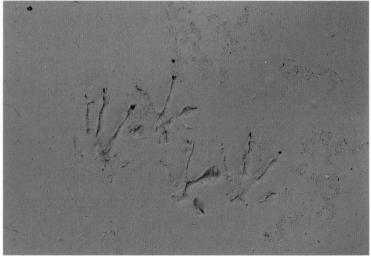

Top: Perfect meadow jumping mouse tracks. (MA) *Bottom:* Meadow jumping mouse tracks. (NH)

Jumping mouse tracks. Note the heels of the hind feet in these tracks, which do not often register. (VT)

Notes:
- Bound when traveling and moving about. I once found a jumping mouse's walking trail.
- These two species overlap significantly in range and habitat; currently, I do not differentiate between them. Literature states that although meadow jumping mice may be found in woodlands, woodland jumping mice do not use open habitats. Research with captive animals may be able to differentiate the two species by trail width or track parameters.
- Jumping mice are hibernators; their tracks are not seen for approximately six months of the year in the northern parts of their range.
- Trails are especially common in riparian areas. These mice are capable swimmers, and on several occasions they have taken to water rather than bound away from me when I've spooked them.

Confusing Trails

Certain other creatures may leave tracks that look very much like mammal tracks. The secret to avoiding misidentification is to be conscious that such mistakes are not only possible but also inevitable. Tracks of frogs and small birds, especially when partially registering, look a lot like those of jumping and pocket mice. Small classic bird tracks are especially likely to mimic mammal tracks. If the three center toes on the rear feet of a jumping or pocket mouse are all that clearly registers, which is often the case, confusion is likely. When their feet land parallel, you may misread the incomplete registration of their feet as being toes 2, 3, and 4 of a small perching bird that is hopping along.

Also look closely in deep substrates, especially snow, where feeding redpoll and junco trails may resemble those of bounding mice or trotting voles. Follow obscure snow trails when in doubt, and see whether flight or wing impressions make things clearer—or whether the trail disappears into a woodpile or down a burrow.

Western Jumping Mouse *(Zapus princeps)*

Track: Front ³/₈–⁹/₁₆ in. (1–1.4 cm) L x ³/₈–⁹/₁₆ in. (1–1.4 cm) W

Very small. Plantigrade. Asymmetrical. Five toes in classic rodent structure: Toe 1 is a vestigial thumb and rarely registers in tracks. Four long and slender toes register in tracks. Toes 2 and 5 point toward the sides or curve backward, and toes 3 and 4 point forward. Some of the metacarpal pads are fused, but the track is composed of three distinct palm pads; there are two additional pads (the heel) at the posterior edge of the track, which may or may not show. Nails may or may not register. Front tracks smaller than rear tracks. Long, slender toes separate this from other mouse species.

Rear ⁷/₁₆–³/₄ in. (1.1–1.9 cm) L x ³/₈–⁵/₈ in. (1–1.6 cm) W

Very small. Plantigrade. Slightly asymmetrical. Five slender, long toes in classic rodent structure: Toe 1, which is very small, and toe 5 point out to either side and are significantly shorter than toes 2, 3, and 4, which point forward. Toes 2 and 4 often curve outward. Toes are long, connected to the palm, and ribbed. Some metacarpals are fused to form larger pads, but distinct pads sometimes show in tracks. Nails are more prominent than in other mouse tracks. Contrary to previous literature, I have found that the heel portion of the feet rarely registers in jumping mouse tracks.

Trail: Bound   Stride: 4–60 in.
(10.2–152.4 cm)
Trail width: 1³/₈–1⁵/₈ in.
(3.5–4.1 cm)

Notes:

- Bound when traveling and moving about. I once found a jumping mouse's walking trail.
- Jumping mice are hibernators, and their tracks are not seen for approximately six months of the year in the northern parts of their range.
- Trails are especially common in riparian areas; they are capable swimmers.

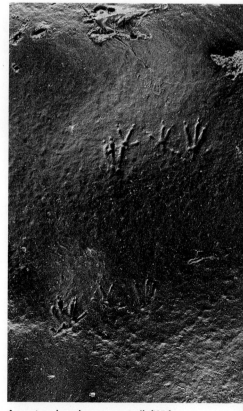

A western jumping mouse trail. (WY)

Pacific Jumping Mouse *(Zapus trinotatus)*

Track: Front $^7/_{16}$–$^5/_8$ in. (1.1–1.6 cm) L
x $^3/_8$–5/18 in. (1–1.6 cm) W

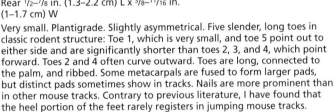

Very small. Plantigrade. Asymmetrical. Five toes in classic rodent structure: Toe 1 is a vestigial thumb and rarely registers in tracks. Four long and slender toes register in tracks. Toes 2 and 5 point toward the sides or curve backward, and toes 3 and 4 point forward. Some of the metacarpal pads are fused, but the track is composed of three distinct palm pads; there are two additional pads (the heel) at the posterior edge of the track, which may or may not show. Nails may or may not register. Front tracks smaller than rear tracks. Long, slender toes separate this from other mouse species.

Rear $^1/_2$–$^7/_8$ in. (1.3–2.2 cm) L x $^3/_8$–$^{11}/_{16}$ in. (1–1.7 cm) W

Very small. Plantigrade. Slightly asymmetrical. Five slender, long toes in classic rodent structure: Toe 1, which is very small, and toe 5 point out to either side and are significantly shorter than toes 2, 3, and 4, which point forward. Toes 2 and 4 often curve outward. Toes are long, connected to the palm, and ribbed. Some metacarpals are fused to form larger pads, but distinct pads sometimes show in tracks. Nails are more prominent than in other mouse tracks. Contrary to previous literature, I have found that the heel portion of the feet rarely registers in jumping mouse tracks.

Notes:

• Bound when traveling and moving about. I once found a jumping mouse's walking trail.

• Jumping mice are hibernators, and their tracks are not seen for approximately six months of the year in the northern parts of their range.

• Trails are especially common in riparian areas; they are capable swimmers.

Porcupines: Family Erethizontidae

North American Porcupine *(Erethizon dorsatum)*

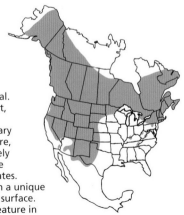

Track: Front $2^1/_4$–$3^3/_8$ in. (5.7–8.6 cm) L
x $1^1/_4$–$1^7/_8$ in. (3.2–4.8 cm) W

Medium. Plantigrade. Asymmetrical. Four very long toes: Toe 1 is absent, and the remaining toes register together and curve inward. Contrary to illustrations in previous literature, the digital pads of porcupines rarely register—rather, only their massive claws are visible in shallow substrates. Metacarpal pads are fused to form a unique palm, with a characteristic pebbly surface. Nails are large and a prominent feature in

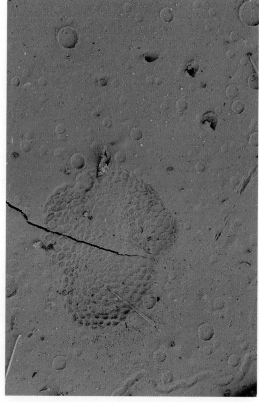

North American porcupine walk.

Perfect front foot of a porcupine. Note the pebbly pad surface. (NH)

tracks, registering far beyond the palm. Front tracks significantly smaller than rear tracks.

Rear 2¾–4 in. (7–10.2 cm) L x 1¼–2 in. (3.2–5.1 cm) W (young: 2½ in. [6.4 cm] L)

Medium. Plantigrade. Slightly asymmetrical. Five long toes: Toe 1 is much smaller than the others and may not register well. Digital pads are absent, unless in deep substrate—look for claw marks well in front of the palm. Palm and heel pads are fused, and the exposed skin is uniquely pebbly. Nails and heel are both prominent in tracks.

Trail: Walk   Stride: 6–10½ in. (15.2–26.7 cm); young, 4–5 in. (10.2–12.7 cm)
Trail width: 5–9 in. (12.7–22.9 cm); young, 3–4 in. (7.6–10.2 cm)

Notes:

- Walk everywhere; occasionally startled into a short-lived loping gait. Typical speeds vary from slow to fast walk and rarely exceed these parameters.
- The diversity of landscapes where porcupines are found is astounding, from snowy, northern woods to dry plains and canyons.

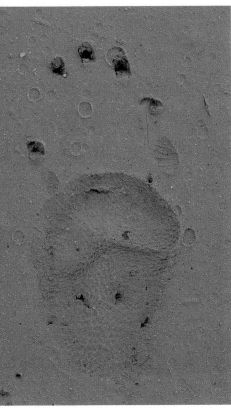

A porcupine hind track accompanying the front track shown on the preceding page. The four squashed holes under the heel are the claws from the front track that preceded it. Also note the two digital pads. (NH)

- Competent climbers; often found feeding or resting in trees, far above the ground. Look up periodically if you encounter porcupine sign, as they often spend the day in the relative safety of the canopy.
- Use all sorts of hollows and cavities to rest and nap, including basements, culverts, tree root systems, and rock ledges.
- Direct register walk in deep snow; plow through snow, creating a deep furrow.
- Have regular runs between areas of denning and feeding, which are apparent in both snow and leaf litter.
- Although considered solitary creatures by many, I counted 17 animals sharing the space created by a single rock ledge one winter in Massachusetts; there were likely twice that number sharing the rocky hillside.

Front and hind (left) porcupine tracks in shallow snow. (NH)

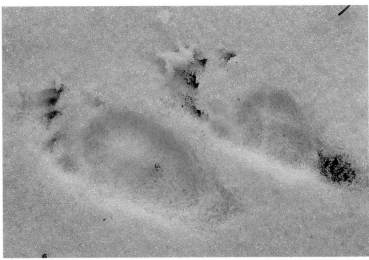

Left: A porcupine's walking trail. Note the quill drag. (TX) *Right:* This porcupine moved toward the camera, plowing through the soft snow. (MA)

Nutrias: Family Myocastoridae

Nutria *(Myocastor coypus)*

Track: Front 1½–2⅞ in. (3.8–7.3 cm) L
x 1⅜–2½ in. (3.5–6.4 cm) W

Medium. Plantigrade. Asymmetrical. Five toes in classic rodent structure: Toe 1 is reduced, but it is clawed and registers in tracks. Toes 2 and 5 point toward the sides, and toes 3 and 4 point forward. Some of the metacarpal pads are fused; there are two additional pads (the heel) at the posterior edge of the track, which may or may not show. Nails are long, sharp, and prominent in tracks. Front tracks significantly smaller than rear tracks. The front tracks are like large

muskrat tracks and are easily differentiated from the front tracks of beavers, with which this animal is often confused.

Rear 2¹/₂–5⁷/₈ in. (6.4–14.9 cm) L x 1⁷/₈–3⁷/₈ in. (4.8–9.8 cm) W

Medium to large. Plantigrade. Asymmetrical. Five long toes: Toes 1 and 2 are not always obvious in tracks. Distal webbing may register between all toes except for toes 4 and 5. Metacarpal pads are partially fused, but distinct in tracks. Nails are large, short, and considerably sharper than those of beavers. If the animal leaves a deep, rounded heel while walking, you've probably found a beaver track. Also compare nails, the straightness of the toes, gait preferences, and tail drag when differentiating between beaver and nutria signs. Young nutria trails can easily be confused with those of muskrats.

Trail:	Walk/overstep walk	Stride: 5–13 in. (12.7–33 cm)
		Trail width: 3³/₄–9¹/₄ in. (9.5–23.5 cm)
	Bound	Stride: 10–30 in. (25.4–76.2 cm)
		Trail width: 7–10¹/₂ in. (17.8–26.7 cm)
		Group length: 6–15 in. (15.2–38.1 cm)

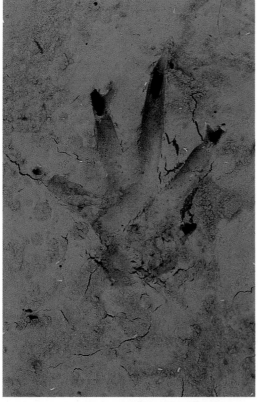

Front track of a nutria. Note toe 1, which registers as a dot. (TX)

Nutria walk.

Entire rear track, taken from within a bound trail. (TX)

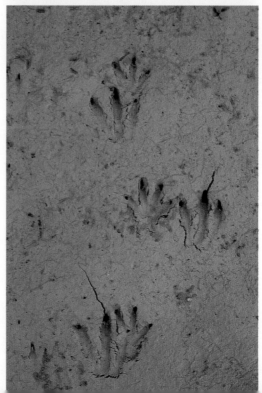

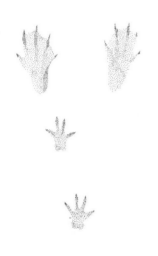

Nutria bound.

Right: Nutria walking trail. (TX)

Notes:

- Explore areas in a walk, but quickly switch to a bound when threatened or alarmed. Large animals tend toward lopes rather than bounds.
- A wetland species originally from South America; released in many areas of the United States and associated with riparian habitats of various kinds.
- Look for burrows near water systems.
- Especially gregarious; where you find one, you'll often find others. It is not uncommon to see obvious size variations among animals in a group, accounted for by the different age groups represented.

Order Lagomorpha

Pikas: Family Ochotonidae

American Pika *(Ochotona princeps)*
Collared Pika *(Ochotona collaris)*

Track: Front $^{11}/_{16}$–$^{7}/_8$ in. (1.7–2.2 cm) L x $^{11}/_{16}$–$^{7}/_8$ in. (1.7–2.2 cm) W

        Small. Digitigrade. Asymmetrical. Five toes: Toe 1 is reduced, but proportionately, it seems larger than in other rabbit tracks. Tracks are round, with bulbous digital pads. Sole is furred. Nails may or may not register. Front tracks similar in size to rear tracks.

        Rear $^{3}/_4$–$1^{1}/_8$ in. (1.9–2.9 cm) L x $^{3}/_4$–1 in. (1.9–2.5 cm) W

        Small. Digitigrade. Asymmetrical. Four toes. Roundish track with a furred and indistinct sole. Nails may or may not register.

Trail: Bound   Stride: $2^{1}/_4$–15 in. (5.7–38.1 cm)

               Trail width: 2–3 in. (5.1–7.6 cm)

               Group length: 2–$4^{7}/_8$ in. (5.1–12.4 cm)

Notes:

- Bound when traveling and foraging.
- Alpine creatures, most often associated with rock jumbles and screes. In some areas, they are also found in higher-elevation forests, again seeking shelter in rock jumbles.
- Their high-pitched alarm calls, which echo among a population in a rock slide, are often the most obvious signs of their presence; use these calls to confirm tracks and trails of this species.
- In deep snow conditions, pikas tend to move below the surface, forming runs and latrines and surviving on hay piles created as summer faded into fall.
- Solitary, but often live in close proximity to other pikas.

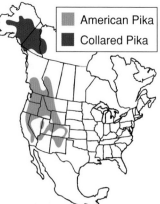

American Pika
Collared Pika

American pika
bound.

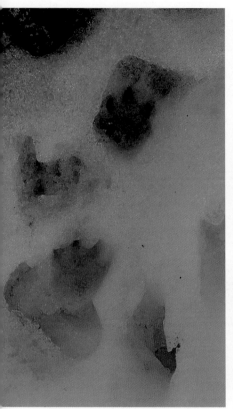 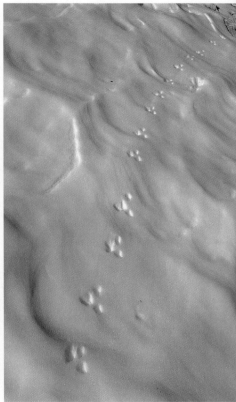

Left: American pika tracks. (CO) *Right:* An American pika bounds toward the camera. (CO)

Rabbits and Hares: Family Leporidae

- Rabbits and hares have five toes on each front foot and four toes on each hind foot. Toe 1 is greatly reduced, raised up on the front feet, but still clawed; therefore, only four toes are obvious in tracks.
- Rabbits and hares have incredibly furry feet and no exposed toe pads.
- This family generally moves in a bounding gait, with rear feet registering beyond the front feet. The trail width tends to decrease as speed increases.
- Rabbits tend to zigzag when being chased—look for trails with lots of sharp turns in rapid succession.
- Rabbits are not climbers, although some are competent swimmers.
- These animals generally ignore roads and trails, crossing them when convenient but rarely following them.
- These species often live in close proximity to both people and other rabbits.
- All these animals form obvious runs.

Double-fronts

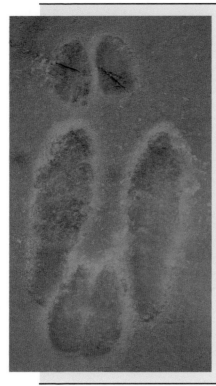

A pause or stop in a bounding animal, such as a cottontail or squirrel, is obvious in a trail section where one pair of rear tracks is accompanied by two sets of front tracks. When the animal is bounding normally, the front tracks touch down and are followed by the rear tracks beyond them. When it is time to stop, the rear tracks stay put, but the front feet, which have just picked up to allow the rear feet to register beyond them, touch down a second time in front of the rear feet to stop forward momentum. When it is time to move on, the front feet are lifted up, and the rear feet push off.

The resulting trail pattern when a snowshoe hare paused. (MN)

Pygmy Rabbit *(Brachylagus idahoensis)*

Track: Front ⁷/₈–1¹/₂ in. (2.2–3.8 cm) L x ⁵/₈–1³/₈ in. (1.6–3.5 cm) W

Small. Digitigrade. Very asymmetrical. Five toes: Toe 1 is greatly reduced but is clawed and occasionally registers in tracks. Tracks are pointy. Digital pads are furred but often evident in tracks. Sole is furred and often indistinct. Nails may or may not register but are often evident in good substrate. Front tracks significantly smaller than rear tracks.

Rear 1¹/₄–2¹/₂ in. (3.2–6.4 cm) L x ³/₄–1¹/₂ in. (1.9–3.8 cm) W

Small to medium. Digitigrade. Asymmetrical. Four toes. Furred sole is often indistinct. Significant furred heel often registers. Nails may or may not register but are often evident in good substrate. Tracks are pointy, unless splayed, in which case the anterior edge becomes rounded.

Trail: Bound   Stride: 4–20 in. (10.2–50.8 cm)
                      Trail width: 2–3³/₄ in. (5.1–9.5 cm)
                      Group length: 4–8 in. (10.2–20.3 cm)

Notes:

- Don't wander far from their burrow systems.
- The only rabbit that digs its own burrows.
- Tracks overlap in size with those of smaller desert cottontails, which are often found sharing the same habitat.

Desert Cottontail *(Sylvilagus audubonii)*

Track: Front 1–1³/₄ in. (2.5–4.4 cm) L x ³/₄–1³/₈ in. (1.9–3.5 cm) W

Small. Digitigrade. Very asymmetrical. Five toes: Toe 1 is greatly reduced but is clawed and occasionally registers in tracks. Digital pads are furred but often evident in tracks. Sole is furred and often indistinct. Nails may or may not register but are often evident in good substrate. Front tracks significantly smaller than rear tracks.

Desert cottontail bound.

Rear 1¹/₄–3 in. (3.2–7.6 cm) L x ⁷/₈–1³/₄ in. (2.2–4.4 cm) W

Small to medium. Digitigrade. Asymmetrical. Four toes. Furred sole is often indistinct. Significant furred heel often registers. Nails may or may not register but are often evident in good substrate. Tracks are pointy, unless splayed, in which case the anterior edge becomes rounded.

Trail: Bound Stride: 5–32 in. (12.7–81.3 cm)

Trail width: 2–5 in. (5.1–12.7 cm)

Group length: 6–14 in. (15.2–35.6 cm)

Notes:

- Bound when moving about and prefer to stay in or near thick cover.
- Often found sharing habitat with one or more jackrabbit species, as well as pygmy rabbits within their range.

Perfect desert cottontail tracks, showing their furry soles. Look closely at the single front track for the impression made by the fifth toe. Two hind tracks are facing the opposite direction. (CA)

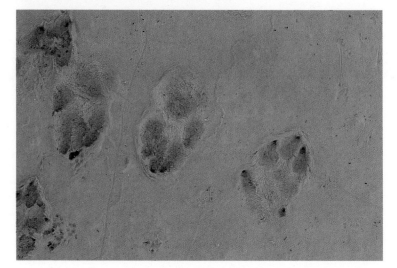

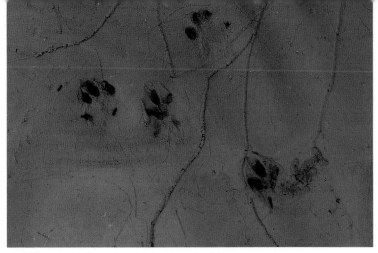

Splayed desert cottontail tracks in soft mud. (UT)

Left: Splayed tracks of mountain cottontail in a bounding gait show the digital pads clearly. (ID) *Right:* A desert cottontail's bounding pattern in which the front feet register next to each other and appear as a single track. (UT)

- Often seek shelter in existing burrows, such as those dug by black-tailed prairie dogs or badgers; they do not dig their own.
- Bound in deep snow, and drag marks are created following the midline of the trail.
- Solitary animals, although they often live in close proximity to others.

Eastern Cottontail
(Sylvilagus floridanus)

Track: Front   1–1⅞ in. (2.5–4.8 cm) L
x ¾–1⅜ in. (1.9–3.5 cm) W
(young: ¹¹⁄₁₆ x ⁷⁄₁₆ in. [1.7 x 1.1 cm])

Small. Digitigrade. Very asymmetrical. Five toes: Toe 1 is greatly reduced but is clawed and occasionally registers in tracks. Tracks are pointy. Digital pads are furred but often evident in tracks. Sole is furred and often indistinct. Nails may or may not register but are often evident in good substrate. Front tracks significantly smaller than rear tracks.

Rear 1¼–3¼ in. (3.2–8.3 cm) L
x ⅞–1¹³⁄₁₆ in. (2.2–4.6 cm) W
(young: 1½ x ⁹⁄₁₆ in. [3.8 x 1.4 cm])

Small to medium. Digitigrade. Asymmetrical. Four toes. Furred sole

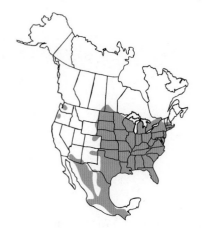

| Eastern cottontail bound. | Eastern cottontail bound (front tracks together). |

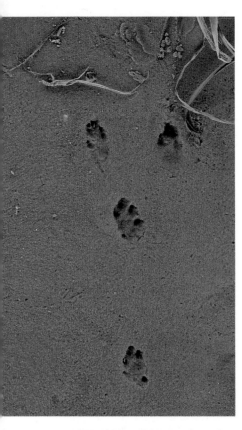

Eastern cottontail tracks in wet sand. (TX)

is often indistinct. Significant furred heel often registers. Nails may or may not register but are often evident in good substrate. Track are pointy, unless splayed, in which case the anterior edge becomes rounded.

Trail: Bound Stride: 5–32 in. (12.7–81.3 cm)

Trail width: 2¼–5 in. (5.7–12.7 cm)

Group length: 6–18 in. (15.2–45.7 cm)

Notes:

- Bound when moving about and prefer to stay in or near thick cover.
- In deep, light snow, all tracks register in one hole, and drags marks connect these holes, following close to the median line of travel. In contrast, squirrels leave drag marks at the outer edge of the trail pattern.
- Solitary animals, although they often live in close proximity to others.

Splayed Eastern cottontail tracks in clay. (NH)

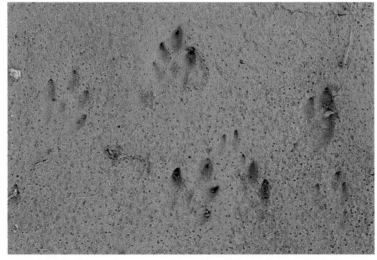

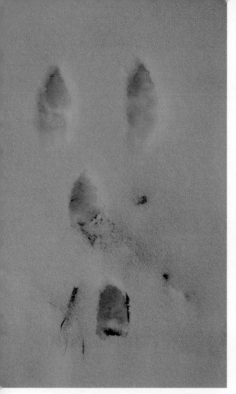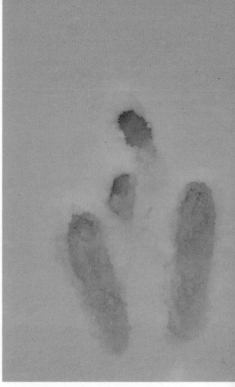

Left: Typical Eastern cottontail bound track pattern. (NY) *Right:* An Eastern cottontail sits and pauses for a moment. (NY)

Marsh Rabbit *(Sylvilagus palustris)*

Track: Front 1–1³⁄₈ in. (2.5–3.5 cm) L x ⁵⁄₈–1¹⁄₈ in. (1.6–2.9 cm) W

Small. Digitigrade. Very asymmetrical. Five toes: Toe 1 is greatly reduced but is clawed and occasionally registers in tracks. Tracks are pointy. Digital pads are furred but often evident in tracks. Sole is furred and often indistinct. Nails may or may not register but are often evident in good substrate. Front tracks smaller than rear tracks.

Rear 1³⁄₈–3¹⁄₄ in. (3.5–8.3 cm) L x ³⁄₄–1¹⁄₈ in. (1.9–2.9 cm) W

Small to medium. Digitigrade. Asymmetrical. Four toes. Furred sole is often indistinct. Significant furred heel may or may not register. Nails may or may not register but are often evident in good substrate. Tracks are pointy, unless splayed, in which case the anterior edge becomes rounded.

Trail: Walk Stride: 3¹⁄₂–6¹⁄₂ in. (8.9–16.5 cm)
Trail width: 3¹⁄₄–4 in. (8.3–10.2 cm)

Bound Stride: 6–30 in. (15.2–76.2 cm)
Trail width: 2³⁄₄–5 in. (7–12.7 cm)
Group length: 2–14 in. (5.1–35.6 cm)

Slow bounding gait of the marsh rabbit. (FL)

Notes:
- Hop and bound like other rabbits and hares when traveling or threatened; frequently walk when exploring, feeding, and stalking away from danger.
- Tend to stay in or near cover.
- Inhabit only the moist woods of the southeastern United States, including Florida, parts of Alabama, and portions of the coastal states up to Virginia.

Marsh rabbit walk.

A marsh rabbit's walking trail. (FL)

Snowshoe Hare
(Lepus americanus)

Track: Front $1^7/_8$–3 in. (4.8–7.6 cm) L
x $1^1/_8$–$2^1/_4$ in. (2.9–5.7 cm) W

Medium. Digitigrade. Very
asymmetrical. Five toes: Toe
1 is greatly reduced but is
clawed and occasionally
registers in tracks. Tracks are
pointy. Digital pads may or
may not be evident in tracks.
Digital pads and sole are
furred and indistinct. Nails
may or may not register.
Front tracks significantly
smaller than rear tracks.

Rear $3^1/_4$–6 in. (8.3–15.2 cm) L
x $1^5/_8$–5 in. (4.1–12.7 cm) W

Medium to very large.
Digitigrade. Asymmetrical.
Four toes. Digital pads and
sole are furred and often
indistinct. Significant furred
heel tends to register. Nails
may or may not register.
Tracks rounder than those
of other rabbits. When
splayed, snowshoe tracks
can be massive and easily
confused with dog tracks.

Trail: Bound   Stride: 8–72 in.
(20.3–182.9 cm) up
to 10 ft. (3.05 m)

Trail width: $3^3/_4$–10
in. (9.5–25.4 cm)

Group length: 8–30
in. (20.3–76.2 cm)

**Snowshoe hare
bound.**

**Snowshoe hare bound
(splayed tracks).**

Front track of a snowshoe hare in mud. (MA)

Notes:
- Although hare trails are often found under cover, they cross forest gaps and other areas frequently.
- Inhabit northern woodlands, especially those at higher altitudes, across the continent; in contrast, jackrabbits tend to be found in drier, more open country.
- Do not use burrows, but rest in forms; I have found them using snow caves when the temperatures were very low.
- I once found a hare that had jumped into the lowest branches of an apple tree and proceeded to climb about, feeding on the cambium layer.
- Tend to keep their rear feet parallel when hopping, except at full speed, when the pattern resembles that of the jackrabbit.
- Rear tracks vary tremendously, depending on substrate conditions and spread of toes. They are often misidentified as large canine, feline, or mustelid tracks.
- Populations are cyclic, peaking every nine years. Although solitary, their sign is found close to other hares.

Splayed snowshoe hare rear tracks in deep mud. (AK)

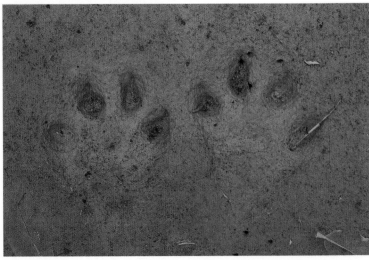

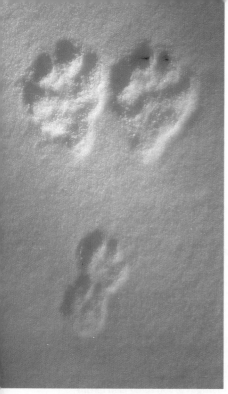
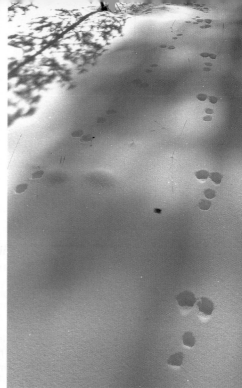

Left: **Splayed rear tracks support this snowshoe hare in 3 feet of snow. (MT)** *Right:* **A snowshoe hare trail moves away from the camera and then back again. (CO)**

Arctic Hare *(Lepus arcticus)*

Track: Front 2³/₄–3³/₄ in. (7–9.5 cm) L x 1³/₄–2¹/₂ in. (4.4–6.4 cm) W

Medium. Digitigrade. Very asymmetrical. Five toes: Toe 1 is greatly reduced but is clawed and occasionally registers in tracks. Tracks are pointy. Digital pads may or may not be evident in tracks. Sole is furred and indistinct. Nails may or may not register. Front tracks smaller than rear tracks.

Rear 4¹/₄–8 in. (10.8–20.3 cm) L x 2³/₈–3⁷/₈ in. (6–9.8 cm) W

Large to very large. Digitigrade. Asymmetrical. Four toes. Furred sole is often indistinct. Significant furred heel tends not to register in shallow substrates. Nails may or may not register. Tracks are pointy, unless splayed, in which case the leading edge becomes rounded. Arctic hare trails are much more similar to jackrabbit trails than snowshoe hare trails. Arctic hares are also significantly larger and heavier animals than snowshoe hares.

All Islands

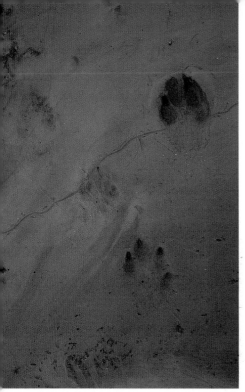

Left: Black-tailed jackrabbit tracks in mud. (CA) *Right:* Look closely at the first and second black-tailed jackrabbit track groups—in the first, the rear feet touch down together and push the animal into a "spy jump" to better assess the area from the crest of this hill; in the second, the animal lands before returning to a typical bounding gait. (CA)

Hind tracks of a black-tailed jackrabbit: Claws are often all that register in lago-morph tracks on hard substrates. (CA)

Notes:

- Use a modified bound in which one rear foot touches down before and in front of the other; because the rear feet do not land simultaneously, these gaits are technically gallops.

- Alternate long, fast bound-gallops with a more vertical jump to get a better view of their environment. Seton (1958) was the first to write about this behavior, and he called them "spy jumps." Since then, they have been discussed in scientific literature as well. Murie (1954) reported watching this species walk on several occasions.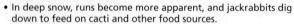

- Considerably smaller than the white-tailed jackrabbit, and in much of the desert Southwest, it is the only jackrabbit species present. Introduced and common on Nantucket Island.

- In deep snow, runs become more apparent, and jackrabbits dig down to feed on cacti and other food sources.

White-tailed Jackrabbit *(Lepus townsendii)*

Track: Front 2$\frac{1}{8}$–3$\frac{3}{4}$ in. (5.4–9.5 cm) L x 1$\frac{1}{2}$–2$\frac{5}{8}$ in. (3.8–6.7 cm) W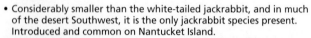

Medium. Digitigrade. Very asymmetrical. Five toes: Toe 1 is greatly reduced but is clawed and occasionally registers in tracks. Tracks are pointy. Furred digital pads and sole may or may not be evident in tracks. Nails may or may not register but often do so in good substrate. Front tracks smaller than rear tracks, but in shallow substrates, the two often have similar dimensions.

Rear 2$\frac{1}{2}$–6$\frac{3}{4}$ in. (6.4–17.1 cm) L x 1$\frac{5}{8}$–3$\frac{3}{8}$ in. (4.1–8.6 cm) W

Medium to large. Digitigrade. Asymmetrical. Four toes. Furred sole is often indistinct. Significant furred heel tends not to register in shallow substrates. Nails may or may not register. Tracks are pointy, unless splayed, in which case they become rounder at the front end. A smaller animal than the white-tailed jackrabbit.

Trail: Bound   Stride: 9–72 in. (22.9–182.9 cm) up to 19 ft. (5.8 m)
Trail width: 4$\frac{1}{2}$–9 in. (11.4–22.9 cm)
Group length: 20–45 in. (50.8–114.3 cm)

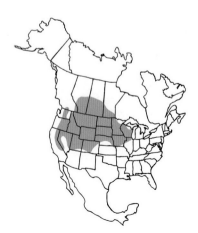

White-tailed
jackrabbit
bound.

Rear tracks of a white-tailed jackrabbit might be mistaken for canine tracks at a glance. (CO)

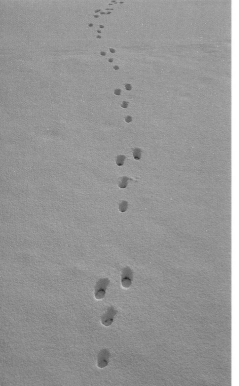

Notes:
- Use a modified bound in which one rear foot touches down before and in front of the other; because the rear feet do not land simultaneously, these gaits are technically gallops.
- The largest rabbit within its range; inhabits open habitats, including sagebrush deserts, high-elevation deserts, open forests, and mountain passes.
- In deep snow, runs become more apparent, and jackrabbits dig down to feed on cacti and other food sources.
- Forms are maintained at ground level, even in deep snow; digs might give the impression of a burrowing animal.

A white-tailed jackrabbit's bounding trail. (CO)

Runs, Ridges, Tunnels, and Eskers   3

After a considerable drive to revisit a wonderful, sandy lakeshore, where bobcats and coyotes run alongside bears and moose, I was disappointed to find that it had rained the night before. All potential tracks had been washed away, leaving a smooth surface of sand many miles long, broken by the occasional chipmunk that had ventured out from its burrow in the morning sun. So I took to an old road that paralleled the shore and decided to spend the morning exploring beyond the area I knew well.

Not long on the track, I crossed a beautiful mole ridge, pushed up as the animal struggled to dig through the compacted earth of the road. I stood and admired the handiwork and was thrilled when the end of the ridge moved and more earth was pushed upward—the mole was still there!

At first, I just watched and enjoyed the process, but then another thought surfaced: Would I be able to catch this mole? And that was the start of an internal argument: Was it right to disturb the animal for selfish reasons? I'd long since done my naturalist homework and knew that although three mole species inhabit New England, the hairy-tailed mole is the one that prefers sandy soils. The area where I stood was nearly completely sand. But I was also aware that the gap between theoretical knowledge, from reading and discussions with others, and experiential knowledge, gained from doing, can be very wide and deep, and the other side can be lost in a fog. I decided to give it a try, which by no means meant that I'd be successful.

Gingerly, I began to pull sandy clumps from the end of the ridge. The moment I made contact with the earth, all digging and movement ceased, so I decided to dig quickly. I soon unearthed all the loose soil and reached the spot where the mole had just been, a mere 8 inches (20.3 cm) under the surface of the dirt road. But there was no mole. Thinking ahead, I walked to the edge of the road where the ridge originated and compressed the ridge inward, knowing that if the mole moved backward the 7 feet (2.1 m) to this point, the ridge would have to be restored to ensure passage. With this safeguard in place, I began excavating the tunnel, moving from the end to the point I'd compressed. Closer and closer I approached the spot where the mole had to pass to escape. And then I reached the end of the road—no mole! I laughed to myself, amazed at the speed of the animal, which must have cleared 7 feet (2.1 m) of tunnel in mere seconds.

I stared at the exposed tunnel, now an excavated channel crossing much of the road. The tunnel surface lay 6 to 7 inches (15.2 to 17.8 cm) below the surface of the road, which did not receive much traffic but was still considerably harder digging than the surrounding woods. I was about to begin filling it all back in when a pink nose appeared from the edge, cautiously smelling the open air in the channel. Suddenly the entire mole burst into the channel and glided in an undulating fashion with remarkable speed toward the dead end. Without thought, I picked him up in my shirt. What a bundle of energy! He never ceased moving and continuously tried to dig through my hands and T-shirt. Quickly I escorted him to the moist sand nearby and placed him down for tracks. He wiggled across in the way that only a mole moves and then began to dig. I picked him up again and rushed him back to his tunnel network. Placed in the channel, he darted for cover, and I filled in the rut as best I could.

I couldn't stop smiling for four days. The experience was a revisit to childhood and catching small critters, and I marveled at the incredible energy of this mole. I'd seen the hairy-tail and had tracks and trails to measure and photograph. At least one gap in my knowledge had been bridged.

Runs

A run is nothing more than an accumulation of footprints over time. Any animal is capable of creating a run—all it requires is that the same route be used again and again by a single animal or by members of a species. Runs may be large and obvious, such as the migration trails of caribou, which are visible from planes, or they may be incredibly subtle, such as those created by stealthy predators. And many species share established runs, making them more difficult to interpret. Bobcat scat is found along porcupine runs, just as coyote scat is found on deer trails.

I interpret runs not only by studying the actual sign itself but also by pulling from my general knowledge of animals and of animals in the specific locale I am tracking. Some animals are more likely to create runs than others, and this likelihood increases with the density of that species in a given area. Fisher runs are uncommon, except in the immediate vicinity of their dens or temporarily around a large cache, but

Left: **Close inspection of a mule deer run reveals the many tracks that created it. (CA)** *Right:* **A black-tailed jackrabbit run in desert sand dunes. (CA)**

ground squirrels, shrews, deer, and bison are among those that commonly create this sign.

Start with an assessment of the width and shape of the run, especially if it has been made in a context where you can deduce vertical height. Is the bottom of the run narrower than the space created by animals passing just several feet above the ground? Is there a V shape to the bottom, which is more characteristic of deer, or more of a U shape or square bottom, which is more characteristic of bears and rabbits? Is there a "roof" of vegetation? The vertical component of runs is extremely helpful in their interpretation.

Be aware that vegetation, debris, or snow may be packed down for other reasons, such as deer yarding or bears feeding extensively. Packed vegetation does not always mean a run. Patience is critical. Search out associated signs for confirmation, such as scat, hair, beds, browse, or burrows. These associated signs add to the certainty of your interpretation. Following are descriptions and measurements of several species, organized from the smallest run width—the distance from one side to the other—to the largest.

Shrew mole. I've found shrew mole trails worn in where they were forced to cross areas of hard-packed soil between debris. Widths range from 5/8 to 1 inch (1.6 to 2.5 cm).

Shrew. Shrew runs are most obvious in the debris layer. Widths range from 5/8 to 1 1/2 inches (1.6 to 3.8 cm).

Vole. Voles tend to form runs under cover, but also cross areas where low vegetation provides some security. Meadow vole run widths range from 1 1/4 to 2 1/2 inches (3.2 to 6.4 cm).

Kangaroo rat. Run width varies, based on the size of the kangaroo rat responsible. Runs spiral out from feeding locations and burrow systems, and can be quite exposed and far-reaching.

Woodrat. Woodrats form runs between areas of good cover; they are found in close proximity to their

A shrew mole run across an old, overgrown road surface. (WA)

An example of the interconnecting runs of meadow voles. (NY)

Left: A desert kangaroo run and burrow. (CA) *Right:* A bushy-tailed woodrat run connects a burrow with foraging areas. (MT)

nests and are much closer to cover than the runs of kangaroo rats, with which they often share habitat. Widths of white-throated woodrat runs range from 2^1/2 to 3^1/4 inches (6.4 to 8.3 cm).

Pika. Pikas form runs in the immediate vicinity of their burrows and haystacks. They are often detectable only in vegetation, which may be sparse in areas of highest activity. In high-elevation forests of the Cascades and elsewhere, greater vegetation makes runs more prominent. Widths are approximately 3 inches (7.6 cm).

Ground squirrel. Many species of ground squirrels form conspicuous runs between burrows and in and around burrow systems. These runs are often well worn, with square, sharp edges. The widths of thirteen-lined ground squirrel runs are between 2^3/4 and 5 inches (7 and 12.7 cm).

Cottontail. Cottontail runs have rounded edges and are found in meadow and edge habitats; look for tunnels in low-growing shrubs and thickets.

Pika trails radiate outward from a cache site. (CO)

Left: A thirteen-lined ground squirrel run and concealed burrow entrance. (CO)
Right: A California ground squirrel run. (CA)

A muskrat run. Note the accumulation of scat on a raised scent mound near the bottom of the photo. (ME)

Muskrat. Muskrats form runs between water sources and leading from burrow systems (in habitats where they do not build lodges) to feeding areas. You can also find them connecting ponds to each other over quite large distances, as well as connecting ponds to feeding areas on land. The walls of muskrat runs are usually vertical, like those of other rodents, and they have square edges. Widths range from $3^1/2$ to $5^1/2$ inches (8.9 to 14 cm).

Snowshoe hare. Snowshoe hare runs are more like cottontail than jackrabbit runs, in that they have softer and rounder edges. Widths range from 4 to 8 inches (10.2 to 20.3 cm).

Jackrabbit. Jackrabbits form runs in a variety of substrates, most easily discernible in snow. Although all species form runs, black-tailed jackrabbit runs are particularly impressive. In southern Idaho, in about 16 inches of snow, the walls of these runs were 10 inches high. Of all the rabbits, the black-tailed jackrabbit makes runs with the most vertical and crisp walls and edges. Widths range from 5 to 9 inches (12.7 to 22.9 cm).

Porcupine. Porcupine runs lead directly from trees, rock ledges, or other cover to feeding areas—often a grove of mast-producing trees or conifers in the winter. Runs are also

A snowshoe hare run. (ME)

Above left: A black-tailed jackrabbit run. (CA) *Above right:* A white-tailed jackrabbit run. (WY)

found following wetland edges. Scat and quills should be evident along the runs. The walls of porcupine runs are not as crisp as those of smaller rodents. Widths range from 6 to 9 inches (15.2 to 22.9 cm).

Collared peccary. Peccary runs are found in all sorts of environments but lead from feeding area to feeding area, with bedding spots in between; watering holes and wallows also tend to have worn runs entering and leaving in several directions. Look for obvious latrines along runs

Left: This porcupine run emerged from the cover of rocky cliffs and led deep into a hemlock grove, where animals foraged during winter seasons. (MA)

(often under cover), at high points of the trail, or in a pass between two elevated areas. Widths range from 5½ to 8 inches (14 to 20.3 cm).

Raccoon. Raccoon runs are common along streams and in wet areas. In the Southeast and in metropolitan suburbs, where populations can be quite high, their runs form vast networks through swamps and thick vegetation. Widths range from 7 to 12 inches (17.8 to 30.5 cm).

Otter. Otters create worn runs connecting water sources, across peninsulas, and occasionally paralleling water sources. Look for scent mounds, rolls, and other marking behaviors anywhere along their length, but most often at exits and entrances into water bodies and at high points on the journey. Widths range from 6 to 12 inches (15.2 to 30.5 cm).

Beaver. Beavers form conspicuous runs leaving water sources and heading into areas for logging and feeding. These trails wear into the earth in a very short time, as beavers concentrate feeding and harvesting efforts in a small area before moving on in search of another. Runs can be long, but they are short when compared with runs of other species, and they always start or end with a water source. Look for a "cut" in the

Below left: **A peccary run leading to and from a regular watering hole. (AZ)** *Below right:* **A raccoon run parallels a nearby stream. (VT)**

bank where they enter and leave the water, and "combed" debris or earth created by beavers towing brush.

Mountain sheep. Dall's and bighorn sheep are responsible for many runs in high, steep terrain. Mountain goats also form runs. These trails are quite conspicuous and can be spotted from a great distance.

Deer. Deer runs are common, and hunters and naturalists quickly become familiar with this sign in the field. Deer runs can be very dramatic, but as with the runs of other ungulates, they are quite narrow, considering the size of the animal. The run is often more V shaped than square, and there is no vertical component—or it is quite high. The occasional low obstacle is not a problem, as deer duck under 2-foot (.6-m) (or lower) overhangs without hesitation.

This beaver run leads from river to cornfield, where animals foraged. (MA)

Dall's sheep runs in high mountain tundra. (AK)

Above left: White-tailed deer runs are especially conspicuous as snow levels rise and animals use packed runs to conserve energy. (MT) *Above right:* A mule deer run. (CA)

They generally do not go over an obstacle unless there is no alternative or they are running.

Pronghorn. Pronghorns form runs very similar to those of deer in open grassland habitats. If you can, follow these trails to a fence, and note that pronghorns always go under rather than over. Look for hair caught on such obstacles.

Elk and moose. Elk and moose runs are larger versions of deer runs. I've walked elk runs in moist habitat in coastal Oregon, and they look

Right: An elk run. (CO)

Left: **Buffalo runs in an open grassland. (WY)** *Right:* **This black bear run formed quickly during heavy foraging of an area during the berry season. (NH)**

similar to human trails in their dimensions. Look for scats and other signs to confirm the presence of moose and elk.

Bison and cattle. Bison and cattle leave obvious runs in open country. Look for them in grasslands and range. Be warned, however, that cattle runs can be encountered in a variety of habitats, including some surprisingly remote places on public lands. Whether buffalo or cow, there should be plenty of accompanying scats to help you interpret their signs.

Bear. Bears create traditional runs, as discussed above, but this is the last phase in an accumulation of sign and trail characteristics over time. The term *bear trail* often refers to a set of worn circles where bears repeatedly place their feet in the same spot each time they pass through the area. Black and brown bears create these trails, which appear as a zigzagging line of worn circles in debris.

Video footage of bears using these trails shows a rather stiff gait, in which the foot is twisted while on the ground, as if to purposefully deepen the trail pattern. Many researchers believe that these trails are a marking behavior, whereby bears leave scent from the glands on their feet and rub it into the earth.

The substrate and litter conditions greatly influence the appearance of these trails. In the Northeast, the trails of black bears are quite common near wetlands but are difficult to see in areas of annual deciduous leaf drop. In mosses, trails become quite obvious and beautiful. I often find these trails following wetland systems and ridgelines in the Northeast, but occasionally near dumps as well. In the West, brown bear trails are often worn in along salmon streams. Bears also frequently use human trails. Bear trails in the West often cut off a hiking trail leading up to a regular mark tree and then cut back in a bit farther on. These trails can also be created relatively quickly, as when a grizzly is feeding at a carcass. Naturally, such trails fade after the bear has moved on.

The next phase of a bear trail is for the worn circles to connect and become two ruts, like an old wagon trail. These trails are most often observed on the tundra, made by grizzlies. The next phase of trail degradation is a worn path. In this case, runs made by black bears tend to measure 10 to 14 inches (25.4 to 35.6 cm) wide, while those made by grizzlies and brown bears can measure up to 20 inches (50.8 cm).

Other carnivores also form runs, which are most obvious near bedding areas and den sites. Cougars, coyotes, and wolves leave subtle runs on the

Left: Look closely for the worn circles of a regular black bear trail. This one followed the edge of a large wetland system. (NH) *Right:* Worn circles are evident in this regular brown bear trail. (AK)

Above left: This wide, worn brown bear trail paralleled a salmon stream in coastal Alaska and was used regularly each year. (AK) *Above right:* Coyotes, especially in the West, form some of the more obvious predator runs. (TX)

landscape, and with training, you'll be able to pick these out. Who would leave a subtle run paralleling obvious deer runs on elevated terrain? I've measured wolf runs, ranging from 8 to 12 inches (20.3 to 30.5 cm) across, near rendezvous sites. Coyotes form more obvious, meandering runs in deep snow, using them to travel between hunting areas and to continue their rounds. Depending on the depth of snow, these runs might be mistaken for deer runs.

Left: A regular coyote run in deep snow, used to travel between foraging areas. (WY)

Channels

Beavers are responsible for creating most channels, which run from ponds or stream up into good logging habitat. The channels are dug only wide and deep enough to hold water and float heavier timber out to the main pond, where it can be used in construction or placed in a winter cache.

From time to time you'll find old channels after water levels have dropped; they are substantial runs that could be confused only with trails or ditches dug by humans. Following such a channel from end to end will likely help in its interpretation. If it is surrounded by old beaver-cut stumps at one end and disappears into a wetland system or slowly revegetating clearing at the other, you likely have found an old beaver channel.

I've also seen muskrats make smaller channels in swampy conditions, but nothing as industrious as beaver channels. Muskrat channels are generally short connections between water sources and are less than half the width of beaver channels. Nutrias may also create channels.

Left: This silted beaver channel was exposed when a dam broke. Note the beaver and raccoon tracks moving to and fro. (MA) *Right:* Muskrat channels in wetland vegetation. (ME)

Ridges in Vegetation and Debris

Raised ridges in the debris layer may be made by moles, but they are more likely the work of shrews, shrew moles, or sometimes voles. Just as moles work underground, shrews tunnel through leaf litter in search of prey. I've spent many afternoons watching short-tailed shrews work an area of leaf litter this way. When I pulled back the cover to reveal what they had been up to, I occasionally found the still writhing remains of earthworms or beetle carapaces left as signs of passage.

I also recommend an afternoon or two following the obvious runs of meadow voles in tall, drooping dry grasses. Runs lead all over the place and are filled with feeding signs, latrines, and, if you are persistent, a nest site tucked in a tight clump of grass. You are likely to hear the screeches of aggressive and territorial voles as you explore. Remember to cover up the runs you've exposed before you leave; otherwise, the predators will be left with an unnatural advantage.

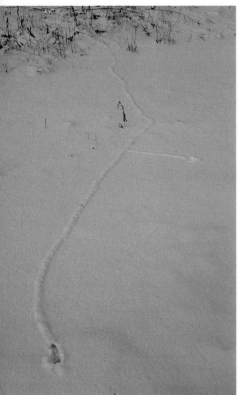

Tunnels under Snow

I've watched voles and shrews make raised ridge trails in light snow cover. The term *subnivean* refers to travel within the snow layer. It is interesting to note, though, that as snow deepens, the tracks and movements of certain small mammals become rarer. Both voles and shrews are active throughout the winter, but they travel atop the snow layer far less frequently than white-footed mouse species, whose tracks are common in winter. Once in a while I come across a shrew trail that travels a great distance over the top of the snow layer. I've often wondered whether this is due to their predatory lifestyle. Do they eat an area out and then set off in search of a new area to exploit? Rarely have I seen voles surface and travel such distances.

A subnivean trail of a meadow vole. (NY)

Actual size exit/entrances to snow tunnels.

A American mink: 1⁷/8 to 2¹/8 in. (4.8 to 5.4 cm)
B Marten: 3 to 3¹/4 in. (7.6 to 8.3 cm)
C Pygmy rabbit and red squirrel: 2¹/2 to 3¹/2 in. (6.4 to 8.9 cm)
D Weasel: ⁷/8 to 1¹/4 in. (2.2 to 3.2 cm)
E Cinereus shrew: ⁵/8 to ¹¹/16 in. (1.6 to 1.7 cm)
F Vole and short-tailed shrew: ³/4 to ⁷/8 in. (1.9 to 2.2 cm)

The only reminder that these small mammals are still with us in winter is the occasional owl print; owls hunt by sound and plunge through the snow to pluck a surprised victim from within. Foxes, coyotes, and bobcats also pounce on voles through the upper snow layer, being able to locate and track animals with their superior hearing.

Larger mammals also travel below the snow surface, increasing their safety as they move across the landscape. Pygmy rabbits and red squirrels are among those that create tunnel systems between homes and feeding sites. All the weasels, from martens down to least weasels, also tunnel in snow, knowing that the hunting may be better within the snow layer than above it.

Raised Ridges and Trails

Obvious raised ridges in the earth are the work of moles, which create extensive, shallow underground networks of tunnels for hunting in warmer months. Moles keep more permanent trail networks deeper underground, where nesting and winter feeding occur. The dirt removed when excavating at this deeper level is pushed up into surface tunnels or into molehills. Surface tunnels, the ridges we see, may be used only once or temporarily while hunting a given area. Whether the tunnels are shallow or deep, moles patrol them relentlessly, consuming all insects and invertebrates that have burrowed through the earth and found themselves in the tunnels.

These trails and tunnels, whether made in earth, leaf litter, or snow, also become common property over time. Moles, voles, shrews, and mice make their own tunnels, but they also readily take to those made by other species.

Insects also create ridges. The most abundant signs of termites in Mexico's tropical forests are the

A raised ridge created by a hairy-tailed mole traveling near the surface. (MA)

muddy trails that follow the trunks of trees up to the foliage. These raised ridges are hollow on the inside, where the termites travel in astounding numbers, keeping them safe from the many predators that would like to make a meal of them.

Trail Castings and Eskers

As the snow recedes with spring temperatures, the signs of some rodents reappear—animals we may have forgotten about during the winter months. You might find tubular deposits of earth, called eskers or trail castings, snaking across the landscape, forking and reconnecting like a network of trails. These are the deposits and

A casting of northern pocket gopher tunnels. (CO)

Numerous northern pocket gopher eskers in sagebrush habitat. (CO)

Soggy trail castings made by meadow voles. (VT)

signs of pocket gophers' underground digging with claws and teeth and their burrow expansions. Snow tunnels made during the winter are used for collecting nest materials, feeding, and moving about. They are also used as holds for dirt moved during continuous underground excavation work. Thus the layout of these eskers reveals where pocket gophers moved through the winter season.

Voles also create eskers, although they have smaller diameters. I've often found small, short sections of dirt deposited by meadow voles during the winter months, but I've yet to find them leaving long sections, beyond several feet, as is common of pocket gophers' eskers.

Murie (1954) states that aplodontia also leave eskers under snow, and that they measure approximately 6 in. (15.2 cm) in diameter.

Beds, Lays, Wallows, Baths, Nests, Burrows, Dens, and Cavities

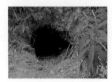

4

While snowshoeing with friends in northern Montana, we discovered a drained beaver pond and an exposed dam and lodge. The dam ringed most of the pond, an 8-foot (2.4-m) wall of sticks, packed earth, and debris. The lodge was one of the largest I've ever seen, easily spanning 25 feet (7.6 m) long and 10 feet (3 m) high. The entrances loomed invitingly—certainly large enough to squeeze inside.

Every condition was perfect. We were wearing less winter clothing than usual, because it was so warm, and the glaring sun was bound to force light into the darkest recesses of the lodge. So we stripped excess bulk, dropped packs, removed snowshoes, and, one at a time, entered the beaver's domain.

The interior of a beaver lodge is breathtaking in its beauty—adobe-style clay walls with the exposed, chewed ends of sticks like massive eyes for adornment. Each of the two entrances had level floors that, depending on the water level, could be used for a shake or preen before entering the main compartment. Both entrances then sloped up to a midlevel, where cleaning and feeding could be done in times of high water. From this point, a central, wide slope led up to the main compartment, which was large and spacious. Two of us easily fit in this compartment on our sides and a bit curled up.

This was an exceptional lodge in wonderful condition and not long abandoned. It was so much larger on the inside than I had imagined, and the smooth walls of packed mud and wood framing made a lasting impression. I've included a sketch of this particular lodge's layout, and encourage anyone to take the opportunity to crawl inside a beaver lodge should the chance arise.

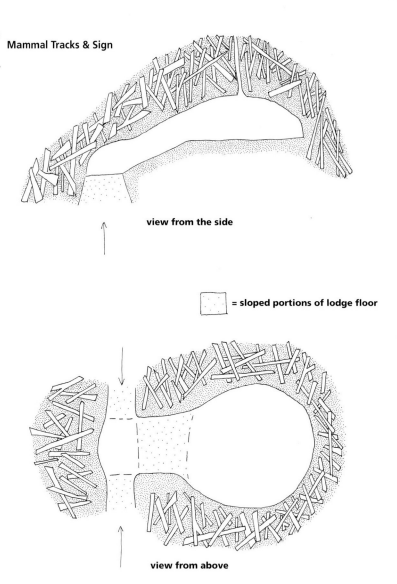

view from the side

□ = sloped portions of lodge floor

view from above

A Montana beaver lodge.

Animals come to rest in beds, burrows, nests, and cavities. They raise young in dens, relax in forms, and wallow in baths. There's something exhilarating about finding the spot where an animal lives or has lain down to rest. These are private places, selected for their secrecy and seclusion. The variety of sign found, from simple beds to complex burrows, is rich and rewarding. During your analysis, keep associated signs in mind, such as fur, scents, scats, or the feeding area or kill site that multiple beds and trails might indicate is near.

Beds, Lays, and Forms

Hoofed Animals

Deer lie on their sides, with their front feet tucked under them and their rear legs out to one side. Thus, the two easily identifiable features in an ungulate bed are the "knees," where the front legs bend back under the body, and the backside, which is a well-defined curve. In a group, animals tend to lie or bed in such a way that their heads face in different directions; this affords greater protection against predators. Ungulates lie down often. Joyal and Ricard (1986) backtracked moose during the winter, studying rates of defecation and bedding in a 24-hour period. The moose in their studies averaged 8.7 lays or beds per day; other researchers have documented averages of 5.

Compare a Dall's sheep lay, just visible in green vegetation, with a well-worn bed found higher on the same mountain. (AK) Dall's sheep beds measure 24 to 35 inches (61 to 88.9 cm) long by 14 to 20 inches (35.6 to 50.8 cm) wide; those of bighorn sheep measure 25 to 40 inches (63.5 to 101.6 cm) long and up to 10 inches (25.4 cm) deep.

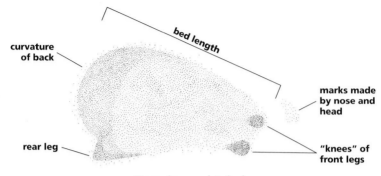

curvature of back

bed length

marks made by nose and head

rear leg

"knees" of front legs

Measuring ungulate beds.

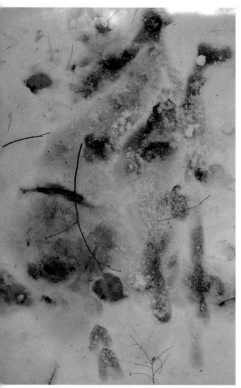

A beautiful white-tailed deer bed. Paired knee prints are clear at the top of the picture, and the curve of the back and hind leg is visible at the bottom. A fisher cruises through as well. Deer beds measure 25 to 42 inches (63.5 to 106.7 cm) long. (NH)

The overall length, the longest measurement across an oval, and ecological clues can help differentiate many ungulate beds. When young animals are involved, identification can be difficult. For example, moose calves fall into the elk range, and elk calves fall within the deer parameters. Often these youngsters are accompanied by adults, which helps alleviate any uncertainty. Remember to consider ecological clues and associated signs such as scats, tracks, parasites, and hair pulled from the beds themselves.

There is still great discussion about how to differentiate the terms *lay* and *bed*. Here is my interpretation: It is a lay when an animal lies down temporarily while out on a feeding circuit. It may take this opportunity to rest, socialize with others, or chew cud. The stay is short, and the animal is unlikely to return to this exact area to lie down for some time. The sign consists of compressed vegetation and does not last long. It is a bed when an animal spends a longer amount of time and returns to an area repeatedly. My fieldwork supports the assertion by

A pronghorn bed in grass. Beds measure 25 to 35 inches (63.5 to 88.9 cm). (WY)

An elk bed. Beds measure 39 to 52 inches (1 to 1.32 m) long. (OR)

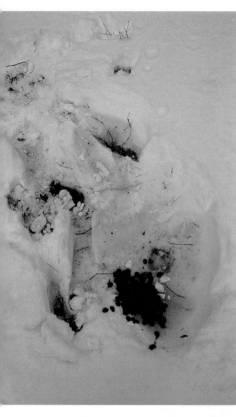

The mark near the front feet of this moose bed was made by the head. Beds measure 52 to 75 inches (1.32 to 1.9 m) long. (VT)

Rezendes (1999) that deer reuse beds. Bighorn and Dall sheep reuse their beds so often that they become quite worn, in contrast to the temporary sign left by their lays. Look for beds on steep ground that provides greater protection at night.

Canines

I tend to use the term *bed* to describe the circle left by a sleeping canine or other animal. The shape of beds is a useful clue when deciphering species. Coyotes, foxes, and wolves sleep in perfect circles in cold months, with their heads wrapped around their legs and their tails covering their noses. In warmer weather, they may

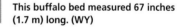

This buffalo bed measured 67 inches (1.7 m) long. (WY)

Arctic fox beds (pictured) measure 9¹/₂ to 11¹/₂ inches (24.1 to 29.2 cm) in diameter. Red fox beds measure 11 to 14 inches (27.9 to 35.6 cm) in diameter. (Canada)

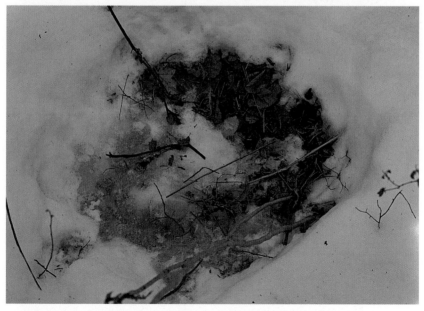

Eastern coyote beds, like this one, measure 14 to 23 inches (35.6 to 58.4 cm) in diameter. Oval beds may be as narrow as 13¹/₂ inches (34.3 cm) (MA)

Circular wolf beds measure 22 to 27 inches (55.9 to 68.6 cm) in diameter. Oval beds such as this one measure 26 to 30 inches (66 to 76.2 cm) long by 21 to 26 inches (53.3 to 66 cm) wide. (MN)

Look closely for the worn ovals in the debris layer created by wolves repeatedly bedding near a rendezvous site. (MN)

sprawl out, leaving ovals and other larger shapes. For the most part, canines lie down without any preparation when a spot is chosen, but they may also scratch to prepare the surface. Look for their beds out in the open, on knolls in shrubby wetlands, in steep terrain, and atop boulders.

I've found areas where wolves have bedded so many times that they have worn ovals into the debris layer. These sites are tucked under cover and are likely linked to rendezvous sites, or "aboveground dens," where packs continue to care for growing pups. Interestingly, it appears that these areas may continue to be revisited through the winter when the pack is in that part of its territory.

Felines

Cats bed on their sides but lie up on their haunches while hunting. Beds are long-term places of rest and are most often found under cover. Cats only occasionally leave the perfect circles of sleeping canines; rather, cat beds are typically kidney or lima bean shaped. Rather than atop a boulder, like a coyote, cougar and bobcat beds are found below boulders or under rock overhangs, upturned root wads of large trees, and low-hanging vegetation. More secure places may also be used, such as caves or other structures that provide greater protection. In some areas, cats bed in trees. While canoeing in the farm country of eastern Kansas, my friends and I spooked two napping bobcats on tree limbs in one day.

Cats "lie" in wait. It is a hunting strategy very different from that of canines. Cats move through areas of rich prey, pausing often or sitting. They also wait in *hunting lays*. These are easily differentiated from resting beds in snow, because the animal is not on its side. Hunting lays are narrow, long beds or, if the cat moved to face various directions during the stay, a wider packed-down area. The cat is not resting but is more

Look closely for the depression made by a resting bobcat in this accumulated leaf litter under a rock overhang. Bobcat beds measure 15 to 22 inches (38.1 to 55.9 cm) long by 11 to 17 inches (27.9 to 43.2 cm) wide. Cougar beds measure 28 to 35 inches (71.1 to 88.9 cm) long by 22 to 28 inches (55.9 to 71.1 cm) wide. (MA)

A lynx bedded in the cover created by these fallen trees and snow. They often lie out in the open, and their oval beds measure 15 to 21 inches (38.1 to 53.3 cm) long by 13 to 17 inches (33 to 43.2 cm) wide. I measured a first-winter kitten bed at 15 by 10 inches (38.1 by 25.4 cm). (ME)

vigilant than ever, waiting for prey to come along. Its feet are tucked under it, ready to react quickly should an opportunity present itself; imagine a sphinxlike posture. Compare the hunting lays of lynx, which measure 16 to 20 inches (40.6 to 50.8 cm) long by 8 to 10 inches (20.3 to 25.4 cm) wide, with their resting beds, which measure 15 to 21 inches (38.1 to 53.3 cm) long by 13 to 17 inches (33 to 43.2 cm) wide.

Bears

Bears bed in varied terrain, but often under the cover of thick vegetation, such as mountain laurel, or in young fir stands. I've also found them on high ground in shrubby wetlands and on small exposed knolls in steep terrain. Black bears often bed at the base of a good climbing tree, such as a mature white pine or hemlock—rather like sleeping next to the fire escape. The beds may be round or oval, depending on the location and the weather, and some beds are used repeatedly. Both black and grizzly bears also prepare beds by tearing limbs from shrubs and trees in the area and building a mattress to keep them off the ground. I asked Lynn Rogers, noted bear biologist, about "constructed beds." He said that it was not unusual to see bears prepare beds in Minnesota when temperatures were below freezing, but he had never observed bears preparing beds in warmer weather. I too have found bear beds only in cold months, and all but one in snowy conditions.

This black bear bed was made in the center of a laurel thicket. Oval beds measure 29 to 39 inches (73.7 to 99.1 cm) long by 22 to 33 inches (55.9 to 83.8 cm) wide, or they may be perfect circles. (NH)

This prepared bed was made by a black bear that was still out and about when significant snow settled and temperatures dropped. The entire mattress was created with mountain laurel branches and foliage and was 8 to 10 inches (20.3 to 25.4 cm) thick. (CT)

A multiuse grizzly bear bed found in the middle of an evergreen stand, near where the bear was feasting on lily bulbs. Beds measure 32 to 42 inches (81.3 to 106.7 cm) long by 24 to 34 inches (61 to 86.4 cm) wide. (MT)

Polar bear beds measure 38 to 48 inches (96.5 to 121.9 cm) long. (Canada)

This striped skunk bed measured 10³/₄ inches (27.3 cm) in diameter and was found in the chicken coop he'd raided. (NH)

Other Carnivores

I've found striped skunks sleeping in perfect circles and have seen raccoons leave nearly perfect circles in forest debris. Some beds may not be on the ground. Cats, coatis, raccoons, and others rest on tree limbs or rock ledges. Raccoons and gray foxes are known to sleep in abandoned bird nests and on abandoned squirrel dreys.

Other animals bed in cavities and burrows, which I generally refer to as "holing up." Raccoons, skunks, and opossums hole up during cold weather, as do gray foxes, which tend to sleep in burrows or wood piles or under other such shelter.

Rabbits

Members of the rabbit family tend to use lays rather than burrows. These resting spots are called *forms,* and they are often used again and again, wearing into the earth. Look for these depressions at the base of shrubs under cover or hidden in a grass clump. It is in the safety of these retreats that rabbits rest and reingest their cecal pellets.

White-tailed jackrabbits continue to rest in forms at ground level, even when snow mounds all about them. The entrances to these forms can be quite conspicuous in snowy terrain, as mud accumulates at the entrance with each use.

Pikas and pygmy rabbits hole up and dig burrows, described later. Pygmy rabbits will also use forms near their burrow entrances.

The well-worn form of an eastern cottontail. Forms measure 6 to 8 inches (15.2 to 20.3 cm) long by 4 to 6 inches (10.2 to 15.2 cm) wide. (NY)

A brush rabbit's form. (CA)

This black-tailed jackrabbit form was hidden in a large grass clump and measured 12 inches (30.5 cm) long by 5 inches (12.7 cm) wide. (TX)

A white-tailed jackrabbit's form that measured 14 inches (35.6 cm) long by 8 1/2 inches (21.6 cm) wide by 4 inches (10.2 cm) deep. (CA)

Birth in the Woods

One of the most amazing wildlife experiences I've ever had occurred while leading a tracking workshop for 24 Boy Scouts in north-central Massachusetts. We were moving through a cutover woods, an area dominated by 6-foot white pine trees growing in loose clusters. Suddenly, she was before me—a porcupine in the throes of giving birth! I stuck out my arms to protect her, and all the Boy Scouts collided and stacked up behind me like dominoes.

She lay at the base of a small pine in a bed of leaves that she seemed to have gathered and packed down in a circular area for the event. She was obviously distressed by our arrival, but it was too late to stop the process, so we witnessed a smaller version of this porcupine appear before our very eyes. The mother paid little attention to the youngster and proceeded to climb the white pine. She reached a height of 4 feet before the thin top began to bend, so there she stayed, eyeing us suspiciously.

All the boys had a good look as they filed past; I stayed to guard the scene and absorb the experience. The young porcupine was soaking wet and glistened as she moved; apparently, the moisture keeps the quills soft during birth to protect the mother. She opened her eyes almost immediately and lay there, wiggling her front toes and blinking at us—such innocence and beauty in eyes seeing the world for the first time.

We were quick to leave, allowing the mother to welcome and care for this new life. At the end of the day, I tried to emphasize how lucky we were to have witnessed such an event, yet the boys seemed to think that it was just another day in the woods, and that anyone who took a workshop with me was sure to see such things.

Dust Baths and Wallows

Dust baths are believed to reduce and remove parasites, maintain coats, scent mark an area, and help remove unwanted fur during shedding. Many rodent species dust bathe, as do bison, Dall's sheep, cottontails, black-tailed jackrabbits, and numerous bird species. I've also found cottontails and grouse dust bathing in the remains of rotting conifer logs.

Dall's sheep inhabit terrain where it's often difficult to roll without risking life and limb. Rather, they dig out areas on steep hillsides and then rub against the vertical wall exposed by their hooves and hard labor. They occasionally bed on these shelves as well. These sites function like vertical dust baths and are easily identified by the shedding fur stuck to the earthen walls.

Merriam's kangaroo rat dust baths measure 4¹/₂ to 5 inches (11.4 to 12.7 cm) long by 2¹/₂ to 3 inches (6.4 to 7.6 cm) wide. (CA)

This golden-mantled ground squirrel dust bath measured 7 inches (17.8 cm) long by 3³/₄ inches (9.5 cm) wide. (CO)

Black-tailed prairie dog dust baths measure 9 to 14 inches (22.9 to 35.6 cm) long by 4 to 8 inches (10.2 to 20.3 cm) wide and are often located in the throw mounds of their burrow entrances. (MT)

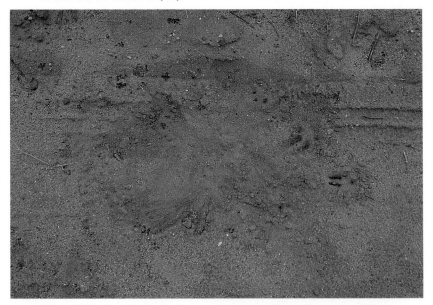

Black-tailed jackrabbit dust baths measure 16 to 17 inches (40.6 to 43.2 cm) long by 11 to 12 inches (27.9 to 30.5 cm) wide; these are similar to the dimensions of roadrunners' dust baths. (CA)

Buffalo dust baths measure 5 to 14 feet (1.5 to 4.3 m) in diameter and are often found with other dust baths, clumped in open grassland habitat. (WY)

The areas dug out and rubbed by Dall's sheep measure 8 to 9 feet (2.4 to 2.7 m) across. Look closely for the white fur clinging to the vertical earthen wall. (AK)

This collared peccary wallow measured 26 by 27 inches (66 by 68.6 cm). Wallows created by feral hogs are much larger. (AZ)

A black bear wallow; this one was heavily used in midspring. (NH)

Wallows in mud and wet areas may serve the same purposes as dust baths, but they are also used when an animal needs to cool down. In addition, a layer of mud provides some protection against biting flies and the like. Bears, hogs, bison, and peccaries wallow. Moose and elk create rut pits and wallow during the rut, but this is strictly a scenting behavior (described in chapter 5).

Nests, Dreys, and Lodges

Mice, Shrews, and Voles

Small rodents and insectivores build circular nests of grasses, tree bark, and other soft, stringy material under the cover of earth, snow, wood-piles, grass clumps, or refuse. Many are constructed underground and will not be visible to a tracker who does not dig. Those that are above-ground require some searching, but occasionally we find them in unex-pected places—tucked close to the engine of a car or in a woodpile. In general, shrews construct nests underground, but smoky shrews and occasionally short-tailed shrews are among those that build nests of grasses under logs or rocks.

Voles, too, often build underground and beneath other cover, such as old plywood left in a field. But when snow settles deep for long periods,

This meadow vole nest measured 9 by 11 inches (22.9 by 27.9 cm), and the inner chamber was 2 by 2¹/₂ inches (5.1 to 6.4 cm). Typical meadow vole nests measure 4 to 5 inches (10.2 to 12.7 cm) in diameter. Southern red-backed vole nests measure 3 to 4 inches (7.6 to 10.2 cm) in diameter. (NY)

Another meadow vole nest. Nests are often built within vegetation, which provides further structure and protection. (WY)

The grass nest of a northern bog lemming is revealed when lush new growth is pulled back. The nest measured 6 inches (15.2 cm) in diameter. (AK)

A pocket gopher nest remains after the snow has melted. Note the mass of scats accumulated on the backside of the nest, which reveals the shape of a tunnel used for a winter latrine. (CO) Photo by Chris Maser.

A deer mouse constructed a roof for this bird nest to create a secure and warm winter nest. White-footed mouse nests measure 3 to 6 inches (7.6 to 15.2 cm) in diameter, and those of jumping mice measure 5 to 6 inches (12.7 to 15.2 cm). (ME)

voles build numerous nests at ground level, and these can be found by those exploring as the snow recedes in spring. Pocket gophers also take advantage of deep snow cover and build nests at ground level. Look for them to be revealed by spring thaws, when the gophers are forced to relocate belowground until the following winter.

Mice commonly build nests aboveground, and these can be found anywhere with ample cover—behind bark slabs or in woodpiles, car vents, old nests, cavities, grass clumps, dense brush, and so on. Mice also build spherical nests up in the air, supported by and attached to tall sedges, grasses, and farm crops, and along the limbs of trees and shrubs. Harvest mice are renowned for their beautiful woven spheres found in fields and in shrubs (3 1/2–6 in., 8.9–15.2 cm), but many mouse species construct such nests. Harvest mice and others often maintain several nests simultaneously; in the case of harvest mice, one may be used as a latrine site.

Mice also move in and refurbish abandoned bird nests, often weaving a roof and creating a new exit in the floor. Look for middens of mast to give away a nest's location; on several occasions, I've found nut and seed remains inside the nests of white-footed mice. There are also documented cases of chipmunks constructing nests in shrubs and trees, although this is rare.

Red Tree Voles

Red tree vole nests are easily mistaken for squirrel nests from the ground. They also renovate old bird or woodrat nests, making long-range identification even more difficult.

The nest of a red tree vole. (OR) Photo by Chris Maser.

Maser (1998) describes the construction of nests as a haphazard affair occurring over time. Harvested and discarded twigs and feces accumulate, creating a base, and then grow until the vole can burrow into the accumulation for cover. Eventually, a scat-free sleeping quarters is established, which is lined with dry resin ducts accumulated while feeding (these ducts transport sap to the foliage and are discarded when voles eat individual needles). There may be numerous tunnels and runs through the nest, but all nests maintain one path heading straight down the center, which is used for escape in case a marten or other predator comes knocking. The entire structure may be 1 to 2 feet (30.5 to 61 cm) in diameter.

Maser also writes that the location of these nests is determined by the age of the tree. Whereas nests are found on the outer limbs of old-growth trees as high as 200 feet (60.96 m) above the ground, they tend to be built near the trunk in younger trees at about 60 feet (18.3 m) off the ground.

Foraging for twigs involves some travel, but food is often brought back and eaten atop the nest. Over time, the layer of scat and resin ducts forms into a sort of plaster roof. This is the sign researchers are looking for when trying to locate and document active red tree vole nests.

Cottontails

Cottontail nests are the creation of both construction and digging. The female digs a hole 4 to 6 inches (10.2 to 15.2 cm) deep and approximately 5 to 8 inches (12.7 to 20.3 cm) in diameter. This is where she leaves her defenseless young while foraging and resting. With hair pulled

A cottontail's nest; the young have matured and dispersed. Note the "roof" constructed of grass and fur. (NY)

from her belly and mixed with surrounding debris, often grasses, she weaves a lid to cover the nest and camouflage her young. These nests are quite common but are difficult to detect.

Squirrels

The squirrel drey, or nest, is a ball of leaves held together by a woven framework of twigs nipped in the vicinity. The ball is stuffed with leaves and eventually lined with softer materials, such as dried and worked inner barks. Squirrels often maintain several dreys within their home range. These structures are most evident just after leaf fall, when suddenly the trees become barren except for the drey, a round ball of leaves somehow suspended in the canopy.

Left: This red squirrel nest was constructed in an outside grill stored on an elevated porch. Grasses and the inner bark of aspens were woven to provide warmth and comfort, and metal substituted for tree branches to provide structural support. (ME)
Right: A gray squirrel drey. Dreys measure 12 to 19 inches (30.5 to 48.2 cm) in diameter. Those of southern flying squirrels measure about 8 inches (20.3 cm.) in diameter, and those of Abert's squirrel measure 12 to 36 inches (30.5 to 91.4 cm). (MA)

Many squirrel species create these nests, but we are most likely to see the work of gray squirrels that live close to us. Fox, flying, and red squirrels also build these structures in which they spend the cold months of winter. Gray squirrels tend to build their dreys out on the limbs of deciduous trees, while red squirrels tend to build their nests near the trunk in coniferous trees. However, these are not hard-and-fast rules. Flying squirrels may also build spherical dreys, although they are more likely to move into and refurbish dreys constructed by another squirrel species or seek shelter in available cavities. Their dreys are typically constructed of finer materials, and I've seen a few that looked like they were made of grasses rather than twigs and leaves. Gray squirrels are also known to build smaller and flatter versions of their nests on which to rest and feed. Look for these resting platforms, especially in the southern portions of their range.

It's possible to confuse the nest of a red tree vole with a squirrel, corvid, or raptor nest. From below, bird nests may be difficult to distinguish—look from an angle to better see the circular construction of squirrel and vole nests, and consider the construction materials. Dried, dead leaves are not a major component in bird nests, but they are in squirrel nests.

Woodrats

Woodrat nests vary according to species and available materials. They may be built among the low-growing prickly pear cactus, placed in between rock slabs, or built up to 50 feet (15.2 m) aboveground in a tree. Regardless of their variety, woodrat nests are easily identifiable by their disorderly appearance, ornamental additions, and the scat accumulations at the entrances, below the nest and in the immediate vicinity. Ornaments vary from rocks and bones of other creatures to cow dung and human garbage. A woodrat may maintain up to three nests, and these structures will continue to be used and maintained over time as one woodrat passes on and others move in to stake a claim. Woodrats are great collectors and continue to use nest sites for long periods of time. Recent research in their middens has resulted in astounding discoveries of artifacts of incredible age.

Consider the variety of nests presented here, two built by the dusky-footed woodrat. These photos emphasize the effects of context on the resulting nest. Any immediately available materials will be used, and the protective shelter provided by houses, other structures, and even dresser drawers is always a welcome addition. Nests vary in a few ways. Some are built completely aboveground, and house a small chamber lined with fine, soft vegetation. Many start with a burrow, which is covered with the bulk of the nest. When the nest is new, the burrows will be quite obvious, sometimes with only a handful of collected materials at the

This dusky-footed woodrat nest is constructed entirely of oak debris and branches and measures 56 inches (1.42 m) high and 77 inches (1.96 m) across at the base. Nests have been recorded up to 8 feet (2.44 m) tall. (CA)

A desert woodrat nest constructed in an abandoned dresser drawer, which was left on the second floor of an abandoned, dilapidated barn. (CA)

A second dusky-footed woodrat nest to emphasize how environment influences the resulting nest. This one was constructed 15 feet (4.6 m) aboveground in a massive pine tree. (CA)

Where white-throated woodrats and prickly pear cacti coincide, look for nests built within the protection of this cactus species. Nests often conceal burrow entrances. (TX)

This large desert woodrat nest was constructed under a rock overhang and measured 5 feet (1.5 m) across. (CA)

front door, but with time and an accumulation of collectibles they will be lost deep under the pile of debris.

From a distance, I once mistook a magpie nest in a small tree in the desert for a woodrat nest. Upon closer inspection the difference was clear—the bird nest was woven of even-diameter branches, unadorned, and was not surrounded in feces. Ample scat is liberally spread around all active woodrat nests and is likely within the nest materials as well.

Muskrats and Beavers

Beaver lodges are impressive, unmistakable shelters of cut wood and mud. Branches and tree trunks are pruned and cut to length before being placed and cemented with a muddy mixture collected from the pond bottom. These structures are strong and over time are often expanded. When abandoned, lodges may be used to raise wolf or otter pups or by denning black bears.

Beaver lodges built along banks often use a different construction strategy. Beavers are competent diggers and tend to excavate bank burrows below the water level when moving into new areas or into habitats with moving and deeper waters. The burrow is the living quarters, and the lodge, if there is one, is a fortification to provide additional protection at the entrance.

Beaver lodges are built, used, and abandoned; used by others; reclaimed by beavers; and eventually collapse in on themselves over time. How do you know if a lodge is occupied? Associated signs, such as fresh scent

The entrance to this beaver lodge was exposed when the lower dam to a large pond broke several years earlier. Since then, this second lodge and dam were constructed, maintaining water levels in a much smaller pond. (MA)

While standing on a beaver's lodge, one gets a close-up look at the exposed ends of the winter cache. Note the run atop the lodge, which the beavers traveled while carrying mud and wood for construction purposes. (NH)

mounds and fresh feeding signs, are the easiest way to tell that beavers are currently using a wetland system, or look for fresh mud or freshly stripped wood decorating the lodge in question. A fish and wildlife biologist once told me that the best way to determine if a lodge is inhabited is to jump on it and see if any beavers appear. I suggest looking for a winter cache, which is a common addition to lodges in the north. Each fall, beavers collect fresh wood and stick it in the mud on the pond's bottom in front of their lodge—the portions of these sticks and saplings breaking water look like a collection of odd shrubbery midpond. A sizable cache is a sure indicator of resident beavers, which will feed from this cache when the ice has sealed the pond shut until the spring thaw.

Beavers also construct dams, which inevitably cause rising water levels and flooding. Beaver dams may be constructed of only mud and plant materials dredged from the pond bottom and measure only a foot high. More often, dams are complex structures of lumber cut and brought to the site, along with mud, other natural cements, and rocks found below the surface of the water.

Beavers start constructing dams by securing large lengths of wood in the stream bottom, one end facing into the current. More wood, often smaller pieces, is piled, held by the longer lengths, and arranged in such a way as to create a lattice wall on which mounds of mud, muck, and other additives are placed and packed down by the force of the water and by the beavers themselves until the dam is nearly waterproof. These dams can be massive, ranging up to 10 feet high and spanning incredible distances. Dams more than a mile (1.6 km) long have been reported. Beavers often create a series of dams in a water system; collectively, these are called *beaver steps* or *terracing*.

Muskrat and round-tailed muskrat lodges are built of softer materials than beaver lodges, avoiding woody branches that require teeth and jaws of a different caliber. Reeds, cattails, and phragmites are typical plants used by muskrats. The lodge is often built in shallow water, to allow a sturdy base, or anchored to logs, snags, or other available resources. Cattails and reeds may be bent over to provide a building base as well.

Muskrat lodges are quite simple affairs; plant materials are mixed with mud and mounded until a suitable size is attained. Then the muskrat hollows out a living compartment. I have taken apart abandoned lodges, and they usually have one entrance-exit, although larger lodges may have several. The entrance leads up to a small chamber created above the water level, where the muskrats congregate and huddle to stay warm. These lodges can be quite small, standing less than 2 feet (.6 m) above the water level, or they can be quite large, holding several muskrats and standing 4 feet (1.2 m) above the water, with an ever wider base.

Muskrat "push-ups" and feeding platforms might be confused with lodges. In winter, a hole is maintained in the ice, and debris is pushed up onto the surrounding ice. These push-ups accumulate debris and feeding signs (often the same plants used for construction) and may reach impressive dimensions.

Muskrats also den in banks and take up residence in beaver lodges as well. Lynn Rogers set up a video camera in a beaver lodge near the

A muskrat lodge. (MA)

A muskrat push-up and hole, which was maintained during winter while the pond was frozen. (NH)

This round-tailed muskrat lodge was collected in the field and placed on display at Payne's Prairie State Preserve. Lodges measure 7 to 24 inches (17.8 to 61 cm) in diameter and are constructed without mud. (FL)

Northwoods Research Center where he works. For the entire winter, he watched a beaver family in their lodge, as well as the pair of muskrats that shared the single chamber. He was even lucky enough to capture a mink on film, which swept in one day and killed one of the muskrats.

The round-tailed muskrat, or Florida water rat, builds a smaller nest, most often of maiden cane grasses, which it also eats. These nests are most often found in shallow freshwater wetlands, where this grass species is abundant. Unlike muskrats, round-tailed muskrats do not use any mud in their nest construction. But like muskrats, they also dig burrows in riverbanks near deep water and in ponds and other wetlands during droughts and low water levels.

Muskrats, round-tailed muskrats, and nutrias also weave mats of buoyant vegetation on which to feed and sun. These mats can be found within tight vegetative growth in shallow waters or floating free in deeper waters. Look for feeding remains sprinkled across their surfaces and associated signs in the area to determine which species is responsible. Also know that vegetation may accumulate and stick together due to currents and storms; this could be confused with mammal sign.

Dirt Mounds

Dirt mounds may or may not reveal the whereabouts of a nest. Moles create molehills when digging at a deep level and pushing the excavated earth into surface tunnels and beyond ground level. Certain species of mole are more likely to create molehills than others. Pocket gophers

Molehills of an eastern mole. (MA)

The mound of a giant pocket gopher. Note the plugged exit hole. (OR)

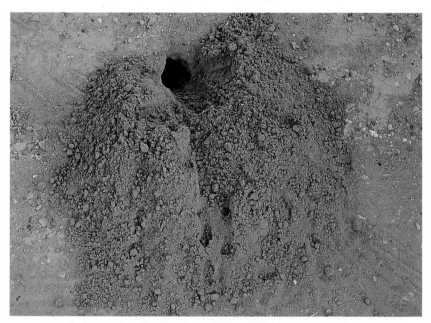

I disturbed this yellow-faced pocket gopher while he was pushing out dirt so that I could photograph a mound with an open entrance. (TX)

This very large mound of a Texas pocket gopher likely holds a nest. (TX)

create mounds when pushing excavated earth out from their burrow systems onto the surrounding ground. When they are finished hauling dirt, pocket gophers tend to plug the exit. Thus, one of the best ways to differentiate between the much smaller molehills, created by moles pushing dirt upward, and the larger gopher mounds, created by pocket gophers pushing dirt out of a hole, is to look for a burrow entrance in the mound, which may be plugged and difficult to detect. Also consider the overall shape of the mound. Molehills are circular, while pocket gopher mounds are fan shaped, with the entrance being the pointy end of the fan from which dirt radiates. Some pocket gopher species, including Texas and Plains pocket gophers, create even larger mounds within which they build their nests. Some Texas pocket gopher mounds I measured were 3 1/2 feet (1.07 m) wide at the base and stood 2 1/2 feet (76.2 cm) tall.

Burrows and Dens

Many mammals make homes, nests, tunnels, caches, and dens beneath the ground. Certain species spend most of their lives beneath the surface, while others divide their time above and below. Still others retreat to underground chambers only to bear and raise young or to escape the heat of the day.

The burrows and dens of North American mammals are distinguished by using a combination of physical characteristics and ecologi-

A desert pocket mouse's burrow. Pocket mouse burrows measure $7/8$ to $1^3/16$ inches (2.2 to 3 cm) in diameter. (TX)

Desert pocket mouse holes. (TX)

This cineurus shrew burrow measured $3/4$ inches tall by $7/8$ inch wide (1.9 by 2.2 cm). Note the accumulation of scats at the entrance. (AK)

Short-tailed shrew burrows such as this one measure 1 to $1^1/4$ inches (2.5 to 3.2 cm) in diameter. (VT)

Meadow vole burrows like this one measure 1 to 1³/₈ inches (2.5 to 3.5 cm) in diameter. (VT)

The burrow of a star-nosed mole at a latrine site. Mole holes are 1 to 1³/₈ inches (2.5 to 3.5 cm) in diameter. (VT)

Kangaroo Rats

Numerous kangaroo rat species live in North America, and their count-less burrows are always apparent in the arid areas they inhabit. Know the natural history of the kangaroo rats in your area, because some species are more communal than others, and groups of burrows are a helpful indicator of which species you have found. Many species plug the burrow entrance for the day, especially in extreme heat. These plugs may not be evident, however, as some are made within the burrow.

Small and medium kangaroo rats, such as Merriam's and Ord's kan-garoo rats, tend to create either round burrows or burrows that are taller than wide. Larger kangaroo rats, such as the giant and desert kangaroo rats, inhabit round burrows and burrows that are a bit wider than tall. These are only tendencies, however; the width of all burrows is influ-enced by two additional factors: soil and length of use. Burrows in soft soils are wider, as are those that have been used for longer periods.

Some species also form communities and create great mounds of dirt in which there are numerous burrow entrances. The chisel-toothed kan-garoo rat is one such species; its mounds are reported to be up to 2 feet (61 cm) high and 13 feet (3.96 m) wide.

Merriam's kangaroo rat burrows measure 1³/₄ to 2³/₄ inches (4.4 to 7 cm) tall by 1³/₄ to 3 inches (4.4 to 7.6 cm) wide and occasionally larger, if you measure the outer-most rim. Merriam's kangaroo rats are not very social; there is generally a single bur-row entrance on each side of a bush, under which the burrows are often made. (CA)

Gulf Coast kangaroo rat burrows measure 2³/₄ to 3¹/₄ inches (7 to 8.3 cm) tall by 2¹/₂ to 3¹/₄ inches (6.4 to 8.3 cm) wide. In loose sand, burrows may be 4¹/₂ by 4 inches (11.4 by 10.2 cm). (TX) For comparison, the circular burrows of agile kangaroo rats measure 1³/₄ to 2¹/₄ inches (4.4 to 5.7 cm) in diameter, and the oval entrances of Ord's kangaroo rat burrows measure 2⁵/₈ to 3¹/₄ inches (6.7 to 8.3 cm) tall by 2¹/₂ to 3¹/₄ inches (6.4 to 8.3 cm) wide.

Giant kangaroo rat burrows measure 2³/₄ to 4¹/₂ inches (7 to 11.4 cm) tall by 2¹/₂ to 4¹/₂ inches (6.4 to 11.4 cm) wide. They also dig vertical tunnels without dirt mounds of about 2¹/₄ inches (5.7 cm) in diameter for emergency escape purposes. (CA)

Desert kangaroo rat burrows measure 2¹/₂ to 4¹/₄ inches (6.4 to 10.8 cm) tall by 3¹/₂ to 6 inches (8.9 to 15.2 cm) wide and are conspicuous in desert dune habitats. (CA)

Chipmunks

These semifossorial mammals (those that spend only a portion of their lives belowground) use burrows year-round for resting and protection. They also slow their metabolism and heart rate in winter, although not to the extent of ground squirrels. Throughout winter, chipmunks wake every few days to feed on a store of seeds and mast in another chamber of their burrow system and occasionally to run aboveground in the snow.

Chipmunk burrows show some variety, but there are features that most share. Many burrows have single entrances, but others have several. Some are used only for escape and evasion, while others are true burrows where animals nest and store food. Regardless of function, entrances are clean—there is no throw mound of dirt or discarded food remains, as is found with many small and medium rodent species. Chipmunks remove debris, soil, and food remains out a "back door," where it is scattered to avoid attracting attention; then this entrance is plugged until it's needed again. Any debris or soil at the "front door" is also scattered and smoothed down.

The entrances made on flat earth tend to go straight down for a hand's length before turning off at an angle. Many similar burrows of kangaroo rats, ground squirrels, and others have angled entrances. Look for chipmunk burrows on well-drained slopes and above the floodplain. In addition, many chipmunk species use existing nooks and crannies in screes and rock jumbles rather than dig burrows.

Least chipmunk burrows measure 1¹/₄ to 1³/₄ inches (3.2 to 4.4 cm) in diameter. (CO)

Eastern chipmunk burrows measure 1¹/₂ to 2 inches (3.8 to 5.1 cm) in diameter. (NY)

Antelope Squirrels

White-tailed and other antelope squirrels may dig their own burrows, which look similar to those of kangaroo rats, but a bit rounder and larger. However, their tendency is to use existing holes rather than construct their own, or to dig their own chambers off an active or abandoned kangaroo rat burrow. White-tailed antelope squirrel burrows range from $1^{3}/4$ to $3^{1}/2$ inches (4.4 to 8.9 cm) tall by $2^{1}/2$ to 4 inches (6.4 to 10.2 cm) wide and are occasionally larger if well established.

Norway Rats

Norway rats use any existing crevice or hole, or they may dig their own burrows if suitable substrate is available. I've not seen many burrows, but those I have seen were tucked up against human structures in root cellars, farm buildings, and the like. The burrows were circular and ranged from 2 to $3^{1}/4$ inches (5.1 to 8.3 cm) in diameter.

Red Squirrels

Red squirrels build nests, use cavities, and use burrows to store food as well as to spend the winter in. Often their burrows require little digging, because they either use an existing hole or create one that allows access to a root system, which has numerous air pockets and chambers for

Red squirrel holes measure $2^{1}/2$ to 3 inches (6.4 to 7.6 cm) tall by $2^{1}/4$ to 3 inches (5.7 to 7.6 cm) wide and are often in close proximity to middens and feeding perches. (MA)

Golden-mantled ground squirrel burrows measure 2¹/₄ to 3¹/₂ inches (5.7 to 8.9 cm) tall by 2¹/₄ to 3¹/₄ inches (5.7 to 8.3 cm) wide. Unlike other ground squirrel species, they do not create throw mounds at burrow entrances. (CO)

Thirteen-lined ground squirrel burrows measure 2 to 3³/₄ inches (5.1 to 9.5 cm) tall by 1³/₄ to 3³/₄ inches (4.4 to 9.5 cm) wide. Note that unlike other ground species, there is no throw mound at the entrance. (CO)

food storage and sleeping quarters. They may sleep amidst their larder or keep separate burrows for living and food storage.

Red squirrel burrows, when used for caching, are often surrounded by a midden or very close to one. The squirrels run down the hole, retrieve a cone, and then return to the entrance to perch and feed, ever watchful for predators. Burrows used only for sleeping are harder to detect, but snow reveals their runs and travels.

Ground Squirrels

Ground squirrel burrows are often conspicuous affairs, with a throw mound of dirt announcing their presence and scat sprinkled in the vicinity. Ground squirrels are diurnal, so obvious signs include the squirrels themselves or their screeching alarms when you enter their range.

Ground squirrels disappear for a portion of the year, those living farther north for the longest time. Many species, including Columbian and Arctic ground squirrels, retire to a separate hibernaculum for the winter months after plugging the entrance with dirt and spreading the throw mound to better camouflage the site.

Uinta ground squirrel burrows measure 2 to 4¹/₂ inches (5.1 to 11.4 cm) tall by 2¹/₂ to 3 inches (6.4 to 7.6 cm) wide. For comparison, Wyoming ground squirrel burrows measure 1³/₄ to 3 inches (4.4 to 7.6 cm) tall by 2 to 2¹/₂ inches (5.1 to 6.4 cm) wide and Columbian ground squirrel burrows measure 3¹/₂ to 5¹/₂ inches (8.9 to 14 cm) tall by 3⁷/₈ to 5¹/₂ inches (9.8 to 14 cm) wide. (MT)

California ground squirrel burrows measure 2³/₄ to 4¹/₂ inches (7 to 11.4 cm) tall by 2³/₄ to 4¹/₂ inches (7 to 11.4 cm) wide, and occasionally up to 6 inches (15.2 cm) in diameter. (CA)

Arctic ground squirrel burrows measure 3¹/₂ to 5 inches (8.9 to 12.7 cm) tall by 3¹/₂ to 5 inches (8.9 to 12.7 cm) wide, and occasionally up to 8 inches (20.3 cm) wide if long established. Iwen (Wilson and Rupp, 1999) writes that they also dig deep pits where they have successfully beaten a rival. (AK)

Black-footed ferret excavations are often referred to as "troughs" and are easily differentiated from the work of prairie dogs. (SD) Photo courtesy of the Black-footed Ferret Program, Badlands National Park.

Black-footed Ferrets

Black-footed ferrets are associated with prairie dogs, which constitute the vast majority of their diet. Ferrets often move into and renovate prairie dog burrows, but they may also dig their own chambers off an existing burrow system. Because the entrance is often a prairie dog burrow and therefore indecipherable, study the signs of excavation to confirm resident ferrets. Rather than pushing dirt back through their legs and creating great fans of earth to create a throw mound, ferrets walk backward holding loads of dirt in their front paws. These long, narrow troughs are unique and are easily distinguished from the digging habits of the prairie dogs that surround them.

White-tailed Prairie Dogs

The burrows of this species look very much like those of other prairie dogs, with the exception of rim craters created by black-tailed and Mexican species (see above). Burrows are either wide mounds of excavated earth surrounding an entrance or escape tunnels, which are more vertical shafts without throw mounds.

Mountain Beavers

Aplodontia, or mountain beavers, dig great networks of shallow tunnels, as numerous angry hikers will attest; I have fallen into their traps many times. They create multientrance burrow systems, with holes approximately 6 inches (15.2 cm) in diameter. There is often a throw mound of dirt at the entrance and a pile of vegetation, either stacked and being dried for later consumption or pulled out and discarded. Good aids in identification are habitat and knowing that where you find one aplodontia burrow, there are certain to be others.

White-tailed prairie dog burrows measure 4 to 6 inches (10.2 to 15.2 cm) tall by 4 to 6 inches (10.2 to 15.2 cm) wide, and occasionally up to 8 inches (20.3 cm) in diameter. (CO)

Mountain beavers are greater architects, constructing additions at the front entrances when terrain or angled slopes create the potential for rain to flood the burrow system. Look for burrows with "tents" of sticks, which function like awnings, woven and placed at exposed entrances on steep terrain.

Armadillos

The few armadillo burrows I've seen were placed in root systems of large trees, stream banks, or steep banks along agricultural fields. Substantial throw mounds of earth are evident,

Aplodontia burrows measure 3¹/₂ to 5¹/₂ inches (8.9 to 14 cm) tall by 4 to 8 inches (10.2 to 20.3 cm) wide. Note the fresh and old discarded ferns that decorate the throw mound. (WA)

This armadillo burrow measured 7 inches (17.8 cm) tall by 7 inches (17.8 cm) wide and had tracks and trails radiating out in every direction. (FL)

but these fade with time and use. Active burrows have ample tracks and trails coming and going.

Nutrias

I have not seen many nutria burrows, but those I have seen were all wider than they were tall and were connected by a worn run to nearby water sources.

Kit Foxes

The kit fox dens I've found were simple holes in the ground, steeply angling down out of sight. Throw mounds tend to be flattened down and to spread out over time. These may be near cover or quite exposed,

Nutria burrows measure 7 to 10 inches (17.8 to 25.4 cm) tall by 8 to 12 inches (20.3 to 30.5 cm) wide. (TX)

Kit fox dens measure 7 to 9 inches (17.8 to 22.9 cm) tall by 7 to 8 inches (17.8 to 20.3 cm) wide. This den was dug on flat ground and angled down steeply into dark depths. (CA)

with only open ground all around them. In dune habitats, I've located dens in islands of tall shrubs whose roots provided support and structure for den systems.

Woodchucks

Woodchucks use burrows throughout the year for resting, safety, and raising young. They also spend the entire winter safely curled up in their burrows, allowing their heart rates to slow from 75 to 4 beats per minute.

Woodchuck burrow systems have between two and ten entrances, although the average is about five. Many have conspicuous throw

A swift fox excavates a new den just above a streambed, at the edge of vast grasslands. (CO)

Woodchuck burrows measure 5¹/₄ to 6¹/₄ inches (13.3 to 15.9 cm) tall by 6 to 11 inches (15.2 to 27.9 cm) wide, and sometimes larger. (NY)

mounds and are easy to locate. Others are more concealed and cleaner and are used for escape and evasion.

Some woodchucks relocate with the winter season, digging additional burrows on slopes in forests near the meadows that are their summer homes. The use of separate winter burrows is often found in areas susceptible to spring flooding. After the waters have settled and the growing season is under way, the animals return to their summer residences.

Yellow-bellied and Hoary Marmots

Hoary and yellow-bellied marmots, like other marmots, either seek refuge in rock slides and natural crevices or dig burrows in suitable terrain. Burrows are obvious affairs, with large throw mounds and often radiating runs into feeding areas and to regular perches, where scat accumulates and sunning is best. When marmots use natural crevices, grasses collected for the nest and beds are often visible peeking out from between rocks—don't confuse this sign with a pika's haystack.

Hoary marmots are considered more gregarious than yellow-bellied marmots, so their burrows may be found in groups. Also consider elevation when you believe you've found a marmot burrow. These creatures inhabit high-elevation forests and are most often seen above the tree line. However, in the far northern parts of hoary and Alaska marmot ranges, burrows are also found at low elevations.

Yellow-bellied marmots live in smaller colonies than do hoary marmots. Their burrows measure 6 to 9 inches (15.2 to 22.9 cm) tall by 6 to 11 inches (15.2 to 27.9 cm) wide but are occasionally a bit larger. (CO)

Badgers

Badgers dig burrows to excavate and catch prey, escape the heat of the day, rest while on forays, and shelter young. Burrows have characteristic throw mounds, which fan out from the entrances and become packed down over time. Badgers tend to work an area over before moving on, and where you find one burrow, you'll likely find many others.

Hoary marmot burrows measure 6 to 9 inches (15.2 to 22.9 cm) tall by 6 to 12 inches (15.2 to 30.5 cm) wide, and occasionally a bit larger. Note the run leading to the left away from this burrow entrance. (WA)

Badger burrows measure 6 to 10¹/₂ by 7 to 10¹/₂ inches (15.2 to 26.7 by 17.8 to 26.7 cm). (ID)

Red Foxes and Coyotes

Red fox and coyote dens are similar in many ways—one a larger version of the other. Two entrances are common, and the main entrance often has a conspicuous throw mound of dirt, where signs of feeding and scat accumulate. Both species often bed at the entrance, so hairs and tracks should also be evident. Both animals move their pups if greatly disturbed, and they often have a backup den or two nearby.

J. D. Henry (1993) studied 65 red fox dens and found that most were in forests, but very near meadows or other forest openings and within 100 yards of water. Dick Decker, a fox biologist in Alberta, found that fox dens were nearer roads and farm buildings than were those of coyotes. He hypothesized that the foxes were better tolerated by ranchers, which offered them some sort of protection, because coyotes that lingered near ranches tended to have shorter life spans.

Beavers

Beaver bank burrows become evident in times of low water levels or when dams are breached and pond levels drop. The entrances are large, between 1 and 2 feet (30.5 to 61 cm) in diameter, and cannot be confused with much else. However, should water levels drop and stay low, these spacious compartments will be used by a host of other mammal species.

The front (above) and rear entrances of a red fox den. Entrances measure 6 to 12 inches (15.2 to 30.5 cm) in diameter. The entrances to coyote dens measure 13 to 24 inches (33 to 61 cm) in diameter. (NY)

A beaver's bank burrow. (MA)

Wolves

Wolf dens are larger versions of other canine dens, but the number of animals present might be greater, because pack members help in the caretaking of the young. When pups reach a certain age, they are relocated to a secure area aboveground, commonly referred to as a *rendezvous site*. These areas have worn beds, well-packed vegetation, and chewed "toys," such as old bones, antlers, and sticks, littering the area.

Wolf dens measure 20 to 30 inches (50.8 to 76.2 cm) tall by 25 to 35 inches (63.5 to 88.9 cm) wide, and may be up to 30 feet (9.14 m) deep. This particular den sloped down gradually about 15 feet (4.57 m) to a large chamber approximately 4 feet (1.22 m) in diameter. (MN)

Black Bears

Black bears den in a wide variety of places, including within blowdowns, excavated root systems, caves, crevices, dense thickets, tree hollows, culverts, or thick brush; under decks and porches; or even at the base of a tree fully exposed. Many researchers believe that bears gain experience with age and choose better den sites with successive years.

Brown Bears

Brown and grizzly bear dens are most often dug into the southern slopes of exposed terrain above the tree line. In the extreme Northwest, the direction of the slope selected for den sites varies much more often than

Left: A black bear den. The entrances vary tremendously but are often between 18 and 23 inches (45.7 and 58.4 cm) in diameter. (NH) *Right:* This grizzly den is in a natural crevice. The interior was hardly excavated—just flattened out for comfort. Den entrances measure 35 to 45 inches (88.9 to 114.3 cm) tall by 35 to 45 inches (88.9 to 114.3 cm) wide and may be 8 feet (2.44 m) deep. (AK)

in other places, and some bears may even dig a den under a downed tree or in a root system in a lower-elevation forest. Bears also use existing cavities or create dens under boulders and other such protection. Often a bear starts several dens before settling down with one. These *den starts* are often visible on high, exposed slopes—large, gaping holes with massive throw mounds of dirt—beginning in early fall.

Polar Bears

Not all polar bears dig dens, and this behavior is most often associated with pregnant females. Unlike black and brown bears, polar bears do not hibernate. In fact, in their southern ranges, such as the Hudson Bay population, they are most active and gain weight during the winter, when ice forms and allows them to hunt seals.

Polar bear dens vary, depending on the amount of snow that has fallen. In southern ranges, bears often dig into the tundra layer and may create caves, much like brown bears. Or they may dig a bowl in the tundra and allow snowfall to provide the roof and insulation. Both methods are common, and these sites are used year after year. In areas with more snow, bears dig snow caves, fully equipped with an entrance and ventilation hole.

The entrance to this polar bear den was 28 inches (71.1 cm) tall, and the circular interior measured 5 by 5 feet (1.5 by 1.5 m). (Canada)

Look for claw marks in the walls of this polar bear den dug in tundra. (Canada)

Secondary Users and Natural Cavities

Should an animal dig a burrow and then move on, that hole in the ground may not stay unoccupied for long. There are many other species willing to take up residence to rest, spend the winter months, or even raise young. These animals are termed *secondary users*. Raccoons, coatis, skunks, opossums, bobcats, fishers, otters, and minks are some of the many mammals that seize the opportunity to use an existing burrow system dug by another. Secondary users are identified with

Exiting and returning trails of a striped skunk revealed the resident of this culvert during the cold winter months. (NH)

Vegetation growing at entrances to natural cavities is an aid in interpretation. Here, 4-inch (10.2-cm) diameter holes reveal where pikas entered and exited the boulder jumble below. (WA)

associated signs, including tracks, scats, and hairs.

Many of those that claim abandoned burrows also take advantage of natural crevices, holes, and other shelter found in the landscape— culverts, rock jumbles, basements, drains, sewers, car engines, grills, old foundations, rock walls, and the like. Existing shelter is valuable, regardless of its structure. You must rely on associated signs to identify who has taken up residence. Tracks, scents, scats, hairs, and any other clues are useful.

Nesting materials are strewn about a rock fortress inhabited by several yellow-bellied marmots. (CO)

Scat flows from beneath these rock overhangs, an obvious sign of resident porcupines. (MA)

Cavities

Cavities of all shapes and sizes are used by a variety of animals. Mammals are not as adept at creating cavities in trees and snags as birds are, so they tend to use what is readily available in nature. Cavities are created in myriad ways, formed where lightning strikes, where pileated woodpeckers have opened a tree in search of carpenter ants, where a dead branch rots and falls away, or by nesting and roosting birds.

As with burrows, when cavities that were created by another animal, likely a bird species, are appropri-

Scat accumulations speak of the length of time a porcupine has resided in this tree cavity. (MA)

A white-footed mouse has taken up residence in this tree cavity. (VT)

ated by a mammal, the mammal is termed a *secondary user.* Flying squirrels are notorious secondary users of old woodpecker nesting and roosting cavities, as are other squirrel species, white-footed mice, and red-tailed chipmunks. In cavities in live trees, rodents of all sizes chew the rim extensively, which is thought to prevent scar tissue from sealing the hole. It may serve the dual purpose of scent marking the entrance.

The list of mammals that use tree cavities to rear young, rest, or sleep is long and varied. Ringtails, raccoons, and coatis all use tree cavities, especially to raise young. Look for where ringtails have gnawed the rim

Red squirrels often nest in live tree cavities, which are conspicuous due to the chewed rims. (NH)

Fox squirrels nest and rest in cavities far more than in leaf nests. This cavity is in an old apple tree. (CO)

around the cavity entrance. Ringtails also use cavities entering the roots at the base of trees, especially when these have already been excavated by a previous animal.

Martens and fishers regularly use tree cavities. Porcupines seek refuge in holes at the bases of trees, and bears climb trees to use cavities that are large enough in which to spend the winter months. Successful interpretation of secondary mammal use relies heavily on associated signs and a flashlight, and it sometimes requires crawling into the hole or reaching in as far as you dare. Look for scat and hair, as well as claw marks in the bark layer.

Scat, Urine, and
Other Secretions

5

John McCarter called me several years ago on my birthday to discuss something he'd found in the woods while scouting an area for a workshop he was leading. He thought he'd found signs of mountain lion in north-central Massachusetts the day before. The ramifications of finding cougar sign in New England are politically unsavory and therefore exciting. So I dropped everything, and we went to investigate and, if necessary, document what he'd found.

John had discovered a peculiar mound of debris while moving stream-side in search of recent signs of otters and beavers. It was large, approximately 14 inches (35.6 cm) across and 5 inches (12.7 cm) high, and composed of dry debris scraped inward in a circular fashion. More amazing was the massive scat—a thick cord approximately 17 inches (43.2 cm) in total length and more than 1 inch (2.5 cm) in diameter over its entire length—that emerged with some prodding and exploring among the needles and debris of the mound.

Then John led me through what he'd discovered the previous day. There were nearby remains of a beaver jaw, broken in half by powerful jaws, and several more scats. Four scats were placed in such a way as to encircle a beaver kill, the remains of which were cached under a leaning snag. The kill site had been surrounded by scent posts, except along the stream, where fewer animals were likely to enter the site.

Three scats were covered by mounded debris, and one was surrounded by collected debris—visible within a volcano of leaves and needles. The scats were all massive—in diameter as well as volume. Three of the four were also covered, which was unusual. Both of us had been tracking that particular area of Massachusetts for some time—John much longer than I—and we *quickly agreed that it was rare to find a covered bobcat scat. Most were just left out, and some were placed in scrapes, but very few were covered completely, and none like those that lay before us.*

And there was not just one massive scat, which could have been a fluke bowel movement, but four (a fifth had appeared at the site the next time John visited, atop the cache remains). The combination of the cache, the covered kill (of which almost nothing remained), and the presence of a predator strong enough to break large bones convinced me that it was cougar sign, and I told John so. Scats were collected, and with the help of tracker Paul Rezendes, they were DNA tested twice by the Wildlife Conservation Society at the Bronx Zoo and by Virginia Tech. Both results confirmed North American mountain lion, Puma concolor—*no question.*

Animal scat, urine, and other secretions offer a wealth of information beyond proving the presence of a species. Overcome any queasiness, and move in for a closer inspection, because scat and urine provide unbeatable insights into diet and behavior. Terminology is colorfully varied (e.g., feces, excrement, pellets, droppings), but *scat* is the term used by trackers to describe the solid waste materials excreted by mammals and many other animals. Mammals void liquid waste as *urine,* unlike birds and some reptiles. Ornithologists prefer the term *droppings* to describe the solid waste deposits of birds.

Bird droppings, such as these of a bobwhite, are easy to distinguish by the white ends, which is uric acid. Look closely for the topmost droppings; these are the softer fecal droppings, which could be mistaken for mammal scats. (TX)

A cherry seed sprouts where it was transported and dropped in a red fox scat. (MA)

Animal scat is filled with an amazing and fascinating array of indigestible hairs, feathers, bones, insect limbs and carapaces, fruit skins, and other plant material. Scat is a real window into the life of an animal. By breaking up scat on the trail (safety issues are discussed in chapter 2 and in this chapter's species accounts), you document a species' dietary habits, which is an aid in identification, as well as begin to envision the environment in a larger way. For example, if the scat is filled with blueberry seeds and skins, and the only blueberry bushes are several miles away in a low wetland, you now know where the animal has been. Ecological relationships are very clear in scatology. Landscapes are viewed as a whole, and species interactions become clear with a study of contents—signs of predator and prey are identified together.

This chapter is predominantly a discussion of mammal scat, rather than urine or other secretions. This is strictly due to my own limitations, as well as the general knowledge in the field of tracking. Urine and other secretions are equally rich, but they are far more subtle and have not received the attention they deserve from trackers and researchers.

Limitations

Animal scats vary tremendously, depending on seasonal food availability, content, and age and health of the animal, and are sometimes challenging to identify in the field and difficult to describe in categories. I continue to find scats that challenge my experience, and from time to

Analysis of this wolf scat revealed hundreds of raspberry seeds. (MN)

time, I leave these encounters with nothing but questions and a photo for my mystery file. Practice and experience will help you identify most scats you encounter in the field, but there will always be those that cannot be positively identified due to visual variations caused by diet, health, or other stresses on the animal.

The three perspectives (see chapter 1) are important in your analysis of scat and urine, because the immediate context and location of the scat are just as vital as the visual characteristics of the scat itself. A scat taken out of context can be incredibly difficult to identify, but when placed within an environment, it can be obvious.

Analyses of scat contents also have limitations. Work by Gamberg and Atkinson (1988) proved that not everything consumed by ermines was reliably detectable in ermine scats. Lynn Rogers proved the same thing with black bears. But researchers such as Weaver (1993), who studied gray wolf scats, have created equations for better interpreting and understanding consumption versus scat content. There is still much to learn in the interpretation of scats and other scents left by wild animals.

Communication

Scat, urine, and scenting behaviors are part of an intricate communication system, potentially relaying information not only about the age, health, and the sex of the individual but also about territorial boundaries or ownership, or to contest the presence of another animal.

Gregory and Cameron (1989) discovered that the frequency of urination and defecation and the placement of urine and feces by hispid cotton rats relayed information about dominance and fertility. They also noted that the reaction of the next rat encountering the scat or urine varied according to its own dominance and fertility status.

We do not completely understand what scats and urine mean when posted and placed with great care by wild animals. Certainly scats and other secretions are used in territorial communication and probably to relay the health and sexual status of an animal. Hope Ryden offers us a glimpse of what all these markers may mean in her *Lily Pond: Four Years with a Family of Beavers*. She observed a resident male's response to a trespassing beaver's scent mound. The male mounted the shore hissing and "growling." He destroyed the scent mound with his front paws and carried a portion of it to the water's edge, sinking it in the pond. Other researchers have recorded similar responses in beavers, as well as observed residents building their own scent mounds atop a trespasser's or secreting their own castoreum in an attempt to cover the scent of a passing beaver.

We know that the noses of wild creatures put ours to shame; we depend on our eyes to decipher and interpret the environment, but many mammals can achieve the same thing with eyes shut and nostrils flaring. I've had many experiences when animals have marked my trails or places I've sat. Recently, while standing on the porch of a lodge in the Arctic and watching the sun rise, I saw an arctic fox run by. He seemed to stare intently at me, and just as he passed out of sight, he turned and

The regular scent post of a muskrat. The lengths of these scats are exceptional. (ME)

A Bobcat's Response

During a workshop, we had spent the second half of the day back-tracking a bobcat, and as the sun sank in the west and the temperature began to dip, we discovered the cat's bed. Tucked under a boulder, and comfortable in a layer of fallen leaves, the cat had napped and rested for much of the previous day before beginning to hunt at twilight.

Rarely are we offered such insight into an animal's private life, so I suggested that we seize the opportunity and place our hands where a wild bobcat had lain. Each person took a turn and in his or her own way connected with our bobcat. We hiked out of the woods and left in every direction, each returning to a life that had become richer after our day tracking a bobcat.

Several days passed, and I happened to be leading a workshop on coyotes in the same area. At the end of the day, we cut up and over a ridge to save time and by chance came to the spot where the bobcat had slept just a few days earlier. I directed everyone to the boulder, sure that they too would be happy to see such a beautiful bobcat bed. I stuck my head under the overhang and nearly knocked myself out when I recoiled and hit the rocks above me. I laughed out loud as the incredibly pungent smell of cat urine spread beyond me and reached the others nearby. In the center of the bed, on the very spot where we had placed our hands, was a pile of leaves scraped together by a bobcat and liberally sprayed with urine.

ran by me again. On his third pass, he stopped, approached slowly, and joined me on the porch. Eyeing me intently, he squatted and left a small pile of scat just several feet from where I stood. Then he loped off out of sight, leaving me wondering what he could have meant. Scat, urine, and other secretions offer a fascinating insight into animal behavior.

Predator and Prey

When a predator takes large prey, one that requires several feedings to finish, scat contents hint as to where the animal was recently feeding on the carcass. Predators tend to eat the internal organs first, which results in black, moist, soft scats with little bone or fur. As they continue to feed, the scats incorporate more bone and fur, and in the end, they are composed entirely of these things.

This was clearly illustrated to me when backtracking a lynx in northern Maine. I encountered my first scat almost immediately after starting on her trail—a thick cord of snowshoe hare fur and bones. All day I backtracked her through her routines. The second scat was similar to the first—a bit less fur and bone. The third was only half fur; the rest was meat and internal organs. The fourth and last I found was black and amorphous—completely internal organs. I continued and found the bed in which she'd spent most of the previous day. It was late, so I had to turn back, but I was sure that a bit further along I'd have come across the remains of the snowshoe hare she had captured—maybe a foot or a skin flap from its back.

Scats also hint at status in wolf and coyote packs. The choicest parts of the kill, the internal organs, are eaten by the alpha pair. As pack status declines, the quality and quantity of meat drop substantially, and those at the bottom of the pecking order may feed more on hide and bones than those at the top. This can all be read in scat composition and shape.

Key Components of Scat Identification

Just as with tracks, there are many important components to scat analysis. Below are some of the most important features.

Twists

If the scat appears to twist along its length, like a rope or a DNA strand, this is important to species identification. Also note the degree to which the scat twists, as both mustelid (weasel) and canine (dog) scats twist when they are composed of fur and bone. In general, weasel scats are extremely twisted and narrow. Those of foxes, coyotes, and wolves may be very twisted or hardly twisted at all, depending on diet.

Cats, bears, and raccoons are among those whose scats do not appear twisted; they have smooth surfaces. Cat scats are extremely twisted inside but appear smooth on the outside.

Tapered Ends

Are the ends of the scat tapered? The most tapered end of the scat is the last to leave the anus of the animal. Canine scats often have one or two tapered ends. Those of weasels generally have very long tapered ends. Scats composed of hair are more tapered than those composed of fruit. Cat scats occasionally have a tapered end, but blunt ends are more characteristic of the cat family, raccoons, coatis, and bears.

Segments

Cats often leave segmented scats, either joined or separated. Canine and mustelid scats tend to be one cord, although canine scats are segmented from time to time. Bear and raccoon scats break easily, leaving blunt ends, giving the impression of segmented scats. Bear scats composed of grasses and roots may be very segmented.

Pellets

Lagomorphs (rabbits) leave pellets throughout the year. Because they are deposited one at a time, a collection of rabbit pellets speaks to a tracker of a period of time. Ungulates, including deer, leave scat in pellet form when browsing from fall through spring and deposit a mass of pellets at one time. Pellets may just drop to the ground or be excreted with incredible force. While tracking a moose in northern New Hampshire, I came across a collection of pellets, the furthest of which had been shot 16 feet (4.9 m) from the animal's trail; the pellets as a whole radiated over an area 25 feet (7.6 m) across.

Color

Dietary variation and age influence the color of scats. As described earlier with the lynx, carnivore scats vary depending on what part of a carcass they are eating. Fruits dye scats a rainbow of colors, and a variety of other ingested items retain their color through digestion.

Study the color of both the exposed portion of scat and the hidden portion found beneath, as well as the color of the ground or vegetation covered by the scat. Scats generally dry and harden with age, whitening as they are left in the open for long periods. (Scats may also be white due to diet.) The area of ground or vegetation under the scat will darken and brown within as little as five days, depending on other variables.

While tracking a bobcat at sunrise in Point Reyes National Seashore, I found a very fresh scat—within an hour of when it was dropped. It was

A colorful black bear scat, filled with blueberries and mountain holly fruits. (MA)

very moist and large, colored black and dark green. I happened by the same spot just three hours later and looked at the scat again. In three hours of sun exposure, the outer portions had completely dried, and the entire scat had become a light tan color. Environmental conditions vary tremendously across North America and are crucial factors when considering color and other aging factors.

Scent

Species have unique odors associated with their scats. Most mammals have scent glands just inside the anus, so scats serve the double purpose of digestive excretion and communication device.

Smells are difficult to describe, but try to smell everything, especially scats and urine, as they are tremendous aids in species differentiation. *Warning:* If you believe you may have found raccoon scat, do not smell it (see the raccoon species account, page 484).

Measurements and Volume

The scats of pikas and snowshoe hares are remarkably similar but are unlikely to be confused due to drastically different diameters. Use a ruler to measure the diameters of round pellets and patties, the width of tubes and ropes, and the lengths and diameters of oblong or rectangular pellets. Judging and comparing volume across species requires some experience.

Contextual Clues

Contextual clues surrounding scats are crucial in overall interpretation. Following are specific environmental features that are particularly useful in scat interpretation.

Scrapes and Scratches

Cat scrapes, in which a scat is placed or urine is sprayed on piled debris, may be quite elaborate and deep or simply a swipe of a paw. Otters occasionally dig scrapes and drop their scat either in it or next to it. Golden-mantled ground squirrels also create small scrapes for both urine and scat deposits, as do arctic ground squirrels. Canines scratch near scats and scent posts from time to time, most often with the back feet.

Covered Scat

Felines do not always cover their scats, but from time to time they take great care in piling earth, snow, or available debris over their scats, leaving a ring of scratch marks about the pile.

Canine scat may also be partially covered. Coyotes that scratch after they defecate may unintentionally shower a scat with debris. However, this sign can be easily distinguished from the care taken when a cat covers a scat.

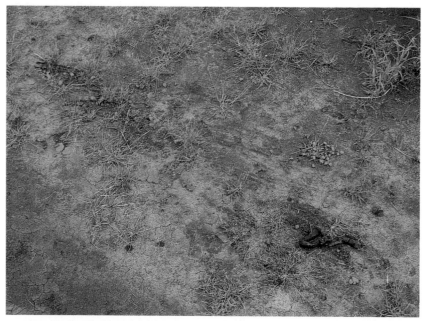

A coyote scat and the accompanying scrapes of both front and rear feet. (TX)

A feral cat has defecated and meticulously covered the scat. (TX)

Trails and Junctions

Canines are renowned for marking established runs, and their scats are common along hiking trails and roads. Martens also mark hiking trails, making their scats quite easy to find, unlike the related fisher, which does not share this tendency. Nowhere is this more apparent than in the Adirondacks in northern New York, where martens inhabit the highest peaks and fishers patrol the lowlands and valleys. Hike any peak and look for marten and fisher scat along the trail. You are not likely to see any until you approach the tree line, when suddenly twisted scats become quite common, posted on raised roots and rocks in the trail.

I counted 49 marten scats along a 6-mile (9.7 km) section of trail in Glacier National Park, where I knew there was a healthy marten population and where fishers are extremely rare if present at all. I counted 1 fisher scat on a 6-mile (9.7 km) section of trail in Pisgah State Park in New Hampshire, where I knew there was a healthy population of fishers and no martens; the single scat was on a log next to the trail. Certainly this comparison does not constitute a study, but it may hint at the results if one were undertaken.

Cats also occasionally mark hiking trails. Justin Shetler, formerly of the Wilderness Awareness Community School, shared a story with me several years ago. His tracking students were in the foothills near Seattle, and they all assumed that every scat in the center of the old logging roads surrounding them had been left by coyotes, because "this is what coyotes do." Then one winter morning, they woke to a thin layer of snow—a rariety in that neck of the woods. All other priorities were dropped, and they were off tracking. Animals had gone about their

An accumulation of coyote scats at a trail junction. (TX)

nightly business, and trails crisscrossed the roads, some highlighted by pauses for defecation. To their surprise, half the scats they found that day along logging roads had been made by bobcats, and the rest by coyotes. By looking closely at each category, they began to create lists of characteristics that helped differentiate scats they encountered in the future.

Look to the smaller trails and runs of voles as well. Oregon and Townsend voles are among the species that create latrines at run junctions, where scat may accumulate impressively.

Raised Surfaces

Many species choose to defecate on a high point along their travel route. This is common for canines and weasels, and felines also do this from time to time. Canines are especially attracted to raised surfaces, such as a root or boulder along a trail. I've found red fox scats placed perfectly atop large mushrooms and dangling from the tiny boughs of white pine saplings.

Martens, fishers, minks, and smaller weasels often place scats along raised surfaces as well. I have followed fishers on numerous occasions when their trails veered off to a stump or rock several inches to several feet high, where they paused only long enough to deposit a scat on their rounds. Martens do this too, and mink and muskrat scats are often found on raised vegetation clumps or rocks and logs in wetlands and streams where these animals commonly move.

Raccoons and ringtails also leave scats above ground level. Both are excellent climbers, and scats can often be found in tree crotches and along limbs where they have spent time. I've stuck my hand in raccoon scat a few times when not paying attention while climbing massive, twisted white pines in the Northeast. The raccoons leave them like land mines along limbs and in crotches—ideal spots for a hand when trying to pull yourself higher.

Bridges

Bridges are features that funnel animal movement. They may be fallen logs over water or tangled forest floor, or beaver dams bridging two land bodies. Even land bridges, such as the narrowest points between two bodies of water, are places where animals move more frequently. For this reason, they are wonderful places to post a scent, as these areas receive higher animal traffic and therefore offer the potential for increased attention.

Follow downed logs for a while and you are bound to find scats of raccoon, coati, ringtail, marten, fisher, weasels, gray fox, or red squirrel. Beaver dams should be regularly checked as well, as they are commonly marked by beavers, otters, coyotes, wolves, foxes, bobcats, raccoons, and fishers.

Left: A red fox scat expertly placed atop a white pine seedling, where it remained suspended. (NH) *Right:* Several raccoon scats mark this log, a regular travel route for several species over a stream. (MA)

Nests and Dens

Scats are also a clue that nests or dens are near or can help in interpreting nests and dens you've found. Woodrat scats are always plentiful near burrows and nests. Voles more often keep clean nests (not always the case), but mice defecate in their nests.

Scat Accumulations and Latrines

Trackers use the term *latrine* to describe a site where an accumulation of scat has been intentionally deposited by an individual or species over time. Many species leave accumulations of scat, but a latrine implies the intent of choosing a particular spot over others to defecate or mark. Scat accumulations may indicate merely a greater length of time spent in one area, such as those found in the resting places of jackrabbits, or areas where mice or rats have been heavily feeding. Raccoons, bears, coyotes, bobcats, lemmings, woodrats, voles, skunks, mustelids, muskrats, and beavers are among those that create latrines.

Aging Scats

As with tracks, aging scats takes some practice and knowledge of the local weather. Over time, meat scats turn white, then crumble and eventually disappear. Scats of hair and bones hold their form longer, and fur retains its color for ages, unless frequently exposed to sun. Fish scales and crayfish shell remains are visible for a long time after a scat deposit, although the form may deteriorate after a short period.

Pellets formed of woody browse and bark may persist many months and are often seen well after the winter when they were dropped. Research by Wigley and Johnson (1981) proved the importance of moisture in deer pellet disintegration; during the wet season in the Southeast, deer pellets disappeared within a month, whereas pellets dropped in drier conditions in the West were identifiable well over a year after they were dropped. With practice and an understanding of the effects of water and wind on scats in the area where you track, aging scats can be done with greater certainty.

Urine and Other Secretions

Like scat, urine and other secretions are used for complex communications between species and individuals and are invaluable to trackers and researchers. Mech and coauthors (1987) proved the usefulness of collecting urine samples while tracking wolves in winter. Analysis of a single urine sample revealed how recently a wolf had eaten, and an analysis of several samples revealed the health of the entire pack.

The contextual clues surrounding urine and other scents are tremendously important. The same contextual clues described for scat interpretation apply to urine and other secretions. Remember that scat is more visible than urine. When a bobcat cuts sideways to walk close to a small rotting stump, you'll want to use your nose to tell you what your eyes might not see.

Urine and some secretions have distinctive smells, and our olfactory memory is excellent at species identification. Feline urine, for example, has a very distinct odor that can easily be learned at home with your own or a neighbor's cat. The wild felines are slightly different but similar enough for identification purposes.

Although smells are quite easy to distinguish, they are remarkably hard to describe. What some describe as tangy, others describe as sharp. You'll just have to get out there and smell animal urine on your own.

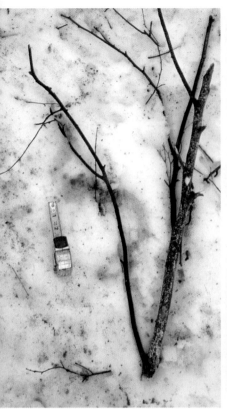

Left: Beaver castoreum. (MA) Photo by John McCarter. *Right:* Mounds and digs made by otters scenting and marking an area. (MA) Photo by John McCarter.

Never pass up an opportunity to refresh your memory or broaden your experience when it comes to confirmed animal scents, such as those associated with sightings, clear tracks, or associated signs that tell you whose scent you are smelling.

Canines and felines gravitate toward raised objects. Canines either raise a leg or squat and often mark old stumps, rocks, low-hanging branches, and assorted of other things. I describe canine urine as fairly musty and dank, with the exception of red and kit foxes, which have exceptionally strong, skunklike urines. The scent of all canine urine is strongest in winter, just before the onset of mating season.

Also check canine urine for blood, indicating that females have come into estrus. The urine may be red to a slight orange, depending on the intensity of her bleeding. The estrous window lasts only a short time, and this is a visual clue for those of us without the amazing sense of

A bobcat approached this stump, sprayed urine backward to mark it, and bounded up the hill. (MA)

smell that communicates information about the readiness and health of the female to prospective mates through glands and pheromones.

Felines may raise a leg or squat but are more likely to squirt their urine backward with incredible accuracy at specific objects. They seem partial to rotten old stumps, which may absorb and hold odors longer, as well as rock overhangs and low branches.

Bears urinate on saplings they walk over, and other species seem to place urine at random. Deer and moose use urine for communication purposes only in the rut. The males create scrapes with their hooves and then urinate in them, making sure that they dribble down the inside of their legs so that the urine picks up scent from glands located near the "knees."

Scents from urine and other secretions are all around us, but for the most part, we remain oblivious. Paul Rezendes uses the analogy that scents for animals are like seeing colors for us. Imagine constantly watching colors float across the landscape and understanding the information in each subtle variation—this is what it would be like to smell as a canine smells.

Species Accounts

Scat collections are invaluable resources for the tracking community. Those at the Antioch Graduate School in Keene, New Hampshire; the Murie Collection at the Teton Science School in Jackson, Wyoming; Jim Halfpenny's A Naturalist's World; and the one to which I contribute, overseen by Keith Badger at the High Mowing School in Wilton, New Hampshire, are sources of volumes of information. We need to make more quality scat collections available to the public. With this in mind, what follows are species descriptions of scat, as well as a visual presentation of the scats of many of North America's mammals, divided into three categories: (1) small scats and pellets (pages 508–27); (2) twists, ropes, and tubes (pages 527–50); and (3) loose and amorphous scats (pages 550–60). Some scats are a combination of categories and cannot be precisely defined, but a category had to be chosen. You will note that many photos include a penny, which is a helpful scale in the field. A penny is exactly 3/4 inch (1.9 cm) in diameter.

The size of scats produced by a single mammal varies dramatically, depending on variations in diet. Thus, there is substantial overlap in scat parameters when comparing across species; as a result, the numbers lose some of their differentiating value to trackers. This is especially true when comparing scat lengths; the diameter of scats, the width, is more reliably diagnostic, because its dimension is predetermined by the animal's internal excretory structures. This measurement comparison, along with shape, contents, location, and other visual and contextual clues, should help you identify the mammal responsible.

Opossums: Family Didelphidae

Virginia Opossum (*Didelphis virginiana*)

Scat: 3/8–1 1/8 in. (1–2.9 cm) diameter,
1–4 1/2 in. (2.5–11.4 cm) L

Scat is highly variable, depending on diet, and rarely encountered in the field.

Marking and other behaviors: Opossums also scent mark trees and other standing structures with glands on the cheeks.

Armadillos: Family Dasypodidae

Nine-banded Armadillo (*Dasypus novemcinctus*), page 534

Scat: 1/2–7/8 in. (1.3–2.2 cm) diameter,
3/4–1 1/2 in. (1.9–3.8 cm) L segment,
with total lengths of 3 to 4 in.
(7.6–10.2 cm).

Pelletish. Armadillos often bury their scats. Dr. Colleen McDonough describes

An armadillo created a latrine in an area of scraped earth. (TX) Photo by Colleen McDonough.

A coyote scrape and urine scent marking. (UT)

A coyote scat and paired marking. The female's urine shows signs of estrus, and the male marked just after her. (MA) Photo by John McCarter.

Marking and other behaviors: Urine and scat scenting is often accompanied by scrapes. These are narrow, short scratches in earth or snow, but debris is thrown up to 10 feet. These scrapes are often done with only the back feet, but sometimes with both front and rears, leaving two depressions in the ground.

When the female is in estrus, her urine includes blood—an obvious orange to red coloration. When in full estrus, blood may drip from the vulva as she moves. Paul Rezendes shared pictures of a female coyote's bed, where puddles of blood had formed when she lay down.

During estrus, pair-bonding becomes especially apparent—look for double scent posts, one with blood in the urine, the other without. Often one animal squats and the other raises a leg, but not always.

Gray Wolf *(Canis lupus)*, pages 546, 554

Scat: $^1/_2$–$1^7/_8$ in. (1.3–4.8 cm) diameter, 6–17 in. (15.2–43.2 cm) L

> Look for scats along travel routes and near kill sites, and accumulations near dens and rendezvous sites. I found a regular bedding area where scats ringed the beds and created a wall of scent no one could ignore.

Marking and other behaviors: Urine and scats are sometimes accompanied by scrapes. These are narrow, short scratches in earth or snow, but debris is thrown considerable lengths. These scrapes are often done with only the back feet, but sometimes with both front and rears, leaving two depressions in the ground.

The alpha pair scent mark by raising their legs, while all other members of the pack squat. In fact, it is not unusual to see the urine of subordinate animals drip down their legs and into a track. Mech and colleagues (1987) collected urine samples and found that analysis of a single sample can tell you how recently an animal has fed; analyzing several samples can determine the health of the entire pack.

When the alpha female is in estrus, her urine includes blood—an obvious orange to red coloration. During estrus, pair-bonding becomes especially apparent—look for double scent posts, one with blood in the urine, the other without.

Paired marking by a gray wolf alpha pair. The female wolf's urine shows signs of estrus; the male marked afterward and then scraped. (MN)

Red Wolf *(Canis rufus)*, page 545

Scat: ¹/₂–1¹/₂ in. (1.3–3.8 cm) diameter, 6–17 in. (15.2–43.2 cm) L

I do not have much experience trailing red wolves, but I imagine that they are similar to coyotes and gray wolves. What I have seen has been along roads used by the wolves for travel purposes.

Arctic Fox *(Alopex lagopus)*, page 531

Scat: ⁵/₁₆–⁵/₈ in. (.8–1.6 cm) diameter, 2–4¹/₂ in. (5.1–11.4 cm) L

Arctic foxes leave scat along travel routes and form latrines in areas where they regularly forage.

Kit Fox *(Vulpes velox)*, page 531

Scat: ³/₁₆–⁵/₈ in. (.5–1.6 cm) diameter, 2–4¹/₂ in. (7.6–11.4 cm) L

Kit foxes are almost completely carnivorous; therefore, fruit scats would be rare. Kit foxes also form latrines; I've most often found them at the base of prominent shrubs in their range.

Urine: Unlike that of other canines, the urine of kit foxes has a powerful skunklike odor. At times, this smell is nearly as strong as that of red foxes.

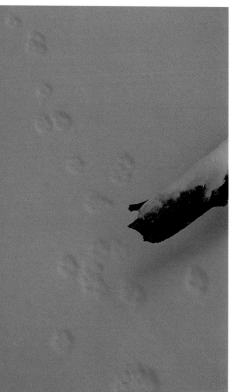

Red Fox *(Vulpes vulpes)*, page 536

Scat: ⁵/₁₆–³/₄ in. (.8–1.9 cm) diameter, 3–6 in. (7.6–15.2 cm) L

Urine: Red fox urine is renowned among trackers because of its incredibly pungent and powerful odor, similar to the odor of striped skunk spray. It is most powerful during the mating season, when I've encountered clouds of scent wafting through the forest. I've backtracked some of these scents with my nose and found scent posts up to 50 yards away.

Common Gray Fox *(Urocyon cinereoargenteus)*, pages 532–33, 553

Scat: ³/₈–³/₄ in. (1–1.9 cm) diameter, 3–5¹/₂ in. (7.6–14 cm) L

Some authors suggest that the darker the color and the greater amount of fruit in a fox scat, the more likely it is that it came from a gray fox rather than a red fox. Scat coloration and content vary for both species day to day and across individual animals as well.

Typical raised surface used for scent marking. Look closely for a red fox's urine. (MA)

Both red and gray foxes create near-black scats at times, and both produce scats composed entirely of fruit remains. I am not comfortable using color or content alone to differentiate between these two species; in fact, without contextual clues, I find it very difficult to do so.

Urine: Gray foxes use urine for scenting purposes in the same way as other canines, marking regularly on rounds.

Bears: Family Ursidae

Scat: Bears defecate often and leave scats in obvious places along travel routes, with what appears to be little awareness of site selection. Bear scat varies tremendously, depending on diet. Fruit scats can be amorphous and loose, or tubular and filled with seeds. Scats break easily and have blunt ends. Scats composed of meat and internal organs are loose patties or very amorphous and do not last long on the landscape. Scats of fur and bone and stringy roots are often linked segments. Look for accumulations of scats at regular bedding sights and near kills or other food-abundant areas.

Urine: Bears use urine to scent mark home ranges and to communicate. They most often do this by straddling shrubs and saplings and urinating while walking over them. Black bears have been documented engaging in this behavior, and I have watched both grizzlies in the greater Yellowstone area and polar bears on the tundra straddle and scent vegetation.

American Black Bear
(Ursus americanus),
pages 547–48, 554

Scat: 1¼–2½ in. (3.2–6.4 cm) diameter, 5–12 in. (12.7–30.5 cm) L, sometimes larger (cubs: can be as little as ½ in. (1.3 cm) diameter; easily confused with that of foxes or raccoons).

Black bears defecate between six and eight times a day.

Urine: Terry DeBruyn noted that the most common scenting behavior in the bears in his study group was straddling trees and urinating on them.

Brown or Grizzly Bear
(Ursus arctos),
pages 549–50, 554

Scat: 1¼–2⅞ in. (3.2–7.3 cm) diameter, 7–20 in. (17.8–50.8 cm) L, sometimes larger

A black bear straddled and urinated on this sapling. Look closely for the wet streak. (MN) Photo by Lynn Rogers.

A large marten scat elevated by rocks on a hiking trail. (MT)

Weasels: Family Mustelidae

Scat: Mustelid scats vary, depending on diet. Fruit and mast scats are tubular, with smooth surfaces, little or no twisting, and often pointy ends. Fur and bone scats are extremely twisted, tapered ropes with very pointy ends. Long scats often fold over on themselves. Scats composed of fish or crayfish may be tubular but are often amorphous.

All mustelids mark elevated surfaces such as stumps, as well as bridges, logs, or other surfaces over water or forest debris. Scats also accumulate at den sites, and piles are quite common at the burrow entrance.

Urine: Weasels use urine for scenting purposes, often in conjunction with other behaviors, such as rolling or rubbing.

American Marten *(Martes americana)*, page 529

Scat: $^3/_{16}$–$^5/_8$ in. (.5–1.6 cm) diameter, 2–5 in. (5.1–12.7 cm) L

Martens eat large amounts of fruit. Look for scats posted in all sorts of circumstances, but especially along trails and small roads on elevated surfaces. Scats accumulate at these sites, and it is not uncommon to find four to six scats together.

Marking and other behaviors: Martens also roll on and mark trees the way fishers and wolverines do. I believe males do this more often than females.

Fisher *(Martes pennanti)*, page 530

Scat: $^3/_{16}$–$^3/_4$ in. (.5–1.9 cm) diameter, 2–7 in. (5.1–17.8 cm) L

Fishers eat large amounts of fruit and other mast. They do not often mark trails, as martens do, but they mark all sorts of elevated surfaces in varied terrain. They often leave scats in raccoon latrines and on other animal trails; I check these places to determine fisher presence during the summer. Fisher scats accumulate impressively at dens and regular holes used for resting.

Fishers, possibly more so than other weasels, are able to control the volume of scat they post. Scat accumulations can be tiny, or they can be full-size scats easily identified.

Marking and other behaviors: Fishers also mark using urine and rolling. They roll on other animals' trails and scent posts, often those of foxes, and roll on and "beat up" small saplings, breaking limbs and defoliating them; urine is often posted while rolling and straddling saplings.

John McCarter also reports trails where fishers have dragged their bodies on the tracks and signs of other animals or done so to scent near caches, beaten saplings, and scent posts. These "troughs" in snow may be 4 to 8 feet (1.2–2.4 m) long. I've noted the same behavior in fishers following other fishers.

John has also found evidence that fishers are marking with glandular secretions that are mucous, light brown, and very small. Look for such sign in the same circumstances you find scats.

Ermine or Short-tailed Weasel *(Mustela erminea)*, page 527

Scat: $^1/_8$–$^5/_{16}$ in. (.3–.8 cm) diameter, $^3/_4$–$2^3/_8$ in. (1.9–6 cm) L

Small weasels are more carnivorous than larger members of this family and are difficult to distinguish from one another without associated signs. They all form latrines near nests.

Long-tailed Weasel *(Mustela frenata)*, page 528

Scat: $^3/_{16}$–$^3/_8$ in. (.5–1 cm) diameter, 1–$3^1/_4$ in. (2.5–8.3 cm) L

Small weasels are more carnivorous than larger members of this family and are difficult to distinguish from one another without associated signs. They all form latrines near nests.

Least Weasel *(Mustela nivalis)*, page 527

Scat: $^1/_8$–$^1/_4$ in. (.3–.6 cm) diameter, $^3/_4$–2 in. (1.9–5.1 cm) L

Small weasels are more carnivorous than larger members of this family and are difficult to distinguish from one another without associated signs. They all form latrines near nests.

American Mink *(Mustela vison)*, page 528

Scat: $^1/_4$–$^7/_{16}$ in. (.6–1.1 cm) diameter, 1–4 in. (2.5–10.2 cm) L

Scats are often found on grass clumps, rocks and logs next to water sources, on vegetative clumps midstream, or in marshes. They may accumulate at regular scent sites. Look for scats amidst muskrat scent posts as well, just as fishers mark raccoon latrines. Minks are also known to form latrines near burrows used for denning or regular resting.

Wolverine *(Gulo gulo)*, page 537

Scat: $^3/_8$–1 in. (1–2.5 cm) diameter, 3–8 in. (7.6–20.3 cm) L

I have little experience with wolverine scats in the wild.

Marking and other behaviors: Wolverines roll on other animals' trails and scent posts and also roll on, climb, bite, and "beat up" small saplings, breaking limbs and defoliating them.

A badger scat and accompanying urine. (CO)

American Badger *(Taxidea taxus)*, page 535

Scat: ³/₈–³/₄ in. (1–1.9 cm) diameter, 3–6 in. (7.6–15.2 cm) L

> Badger scats vary in shape and dimensions considerably, but they almost always reek when opened up to study their contents. Although I have occasionally found tubular scats, they are often twisted, folded, pointy piles of somewhat segmented scats. Look for them along travel routes and occasionally marking ground squirrel and prairie dog burrow entrances. Badgers will also roll and drag their body when marking along travel routes.

Northern River Otter *(Lontra canadensis)*, pages 534, 552

Scat: ³/₈–1 in. (1–2.5 cm) diameter, 3–6 in. (7.6–15.2 cm) L

> The scats of river otters are unique among mustelids, due to their fish diet. Scats vary from amorphous, pattylike squirts to tubular structures, but regardless of shape, they often disintegrate into a pile of fish scales and reek of fish. Scats composed of crayfish or terrestrial prey are more tubular. Scats are often part of a larger roll (described below). Sites are used time and again, and these areas can sometimes be identified by the dead and dying vegetation, which recoil from the urine and acid buildup. These areas are called *brown-outs.*

Marking and other behaviors: Otters also secrete a white, gooey substance that some believe is from the intestinal tract and others believe is from the anal glands. Look for this sign where you find scats. Scats accumulate at regular rolls, where otters come ashore and roll, scat, and urinate. Some researchers believe that rolling is necessary to maintain oils in the coat, thus keeping the animals warm and waterproof. Also look for mounds and digs at roll sites. Debris or earth may be mounded, and scats are often placed on top or nearby. Otters also create scrapes in mud and sand, which look somewhat catlike, and scats may appear in or near them. A collection of scrapes or digs found together is common. In addition, otters collect vegetation and create circular globs or mounds on which to scent, as well as twist and form grasses and vegetation that are still rooted and scent them with urine and anal gland secretions. These behaviors are often

An otter brown-out. Look closely for fish scales from long-dissolved scats. (NH)

A scraped mound and the yellowish white secretion otters occasionally use for marking. (MA)

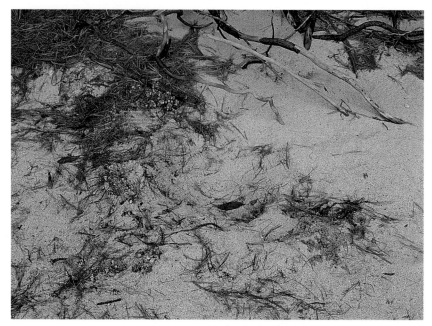

Typical otter roll with accompanying scats and urine. (MA)

A grass ball formed by an otter and then scented. (MA)

associated with rolls, as well as runs that connect water sources. Rolls may occur anywhere but are especially common under the following circumstances: the narrowest strip of land between water bodies; any narrow peninsula jutting out into a river, pond, or lake; along runs; and near holes in banks where otters enter and exit the water.

Sea Otter *(Enhydra lutris)*, page 551

Scat: 1/2–1 1/2 in. (1.3–3.8 cm) diameter

Tubular scats are formed when feeding on shellfish, but are less common than the small amorphous scents created when feeding on clams and shrimp. Most often sea otters defecate in the water, but occasionally scats will be found at haul-outs along the shore.

Skunks: Family Mephitidae

Skunk scats vary somewhat, according to diet, but are often tubular with smooth surfaces and blunt ends and break easily when prodded.

Western Spotted Skunk *(Spilogale gracilis)*

Scat: 1/4–3/4 in. (.6–1.9 cm) diameter

Striped Skunk *(Mephitis mephitis)*, page 533

Scat: 3/8–7/8 in. (1–2.2 cm) diameter, 2–5 in (5.1–12.7 cm) L

Striped skunks both place scats with care and at other times drop them at random. I've found several instances when skunks did not even stop to defecate but kept moving forward; the resulting sign was spread over four or five steps. Striped skunks form latrines at den sites, under overhangs, or near prominent features along travel routes, such as a stump in a field.

A striped skunk latrine located under a rock overhang in front of its winter den. (ID)

Seals: Family Phocidae

Harbor Seal *(Phoca vitulina)*, page 555

I have found only amorphous, pattylike scats of harbor seals, but Olaus Murie reports finding tubular scats of sea lions. Scats are not uncommon at haul-outs.

Ringtails, Raccoons, and Coatis: Family Procyonidae

Ringtail *(Bassariscus astutus)*, page 529

Scat: ³/₁₆–⁵/₈ in. (.5–1.6 cm) diameter, 2¹/₂–5 in. (6.4–12.7 cm) L

Ringtail scats are highly variable, depending on diet. When composed of fur and bone, they are twisted, tapered ropes that resemble those made by weasels. Scats are placed along travel routes and accumulate near holes in rocks or trees where animals are denning or resting. Ringtails also mark with urine.

Northern Raccoon *(Procyon lotor)*, pages 538–39, 552

Scat: ⁵/₁₆–1³/₁₆ in. (.8–3 cm) diameter, 3¹/₂–7 in. (8.9–17.8 cm) L

Warning: Raccoon scats can carry the parasitic roundworm *Baylisascaris procyonis,* which can be fatal in humans. Handle with caution.

Raccoons form large latrines at the bases of dominant conifers, especially those near wetland systems and water sources. Latrines are most often on the side facing away from the water source. Raccoons also form large latrines under rock overhangs and in other human structures that mimic such circumstances.

Ough (1982) studied a group of captive raccoons sharing an enclosure and found that individuals maintained their own personal scent posts with neck and anus rubs but formed communal latrines of scat.

A raccoon latrine found under a rock overhang near a site used for winter denning. (MA)

White-nosed Coati *(Nasua narica)*, pages 537, 552

Scat: 5/16–1 in. (.8–2.5 cm) diameter, 2³⁄4–6 in. (7–15.2 cm) L

I have little experience with coati scat. Those that I have found were along travel routes and in papaya plantations where the animals were regularly feeding.

Cats: Family Felidae

Scat: Cat scats are often tubular, long ropes that may be either segmented and folded in on themselves or one great length. Cougar scats may twist, but in general, cat scats are not twisted; they have a smooth outer surface (however, scats of fur and bone are very twisted inside). Scats are often segmented in appearance and have blunt ends or just one pointy end, which was the last to exit the anus. Cats are more carnivorous than canines, and scats full of fruits and mast crops are never found. However, grasses are consumed at times and may appear in scats.

Also look for scats placed in scrapes, which may be obvious and deep or just a swipe of the paw. Felines also cover their scats from time to time and pull material in a circular fashion from all directions. The length of the resulting scrapes is a useful tool for interpretation. House cat scrapes to cover scats measure 7 to 10 inches (17.8 to 25.4 cm), bobcat 12 to 18 inches (30.5 to 45.7 cm), and cougar 20 to 36 inches (50.8 to 91.4 cm).

Urine: Like canines, felines use urine to communicate and scent mark. Although various postures are employed, including squatting and raising a leg, cats often squirt their urine backward with incredible accuracy at stumps, rocks, low-hanging foliage, lower branches, and a variety of other targets. Look for trails to cut close to such objects, and a rear track to fall outside the line of travel when taking aim and shooting urine.

All cat urine smells similar, but there are subtle differences. For this reason, house cats provide a wonderful starting point from which to launch a study and build recognition of cat urine. Lynx is somewhat subtler than bobcat, and cougars have their own twist. Build experience slowly, and never pass up the opportunity to smell cat scent posts.

A cougar's scat and scrape. (AZ) Photo by Sue Morse.

Typical cougar scrape, or scratch, and scent mound created by the hind feet; urine is squirted on the mounded debris. I followed just behind this male, and each of the many scrapes and mounds I found that morning were still wet with his urine. (CA)

Cougar or Mountain Lion *(Puma concolor)*, pages 544–45

Scat: 3/4–1 5/8 in. (1.9–4.1 cm) diameter, 6 1/2–17 in. (16.5–43.2 cm) L

Scats are placed in scrapes, covered, left on open ground near bedding sites or kills, or used in conjunction with other scenting behaviors.

Marking and other behaviors: Cougars scent in all the ways described above, as well as create scrapes (or scratches) and mounds of debris on which they squat and urinate. Literature emphasizes that this behavior is the work of males, but I tracked a lion with two kittens that made several such scrapes in less than a mile of trail. I find such scrapes under large, low-hanging junipers and pines and along vertical rock ledges, under overhangs, in caves, and along ridge lines. According to Sue Morse, the width of these scrapes is the key when distinguishing them from those of bobcats: cougar scratches are 8–12 in. (20.3–30.5 cm) wide.

House Cat *(Felis domesticus)*, page 535

Scat: 3/8–7/8 in. (1–2.2 cm) diameter

Scats are often found in scrapes and are often covered as well. House cats seem particularly attracted to soft substrates, the "sandbox phenomenon," in which it is easier to cover scats.

Urine: When house cats urinate backward on objects, the urine is usually 8 to 9 inches off the ground.

Ocelot *(Leopardus pardalis)*, page 539

Scat: 1/2–7/8 in. (1.3–2.2 cm) diameter, 4–9 in. (10.2–22.9 cm) L

Urine: Like other felines, ocelots squirt urine backward to scent mark. In dry habitats of Mexico, Marcelo Aranda has found trees stained from regular scenting by ocelots. I do not know if ocelots make scratches and scent mounds like bobcats.

The regular scent post of this ocelot is visible by the stains on the tree bark. (Mexico) Photo by Marcelo Aranda.

Canada lynx *(Lynx canadensis)*, page 540

Scat: ½–¹⁵⁄₁₆ in (1.3–2.4 cm) diameter, 3–10 in. (7.6–25.4 cm) L

Tumilson (Wilson and Ruff, 1999), a lynx researcher, wrote that kittens sharing a mother's range cover their scats. In tracking adults, however, I have not yet found a covered scat. Scats are often posted on elevated terrain, which may be as insignificant as a bump in the snowy landscape.

Bobcat *(Lynx rufus)*, pages 540–41

Scat: ⁷⁄₁₆–1 in. (1.1–2.5 cm) diameter, 3–9 in. (7.6–22.9 cm) L

Bobcats form latrines along travel routes, especially at game trail junctions. They do not cover scats often and may leave them

A simple bobcat scrape. Look closely, and you can see the footprint that ended the scrape, next to the scat. (NH)

A bobcat's leaf scent mound, liberally sprayed with urine. (MA)

midtrail. They also place scats in scrapes, which may be a simple swipe of a hind paw or quite elaborately dug with both hind feet.

Urine: When bobcats urinate backward on objects, the urine is usually 9 to 17 inches (22.9 to 43.2 cm) off the ground. John McCarter documented 32 such scent posts and 1 scat in less than a mile (1.6 km) of trail, 23 scent posts and 1 scat in $^1/2$ mile (.8 km), and, on one incredible occasion, 31 scent posts and 2 scats in less than $^1/4$ mile (.4 km).

In addition, bobcats create small scrapes and mounds, much like cougars. In the Northeast, these leaf mounds are most often found under rock overhangs or along runs that follow vertical rock ledges. These mounds may be sprayed with urine or placed next to a scent post. Based on data provided by John McCarter, the parameters of these scrapes are 6 to 20 inches (15.2 to 50.8 cm) long by 3 to 7$^1/2$ inches (7.6 to 19.1 cm) wide. These numbers do not include the mounded debris.

Jaguar *(Panthera onca)*, page 547

Scat: $^7/8$–1$^3/4$ in. (2.2–4.4 cm) diameter, 8–17 in. (20.3–43.2 cm) L

Often leave scat midtrail.

Urine: Jaguars were not believed to create scrapes or debris mounds for urine, like those created by cougars. Recently, Jack Childs (1998) documented jaguar scrapes, or scratches, although mounded debris scent posts are still in question. And Alan Rabinowitz has shown that in areas of higher jaguar densities, posted scats and scrapes were more common.

Feral Horses: Family Equidae

Feral Horse or Wild Pony *(Equus cabillus)*, page 559

Scat: Pellets 1–1$^3/4$ in. (2.5–4.4 cm) diameter, 2–3 in. (5.1–7.6 cm) L

Varies from amorphous clumps to large, pellet-shaped scats, dependent upon moisture in diet. In the wild, dominant males form latrines to mark their territory.

Wild Boars: Family Suidae

Wild Boar *(Sus scrofa)*, page 547

Scat: 1–2 in. (2.5–5.1 cm) diameter, 4–14 in. (10.2–35.6 cm) L

A peccary's latrine site. The freshest scat has not yet turned white. (AZ)

Boar scat is often tubular, filled with mast crops and vegetation, and can easily be confused with that of black bears, with which boars often share range. A diet of lush vegetation results in loose tubes and amorphous patties.

Marking and other behaviors: Boars also rub trees and other hard surfaces when marking; occasionally, mud is left behind as a visible clue.

Peccaries: Family Tayassuidae

Collared Peccary *(Pecari tajacu)*, pages 541–42

Scat: 1/2–11/2 in. (1.3–3.8 cm) diameter, 4–13 in. (10.2–33 cm) L

Scats are highly variable, depending on diet. They are often tubular and may or may not be segmented. Peccary scats can be very large, considering the size of the animal, and may be similar in dimension and shape to cougar scats. Smaller peccary scats can easily be confused with those of foxes and coyotes. This is one of the more challenging scats to identify.

Peccaries leave scats along travel routes and midtrail, but they do not mark raised surfaces like canines do. They form substantial latrines along runs, and scats of every age should be apparent at such sites. I've found latrines along runs under prominent vegetation; in low passes; and on the edge of dry creek beds, posted on the lips just before dropping in and crossing them.

Urine: Urine is often found with scat.

Deer and Relatives: Family Cervidae

Scat: Deer scats vary with diet and, more importantly, the moisture content in that diet, both of which are dependent on seasonal availability and weather. Summer scats are loose and amorphous due to the high moisture content of herbaceous plants. As diets shift into drier vegetation in the fall, pellets become obvious within scats, but they are soft and clumped together. During the colder months, a woody diet produces harder pellets, which hold their shape well and last long into summer and sometimes beyond. Amorphous patties and hard pellets are the extremes of the possible variations. Be flexible in your interpretations.

When defecating pellets, members of the deer family expel numerous pellets simultaneously, as opposed to rabbits, which excrete one at a time.

Urine and other marking behaviors: Deer have unique ways of scenting and communicating in their respective ruts (described below).

Elk *(Cervus elaphus)*, pages 525–26, 557–58

Scat: Pellets $7/16$–$11/16$ in. (1.1–1.7 cm) diameter, $1/2$–1 in. (1.3–2.5 cm) L

Rut behaviors: Bull elk dig large wallows in the fall, in which they urinate and roll, much as moose do.

Mule Deer *(Odocoileus hemionus)*
White-tailed Deer *(Odocoileus virginianus)*, pages 524, 556

Scat: Pellets $3/16$–$5/8$ in. (.5–1.6 cm) diameter, $1/2$–1$3/4$ in. (1.3–4.4 cm) L

Deer pellets are highly variable. Often there is a dimple at one end and a point at the other, but they may be rounded at both ends as well. Pellets may be short and stout or long and skinny. Wigley and Johnson (1981) studied the disappearance rates of deer pellets and found that they were unrecognizable within a month during the wet season in the Southeast but were identifiable for well over a year in dry areas in the West.

Urine: Urine often smells piney, light, and somewhat pleasant.

Rut behaviors: Bucks form triangular scrapes during the rut, with the area of exposed earth from 1$1/2$ to 4 feet (45.7–121.9 cm) long and debris thrown as far as 15 feet (4.6 m) away. Bucks urinate down the insides of their legs, where glands contribute scents and chemicals, and then into the scrape. Often they choose a site where there is also low-hanging vegetation. A branch may be broken and left dangling above the scrape, as well as scented with glands near

A mule deer's typical winter pellets; this is a single excretion. (AZ)

A white-tailed deer scrape. Note the broken hemlock branch above, on which facial glands were rubbed as well. (MA)

the eye. Look for scrapes along runs. Miller and colleagues (1987) studied a captive white-tailed deer population and noted that bucks less than 2½ years old did not create scrapes during the rut.

Moose *(Alces alces)*, pages 529, 559–60

Scat: Pellets ½–⅞ in. (1.3–2.2 cm) diameter, ⅞–1¾ in. (2.2–4.4 cm) L

Patties are often a result of feeding on wetland vegetation. Pellets are rounded or blocklike. MacCraken and Van Bellenberghe (1987) did research to determine whether it was possible to differentiate males, females, and yearlings from pellet samples in central Alaska. They found that comparing the three measurements used to create the volume for each pellet would likely differentiate the three age and

A moose's rut pit. I could smell this pit from over 100 yards (91.4 m) away. (VT)

sex classes. The length and width measurements overlapped considerably between males and females and between yearlings and females. But a width less than 1.63 cm was not a male, and a width greater than $^3/_5$ inch (1.64 cm) was not a yearling. They also noted oven-dried pellets greater than .07 ounce (2 g) were always from males. This, at least, provides a starting point for quick analysis in the field.

Others suggest that bull moose pellets can be differentiated from those of cows because they are blockier than the rounded pellets of females. I have never had the opportunity to test this, but it is worth pursuing. Elk and muskox scats also fall into two categories: blocklike and rounded pellets. If this were a sex determiner, it would be a useful one.

Rut behaviors: Bull moose dig large wallows in the fall, in which they urinate and roll. Females also roll in wallows. Wallows measure between 3 and 10 feet (.91 and 3.05 m) long.

Caribou *(Rangifer tarandus)*, pages 525, 557

Scat: Pellets $^3/_8$–$^5/_8$ in. (1–1.6 cm) diameter, $^3/_8$–$^7/_8$ in. (1–2.2 cm) L

Pronghorns: Family Antilocapridae

Pronghorn *(Antilocapra americana)*, pages 523, 555

Scat: $^3/_{16}$–$^1/_2$ in. (.5–1.3 cm) diameter, $^3/_8$–$^3/_4$ (1–1.9 cm) L

Pronghorn scats, much like deer scats, vary with diet and moisture content, both of which are dependent on seasonal availability and weather. Summer scats are looser due to the high moisture content of herbaceous plants. As diets shift into drier vegetation in the fall, pellets become obvious within scats, but they are soft and clumped together. During the colder months, a woody diet produces harder pellets, which hold their shape well and last long into summer and sometimes beyond. I've also found strings of connected pronghorn pellets—20 or so per string. I have yet to see deer produce such sign.

A pronghorn's scat and territorial scrape. (CO)

Urine and other marking behaviors: Pronghorns urinate or leave scat to mark territorial boundaries, and this is often accompanied by a scrape in the earth made by the hooves. These scrapes are made in every season.

Bison, Goats, Muskox, and Sheep: Family Bovidae

Scat: Like deer scats, the scats of members of this family vary with diet and moisture content, both of which are dependent on seasonal availability and weather. Summer scats are loose and amorphous due to the high moisture content of herbaceous plants. As diets shift into drier vegetation in the fall, pellets become obvious within scats, but they are soft and clumped together. During the colder months, a woody diet produces harder pellets, which hold their shape well and last long into summer and sometimes beyond. Amorphous patties and hard pellets are the extremes of possible variations. Be flexible in your interpretations.

Cows and buffaloes do not follow the same pattern, but rather shift from patties in summer to "chips" in winter, which are smaller, layered patties that hold their form.

American Bison
(Bison bison),
page 560

Scat: Patties 10–16 in. (25.4–40.6 cm) diameter

The patties of buffaloes are nearly identical to those of domestic cows.

Chips 3–4¹/₂ in. (7.6–11.4 cm) diameter

Other scenting behaviors: Bison mark trees often, discussed in chapter 6.

Mountain Goat
(Oreamnos americanus),
pages 525, 557

Scat: Pellets ¹/₄–⁵/₈ in. (.6–1.6 cm) diameter, ³/₈–1 in. (1–2.5 cm) L

Other scenting behaviors: Although mountain goats do not horn trees during the rut like bison do, they rub them for marking purposes. These signs are hard to detect in the field, but the goats are attracted to injured trees, where sap helps catch their scent and hold it.

This tree was damaged by falling debris but was also marked by a mountain goat during the rut. Look closely for his white hairs. (MT)

Muskox *(Ovibos moschatus)*, pages 527, 558

Scat: Pellets $^7/_{16}$–$^3/_4$ in. (1.1–1.9 cm) diameter, $^5/_8$–1 in. (1.6–2.5 cm) L
I expected scats of muskox to be similar to those of buffaloes, but they look much more like elk scats.

Bighorn Sheep *(Ovis canadensis)*, pages 524, 556

Scat: Pellets $^1/_4$–$^5/_8$ in. (.6–1.6 cm) diameter, $^3/_8$–1 in. (1–2.5 cm) L

Dall's Sheep *(Ovis dalli)*, pages 524, 555

Scat: Pellets $^1/_4$–$^7/_{16}$ in. (.6–1.1 cm) diameter, $^3/_8$–1 in. (1–2.5 cm) L

Mountain Beavers: Family Aplodontidae

Mountain Beaver or Aplodontia *(Aplodontia rufa)*, page 11

Scat: $^3/_{16}$–$^5/_{16}$ in. (.5–.8 cm) diameter, $^1/_2$–$^{11}/_{16}$ in. (1.3–1.7 cm) L
Mountain beavers eat their cecal pellets, much like rabbits.

Squirrels: Family Sciuridae
Chipmunks

Like other rodents, chipmunk scats vary, depending on the moisture content in their diet. Scats can be soft and pointy and stick together in clumps, or they can be individual pellets like those of squirrels; on occasion, they may be linked. I often find chipmunk scats at regular perches in their home range.

Eastern Chipmunk *(Tamias striatus)*, page 513

Scat: Pellets $^3/_{32}$–$^5/_{32}$ in. (.2–.4 cm) diameter, $^1/_8$–$^9/_{32}$ in. (.3–.7 cm) L

Marmots and Woodchucks

Scats vary tremendously, based on the moisture content in their diet. Most of my experience is with marmot scats, rather than those of woodchuck. They vary from moist, very soft, dark green dollops to tubular scats of various colors. Sometimes, great chains of linked pellets are produced, much like those created by prairie dogs.

Hoary Marmot *(Marmota caligata)*, page 538

Scat: $^3/_8$–$^{15}/_{16}$ in. (1–2.4 cm) diameter, 1 $^1/_2$–3$^1/_2$ in. (3.8–8.9 cm) L, sometimes in chains much longer
I have found large latrines (up to 100 scats) made by this species, but not by any other marmot species. Hoary marmots are considered more gregarious than yellow-bellied marmots, which may be connected with this behavior. Look for latrines near prominent perches and under overhangs on regular travel routes.

Yellow-bellied Marmot *(Marmota flaviventris)*, page 538

Scat: $^3/_8$–$^3/_4$ in. (1–1.9 cm) diameter, 1$^1/_2$–2 in. (3.8–5.1 cm) L, sometimes in chains much longer

A hoary marmot's latrine. (AK)

Scats are easy to find along travel routes and near burrows and natural crevices. Although scats accumulate at crevices inhabited by several animals, I have yet to find them creating large latrines like those of the hoary marmot.

Woodchuck or Groundhog *(Marmota monax)*, pages 521, 537

Scat: $^7/_{16}$–$^3/_4$ in. (1.1–1.9 cm) diameter, $1^1/_2$–$2^1/_2$ in. (3.8–6.4 cm) L

Woodchuck scat is hard to find; it is most often left in special underground chambers or on the throw mound, where it is trampled or buried. On one occasion I found a latrine near an active burrow where young woodchucks repeatedly buried their scats.

Ground Squirrels

Ground squirrel scats vary with the moisture content in their diet. High moisture content results in soft scats that are often twisted, with tapered ends, or in pellets clumped together. Scats also vary in shape and size. The larger ground squirrels create pellets similar to those of gray squirrels, which are reminiscent of deer pellets, in that they are often pointed at one end and have a dimple at the other. Moister scats are less defined, more wrinkled, and likely pointy at both ends.

Many ground squirrel species leave scats sprinkled around their burrow systems. Some are more particular in site selection.

Uinta Ground Squirrel *(Spermophilus armatus)*

Scat: $^1/_8$–$^5/_{16}$ in. (.3–.8 cm) diameter, $^3/_8$–$^{13}/_{16}$ in. (1–2.1 cm) L

Scats are easily found near burrow entrances.

California Ground Squirrel *(Spermophilus beecheyi),* page 520

Scat: ⁵/₃₂–⁵/₁₆ in. (.4–.8 cm) diameter, ¹/₄–³/₄ in. (.6–1.9 cm) L
Scats are easily found near burrow entrances.

Columbian Ground Squirrel *(Spermophilus columbianus),* page 520

Scat: ¹/₈–⁹/₃₂ in. (.3–.7 cm) diameter, ⁵/₁₆–¹³/₁₆ in. (.8–2.1 cm) L
Scats are easily found near burrow entrances.

Wyoming Ground Squirrel *(Spermophilus elegans),* page 519

Scat: ⁵/₃₂–⁹/₃₂ in. (.4–.7 cm) diameter, ⁵/₁₆–⁷/₈ in. (.8–2.2 cm) L
Scats are easily found near burrow entrances.

Golden-mantled Ground Squirrel *(Spermophilus lateralis),* page 519

Scat: ³/₁₆–⁵/₁₆ in. (.5–.8 cm) diameter, ³/₁₆–¹/₂ in. (.5–1.3 cm) L
Golden-mantled ground squirrels do not litter their burrow entrances and throw mounds with scats, as do other ground squirrels. Instead, look for scats to be placed on prominent perches and along nearby travel routes. In addition, these squirrels create circular scrapes, between 1¹/₄ and 2 inches (3.2–5 cm) in diameter, and urinate or defecate within them. These scrapes are found near burrow entrances, often ringing them completely.

A golden-mantled squirrel's scrape and carefully placed scat. (CO)

Arctic Ground Squirrel *(Spermophilus parryii)*, pages 520–21

Scat: Hard $5/32$–$7/32$ in. (.4–.6 cm) diameter, $5/16$–$3/8$ in. (.8–1 cm) L
Soft $3/8$–$1/2$ in. (1–1.3 cm) diameter, $3/8$–$11/4$ in. (1–3.2 cm) L
Scats are easily found near burrow entrances. This species also places scats in scrapes, like golden-mantled ground squirrels.

Prairie Dogs

Prairie dog scats are larger versions of ground squirrel scats, and they vary with the moisture content in the diet. When the animals are eating green materials, scats are soft or clumped pellets; when they are subsisting on drier diets, scats form harder pellets. Sometimes, pellets are linked and form large chains. Scats are conspicuous around burrows and throughout "towns," or groups of burrows.

White-tailed Prairie Dog *(Cynomys leucurus)*, page 522

Scat: $3/16$–$1/2$ in. (.5–1.3 cm) diameter, $1/2$–$21/8$ in. (1.3–5.4 cm) L, occasionally in chains of considerable length
In addition to leaving scats littered all over, white-tailed prairie dogs defecate in small pits in or near the throw mound.

Black-tailed Prairie Dog *(Cynomys ludovicianus)*, page 522

Scat: Hard $3/16$–$7/16$ in. (.5–1.1 cm) diameter, $1/2$–2 in. (1.3–5.1 cm) L, occasionally in chains of considerable length
Scat accumulates around burrows, and considerable amounts may be removed and pushed out of entrances during bouts of "cleaning."

Tree Squirrels

Scats vary, depending on the moisture content in the diet. High moisture content results in soft scats that are often twisted, with tapered ends, or in clumps of pellets stuck together. More common are small scats reminiscent of deer pellets, in that they are often pointed at one end and have a dimple at the other. Moister scats are less defined, more wrinkled, and likely pointy at both ends.

Eastern Gray Squirrel *(Sciurus carolinensis)*, page 519

Scat: $1/8$–$7/32$ (.3–.6 cm) diameter, $5/32$–$3/8$ (.4–1 cm) L
The pellets of gray squirrels, as opposed to those of red squirrels, seem to be dropped at random. I usually find them where squirrels have spent ample time feeding in an area. Pellets are quite easy to find in new, wet snow. Pellets are dropped as squirrels travel overhead, and they swell in the wet snow. You may find the bloated gray to brown pellets under tree canopies sprinkled about. Those that have soaked up more snow may "explode," leaving a brown or gray stain with the residue of the pellet in the center.
Marking and other behaviors: Gray squirrels rub, roll, and tear up elevated moss patches in their home range. I've watched them engage in this behavior on several occasions but do not know its significance—a marking behavior of some kind. Grays also bite and rub along travel routes. This sign is similar to that of red squirrels.

Site of an unusual gray squirrel marking behavior. He flung himself into the moss repeatedly, tearing and rolling about for several minutes. (NY)

Red Squirrel (*Tamiasciurus hudsonicus*), page 518

Scat: $^3/_{16}$–$^1/_4$ in (.5–.6 cm) diameter, $^3/_{16}$–$^7/_{16}$ in (.5–1.1 cm) L

The scats of red squirrels may be dropped at random but are often placed carefully along travel routes, on bridges over water and forest debris, and in other high-traffic areas. As with canines, high points in the trail are often marked—often a branch stub or burl on a limb.

Marking and other behaviors: Red squirrels bite and rub their cheeks along travel routes, especially on raised surfaces such as burls or knobs.

Southern flying squirrel scats flow freely from this tree cavity, giving away a nesting site. The larger scat was left by a passing porcupine. (MA)

Northern Flying Squirrel *(Glaucomys sabrinus)*, page 514

Scat: Pellets 3/32–3/16 in. (.2–.5 cm) diameter, 1/8–3/8 in. (.3–1 cm) L

Southern Flying Squirrel *(Glaucomys volans)*, page 514

Scat: Pellets 1/16–5/32 in. (.2–.4 cm) diameter, 3/16–5/16 in. (.5–.8 cm) L
        Scat accumulates in cavities and hollows where the squirrels nest and
        cache. Look for scat flowing out of holes low down on trees or for
        accumulations in hollows of logged and stacked wood. These accumu-
        lations can be impressive; I have never measured all the scats in one
        location, but I recall one flow that could have filled two 1-gallon
        buckets, not including what was hidden in the tree trunk.

Pocket Gophers: Family Geomyidae

Plains Pocket Gopher *(Geomys bursarius)*, page 517

Scat: Pellets 1/8–3/16 in. (.3–.5 cm) diameter, 5/16–7/16 in. (.8–1.1 cm) L
        Scats are capsule shaped, with smooth surfaces and rounded ends.
        Contents of the scats are woody; summer scats might be softer and vary
        more in shape, but I've never found them.
        Pocket gopher scat is not common aboveground but can be found just
        after the snow recedes, in latrines made aboveground, or by pulling apart
        "eskers." I've also found scats where predators have attempted to dig up
        and capture pocket gophers.

Pocket Mice: Family Heteromyidae

Giant Kangaroo Rat *(Dipodomys ingens)*, page 512

Scat: 3/32–5/32 in. (.2–.4 cm) diameter, 1/4–7/16 in. (.6–1.1 cm) L
        Scats are slightly curved, with tapered ends. They can be found sprinkled
        near burrow entrances and within precincts.

Merriam's Kangaroo Rat *(Dipodomys merriami)*, page 511

Scat: 1/16–3/32 in. (.2 cm) diameter, 3/32–3/16 in. (.2–.5 cm) long
        I have identified Merriam's kangaroo rat scats in the wild on only one occa-
        sion. They were just slightly larger and rounder than those pictured here.

Ord's Kangaroo Rat *(Dipodomys ordii)*, page 512

Scat: 3/32–1/8 in. (.2–.3 cm) diameter, 1/4–1/2 in. (.6–1.3 cm) L
        Scats can be found near burrow entrances and in areas of heavy foraging.

Beavers: Family Castoridae

American Beaver *(Castor canadensis)*, page 544

Scat: 3/4–11/2 in. (1.9–3.8 cm) diameter, 11/4–3 in. (3.2–7.6 cm) L
        Scats are often composed of three to five separate pellets or may be
        tubular; they are always filled with tiny bits of woody material and
        other plant fibers. Beavers defecate in the water but occasionally do
        so in shallow puddles or in areas that dry up. I once found an inlet to a
        stream that had dropped during a drought and discovered that a beaver
        had been using the site for a latrine; it contained approximated 30 scats.

A beaver's scent mound, created entirely from dry materials collected on land. (NH)

Two large scent mounds, which are the culmination of numerous beaver scenting behaviors. (MA)

Typical beaver scent mound, with wet, dark materials dredged from the pond's bottom. (NH)

Like rabbits, beavers engage in coprophagy and reingest scats to better break down the cellulose in vegetation. Their initial scats are soft and green, but you are unlikely to find them without disturbing a beaver during the process.

Other marking behaviors: Beavers have two musk glands located near the cloaca that secrete a substance called *castoreum*. Castoreum may be either liquid or somewhat jellylike in consistency, and it has a remarkably strong odor. Beavers walk over grass clumps and other rises in the landscape at water's edge and deposit castoreum. They also construct mounds, called scent mounds, of materials dredged from below the water's surface and hauled onto land. After a suitable mound is created, which may be either a handful or bucketful of material, the beaver walks over the pile and deposits castoreum. Scent mounds may also be created from materials collected on land, although this is less common. These mounds may be quite large, especially if reused. I have found mounds 2 feet high on several occasions. Researchers believe that scent mounds play a role in territorial communication. John McCarter has also recorded instances in which beavers have come ashore and scratched together small mud piles with the front paws, which is likely a scenting behavior as well.

Rats and Mice: Family Muridae

Marsh Rice Rat *(Oryzomys palustris)*, page 513

Scat: 1/16–1/8 in. (.2–.3 cm) diameter, 1/4–15/32 in. (.6–1.2 cm) L
        I have not identified this scat in the field.

White-footed Mouse *(Peromyscus leucopus)*, page 512
Deer Mouse *(Peromyscus maniculatus)*

Scat: 1/32–1/16 in. (.1–.2 cm) diameter, 3/32–7/32 in. (.2–.6 cm) L
        These mice produce irregular, wrinkled, twisted, and tapered scats. They seem to be dropped at random and can be found wherever mice have spent time, accumulating along travel routes and where they have been actively foraging.

Hispid Cotton Rat *(Sigmodon hispidus)*, page 513

Scat: $^1/_{32}$–$^5/_{32}$ in. (.1–.4 cm) diameter, $^5/_{32}$–$^3/_8$ in. (.4–1 cm) L

Scats are common along runs and in areas of feeding. Gregory and Cameron (1989) discovered that hispid cotton rats select sites for scat and urine according to their dominance within a population. In addition, their reactions when encountering other rats' scats and urine vary, depending on their level of dominance.

Woodrats

Where there are woodrats, there will be ample scat and other signs; great accumulations can be found along travel routes and in and around burrows and nests. Scats are tubular pellets, much longer than wide, and are similar across species. Woodrats also excrete a soft, dark, tarlike scat, which they often post along travel routes and near nests. These scent posts are used repeatedly, and the black goo accumulates impressively over time.

Woodrats also use urine for scenting purposes, and in dry climates, the spots where woodrats urinate become white with calcareous deposits. These also form below nests in rock cliffs.

White-throated Woodrat *(Neotoma albigula)*, page 517

Scat: $^1/_8$–$^3/_{16}$ in. (.3–.5 cm) diameter, $^1/_4$–$^9/_{16}$ in. (.6–1.4 cm) L

Bushy-tailed Woodrat *(Neotoma cinerea)*, page 518

Scat: $^1/_8$–$^3/_{16}$ in. (.3–.5 cm) diameter, $^5/_{16}$–$^5/_8$ in. (.8–1.6 cm) L

Desert Woodrat *(Neotoma lepida)*, page 517

Scat: $^1/_8$–$^3/_{16}$ in. (.3–.5 cm) diameter, $^1/_4$–$^9/_{16}$ in. (.6–1.4 cm) L

Look closely for the black, sticky substance accumulating in two spots along this woodrat travel route. These are small examples; over time, accumulations can be massive. (UT)

Calcareous deposits accumulate where bushy-tailed woodrats regularly urinate. (ID)

Voles

Vole scats are capsule shaped, with smooth surfaces and rounded ends; they are very symmetrical and regular. Vole scats may be found anywhere the animals have been, but they accumulate in latrines and dead-end runs, near nests, and at trail junctions along runs. Northern bog lemmings and rock voles prefer to create latrines on elevated surfaces near runs.

Red Tree Vole *(Arborimus longicaudus)*, page 515

Scat: $^1/_{16}$ in. (.2 cm) diameter, $^5/_{32}$–$^3/_{16}$ in. (.4–.5 cm) L

Tundra Vole *(Microtus oeconomus)*, page 515

Scat: $^1/_{16}$–$^1/_8$ in. (.2–.3 cm) diameter, $^3/_{16}$–$^1/_4$ in. (.5–.6 cm) L

Meadow Vole or Field Mouse *(Microtus pennsylvanicus)*, page 516

Scat: $^1/_{16}$–$^1/_8$ in. (.2–.3 cm) diameter, $^1/_8$–$^5/_{16}$ in. (.4–.8 cm) L

Scat is found along runs, especially in small dead-end tunnels that are often used for latrines. Meadow voles also form latrines next to nests; these are especially apparent at exposed nests built during snow cover. White calcareous deposits may also form in dry climates, where voles repeatedly urinate to scent mark. This is similar to that of woodrats, but in miniature.

Muskrat *(Ondatra zibethicus)*, pages 521, 551

Scat: Hard $^3/_{16}$–$^5/_{16}$ in. (.5–.8 cm) diameter, $^3/_8$–1 in. (1.–2.5 cm) L
         Soft $^3/_8$–1 in. (1–2.5 cm) diameter, $^7/_8$–1$^3/_4$ in. (2.2–4.4 cm) L

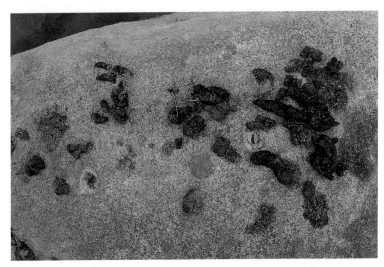

A variety of muskrat scats accumulating on a favorite scent post at the water's edge. (NH)

Scats vary depending on the moisture content in the diet. They may be soft and amorphous; clumped pellets stuck together; or harder, with individual pellets obvious. Muskrats form scent posts, where tremendous amounts of scat may accumulate. Look for scent posts along runs, as well as on prominent elevated surfaces in and around water sources, such as rocks, grass clumps, or stumps. On occasion, muskrats construct small mounds of earth and debris on which to defecate.

Northern Bog Lemming *(Synaptomys borealis)*, page 516

Scat: $^3/_{32}$–$^3/_{16}$ in. (.2–.5 cm) diameter, $^1/_4$–$^7/_{16}$ in. (.6–1.1 cm) L

Norway Rat *(Rattus norvegicus)*, page 518

Scat: $^1/_8$–$^1/_4$ in. (.3–.6 cm) diameter, $^1/_4$–$^{15}/_{16}$ in. (.6–2.4 cm) L
        Scats accumulate wherever rats spend time, especially near nest sites, along travel routes, and wherever they have spent time feeding.

Jumping Mice: Family Dipodidae

Jumping Mice (*Zapus* and *Napaeozapus* species), page 513

Scat: $^1/_{16}$–$^1/_8$ in. (.2–.3 cm) diameter, $^1/_8$–$^1/_2$ in. (.3–1.3 cm) L
        I have not identified jumping mouse scat in the field.

Porcupines: Family Erethizontidae

North American Porcupine *(Erethizon dorsatum)*, page 523

Scat: $^1/_4$–$^1/_2$ in. (.6–1.3 cm) diameter, $^1/_2$–$1^1/_4$ in. (1.3–3.2 cm) L

A river of porcupine scat flows freely from a rock crevice used for some time to provide safety and warmth. (MA)

Porcupine scat can be found wherever there are porcupines, accumulating anywhere they feed or walk; it may be especially thick in crevices and hollows or even basements, where they rest. In fact, scat accumulations may be so high at resting places that porcupines have to burrow through their own excrement to exit and enter. Look for rivers of scat flowing from rock ledges where they hole up in winter. Some researchers suggest that this behavior may aid in providing shelters with insulation; winter scat is composed completely of tiny wood chips.

Scats are small, irregular tubes and pellets with rounded or pointy ends. Most scats curve over their length—this asymmetry helps differentiate them from deer scats. Scats may also be linked and form chains.

Nutrias: Family Myocastoridae

Nutria *(Myocastor coypus)*, page 522

Scat: $^3/_{16}$–$^1/_2$ in. (.5–1.3 cm) diameter, $^3/_4$–1$^1/_2$ in. (1.9–3.8 cm) L

Nutria scat is tubular and very symmetrical. The clear, parallel grooves that run their length make these scats easy to identify in the field. Scats are sprinkled wherever nutrias move and can be seen floating in water sources they use and inhabit. Grass clumps and elevated surfaces are also used repeatedly, and accumulations can be found at such locations.

Pikas: Family Ochotonidae

American Pika *(Ochotona princeps)*, pages 508, 551
Collared Pika *(Ochotona collaris)*

Scat: Pellets $^3/_{32}$–$^1/_8$ in. (.2–.3 cm) diameter

Pika scat comes in two forms. The first is the round pellet, typical of all lagamorphs. In the case of pikas, these pellets are very small. The second

An American pika's winter latrine is revealed as the snow recedes. (WA)

is a soft, dark green to black scat that looks like toothpaste pushed out of the tube. This variation is less common but is not difficult to find; according to Olaus Murie, it is a result of a moister diet.

Marking and other behaviors: Most lagomorphs drop pellets at random, and this is occasionally true of the pika as well. But pikas clearly use urine and pellets for marking purposes. I often see the entrances to burrows with regular urine stains (in snow), and scat is posted in high-traffic areas. Pikas also form large latrines during winter, which are revealed when the snow melts in the spring.

Rabbits and Hares: Family Leporidae

Scat: All rabbits and hares engage in coprophagy, ingesting their feces to better digest plant materials. The first scat is very hard to find in the field, but the pellets produced after the second ingestion are plentiful. Rabbit and hare scats all look similar—round pellets or discs; they tend to look like squashed spheres but are occasionally teardrop shaped as well. Pellets are composed entirely of plant material; in winter, the woody material is obvious.

Rabbits release one pellet at a time, rather than the shotgun approach used by deer. Therefore, an accumulation of rabbit pellets requires a length of time. Why did a rabbit pause in one place for so long? Scats seem to be placed at random, although a notable exception is the swamp rabbit. Zoller and colleagues (1996) found that 91 percent of swamp rabbit scat was found on decaying logs, making it very likely that scat plays a role in territorial communication. Scat was found on logs least often in spring and summer.

Urine: Rabbit urine tends to be orange to red in color and is easily confused with blood. Likely, diet influences coloration.

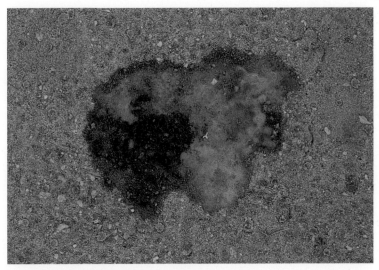

The urine of a black-tailed jackrabbit. (CA)

Pygmy Rabbit *(Brachylagus idahoensis)*, page 508
Scat: Pellets 1/8–9/32 in. (.3–.7 cm) diameter

Desert Cottontail *(Sylvilagus audubonii)*, page 509
Scat: Pellets 1/4–7/16 in. (.6–1.1 cm) diameter

Brush Rabbit *(Sylvilagus bachmani)*, page 509
Scat: Pellets 3/16–3/8 in. (.5–1 cm) diameter

Eastern Cottontail *(Sylvilagus floridanus)*, page 509
Scat: Pellets 3/16–7/16 in. (.5–1.1 cm) diameter

Snowshoe Hare *(Lepus americanus)*, page 510
Scat: Pellets 5/16–9/16 in. (.8–1.4 cm) diameter

Alaskan Hare *(Lepus othus)*, page 511
Scat: Pellets 1/2–11/16 in. (1.3–1.7 cm) diameter

Black–tailed Jackrabbit *(Lepus californicus)*, page 510
Scat: Pellets 3/8–1/2 in. (1–1.3 cm) diameter

White-tailed Jackrabbit *(Lepus townsendii)*, page 510
Scat: Pellets 3/8–11/16 in. (1–1.7 cm) diameter

Scat Identification

PART 1:
Small Scats and Pellets

Collared pika (AK): $3/32$ to $1/8$ inch (.2 to .3 cm) in diameter. Description on page 505.

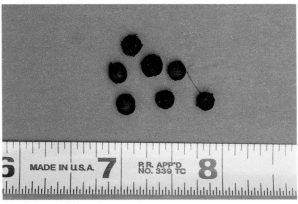

American pika (WA): $3/32$ to $1/8$ inch (.2 to .3 cm) in diameter. Description on page 505.

Pygmy rabbit (WY): $1/8$ to $9/32$ inch (.3 to .7 cm) in diameter. Description on pages 506–7.

Brush rabbit (CA): 3/16 to 3/8 inch (.5 to 1 cm) in diameter. Description on pages 506–7.

Desert cottontail (UT): 1/4 to 7/16 inch (.6 to 1.1 cm) in diameter. Description on pages 506–7.

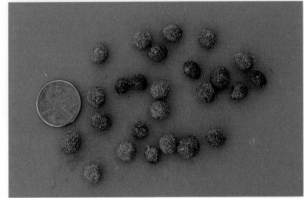

Eastern cottontail (NY): 3/16 to 7/16 inch (.5 to 1.1 cm) in diameter. Description on pages 506–7.

Scat Identification

Snowshoe hare (ID, MA): $5/16$ to $9/16$ inch (.8 to 1.4 cm) in diameter. Description on pages 506–7.

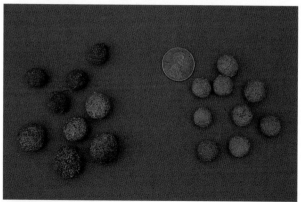

White-tailed and black-tailed jackrabbits (NV); the black-tailed are the smaller. Black-tailed: $3/8$ to $1/2$ inch (1 to 1.3 cm) in diameter. Description on pages 506–7.

White-tailed jackrabbit (WY): $3/8$ to $11/16$ inch (1 to 1.7 cm) in diameter. Description on pages 506–7.

Alaskan hare (AK): 3/8 to 11/16 inch (1 to 1.7 cm) in diameter. Description on pages 506–7.

Cinereus shrew (AK): 1/16 inch (.2 cm) in diameter, 3/16 inch (.5 cm) long. Description on page 472.

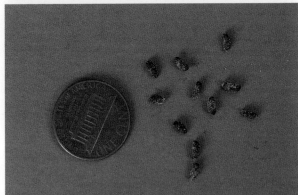

Merriam's kangaroo rat (captive): 1/16 to 3/32 inch (.2 cm) in diameter, 3/32 to 3/16 inches (.2 to .5 cm) long. Description on page 499.

Deer mouse (MN): $1/32$ to $1/16$ inch (.1 to .2 cm) in diameter, $3/32$ to $7/32$ inch (.2 to .6 cm) long. Description on page 501.

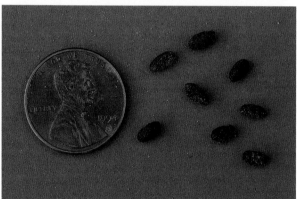

Ord's kangaroo rat (UT): $3/32$ to $1/8$ inch (.2 to .3 cm) in diameter, $1/4$ to $1/2$ inch (.6 to 1.3 cm) long. Description on page 499.

Giant kangaroo rat (CA): $3/32$ to $5/32$ inch (.2 to .4 cm) in diameter, $1/4$ to $7/16$ inch (.6 to 1.1 cm) long. Description on page 499.

Jumping mouse (captive): $^1/_{16}$ to $^1/_8$ inch (.2 to .3 cm) in diameter, $^1/_8$ to $^1/_2$ inch (.3 to 1.3 cm) long. Description on page 504.

Eastern chipmunk (MA): $^3/_{32}$ to $^5/_{32}$ inch (.2 to .4 cm) in diameter, $^1/_8$ to $^9/_{32}$ inches (.3 to .7 cm) long. Description on page 494.

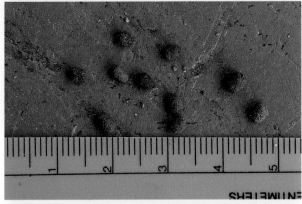

Rice and cotton rats (captives). Marsh rice rat: $^1/_{16}$ to $^1/_8$ inch (.2 to .3 cm) in diameter, $^1/_4$ to $^{15}/_{32}$ inch (.6 to 1.2 cm) long; the smaller scats are hispid cotton rat: $^1/_{32}$ to $^5/_{32}$ inch (.1 to .4 cm) in diameter, $^5/_{32}$ to $^3/_8$ inch (.4 to 1 cm) long. Descriptions on pages 501–2.

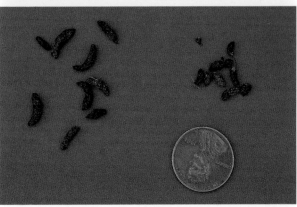

Southern flying squirrel (VT): $1/16$ to $5/32$ inch (.2 to .4 cm) in diameter, $3/16$ to $5/16$ inch (.5 to .8 cm) long. Description on page 499.

Northern flying squirrel (OR): $3/32$ to $3/16$ inch (.2 to .5 cm) in diameter, $1/8$ to $3/8$ inch (.3 to 1 cm) long. Description on page 499. Photo by Chris Maser.

Northern short-tailed shrew (NY): $1/16$ to $3/16$ inch (.2 to .5 cm) in diameter, $1/4$ to $11/16$ inch (.6 to 1.7 cm) long. Description on page 472.

Little brown myotis (NH): $^1/_{16}$ to $^1/_8$ inch (.2 to .3 cm) in diameter, $^1/_8$ to $^{11}/_{16}$ inch (.3 to 1.7 cm) long. Description on page 473.

Tundra vole (AK): $^1/_{16}$ to $^1/_8$ inch (.2 to .3 cm) in diameter, $^3/_{16}$ to $^1/_4$ inch (.5 to .6 cm) long. Description on page 503.

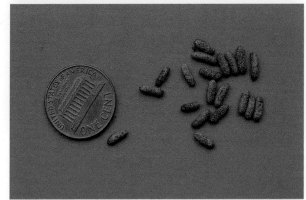

Red tree vole (OR): $^1/_{16}$ inch (.2 cm) in diameter, $^5/_{32}$ to $^3/_{16}$ inch (.4 to .5 cm) long. Description on page 503.

Scat Identification

Meadow vole (NY): $^{1}/_{16}$ to $^{1}/_{8}$ inch (.2 to .3 cm) in diameter, $^{1}/_{8}$ to $^{5}/_{16}$ inch (.4 to .8 cm) long. These scats are part of a larger latrine located near the entrance to a nest. Description on page 503.

Northern bog lemming (AK): $^{3}/_{32}$ to $^{3}/_{16}$ inch (.2 to .5 cm) in diameter, $^{1}/_{4}$ to $^{7}/_{16}$ inch (.6 to 1.1 cm) long. Description on pages 503–4.

Mole species (NH): $^{3}/_{32}$ to $^{3}/_{16}$ inch (.2 to .5 cm) in diameter, $^{3}/_{8}$ to 1 inch (1 to 2.5 cm) long. Description on pages 503–4.

Plains pocket gopher (CO): $1/8$ to $3/16$ inch (.3 to .5 cm) in diameter, $5/16$ to $7/16$ inch (.8 to 1.1 cm) long. Description on page 499.

White-throated woodrat (TX): $1/8$ to $3/16$ inch (.3 to .5 cm) in diameter, $1/4$ to $9/16$ inch (.6 to 1.4 cm) long. Description on page 502.

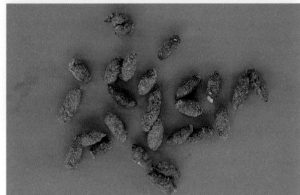

Desert woodrat (CA): $1/8$ to $3/16$ inch (.3 to .5 cm) in diameter, $1/4$ to $9/16$ inch (.6 to 1.4 cm) long. Description on page 502.

Scat Identification

Bushy-tailed woodrat (MT): $1/8$ to $3/16$ inch (.3 to .5 cm) in diameter, $5/16$ to $5/8$ inch (.8 to 1.6 cm) long. Description on page 502.

Norway rat (VT): $1/8$ to $1/4$ inch (.3 to .6 cm) in diameter, $1/4$ to $15/16$ inch (.6 to 2.4 cm) long. Description on page 504.

Red squirrel (MN): $3/16$ to $1/4$ inch (.5 to .6 cm) in diameter, $3/16$ to $7/16$ inch (.5 to 1.1 cm) long. Description on page 498.

Golden-mantled ground squirrel (CO): $3/16$ to $5/16$ inch (.5 to .8 cm) in diameter, $3/16$ to $1/2$ inch (.5 to 1.3 cm) long. Description on page 496.

Gray squirrel (NH): $1/8$ to $7/32$ inch (.3 to .6 cm) in diameter, $5/32$ to $3/8$ inch (.4 to 1 cm) long. Description on page 497.

Wyoming ground squirrel (CO): $5/32$ to $9/32$ inch (.4 to .7 cm) in diameter, $5/16$ to $7/8$ inch (.8 to 2.2 cm) long. Description on pages 495–96.

Columbian ground squirrel (MT): $1/8$ to $9/32$ inch (.3 to .7 cm) in diameter, $5/16$ to $13/16$ inch (.8 to 2.1 cm) long. Description on pages 495–96.

California ground squirrel (CA): $5/32$ to $5/16$ inch (.4 to .8 cm) in diameter, $1/4$ to $3/4$ inch (.6 to 1.9 cm) long. Description on pages 495–96.

Arctic ground squirrel (AK): Hard scats. $5/32$ to $7/32$ inch (.4 to .6 cm) in diameter, $5/16$ to $3/8$ inch (.8 to 1 cm) long. Description on pages 495–96.

Arctic ground squirrel (AK): Soft scats. $3/8$ to $1/2$ inch (1 to 1.3 cm) in diameter, $3/8$ to $1^{1}/4$ inches (1 to 3.2 cm) long. Description on pages 495–96.

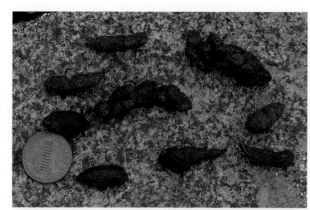

Young wood-chuck (NY): Scats were buried near a burrow entrance. Description on pages 494–95.

Muskrat (ME): Hard scats. $3/16$ to $5/16$ inch (.5 to .8 cm) in diameter, $3/8$ to 1 inch (1. to 2.5 cm) long. Description on pages 503–4.

Scat Identification

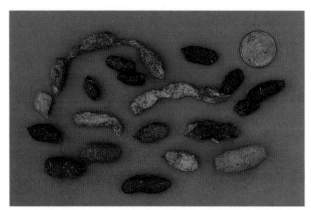

Black-tailed prairie dog (MT): $3/16$ to $7/16$ inch (.5 to 1.1 cm) in diameter, $1/2$ to 2 inches (1.3 to 5.1 cm) long. Description on page 497.

White-tailed prairie dog (CO): $3/16$ to $1/2$ inch (.5 to 1.3 cm) in diameter, $1/2$ to $2^1/8$ inches (1.3 to 5.4 cm) long. Description on page 497.

Nutria (TX): $3/16$ to $1/2$ inch (.5 to 1.3 cm) in diameter, $3/4$ to $1^1/2$ inches (1.9 to 3.8 cm) long. Description on page 505.

Porcupine (MA): Spring scats. Description on pages 504–5.

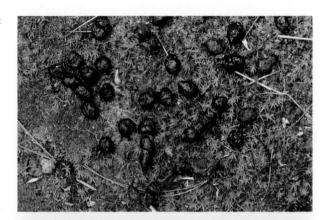

Porcupine (MA): Winter scats. 1/4 to 1/2 inch (.6 to 1.3 cm) in diameter, 1/2 to 1 1/4 inches (1.3 to 3.2 cm) long. Description on pages 504–5.

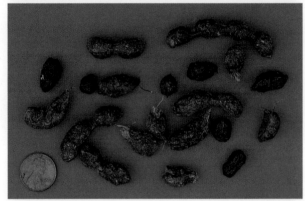

Pronghorn (WY): Pellets. 3/16 to 1/2 inch (.5 to 1.3 cm) in diameter, 3/8 to 3/4 inch (1 to 1.9 cm) long. Description on pages 492–93.

Scat Identification

Dall's sheep (AK): Pellets. $^1/_4$ to $^7/_{16}$ inch (.6 to 1.1 cm) in diameter, $^3/_8$ to 1 inch (1 to 2.5 cm) long. Description on pages 493–94.

White-tailed deer (MN, MA): Pellets. $^3/_{16}$ to $^5/_8$ inch (.5 to 1.6 cm) in diameter, $^1/_2$ to 1$^3/_4$ inches (1.3 to 4.4 cm) long. Description on pages 489–91.

Bighorn sheep (CO): Pellets. $^1/_4$ to $^5/_8$ inch (.6 to 1.6 cm) in diameter, $^3/_8$ to 1 inch (1 to 2.5 cm) long. Description on pages 493–94.

Mountain goat (CO): Pellets. $1/4$ to $5/8$ inch (.6 to 1.6 cm) in diameter, $3/8$ to 1 inch (1 to 2.5 cm) long. Description on page 493.

Caribou (AK): Pellets. $3/8$ to $5/8$ inch (1 to 1.6 cm) in diameter, $3/8$ to $7/8$ inch (1 to 2.2 cm) long. Description on pages 489, 492.

Elk (CO): Hard pellets. $7/16$ to $11/16$ inch (1.1 to 1.7 cm) in diameter, $1/2$ to 1 inch (1.3 to 2.5 cm) long. Description on pages 489–90.

Scat Identification

Elk (CO): Very soft pellets. Description on pages 489–90.

Moose (VT): Winter pellets. $1/2$ to $7/8$ inch (1.3 to 2.2 cm) in diameter, $7/8$ to $1^3/4$ inches (2.2 to 4.4 cm) long. Description on pages 489–92.

Moose (VT): Soft pellets. Description on pages 489–92.

Muskox (AK): Winter pellets. $7/16$ to $3/4$ inch (1.1 to 1.9 cm) in diameter, $5/8$ to 1 inch (1.6 to 2.5 cm) long. Description on pages 493–94.

PART 2: Twists, Ropes, and Tubes

Least weasel (AK): $1/8$ to $1/4$ inch (.3 to .6 cm) in diameter, $3/4$ to 2 inches (1.9 to 5.1 cm) long. Description on pages 478–79.

Ermine (NH): 9 scats. $1/8$ to $5/16$ inch (.3 to .8 cm) in diameter, $3/4$ to $2^{3}/8$ inches (1.9 to 6 cm) long. Description on pages 478–79.

Long-tailed weasel (WA): ³/16 to ³/8 inch (.5 to 1 cm) in diameter, 1 to 3¹/4 inches (2.5 to 8.3 cm) long. Description on pages 478–79.

Long-tailed weasel (NY): ³/16 to ³/8 inch (.5 to 1 cm) in diameter, 1 to 3¹/4 inches (2.5 to 8.3 cm) long. Description on pages 478–79.

American mink (NH): ¹/4 to ⁷/16 inch (.6 to 1.1 cm) in diameter, 1 to 4 inches (2.5 to 10.2 cm) long. Description on pages 478–79.

Ringtail (TX): $3/16$ to $5/8$ inch (.5 to 1.6 cm) in diameter, $2^1/2$ to 5 inches (6.4 to 12.7 cm) long. Description on page 484.

Marten (MT): 5 fruit. $3/16$ to $5/8$ inch (.5 to 1.6 cm) in diameter, 2 to 5 inches (5.1 to 12.7 cm) long. Description on page 478.

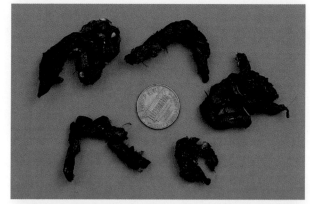

Marten (MT): 5 meat. $3/16$ to $5/8$ inch (.5 to 1.6 cm) in diameter, 2 to 5 inches (5.1 to 12.7 cm) long. Description on page 478.

Fisher (NH): $3/16$ to $3/4$ inch (.5 to 1.9 cm) in diameter, 2 to 6 inches (5.1 to 15.2 cm) long. Description on pages 478–79.

Fisher (NH): 4 scats. $3/16$ to $3/4$ inch (.5 to 1.9 cm) in diameter, 2 to 6 inches (5.1 to 15.2 cm) long. Description on pages 478–79.

Fisher (VT): Apple. $3/16$ to $3/4$ inch (.5 to 1.9 cm) in diameter, 2 to 6 inches (5.1 to 15.2 cm) long. Description on pages 478–79.

Kit fox (CA): Four scats. $^3/_{16}$ to $^5/_8$ inch (.5 to 1.6 cm) in diameter, 2 to $4^1/_2$ inches (7.6 to 11.4 cm) long. Description on pages 473, 476.

Kit fox (CA): Three scats. $^3/_{16}$ to $^5/_8$ inch (.5 to 1.6 cm) in diameter, 2 to $4^1/_2$ inches (7.6 to 11.4 cm) long. Description on pages 473, 476.

Arctic fox (Canada): Three scats. $^5/_{16}$ to $^5/_8$ inch (.8 to 1.6 cm) in diameter, 2 to $4^1/_2$ inches (5.1 to 11.4 cm) long. Description on pages 473, 476.

Gray fox (CA): Juniper berries. $3/8$ to $3/4$ inch (1 to 1.9 cm) in diameter, 3 to $5^1/2$ inches (7.6 to 14 cm) long. Description on pages 473, 476–77.

Gray fox (TX): 2 fruit scats. $3/8$ to $3/4$ inch (1 to 1.9 cm) in diameter, 3 to $5^1/2$ inches (7.6 to 14 cm) long. Description on pages 473, 476–77.

Gray fox (OR): Blueberries. $3/8$ to $3/4$ inch (1 to 1.9 cm) in diameter, 3 to $5^1/2$ inches (7.6 to 14 cm) long. Description on pages 473, 476–77.

Gray fox (TX): Two scats—one meat, one fruit. $^3/_8$ to $^3/_4$ inch (1 to 1.9 cm) in diameter, 3 to $5^1/_2$ inches (7.6 to 14 cm) long. Description on pages 473, 476–77.

Striped skunk (ID): Tubular scats. $^3/_8$ to $^7/_8$ inch (1 to 2.2 cm) in diameter, 2 to 5 inches (5.1 to 12.7 cm) long. Description on page 483.

Striped skunk (NH): Tubular meat scats. $^3/_8$ to $^7/_8$ inch (1 to 2.2 cm) in diameter, 2 to 5 inches (5.1 to 12.7 cm) long. Description on page 483.

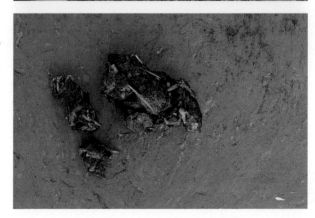

Armadillo (TX): 1/2 to 7/8 inch (1.3 to 2.2 cm) in diameter, 3 to 4 inches (7.6 to 10.2 cm) long. Description on pages 471–72.

Otter (NC): Tubular scats. 3/8 to 1 inch (1 to 2.5 cm) in diameter, 3 to 6 inches (7.6 to 15.2 cm) long. Description on pages 478, 480–83.

Otter (VT): Tubular crayfish scats. 3/8 to 1 inch (1 to 2.5 cm) in diameter, 3 to 6 inches (7.6 to 15.2 cm) long. Description on pages 478, 480–83.

House cat (VT): $3/8$ to $7/8$ inch. (1 to 2.2 cm) in diameter, 4 to $5^{1}/_2$ inches (10.2 to 14 cm) long. Description on pages 485–86.

Badger (SD): $3/8$ to $3/4$ inch (1 to 1.9 cm) in diameter, 3 to 6 inches (7.6 to 15.2 cm) long. Description on pages 478, 480.

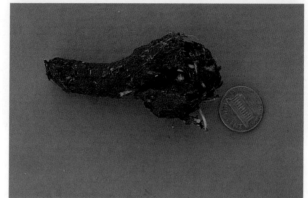

Badger (ID): Two scats. $3/8$ to $3/4$ inch (1 to 1.9 cm) in diameter, 3 to 6 inches (7.6 to 15.2 cm) long. Description on pages 478, 480.

Scat Identification

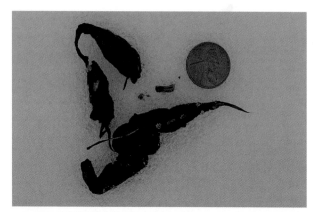

Red fox (MN): Meat. 5/16 to 3/4 inch (.8 to 1.9 cm) in diameter, 3 to 6 inches (7.6 to 15.2 cm). long. Description on pages 473, 476.

Red fox (MN): Meat. 5/16 to 3/4 inch (.8 to 1.9 cm) in diameter, 3 to 6 inches (7.6 to 15.2 cm). long. Description on pages 473, 476.

Red fox (NH): Apple. 5/16 to 3/4 inch (.8 to 1.9 cm) in diameter, 3 to 6 inches (7.6 to 15.2 cm) long. Description on pages 473, 476.

Wolverine (captive): $3/8$ to 1 inch (1 to 2.5 cm) in diameter, 3 to 8 inches (7.6 to 20.3 cm) long. Description on pages 478–79.

Coati (captive): $5/16$ to 1 inch (.8 to 2.5 cm) in diameter, $2^3/4$ to 6 inches (7 to 15.2 cm) long. Description on page 485.

Woodchuck (NY): $7/16$ to $3/4$ inch (1.1 to 1.9 cm) in diameter, $1^1/2$ to $2^1/2$ inches (3.8 to 6.4 cm) long . Description on pages 494–95.

Scat Identification

Yellow-bellied marmot (CO): 5 scats. $3/8$ to $3/4$ inch (1 to 1.9 cm) in diameter, $1\frac{1}{2}$ to 2 inches (3.8 to 5.1 cm) long. Description on pages 494–95.

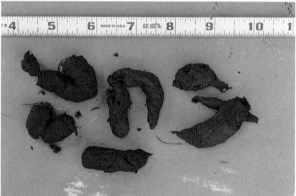

Hoary marmot (WA): 6 scats. $3/8$ to $15/16$ inch (1 to 2.4 cm) in diameter, $1\frac{1}{2}$ to $3\frac{1}{2}$ inches (3.8 to 8.9 cm) long. Description on page 494.

Raccoon (MA): $5/16$ to $1\frac{3}{16}$ inches (.8 to 3 cm) in diameter, $3\frac{1}{2}$ to 7 inches (8.9 to 17.8 cm) long. Description on page 484.

Raccoon (MA): 5/16 to 1³/16 inches (.8 to 3 cm) in diameter, 3¹/2 to 7 inches (8.9 to 17.8 cm) long. Description on page 484.

Raccoon (NH): Fall latrine. 5/16 to 1³/16 inches (.8 to 3 cm) in diameter, 3¹/2 to 7 inches (8.9 to 17.8 cm) long. Description on page 484.

Ocelot (Mexico): ¹/2 to 7/8 inch (1.3 to 2.2 cm) in diameter, 4 to 9 inches (10.2 to 22.9 cm) long. Description on pages 485–87. Photo by Sue Morse.

Canada lynx (ME): 3 scats. $1/2$ to $15/16$ inch (1.3 to 2.4 cm) in diameter, 3 to 10 inches (7.6 to 25.4 cm) long. Description on pages 485, 487.

Bobcat (NH): Note the scrape. $7/16$ to 1 inch (1.1 to 2.5 cm) in diameter, 3 to 9 inches (7.6 to 22.9 cm) long. Description on pages 485, 487–88.

Bobcat (MA): $7/16$ to 1 inch (1.1 to 2.5 cm) in diameter, 3 to 9 inches (7.6 to 22.9 cm) long. Description on pages 485, 487–88.

Bobcat (CA): $7/16$ to 1 inch (1.1 to 2.5 cm) in diameter, 3 to 9 inches (7.6 to 22.9 cm) long. Description on pages 485, 487–88.

Collared peccary (TX): Fresh and old scats side by side. $1/2$ to $1^1/2$ inches (1.3 to 3.8 cm) in diameter, 4 to 13 inches (10.2 to 33 cm) long. Description on page 489.

Collared peccary (TX): $1/2$ to $1^1/2$ inches (1.3 to 3.8 cm) in diameter, 4 to 13 inches (10.2 to 33 cm) long. Description on page 489.

Collared peccary (TX): $1/2$ to $1^1/2$ inches (1.3 to 3.8 cm) in diameter, 4 to 13 inches (10.2 to 33 cm) long. Description on page 489.

Coyote (MA): Apple. $3/8$ to $1^3/8$ inches (1 to 3.5 cm) in diameter, 5 to 13 inches (12.7 to 33 cm) long. Description on pages 473–75.

Coyote (CA): Juniper berries. $3/8$ to $1^3/8$ inches (1 to 3.5 cm) in diameter, 5 to 13 inches (12.7 to 33 cm) long. Description on pages 473–75.

Coyote (UT): Insects. $3/8$ to $1 3/8$ inches (1 to 3.5 cm) in diameter, 5 to 13 inches (12.7 to 33 cm) long. Description on pages 473–75.

Coyote (NH): Grasses. $3/8$ to $1 3/8$ inches (1 to 3.5 cm) in diameter, 5 to 13 inches (12.7 to 33 cm) long. Description on pages 473–75.

Coyote (CA): Juniper and meat. $3/8$ to $1 3/8$ inches (1 to 3.5 cm) in diameter, 5 to 13 inches (12.7 to 33 cm) long. Description on pages 473–75.

Scat Identification

Coyote (VT): Meat. $^3/_8$ to $1^3/_8$ inches (1 to 3.5 cm) in diameter, 5 to 13 inches (12.7 to 33 cm) long. Description on pages 473–75.

Beaver (TX): $^3/_4$ to $1^1/_2$ inches (1.9 to 3.8 cm) in diameter, $1^1/_4$ to 3 inches (3.2 to 7.6 cm) long. Description on pages 499–501.

Cougar (MA): $^3/_4$ to $1^5/_8$ inches (1.9 to 4.1 cm) in diameter, $6^1/_2$ to 17 inches (16.5 to 43.2 cm) long. Description on pages 485–86.

Scat Identification

Cougar (CO):
3/4 to 1 5/8 inches
(1.9 to 4.1 cm) in
diameter, 6 1/2 to
17 inches (16.5
to 43.2 cm) long.
Description on
pages 485–86.

Cougar (CA): 3/4
to 1 5/8 inches
(1.9 to 4.1 cm) in
diameter, 6 1/2 to
17 inches (16.5
to 43.2 cm) long.
Description on
pages 485–86.
Photo by Doniga
Murdoch, Shikari
Tracking Guild.

Red wolf (NC):
1/2 to 1 1/2 inches
(1.3 to 3.8 cm) in
diameter, 6 to
17 inches (15.2
to 43.2 cm) long.
Description on
pages 473, 476.

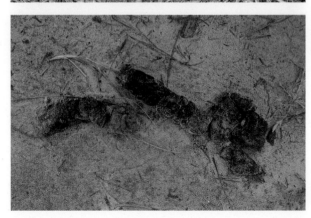

Scat Identification

Gray wolf (MN): 1/2 to 17/8 inches (1.3 to 4.8 cm) in diameter, 6 to 17 inches (15.2 to 43.2 cm) long. Description on pages 473, 475.

Gray wolf (MN): 2 scats. 1/2 to 17/8 inches (1.3 to 4.8 cm) in diameter, 6 to 17 inches (15.2 to 43.2 cm) long. Description on pages 473, 475.

Gray wolf (MN): 1/2 to 17/8 inches (1.3 to 4.8 cm) in diameter, 6 to 17 inches (15.2 to 43.2 cm) long. Description on pages 473, 475.

Jaguar (Mexico): 7/8 to 1 3/4 inches (2.2 to 4.4 cm) in diameter, 8 to 17 inches (20.3 to 43.2 cm) long. Description on page 488.

Feral hog (TX): 2 scats. 1 to 2 inches (2.5 to 5.1 cm) in diameter, 4 to 14 inches (10.2 to 35.6 cm) long. Description on pages 488–89.

Black bear (NH): Beech-nut and winterberry. 1 1/4 to 2 1/2 inches (3.2 to 6.4 cm) in diameter, 5 to 12 inches (12.7 to 30.5 cm) long. Description on page 477.

Black bear (MA): Acorn. 1¹/₄ to 2¹/₂ inches (3.2 to 6.4 cm) in diameter, 5 to 12 inches (12.7 to 30.5 cm) long. Description on page 477.

Black bear (AK): Fruit. 1¹/₄ to 2¹/₂ inches (3.2 to 6.4 cm) in diameter, 5 to 12 inches (12.7 to 30.5 cm) long. Description on page 477.

Black bear (MA): Black cherry. 1¹/₄ to 2¹/₂ inches (3.2 to 6.4 cm) in diameter, 5 to 12 inches (12.7 to 30.5 cm) long. Description on page 477.

Grizzly bear (MT): Glacier lily bulb. 1 1/4 to 2 7/8 inches (3.2 to 7.3 cm) in diameter, 7 to 20 inches (17.8 to 50.8 cm) long. Description on page 477.

Grizzly bear (AK): Pea vine roots. 1 1/4 to 2 7/8 inches (3.2 to 7.3 cm) in diameter, 7 to 20 inches (17.8 to 50.8 cm) long. Description on page 477.

Grizzly bear (MT): Fruit. 1 1/4 to 2 7/8 inches (3.2 to 7.3 cm) in diameter, 7 to 20 inches (17.8 to 50.8 cm) long. Description on page 477.

Grizzly bear (AK): Grasses. $1^{1}/_{4}$ to $2^{7}/_{8}$ inches (3.2 to 7.3 cm) in diameter, 7 to 20 inches (17.8 to 50.8 cm) long. Description on page 477.

Grizzly bear (MT): Meat. $1^{1}/_{4}$ to $2^{7}/_{8}$ inches (3.2 to 7.3 cm) in diameter, 7 to 20 inches (17.8 to 50.8 cm) long. Description on page 477.

PART 3:
Loose and Amorphous Scat

Mole (NY): Description on pages 472–73.

American pika (WA): Description on pages 505–6.

Muskrat (MN): Soft. 3/8 to 1 inch (1 to 2.5 cm) in diameter, 7/8 to 1 3/4 inches (2.2 to 4.4 cm) long. Description on pages 503–4.

Sea otter (captive on diet of clams and shrimp): Tubular scats. 1/2 to 1 1/2 inches (3 to 3.8 cm) in diameter. Description on page 483.

Scat Identification

Otter (MA): Description on pages 478, 480–83.

Raccoon (MA): Black cherry. Description on page 484.

Coati (AZ): Description on page 485.

Gray fox (MA):
Black cherries.
Description on
pages 473,
476–77.

Coyote (AK):
Description
on pages 473–75.

Coyote (TX):
Coyotes are con-
sidered the pri-
mary distributor
for sabal palm
seeds. Descrip-
tion on pages
473–75.

Scat Identification

Wolf (ID): Description on pages 473, 475. Photo by Kevin Jarvis, Shikari Tracking Guild.

Black bear (AK): Blueberry. Description on page 477.

Grizzly bear (MT): Glacier lily bulbs and ground squirrel. Description on page 477.

Harbor seal (OR): Description on page 484.

Pronghorn (WY): Description on pages 492–93.

Dall's sheep (AK): Description on pages 493, 494.

Scat Identification

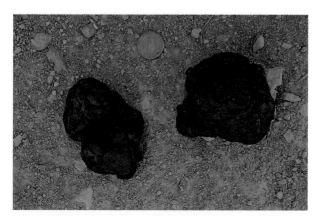

Bighorn sheep (CO): Description on pages 493–94.

White-tailed deer (NH): Description on pages 489–91.

White-tailed deer (MN): Description on pages 489–91.

Caribou (AK):
Description
on pages
489–90, 492.

Mountain goat
(MT): Description
on page 493.

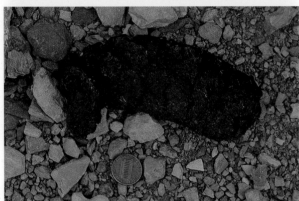

Elk (OR):
Description on
pages 489–90.

Elk (OR): Description on pages 489–90.

Muskox (AK): Description on pages 493–94.

Muskox (AK): Description on pages 493–94.

Feral horse (VA):
Description on
page 488.

Moose (NH):
Description on
pages 489–92.

Moose (NH):
Description on
pages 489–92.

Scat Identification

Moose (NH): Description on pages 489–92.

Buffalo (WY): Patties. 10 to 16 inches (25.4 to 40.6 cm) in diameter. Description on page 493.

Buffalo (WY): Chips. Diameter of individual chips ranges from 3 to 4 1/2 inches (7.6 to 11.4 cm). Description on page 493.

Sign on Vegetation and Fungi

6

While awaiting coworkers in the Cascade range of Washington, I sat down and watched a Townsend's chipmunk duck in and out of an impressive blackberry patch. He was often hard to see, deep among the tangled growth, but for a moment, he worked in the open. After chewing off a large, half-moon-shaped section from one of the thick green stems, he retired to a perch near me and proceeded to attack and demolish the entire great chunk, just as children do with a large slice of watermelon. With only a pause to lick his paws, he dashed to a nearby stem and cut another, and when that one was done, another. Suddenly, I was able to see myriad chews of every age throughout the understory of blackberry, where half-moon-shaped slices of juicy blackberry stem had been taken. Amazing. I also found identical sign in four of five blackberry patches we passed on our hike that day. It is always worthwhile to sit and observe what is all around us.

Everything an animal does shapes the environment, and ultimately the world, in which it lives. A track compresses earth, making it more or less suitable for a specific plant species. A scat transports seeds, and a dig exposes earth for seedlings to propagate. Nowhere is this more apparent than in interpreting mammal sign on vegetation. Trees are shaped and even killed by mammals. A squirrel may cut the ends of spruce twigs from 100 limbs in a single tree, later eating the terminal buds on the forest floor. This act shapes the canopy and thus the shade structure on the forest floor, and shade quantity and quality greatly influence the potential list of plants participating in the herbaceous layer under this great tree; thus, a feeding squirrel influences the structure of the herbaceous layer. In another scenario, Miquelle and Van Bellenberghe (1989)

Green blackberry stem harvested by a Townsend's chipmunk. (WA)

reported that intense feeding of winter moose, which stripped the bark of 75 percent of willows and aspens in an area and broke a large percentage of saplings in the understory, was greatly speeding up successional changes in the forest.

How is the forest influenced when beavers remove all the hardwoods from a wetland edge, or an overpopulation of deer suppresses sapling growth, or bears rip the limbs from old apple trees and beeches on a mountain slope? How is the earth and vegetation altered when a grizzly turns over hundreds of cubic feet of alpine meadow feeding on glacier lily bulbs, or when pocket gophers leave miles of tunnels and eskers under aspen groves? Our culture and science are just beginning to probe such ecological relationships.

Mushrooms and Other Fungi

Many mammals eat fungi in their entirety, but you may find caches, drying mushrooms, or partially eaten fungi in your travels. Chipmunks, ground squirrels, porcupines, squirrels, voles, birds, and deer are among the many animals that eat mushrooms and other fungi. Here are a few signs to look for in your explorations. Truffles, an underground fungi, are discussed under digs in chapter 7, as often the hole is all that remains to interpret.

Birch Polypore

Birch polypore *(Piptoporus betulinus)* grows only on dead birches and is a reliable source of animal signs. Insects leave their signs, pursuing birds leave theirs, and squirrels and white-tailed deer actually eat the bracket fungus itself. The two mammal species can be differentiated by looking

Top: Birch polypore nibbled by a red squirrel. Squirrels often eat them down to a nub. (MN) *Bottom:* This birch polypore holds the perfect bite of a white-tailed deer. (MA) Photo by Paul Rezendes.

for clear incisors in the remaining fungi walls. The small paired upper and lower incisors of squirrels are easy to differentiate from the lower incisors of deer. In some cases, when the polypores have been completely consumed and only a nub remains, the sign is harder to interpret. In this case, consider the height of the sign, because squirrels can climb higher than deer can reach.

Hanging Mushrooms

Red squirrels harvest and hang mushrooms to dry for later caching and consumption. I have found trees laden with mushrooms in crotches and branches, hanging like Christmas tree ornaments. I have yet to find gray squirrels or other small rodents hanging mushrooms in this way.

Eating Mushrooms

On several occasions, I've watched red-backed voles shuttle parts of mushrooms back and forth to a nearby burrow. Large mushrooms are dismantled where they are found, then moved in manageable chunks. In the end, all that remains is the stem, just visible below the earth's surface. Many others also eat mushrooms, and their signs may be difficult to find at times. Larger mammals eat mushrooms in their entirety, pluck

Left: A red squirrel hung this mushroom in the canopy, along with many others. When dry, the mushrooms will be moved to a cache. (NH) *Right:* This dismantled mushroom was transported belowground in manageable chunks by a red-backed vole. The work is still in progress. (NY)

and store them, or hang them up to dry (see Hanging Mushrooms). Slugs and snails consume vast amounts of mushrooms, and their signs are also quite easy to find.

Grasses and Forbs

During the warmer months, a variety of wildlife takes advantage of the lush green herbaceous layer that fills fields and creates understories in forested landscapes. An animal is *grazing* when feeding on herbaceous plant material during the bountiful summer months. Often, these same animals turn to *browsing* on woody stalks and bark when the temperatures plummet and the green grasses, flowers, and leaves curl up, fade away, and become scarce.

It is difficult to distinguish the grazing of one species from that of another. I have watched deer, elk, and bison graze and then, after their departure, investigated the area where they were feeding. The grasses and other vegetation appeared to be ripped, often leaving ragged, flat ends. Rather than attempt to differentiate among ungulates when interpreting grazing sign, I rely on associated signs, most often scats.

Rodents and lagomorphs, many of which graze during the lush season, slice their meals from the stalk. With incisors on top and bottom, they should (in theory) leave neat, 45-degree-angle cuts on grass and other vegetation. Sometimes this is the case, especially with smaller mammals or when animals cut and feed on larger greenery. I once

Green skunk cabbage browsed by elk. (OR)

Grass cut and accumulating where a meadow vole returned to feed under cover (which I removed for the photograph). (NY)

watched a meadow vole feeding on red clover in a field. Each stalk was sliced individually and then eaten in its entirety. Upon inspection, I found a 45-degree cut on each of the stalks, but these signs were impossible to notice unless I was on my hands and knees. In other cases, after watching cottontails feed, I was not always able to find neatly angled cuts—some were angled, but many went straight across, and others looked torn. Certainly the angle of attack influences the resulting signs, but variety is the point I want to emphasize.

Otter-chewed sedges at a roll site. Many carnivores eat grass to help clean their digestive systems. Otters also chew and manipulate grasses when scent marking. (VT)

Top: Cornstalks harvested and carried away by a beaver. (MA) *Bottom:* Green false hellebore harvested by an American pika. (MT)

When muskrats and nutrias feed on larger wetland plants, such as cattail or phragmitis, they reliably leave angled cuts, with clear incisors in the plant tops and stems left behind. Signs of feeding may be seen floating in ponds and marshes where these species are active, or stacked waterside by muskrats that have already eaten the tubers and choice portions of the stalks. Muskrats pile the discarded plant remains at favorite feeding stations.

I once spent an afternoon watching marmots feed on alpine flowers, a summer staple for this species. Flowers were plucked as often as they

Top: Cattails harvested by a porcupine. (NH) *Bottom:* Floating cattail remains cover the surface where nutrias fed. (TX)

were neatly cut, leaving a great variety of sign. Clearly the size of the stem and the size of the animal are factors in the sign left behind. It's also evident that rodents and lagomorphs do not always leave clean, angled cuts; therefore, their grazing sign could be confused with that of ungulates and other animals, such as grouse and turkeys.

The giant kangaroo rat mows vegetation in an easily identifiable fashion. These rats cut vegetation to establish a territory, called a *precinct;* these areas function much like our suburban yards. Each person keeps

Top: Vegetation cut and partially eaten by muskrats. (ME) *Bottom:* Discarded portions of phragmitis stems accumulate at a muskrat's favorite feeding perch. (MA) Photo by John McCarter.

his or her yard maintained and objects when other humans trespass. In the same way, kangaroo rats live within a *colony,* which is a collection of fiercely guarded precincts. These areas are easy to detect in areas of long grasses, where you'll see mowed circular and amoeba-shaped areas, up to 30 feet (9.14 m) across, sprinkled across the landscape.

Ground squirrels and black-tailed prairie dogs are also known to cut the vegetation around their burrows to allow for easier spotting of preda-

A clear edge of cut grass defines the boundary of a giant kangaroo rat's precinct, or defended territory. (CA)

tors and interlopers. Long-established black-tailed prairie dog towns appear devoid of vegetation, whereas other prairie dog species often leave tall vegetation standing within colony boundaries.

Seeds

The seeds of grasses and other forbs are eaten by many small mammals, as well as numerous bird species. Signs of feeding on these tiny seeds are often hard to detect; it may be easier to detect caches. Consider natural caches on the landscape when looking for signs of small rodents, such as areas where seeds blow and collect in great numbers; these places provide a greater return on time invested in harvesting.

Giant kangaroo rats make another unusual sign. A few mammal species create piles of green vegetation (see Haystacks), but giant kangaroo rats create piles of seeds—often entire seed heads of nearby grasses—which they dry aboveground for up to six weeks before moving them below into their burrow system. These wonderful creatures live in only a fragment of their previous range, so unless you are in or near San Luis Obispo County in California, you should consider alternative interpretations.

Haystacks

Those who are familiar with farm country may recall the smell of fresh-cut hay, which fills the air several times each growing season. Humans are not the only mammals that have learned to harvest herbaceous greens and then stack them neatly in ways that actually increase their

Top: Large pile of seed heads gathered and left to dry by a giant kangaroo rat. When dried completely, the seeds will be moved into the burrow and stored. (CA)
Bottom: Look closely for the hay pile of an American pika amidst this rock jumble, which is commonly where they make their homes. (MT)

nutritional value. Four other mammals come to mind immediately: the collared pika, American pika, mountain beaver, and singing vole.

Each of these species is known to create larders of grasses and other herbaceous plants and store them for the long winter months. Pikas are high-altitude creatures, most often making their homes in screes and rock jumbles near or above the tree line. When summer finally arrives at

Hay pile of a collared pika. (AK)

their elevation, and the grasses and alpine flowers burst forth in waves of color, the pikas go to work for the upcoming winter, which comes all too soon where they live.

Pikas cut grasses, flowers, and an assortment of other vegetation and pile them in large haystacks. Their handiwork can often be seen peeking out from nooks and crevices between boulders, from under rock overhangs, and sometimes overflowing and blowing about on surrounding rocks.

Pikas are expert hayers. Research has shown that there is more to their haystacks than just piling vegetation. Dearing (Smith, 1997) discovered that some of the plants harvested by pikas inhibit bacterial growth, thus

Compare the contents of the hay piles presented. This one was created by an American pika. (CO)

Small hay piles created by a singing vole. (AK)

preserving them. These same plants are actually poisonous to pikas, but when they are stored for a long time, they lose their toxicity and can be consumed. These "preservative" plants in haystacks are crucial to winter survival and provide a fascinating leap in our understanding and acknowledgment of how complicated some animal behaviors really are.

The singing vole, also called the Alaska vole, also creates haystacks for the winter. These voles tend to stash their stores under rocks and logs, but I've occasionally found them in the open as well. Be careful not to confuse dilapidated nests for haystacks in your explorations. Adolf Murie (1961) invested significant time and energy studying this behavior. He found their piles as I described above, as well as held aloft and cradled in shrubs and low-growing vegetation—presumably to help keep caches dry. Murie found these haystacks in every habitat of Denali National Park, along with large caches of roots that were dug and transported by these same voles and stored underground.

Burt and Grossenheider (1952) wrote that singing voles create haystacks of between 1 and 7 quarts (.95 and 6.6 l). All such piles found at low elevations are definitely those of voles rather than collared pikas, with which they share a range; those found at higher elevations should be considered along with associated sign. Vole and pika scats are easily differentiated and are often found in and around haystacks. And if you've found a pika haystack, you will likely hear and see its maker dashing between boulders and across rock jumbles, screaming alarm to others who share its rocky home.

The aplodontia, or mountain beaver, found in the Pacific Northwest, also stacks and dries materials near its burrow. Ferns are a major component of its diet and are found drying in piles near entrances. Once they are dry enough, they are moved below.

Cacti and Lechugillas

The soft, succulent vegetation of dry, desert ecosystems is popular fare for many species, which rely on it for water as well as nutrition. Cholla are ringed by hispid cotton rats. Prickly pear species are widespread in the southern and southwestern United States and Mexico and are eaten by numerous mammals. The "pads" of prickly pear cacti are chewed by black-tailed jackrabbits, white-throated woodrats, mule deer, and collared peccaries, to name a few.

Peccaries are notorious for eating prickly pears; they tear bite-sized chunks with no concern for the pear's large spikes or the thousands of spiny hairs that cover its pads and are harder to see. When peccaries feed straight from the plant, their sign is quite obvious: ripped and shredded pads hanging limply from the cactus. Peccaries also remove entire pads and retire to cover to continue eating; thus, their sign on the actual plant may be more subtle, and additional signs of feeding may appear quite far from the plant—half-eaten pads trailing to nearby shade and shrubbery.

Classic example of collared peccaries feeding on prickly pear cactus. Compare the fresh sign, which is minutes old, with the older sign, which has healed and browned. (TX)

Mule deer leave similar signs. Look for associated signs to confirm your suspicions, and consider the height of the sign as well. Deer loom over peccaries. If teeth marks are clear, they are also an aid. The pointy incisors of peccaries are distinct.

Jackrabbit and woodrat signs on prickly pears are similar. Jackrabbits tend to bite through the entire pad, which woodrats do only to the thinnest of pads. Woodrats often peel back the outer skins of pads and

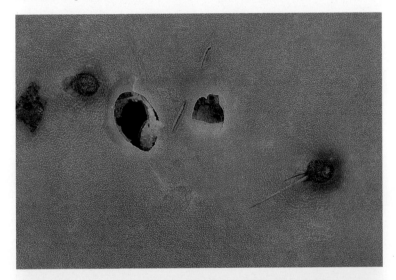

Top: The pointed incisors of a peccary are clearly visible in this prickly pear pad pulled from the cactus. (TX) *Bottom:* Prickly pear pads eaten by a mule deer. (TX)

scrape out the pulpy insides. If jackrabbits have fed for any length of time, there are likely to be pellets on the ground, and if woodrats are responsible, a nest should be very close by.

The fruits of many other cacti are also eaten by numerous animals. The fruits of saguaros attract birds of all kinds and are also eaten by foxes,

Top: Prickly pear cactus eaten by a black-tailed jackrabbit. Also note the accumulation of pellets. (TX) *Bottom:* Prickly pear cactus peeled and eaten by a white-throated woodrat. (TX)

Barrel cactus surrounded by fruit remains discarded by feeding peccaries. (AZ)

coyotes, antelope squirrels, and peccaries, when they drop to the ground. Barrel cactus fruits are also relished by many. With barrel cactus, woodpeckers tend to create a hole in the fruit from which to retrieve the seeds, while peccaries and other mammals eat the whole thing.

The soft core and roots of the lechugilla are prized by peccaries and Botta's pocket gophers, and signs of both species are easy to find. Mammals strip the thick, sharp leaves from the plant to work down to the soft core—a bit like eating an artichoke. When you encounter such

Compare the nearly intact fruit left by gila woodpeckers, which remove the seeds through a single hole, with the remains of fruit left by collared peccaries, which eat the fruit in its entirety. (AZ)

A lechugilla core stripped and eaten by a peccary. Note the direction of attack and the scattered leaves. (TX)

signs, it is important to note the direction of attack. Peccaries attack from above, gripping spiny leaves in their teeth and pulling them out one at a time. The leaves will be strewn about the plant, and the core will be eaten. Pocket gophers attack from below and sever all the leaves right where they are, leaving a neat ring of cut leaves, each with the 45-degree angle characteristic of rodents. In areas where gophers have worked many lechugillas growing in close proximity, their mounds will be sprinkled through the area as well.

A Botta's pocket gopher has come from below and neatly removed the soft core of this lechugilla. (TX)

Live Trees and Shrubs

When assessing signs associated with woody perennials, shrubs, and trees, first consider whether the sign was created while the plant was alive or dead. This is an important question, because dead trees offer no nutritional value to a browser or an animal debarking the cambium layer beneath the outer bark. Maybe the sign was made while the tree lived and caused its demise. The greater your field experience, the easier this task will become. The greatest challenge is interpreting signs created on living trees that have since died.

Fresh signs are easy to differentiate from old. And the bark of trees and shrubs holds signs for years, offering a wonderful opportunity to age signs and track past events. With practice and patience, the observer can follow moose incisor scrapes from past winters and then read a history of use in a given area by a particular species. Consider an unpublished study by Daniel Wolfson, who created age categories for bear claw marks on beech trees in the Northeast and tested wildlife professionals using photographs. Thus, habitat assessments could determine not only that bears had been in an area but also for how long or how long ago if they were no longer there. (Details of this study are presented later in this chapter.)

The incredible diversity of animal signs associated with live trees and shrubs can be divided into three large categories: (1) removal of or marks in the bark or cambium layer; (2) breaking, cutting, or browsing twigs, limbs, or trunks; and (3) sign on mast and fruit crops.

1) Sign in Bark or Cambium

This massive category of sign can be further subdivided into three sections: feeding, marking, and other activities. Signs in the cambium (the inner bark) and the outer bark layer are most often attributed to feeding or marking animals. Other signs, such as those made by climbing or lightning, are discussed last.

Feeding

Numerous animals feed on the inner bark of living trees during the colder months to carry them through to the next growing season. The inner bark, where the xylem and phloem carry sugar and other vitamins, is the only living portion of the trunk and limbs and the only area that provides any sustenance for hungry mammal species. Both the inner wood, which provides the structural support, and the outer bark, which provides protection, are dead and offer nothing in terms of food for animals. The exception is dead wood impregnated with fungal mycelia, upon which squirrels sometimes feed.

Root Systems. Voles and pocket gophers feed on the cambium layers of roots beneath the ground. If they do enough damage to a root system, the signs will spread aboveground, and a tree may wilt or die off completely. In many cases, only a portion of the root system is eaten or stripped, and one portion or side of the tree dies back in reaction. In extreme cases, there is little left of the root system, and the shrub just

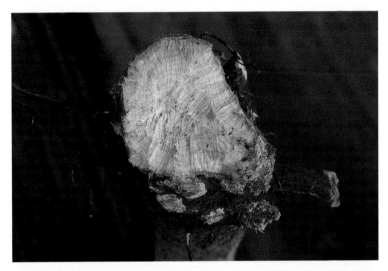

Top: This beech sapling had its entire root system eaten by a vole, likely a woodland vole, and subsequently tipped over. (NH) *Bottom:* A snowshoe hare has eaten the cambium layer of this exposed spruce root. (ME)

Left: Exposed fir root bitten by a black bear. It has been theorized that the height of such sign is significant in dominance communication, but you will find bites on trees at every level in the field. (NH) *Right:* Wild rose stalks debarked by meadow voles. (MA)

tips over. On a number of occasions, I've poked at dying rosebushes and had them fall over because voles had completely removed the support system over the course of a winter.

Other mammals chew or bite at exposed roots. Beavers, rabbits, and porcupines feed on the cambium, and bears may bite roots for marking purposes. Red squirrels and chipmunks also bite along exposed roots for communication purposes, especially in areas surrounding the entrance to a burrow or cache, and on bulbous growths and knobs.

Debarking. Rodents and lagomorphs of every size feed on the cambiums of numerous shrub and tree species in similar fashion—leaving visible incisor marks in the inner bark layer. This feeding strategy is termed *debarking*. The size of the teeth marks is helpful in interpretation, as is the location of feeding on the tree. Let us consider signs found from ground level upward.

Voles and pocket gophers. Tiny teeth marks low on shrubs and trees are likely the work of voles. This sign is often most evident after a deep

Alder twigs, debarked and cut into lengths by a heather vole. An accumulation of these twigs was found under a rock near the shrub. (WA)

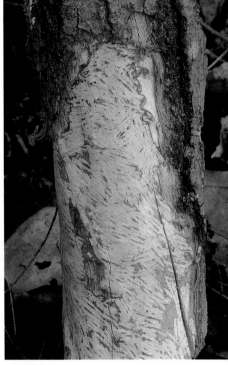

Left: A sugar maple sapling completely girdled by a meadow vole. Numerous tree and shrub species are debarked by meadow voles under the protection of snow during the winter. (VT) *Right:* This large-diameter branch of a northern red oak fell during a storm and was debarked by red-backed voles. (MA)

snow that persists for some time and then melts away with the spring sun and warm temperatures. The voles, while tunneling and exploring within the snow level, often feed on shrubs and trees they encounter, diligently girdling saplings and medium-sized trees. The list of shrubs and tree species I've seen debarked by voles is long and includes ash, sumac, maple, birch, rose, alder, mountain ash, and fruit trees. Voles are also quick to take advantage of storm-broken branches that drop to the ground or slash left by people. On several occasions, I've even found cut and stacked firewood that had been discovered and celebrated by voles. I have never found a mouse debarking trees or shrubs for food; mice are more dependent on stores of mast crops to survive the winter. Pocket gophers also debark shrubs and trees within the snow layer in the winter months. Olaus Murie (1954) reported finding such signs of their feeding on aspens when snows receded in the spring.

Rabbits, muskrats, and woodchucks. Rabbits feed on the bark of numerous species at ground level or as high as a given year's snowpack. Signs of feeding rabbits can often be differentiated from those of porcupines and others by the location of the sign and the tendency for lagomorphs to eat more than the cambium layer and to do considerable damage to the inner wood as well. This "going beyond" the cambium layer, though rare in rodents, is characteristic of all members of the pika and rabbit families, from cottontails to snowshoe hares.

Muskrats and woodchucks also feed at ground level on occasion, and the size of their incisors is similar to that of rabbits. I have not found

Pikas debarking red huckleberry stalks. I've also found them debarking mountain hemlock and alders. (WA)

Left: Blackberry stalks debarked by eastern cottontails. (MA) *Right:* A sumac trunk holds the clear incisors of feeding eastern cottontails. Cottontails also debark fruit trees. (MA)

A close-up look at how rabbit species go beyond the cambium layer and cut into the wood. Here, a snowshoe hare has been feeding on a beaked hazelnut. (NH)

Many species take advantage of fallen branches for browse or to debark the tender cambium layer. Here, snowshoe hares have completely cleaned a large quaking aspen branch. (MN)

muskrats debarking often, but you may find this sign. Charlie Perakis found Maine's coastal populations feeding on bark on offshore islands. The incisors create a sporadic pattern, because feeding is approached from every angle. Woodchucks have most often been documented debarking fruit trees, but I have not found this sign personally. Woodchucks do bite trees for marking purposes (discussed later).

Both biting and bark stripping are used by this snowshoe hare as he feeds on an apple tree. Hares also regularly debark red maple, striped maple, willow, alder, mountain ash, balsam fir, and dogwood. (ME)

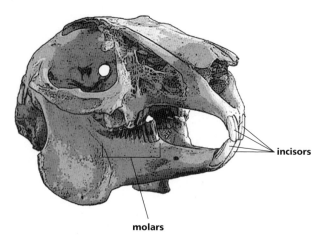

incisors

molars

Snowshoe hare skull.

Beavers. The most notorious bark-eating mammal in North America is the beaver, which also works at ground level. Beavers strip a tree from base to crown, leaving a glowing yellow landmark as a testament to their logging abilities and their presence in a given water system. Their work often accompanies felled trees and shrubs (discussed later).

Beavers may also chew into wood and then abandon the project, allowing the tree to persist and heal over time. Often with conifer species, beavers strip the cambium layer off the base of the tree as high as they can reach and then move on, never making an attempt to fell the whole tree to harvest bark beyond their reach. I've found groves of young hemlocks killed by beavers girdling only the base and never attempting to cut any down.

A beaver has stripped and eaten the bark of this white pine as high as it could reach. Beavers feed on many conifer species in this way, never attempting to fell them. (MA)

Tassel-eared squirrels debark masses of ponderosa pine twigs, which they first cut free while in the canopy. (AZ)

Squirrels, porcupines, and mountain beavers. Sign found higher aboveground may be feeding squirrels but is more likely to be the work of climbing porcupines or mountain beavers. These two species are notorious bark eaters and have gained poor reputations among the foresters who cherish young stands of planted trees.

Porcupines can do incredible damage to trees. While hiking with John McCarter several years ago, we came over a rise and couldn't help but stop and gaze at a bright yellow tree farther down the ridge. Porcupines had debarked an entire 40- to 50-foot (12.2- to 15.2-m) red oak tree,

A fox squirrel debarked and scraped this cottonwood branch with its incisors. The diameter of the branch is 1¹/₈ inches (2.9 cm). (CO)

Fox squirrels also scrape the insides of peeled bark strips to feed on cottonwood cambium. Look closely for teeth marks. (CO)

Left: Missing patches of red pine bark high on the trunk are a sure sign of feeding porcupines. (MA) *Right:* Hardwoods, such as this American beech, hold the signs of porcupine incisors beautifully. Also note the distinctive colors of porcupine feeding sign from three different periods; the oldest is several years old. (NH)

A young white pine damaged by a porcupine. (MA)

10 inches (25.4 cm) in diameter, from ground to crown, except for a 1-foot (30 cm) section at head level on one side. Any such work done during a winter season remains bright yellow until the sap begins to flow again and the tree heals or starts to die; at this point, bright yellow patches of exposed inner wood dull and fade to grays and browns. Look for bright patches high in trees, where porcupines are safe from many predators and the outer bark is thinner, allowing easier access to the cambium layer. The variety of trees eaten is incredible and includes aspens, willows, hemlocks, beeches, maples, pines, fruit trees, hickories, oaks, and ashes.

Mountain beavers also climb and chew patches in firs, spruces, and other conifers, as well as vine and big-leaf maples. Nearby burrow systems should aid in the interpretation where nipped branches may be found protruding.

Tapping. Squirrels are reliable tappers of many tree species during the spring sap flow and sometimes again in the fall. Red squirrels tap trees often; I have also observed gray squirrels tapping, though less often, and researchers have observed southern flying squirrels tapping trees. Differentiating among squirrel species can be a challenge.

Squirrels bite into the cambium layer with their heads turned sideways. Just as we bite into an apple, they anchor with the upper incisors and then cut upward with the lower incisors. They may also anchor with the upper incisors and repeatedly slice with the lower incisors as they approach and join the upper incisors. Either way, sap oozes freely from the cut bark, surging with the sap flows and spring temperature swings. After biting different places along sapling trunks and mature tree limbs, the squirrel leaves to attend to other business. My observations support work done by Heinrich (1992), who also noted squirrels biting and then leaving the site. They return sometime later to lick what remains after most of the water has evaporated, condensing vitamins

Left: **A fresh red squirrel tap in a red maple, with recent surges of sap evident in the circular stains. (NH)** *Right:* **What may look like disease in a red maple, is actually the healed signs of numerous red squirrel taps many years ago. Look closely for the dot-dash patterns. (NH)**

and sugars for a better resource and reward for energy expended. According to one researcher, sugars are condensed from 2 to 55 percent through evaporation.

Sue Morse coined the phrase "dot-dash pattern" to describe bear bites, but I use it to describe tapping sign. The anchor point of the upper incisors leaves a small cut in the bark, the dot, while the slashing lower incisors create a longer cut, the dash. In this way, you can envision which way the animal turned its head to tap the tree. Look for their sign along the trunks of young saplings, as well as along the smooth limbs of larger furrowed trees. I have noted a number of tree species being tapped. All the maples are tapped, including big-leaf maple in the West and striped maple in the East. Serviceberry is often tapped, and occasionally birches and apple trees.

Tapping is a common sign in woodlands and persists for many years. Be warned that the horizontal expansion of bark and tree over many years may expand original sign of a mere 3/8 inch (1 cm) into dot-dash patterns up to 4 inches (10.2 cm) across.

Incisor scraping. Deer, moose, elk, horses, domestic goats, and sheep feed on the bark of trees during the winter months, but it is more common in particular regions of the continent. I have followed large deer herds in parts of the West and not been able to find this sign, yet signs of incisor scraping are incredibly common in much of New England. We must constantly remind ourselves that animals do different things in different places. Bears also strip off the outer bark of evergreens and feed on the inner cambium layer, leaving obvious signs of scraping teeth and claws. This sign is especially prevalent in the Northwest, where a great deal of time and money has been spent to determine how to stop black bears from feeding in evergreen timber plantations in the spring.

Ungulates. The structure of the mouth is especially important in understanding the sign of ungulates eating inner bark. Upon close inspection of the sign, you will note that all the motion is made upward, or angled upward, depending on the position of the head. This important feature helps differentiate feeding sign from antler rubs, which result from two-directional movement—up and down. Ungulates can only scrape bark up, because they have no teeth on the upper jaw at the front of the mouth. Horses have both upper and lower teeth, which makes their sign on bark easy to differentiate from that of deer, elk, and moose.

Deer, elk, and moose are particular about tree species when incisor scraping, each having a short list of species they feed on most often. White-tailed deer sign tends to be found on young hemlock, sumac, witch hazel, viburnum, young spindle tree, willow, and occasionally young

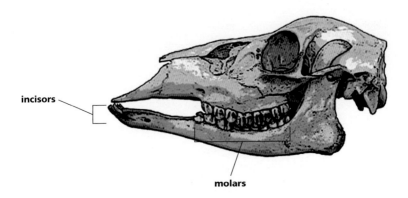

incisors

molars

White-tailed deer skull.

Left: When horses feed on bark, sign is distinctly two-directional, in that upper and lower incisors bite down and up and meet in the middle. (NH) *Right:* A hemlock incisor scrape by a white-tailed deer. (NH)

apple, cherry, and red maple. I've found mule deer incisor scraping only on willows, and only on a few occasions. Moose sign tends to be found on red and striped maple, willow, quaking aspen, balsam fir, and mountain ash, but occasionally on young cherry, witch hazel, and others.

In addition to incisor scraping, moose employ a strategy I term *spaghetti feeding.* Incisors are used to cut into and under the cambium layer, which is then gripped between the teeth and the hard palate. With a jerk of the head, a sizable strip of bark can be peeled, running straight up the trunk. A moose with a 4-foot (1.2 m) strip of bark hanging from its mouth probably looks something like we do with a long piece of spaghetti hanging from ours, pulling it in slowly and chewing as we go.

Elk sign is found predominantly on quaking aspen trees, but occasionally on willows and alders. Winter elk herds can be rather sedentary, so significant signs on bark can accumulate quickly. In areas of the Rockies, every aspen from 6 feet (1.8 m) down is scarred black with the accumulation of signs of elk feeding during past winters.

The species of tree is an excellent clue to which animal has fed on the bark, as there is little overlap. The width of the teeth is helpful as well, especially when differentiating between deer and moose, but differentiating between elk and moose is more difficult. Also remember that incisor scraping is not done with the largest of the incisors, because the nose would get in the way. Scraping is done with the smaller teeth found to either side, and the width of these teeth marks depends on how deeply they gouge the bark surface; deeper gouges create wider teeth marks. Deer incisor marks generally measure between 1/8 and 3/16 inch (.3 and .5 cm), and moose measure between 3/16 and 3/8 inch (.5 and 1 cm).

The height of the sign may also be a useful indicator when determining species. I have seen moose scrape as low as 9 inches off the ground, and elk and deer sign may be found quite low as well. The upper reach may be a more useful study. I have measured moose incisor scrapes as high as 95 inches (2.4 m) off the ground, elk up to 85 inches (2.16 m), and deer as high as 72 inches (1.8 m). Unfortunately, these upper measurements are potentially misleading, as they depend on the snowpack in a given year. You may be interpreting sign created in February, when a 3-foot (91 cm) snowpack elevated the deer, in the summer, after the snow has melted away. Use the three perspectives (lying, standing, flying) to slow yourself down and avoid rash interpretations.

Left: Witch hazel scraped by a white-tailed deer. (NH) *Right:* A red maple incisor scrape by a moose. (VT)

Left: Moose incisor scraping on willow. (MT) *Right:* Spaghetti feeding, in which a moose pulled strips of bark from this striped maple. (NH)

Fresh elk sign sits above the accumulation of healed, scarred quaking aspen bark. Elk hit the same trees year after year, until the bark is so thickly scarred that the cambium is protected from further assault and fresh bark is out of reach. (CO)

A western larch stripped and scraped by a black bear feeding on the spring sapwood. (MT)

Bears. Although much has been written about black bears engaging in incisor scraping, some authors also note that grizzlies feed on the sapwood of trees. These notations are always brief and without further explanation, so I pursued the question by reviewing several long-term, large-scale studies of grizzly bear dietary habits and could find no mention of this behavior.

The signs of bears feeding on the sapwood of conifers are dramatic. Trees are stripped of bark up to 88 inches (2.24 m) aboveground, and the strips lie strewn about the base. In some cases, the bears may girdle an entire tree. The extent of the sign and the numerous teeth marks make bear sign hard to confuse with others. Claw marks may also be visible where bark was gripped and pulled.

Marking

Deer, elk, moose, caribou, and bison. During the rut, many antlered and horned mammals leave obvious signs on the trunks and limbs of trees. Male deer, elk, moose, caribou, and bison create visual and olfactory marks along travel routes and in areas of congregation. The details of such signs and their height above ground level are useful clues in determining which species is responsible.

Trackers use the term *antler rub* to describe the area where a male deer, elk, or moose has rubbed the bark of a tree trunk or limb with his head and antlers. Each fall, when antlers reach their peak size and weight and the velvet, which nourished the growing antlers, begins to dry, crack, and fall off, antler rubs begin to appear on the landscape. I have the most experience watching deer create this sign, and there has been significant research on this subject due to the popularity of the deer hunt.

Bucks approach the selected tree and lower their heads. This tree may be the same one used in previous years, but if not, it is likely to be

Left: Close-up of a recent white-tailed deer antler rub on a balsam fir. (NY)
Right: White-tailed deer rubs on staghorn sumacs. Fresh rubs glow and are easily detected on the landscape until the following spring, when the sap flow allows the bark to brown and heal. (VT)

in the immediate vicinity of previous antler rubs. Research has also proved that the diameter of the tree selected directly correlates with the size of the deer. Smaller bucks choose smaller trees.

The trees used tend to be $^1/2$ to 3 inches (1.3 to 7.6 cm) in diameter, but I've found antler rubs on serviceberry and basswood trees measuring $8^1/2$ inches (21.6 cm) or larger. If basswood trees are present, they are often utilized, but aromatic conifers are favorites; numerous other species are used as well.

Antler rubs are not always the violent acts I had imagined. Rubbing may be vigorous and rough or slow and calm. The area between the antlers is often rubbed as much as the antlers themselves. It was once believed that antler rubs were intended to relieve itching—which we assumed occurred due to the rapid bone growth and shedding of the velvet—and to remove the velvet from the antlers. These may be contributing factors in antler rubbing, but we've learned that these rubs are olfactory and visual markers that may allow females and other males to assess the health, vigor, and dominance of the buck that created the rub. Deer rub the glands on the head and face along the tree trunk, and the odor secreted is spread onto the antlers again as the buck continues to rub or even spar with the sapling in readiness for the rut. This scent is then paraded through the forest as the buck leaves the area. More is written about antlers and their functions in chapter 8. When the deer moves on, the resulting rub on the tree trunk is between 10 and 45 inches (25.4 and 114.3 cm) off the ground.

Behaviors are similar in elk, although their antler rubs seem to fall into two distinct categories. Elk create either long and high antler rubs on small-diameter trees, falling between 14 and 80 inches (35.6 and 203.2 cm) off the ground, or shorter rubs, between 23 and 60 inches (58.4 and 152.4 cm) off the ground, on stout, wider trees that are several inches in diameter. Whereas hair is not commonly found on deer antler rubs, it is often prominent on elk antler rubs, especially those on larger-diameter trees.

Moose also create two categories of antler rubs. The first is classic and similar to those of elk and deer, ranging between 15 and 99 inches (38.1 and 251.5 cm) off the ground. The second category of rubs are those done in bushes and shrubbery. Thrashing their heads from side to

Left: An example of an elk rub on a sapling. (CO) *Right:* A recent elk rub on a stout tree trunk. Note the copious hair stuck in the sap. (ID)

A moose antler rub on a single trunk. (NH)

side rather than vertically, moose destroy bushes. The resulting sign is a bush with numerous broken limbs and scraped bark. Caribou use the shrubby vegetation they encounter in their tundra habitats.

Buffaloes may horn trees at any time of year, but this behavior is especially prominent in the fall rut, when males horn numerous trees. Horns, unlike antlers, do not fall off but continue to grow over an animal's lifetime. Buffalo "horned trees" are often very conspicuous, and where you find one, you'll often find others. I have wandered through entire groves of lodgepole pine where every tree was hammered, and yellow sap glistened in the sunlight all around me. Trees selected are often 5 to 10 inches (12.7 to 25.4 cm) in

A moose antler rub in shrubbery. (NH)

A grove of lodgepole pines horned and rubbed by bison. (WY)

diameter, and the bark is stripped between 6 and 66 inches (15.2 and 167.6 cm) off the ground. Deep gouges are common, and the bark, which is peeled off in strips, litters the base of the tree if the sign is fresh. Horning tends to be followed by rubbing the trunk of the tree with neck and shoulders, and great clumps of buffalo fur often confirm who is responsible for the sign.

Squirrels. John McCarter was the first person to point out the unusual sign left by gray squirrels on black locust trees. It appeared as if the squirrels were chewing grooves into the outer bark layer, which was unlikely to provide any nutritional value. Together we pursued this phenomenon further and eventually discovered that these "stripes" chewed into the bark layer could be found both vertically and horizontally. Although John and I speculated that the stripes were the result of marking behaviors, no one I knew had witnessed a squirrel actually working a stripe, nor are these stripes discussed in the literature. Finally, I had an opportunity to witness the activity firsthand.

Two gray squirrels were caching acorns in someone's yard, while a third sat high in a black locust tree watching intently. The tree was distinctive for its massive size and presence, but also for the three long, bright orange stripes along its trunk, created by myriad chews and bites over time. While I watched, one of the squirrels in the yard approached the tree and hopped up onto the trunk, pausing at the bottom of the first stripe. She moved up along the chewed bark surface, smelling its entire length. At times, she paused to rub her cheeks or bite and add to the existing sign. When she got to the end of that stripe, she bounded up the

Left: Conspicuous vertical stripe chewed by many gray squirrels over time on a black locust trunk. (NH) *Right:* A closer look at a gray squirrel's vertical stripe on a northern red oak, which holds clear incisor marks. (NH)

tree to the next stripe, and the whole process of investigation and marking began again. Above the second stripe, she encountered the squirrel perched on a small limb, and the two began to chase each other about the tree. Clearly these stripes were part of an intricate communication shared by gray squirrels.

Since this first sighting, I have watched both gray and fox squirrels creating and adding to these markers across eastern America. I studied 64 vertical stripes created by gray squirrels on 37 species of trees in the East, and this is what I found:

1. The incisor marks rarely enter the cambium layer; therefore, no nutritional value is obtained.

2. The tree species used are distinctly different colors when comparing the outside bark with the area exposed when bitten.

Vertical stripes chewed by fox squirrels on a massive willow tree. (CO)

3. Stripes are an accumulation of sign over time—years and generations of squirrels may use them.

4. Stripes are made on the side of the tree least effected by weather—under the leaning side or under a large lower limb, if present.

5. Stripes are most often made on dominant trees in a given area. In the 64 trees studied, diameter at breast height ranged from 13 to 48 inches (13 to 129 cm) and averaged 29.15 inches (73.9 cm).

6. Ninety percent of the stripes were between 13 and 70 inches (33 and 177.8 cm) off the ground.

7. In every case in which the tree had a large lower limb, the stripe was found below it.

8. Stripes are also made on fence posts and other human-made structures.

9. Red squirrels occasionally chew vertically on trunks—most often on saplings, but occasionally on large conifers near the ground. These stripes are miniature versions of what gray and fox squirrels typically produce.

Red squirrels also chew and bite to mark and communicate with other squirrels. I watched a few red squirrels for a four-day period to improve my understanding of their territorial marking. My position seemed to be on the border of two squirrel properties, marked by a large hemlock with a gnarled root system. The tree stood just within the range of one squirrel and was fiercely guarded. On one of the dead lower branches, the resident squirrel maintained a horizontal stripe along the branch—the result of an accumulation of biting over time. In the root system of the same tree was also the start of a winter cache. But when this squirrel was away collecting or working in another part of its range, the neighboring red squirrel would sneak over, explore, and occasionally rob his neighbor's cache. It wasn't long before the resident squirrel

Classic horizontal stripe chewed by a red squirrel on the dead lower limb of an eastern hemlock. (NH)

became aware of this and sent up a shrill alarm from some distant tree-top. Quickly he reappeared and pursued the trespasser back to his own property. Once the trespasser was out, the resident ran to this particular hemlock on the boundary and visited the branch with the stripe. He smelled its length, often pausing to rub his cheek along it and add additional bites. I wonder if he checked the stripe to make sure it had not been desecrated by an outsider. Red squirrels are fiercely territorial, so it makes sense that this sign would be created by an individual, whereas gray squirrels tend to have overlapping ranges, and their marking sign is likely the result of several individual efforts.

Regardless of whether the stripe is horizontal or vertical, it is a visual and olfactory mark left by the squirrel that created it. Rubbing cheek glands and biting are both important components of the sign. Look for red squirrel stripes on the dead, lower branches of conifers. If you are willing to climb, you can often find their sign on higher limbs as well, especially if the tree holds a drey, or leaf nest. Travel routes from tree to tree are also heavily marked. Look for gray squirrel stripes vertically along large trunks of locust, black gum, ginkgo, pine, ash, and others. Gray squirrels, like all other species, also bite along travel routes, although I haven't found them creating horizontal stripes like red squirrels. In general, a vertical stripe means a gray or fox squirrel, and a horizontal stripe means a red or Douglas squirrel.

It is worth noting that squirrels bite just about anything to mark travel routes, be it twig, trunk, porch railing, wooden stairs, or other resources

Red squirrels also chew and bite green wood to mark. Here are fresh signs along the limb of a hemlock sapling. (MA)

just off the trail. In a house where I stayed in Minnesota, there was an established red squirrel route following the porch stairs from the second to third floor. Just where the squirrel leaped off into the tree, there was a wooden bowl on the deck that it marked, both coming and going. This large wooden bowl was repeatedly bitten along its rim and held over 25 scats, which accumulated in its center.

Woodchucks. Woodchucks often mark trees and shrubs in the immediate vicinity of burrow entrances. Look for bite marks on trunks and the lowest branches, as well as the remains of bark or cambium dropped next to the tree.

A gnarled hemlock root bitten and marked by a red squirrel. (MA)

Left: A cherry tree marked by a woodchuck. The tree stood about 5 feet (1.52 m) away from the nearest burrow entrance. (NY) *Right:* A feral farm cat's scratching post on common elderberry. (NH)

Felines. Felines are thought to scratch trees, shrubs, furniture, and other resources to keep their claws sharp and ready for use. Scratching may well serve the dual purpose of scent marking, as there are numerous glands in the feet; thus, there is likely to be some communication purpose in scratching posts.

This behavior is commonly observed in house cats both indoors and out. I've measured house cat scratch posts on shrubs, ranging from 5 to 23 inches (12.7 to 58.4 cm) off the ground, and seen them scratch higher on wooden decking, walls, and other human-made structures. All felines scratch horizontal surfaces such as logs as well.

I have found few scratching posts of wild felines on my forays, even though I've looked for them. Jen Vashon, a lynx biologist responsible for the Maine lynx project, could recall finding only one lynx scratching post on northern white cedar in all her winter backtracking. John Laudré, a

One of the benefits of scratching is removing the old, worn outer layers of the claws, which keeps them sharp and ready. These are the remains of a bobcat's claws. (CA)

longtime cougar researcher, could not recall ever seeing one in his 15-plus years of winter backtracking. John McCarter has found four in his 15 years of tracking bobcats in Massachusetts, and Paul Rezendes has found two in his 30 years of experience.

Scratching posts do exist, but they may be more subtle or temporary than we expect, especially if punky deadwoods are preferred. Including those seen by John McCarter and Paul Rezendes, with whom I often work, our combined bobcat scratching posts have all been on deadwood, except one I found years ago in Oregon on an elderberry.

A small-diameter log scratched by a bobcat. (MA) Photo by Paul Rezendes.

A cougar's scratching post. (Mexico) Photo by Sue Morse.

Big cats, including cougars and jaguars, scratch horizontal logs as well as vertical trunks. I found one such log, scratched by a cougar in Washington, on an old, overgrown logging road that was well traveled by big cats. I've also seen one trunk, scratched by a cougar, that was between 3½ and 5 feet (1.07 and 1.52 m) off the ground along a regular travel route in a dry streambed in Mexico. Any feline scratching post you find is cause for celebration.

Bears. Bears are responsible for many clawed, bitten, and rubbed trees on the landscape. Trees, utility poles, and other resources are selected along travel routes and near food resources and bedding areas, and they are used for commu-

A large log scratched and marked by a cougar. (WA)

A trail sign bitten and broken by a resident black bear. (NH)

Left: Carefully compare the coloration of the bark on each side of this tree; the lighter side is regularly rubbed by grizzly bears. (MT) *Right:* Hair is a wonderful find on rub trees. Note the silver-tipped guard hairs caught in this branch stub, which can belong only to a grizzly. (MT)

Compare the subtle claw marks on this red pine with the years of accumulated bites and claw marks on this second red pine. (NH, MA)

nication of health, sex, mating status, territorial boundaries, and who knows what else. Bears mark in one of three ways: rubbing the back and body, biting (often done over the shoulder while rubbing the back), and clawing (also often done over the shoulder while rubbing the back). A tree likely receives a combination treatment, so bitten or clawed trees are likely to provide hairs for those who look closely, caught while the animal also rubbed. Bears also break trunks and limbs while marking, and these signs are described later.

Some sources state that the height of claw marks or bites on a tree trunk may play a role in communicating dominance. I've heard from many sources that when a bear moves through a new area and finds a tree previously marked by another bear, it stands and checks its height against the sign; if it's obvious that a taller and larger bear marked the tree, it leaves quickly and doesn't look back. I haven't been able to find support for this theory. In fact, bears mark with all four feet on the ground and often climb to mark higher in the tree. If height were important, any bear could climb and mark higher than previous bears. Lynn Rogers shared a story with me about a female bear in his study group. She had a regular fence post (way out in a woods that had grown up and swallowed an old homestead) that she rubbed whenever she passed by.

One day, Lynn and the bear arrived together to find the post lying on the ground. This did not stop the bear—she rolled all over it, rubbing as low to the ground as she could get. Lynn pointed out that the height of this sign would certainly not impress any other bears.

Bears mark telephone poles (very common), trail signs, sheds, and other human-made structures placed in their domain. In fact, a simple bear presence/absence inventory can be done near your home by hiking the power lines and checking utility poles for bear bites and hair.

Marking is not aggressive behavior but a communication strategy. Lynn Rogers' research showed that females mark most often in the spring and that the behavior tapers off in summer and fall. Males do the opposite, marking less at the start of the year and slowly building up and marking most in late summer and fall. Remember that marked trees are not a release of pent-up aggression. Bears are very shy and are often fearful of human interaction; marked trees and signs in areas where humans are active are attempts to communicate *without* physical interaction.

I've had several interactions with bears that made me wonder if marking might also be some sort of displacement behavior. On two occasions,

Left: This balsam fir has been repeatedly bitten by black bears over many years and now survives at a portion of its previous diameter. (NH) *Right:* A telephone pole marked by a black bear. (NH)

This park service cabin wears years of grizzly sign—the freshest is yellow, as the building had just been repainted, covering the older signs. (MT)

I've come face-to-face with cornered, scared bears that were unable to escape. Both bears stood up and repeatedly raked their claws on tree bark, leaving impressive and unmistakable signs while staring me down, vocalizing, and jaw-popping. Sue Morse also told me of an occasion when she was asked to follow a bear and keep it in sight until Fish and Wildlife officials arrived. She said that the bear stood several times, clearly intimidated, and glared at the state trooper who accompanied her, while marking a tree vigorously. There is much more to learn about what is communicated with marked trees.

A cornered black bear shredded this balsam fir in an Adirondack campground before finding an escape route. (NY)

Other Activities

Abrasions and Climbing Sign

Feeding and intentional marking behaviors are responsible for only a portion of the signs found on vegetation. Abrasions from wildlife passage, falling trees, and other objects that come in contact with vegetation all leave signs.

Signs of climbing mammals may be difficult to decipher on some tree species but incredibly easy on others. The tree species, age, bark structure, mammal species creating the sign, and weight of the animal are all variables to consider. Climbing signs of squirrels, porcupines, and bears are quite easy to find, but also look for areas where cougars, bobcats, raccoons, coatis, fishers, and martens have left signs of passage.

When climbing sign is discovered, ask yourself why an animal is climbing that particular tree. Is there a cavity or nest it is residing in? Is

Left: Signs of a red squirrel's numerous travels up and down a Douglas fir. (MT)
Right: Birch trees hold the claw marks of numerous species well. The larger claw marks are the climbing signs of a gray squirrel. (MA)

Left: Raccoons foraging for the fruits of sea grapes leave ample signs in the soft bark. (FL) *Right:* Signs of foraging coatis are held by the bark of this wild papaya tree. (Mexico)

the tree providing food, possibly mast or fruit, or foliage? Is the tree in an area where the animal was likely to have been alarmed or surprised? Climbing requires a tremendous amount of energy and is done only with purpose. Certain species, such as squirrels, live in the trees and spend large amounts of time climbing up and down trunks; their potential reasons for climbing are therefore endless. Other animals, such as black bears, tend to climb for one of three reasons: fear, shelter or rest, or foraging.

Bears take to trees when they have been surprised or are scared. In areas where bears and people overlap, you'll often find trees that are repeatedly used by frightened bears. Bears also scare other bears up trees. Any congregation of black bears tends to result in bigger bears chasing smaller bears up trees.

Bears may also climb into trees to take cover in the shade provided by the canopy of a conifer or to rest in a safe crotch, where they can worry less about other bears and predators. Sue Morse introduced me to the concept of "baby-sitter" trees. These are large-diameter softwoods with furrowed bark (easy for cubs to climb), a full canopy, and ample branches and places to rest and relax. Females use such trees to protect their cubs while they go off exploring and foraging by themselves. John McCarter told me about one such tree he recently found surrounded by 32 scats—of both mother and cubs. I have found marked trees in close proximity to baby-sitter trees, so be sure to study nearby saplings and trunks.

The final reason that bears climb trees is food. Beech, aspen, cherry, ash, oak, hickory, shadbush, apple, and other food-producing trees are often climbed by bears in the appropriate season for foraging. They tend to climb trees in two ways, one much faster than the other. They may walk up a tree, in which case moving each leg is similar to walking on the ground. The strength of the upper body and front legs is tremendous and can support the bear propped in such a way that its rear feet can be placed flat against the trunk. The claws of the rear feet are used only if the bear slips, so there may not be evidence of every step up and down.

The second way to move up a tree is to run—really a modified hop in which the front legs stretch up together, followed by both rears moving

Left: Porcupines climb these aspens each spring to feed on the nutritious leaf shoots and early foliage. (NY) *Right:* Quaking aspen trees covered with climbing signs of foraging black bears, which feed heavily on leaf shoots and early foliage. (WY)

Left: A well-used American beech tree, which black bears climb to harvest mast in late summer and early fall, just before the nuts drop to the ground. (MA)
Right: Black bears also climb serviceberries to feast on the fruits at the start of summer. (MA)

Aging Bear Claw Marks on Beech Trees: A Study by Daniel Wolfson

Using three age categories, Daniel Wolfson attained up to 90 percent agreement when querying wildlife officials about the age of scars on beech trees created by climbing black bears. Initially, he tried to define more age classes, allowing for a much narrower and therefore more specific way of aging the sign, but agreement was significantly lower. Wolfson believes that people most accurately identify claw marks in the "Fresh" category. The three categories are as follows:

• **Fresh** (up to 3 years old): Scar orange (less than a year) to brown; importantly, edges have gained no height. Between the second and third year, there may be some widening.

• **Recent** (3 to 7 years old): Scar may still show some brown but is more likely to be gray and black. Definite cracking within the scar, and some widening. Edges are slightly puckered and raised.

• **Old** (7 years or older): Scar is gray or black. Cracking and widening are obvious, with widening of 1/2 inch (1.27 cm) or greater. The scar itself is roughened, and its edges are significantly raised.

together, much as a squirrel moves up a tree. Coming down, bears, raccoons, and many other species must come rear-end first. Fishers, martens, and coatis are able to rotate their rear feet 180 degrees and can move down trees head-first, just like squirrels, chipmunks, and mice.

Barking

Rodents, including white-footed mice, squirrels, and woodrats, gather tremendous amounts of nesting material throughout the year from their environments. The sign associated with this behavior is most easily recognizable when they are collecting the dry cambium layer, or inner bark, of dead or dying shrubs and trees. Look for clear tooth marks on tree species that provide good, fluffy, stringy inner bark, such as maples, aspens, and willows. Certain tree species yield little or no decent nesting material. Sign on dead wood is discussed at the end of this chapter.

I've found areas where gray squirrels have stripped live trees for nesting materials, although this is not common. In each case, they were in suburban areas where there was no standing deadwood to provide an alternative.

Still other tree species provide a fibrous outer bark layer. Rodents and mammals collect nesting materials from the outer bark of live cedars, blueberries, and maleberries, among others.

Gray squirrel barking on a live red maple. (NH)

2) Broken, Cut, Felled, and Browsed Twigs, Limbs, and Trunks

Browse

Browsing refers to feeding on the buds and bark of woody perennials. It is most common from fall to spring, when herbaceous plants become available again and grazing becomes an option.

Members of the deer family tear buds from twigs, leaving a ragged but straight cut across the twig. This tear and ragged appearance are directly related to deer's mouth structure—

Left: White-tailed deer have overbrowsed this hemlock sapling. Deer browse many species of shrubs and trees, including elderberry, hemlock, maple, beech, oak, huckleberry, blueberry, rose, ribes, and yew. Moose often browse birch, hobblebush, maple, mountain ash, and balsam fir. (NY) *Below:* A white-tailed deer browse line in an arborvitae stand. (NY)

they lack teeth on the upper jaw at the front of their mouths. Rather, they have a hard palate, a tough layer of skin and bone. Buds are grabbed tight between the hard palate and lower incisors, and the head jerks back to tear the buds free. There are times when branches, and even trunks, are broken in the browsing process. These instances are described later, contributing to a full discussion of broken branches.

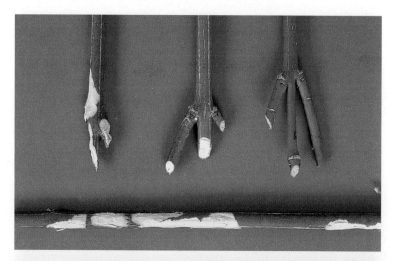

Top: Eastern cottontails browse on winged euonymus. Cottontails browse many species, including ribes, maple, oak, birch, dogwood, black cherry, hawthorn, blueberry, beech, and sumac. (NY) *Bottom:* Pitch pine browsed by eastern cottontails. (MA)

Rodents and lagomorphs also browse, leaving signs characteristic of their mouth structure—four large incisors, two each on top and bottom. (Lagomorphs actually have six incisors—the two additional ones are very small teeth that sit directly behind the larger upper incisors.) Large, sharp incisors cleanly slice buds from smaller-diameter twigs, almost always leaving a smooth, angled cut. Many authors refer to this

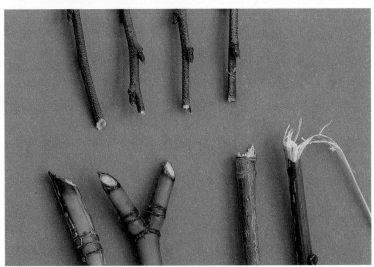

Top: Desert cottontails browse on fremont mahonia. (UT) *Bottom:* Ruffed grouse browse on lowbush blueberry (top), snowshoe hare on striped maple (bottom left), and white-tailed deer on red maple (bottom right). (NH) Hares browse many species, including ribes, maple, oak, hawthorn, blueberry, willow, Douglas fir, alder, birch, beech, and sumac.

as the 45-degree angle characteristic of all rabbits and rodents. The exact angle varies, but recognizing the slanted slice is important. Larger-diameter twigs and branches are chewed through, and these too show the characteristic angle. In these cases, there are also numerous lines running across the exposed inner wood perpendicular to the grain, each the result of a single bite.

Top: A clear browse line 28 to 30 inches (71.1 to 76.2 cm) off the ground created by snowshoe hares. (ME) *Bottom:* Sagebrush browsed by a black-tailed jackrabbit. Jackrabbits also browse mesquite, greasewood, saltbush, and rabbitbrush. (CA)

The diameter of twigs browsed is not a reliable basis for differentiating among species, because the density of the particular species of plant and mammal influences the "depth" of the bite and the resulting sign. In other words, high-density cottontail areas may result in larger-diameter browse than low-density jackrabbit areas.

Grouse and ptarmigan are two of the birds that browse in the winter months. This can create potentially confusing signs when looking for and interpreting mammal signs. Buds are often plucked without leaving any damage to the stem at all. If the bite is deeper on the stem, there may be some tearing. Use judgment on these occasions. Is the stem so large that a grouse or a deer would leave a ragged end?

Nipped Twigs

The twigs of many species of trees and shrubs are cut free throughout the year and may be found carpeting the forest floor in a mass, alone, or hanging with others in the canopy of the original tree or surrounding vegetation. Twigs are nipped by mammals, insects, and sometimes birds for various reasons, although most often for feeding. Always check the severed ends of nipped twigs carefully, because branches of every size, alive and dead, are constantly being shed in wind, ice storms, and other life events of trees. Look for "steps" created by the horizontal lines, each representing the slice of rodent or rabbit teeth.

Squirrels. Feeding mammals cut twigs free for a variety of reasons. In the case of the red squirrel, it seems to be a more efficient means of food collection. Mass amounts of food are cut free and dropped, and then the food is collected on the ground and moved to a cache or eaten on the safety of a perch.

Squirrels also nip twigs throughout the year to construct dreys, the spherical nests built high up in canopies or tucked safely against a

Twigs nipped by red squirrels litter a hiking trail in the Oregon Dunes. (OR)

Top: Lodgepole pine twigs nipped by snowshoe hares feeding on the tender twigs. (ID) *Bottom:* Look closely at the ends of these pitch pine twigs nipped by a red squirrel and note the characteristic "steps" created when rabbits or rodents nip branches. The diameter of these twigs was up to $5/8$ inch (1.6 cm). (MA)

tree trunk. Branches are often dropped during the construction, and old nests shed branches with time. However, you are more likely to encounter nipped twigs cut by feeding squirrels.

Always consider the season in which you are tracking. During the spring, red and gray squirrels cut twigs of red maples to feed on the buds, and just a bit later to feed on the seeds. I've also watched gray

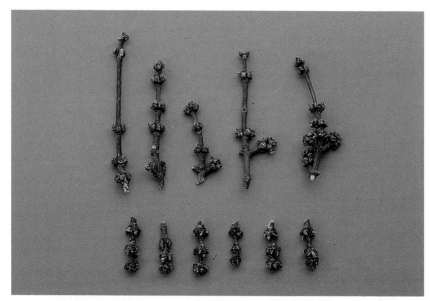

Compare the nipped twigs of red and gray squirrels feeding on the swollen buds of red maples. Gray squirrel nips measured 2⅞ to 3¾ inches (7.3 to 9.5 cm) long, while those of red squirrels measured 1⅛ to 1½ inches (2.9 to 3.8 cm). (NH)

Nipped hemlock twigs and cone remains—both signs of a foraging and feeding red squirrel. Nipped hemlock twigs measured 2½ to 7 inches (6.4 to 17.8 cm) long (occasionally up to 14 inches [35.6 cm] and ⅛ to ¼ inch [.3 to .6 cm] in diameter). (MA)

Red pine twigs nipped and dropped by red squirrels, which then cut free the attached cones and carried them off to cache. (MN)

squirrels cut the twigs of red oaks when harvesting immature one-year-old acorns.

In fall, acorns are the crop of choice, but squirrels do not generally nip twigs during their collection rounds. Red squirrels, however, nip masses of hemlock, pine, and spruce branches to collect cones on the ground for winter caches. Western gray squirrels also harvest bay-leaf maple seeds in this manner. This is a different feeding strategy from porcupines, which feed in the tree before dropping the branch they have cut free. In winter, red squirrels nip spruce branches to feed on the

Spruce twigs nipped by a red squirrel in winter carpet the forest floor. The squirrel then harvested the terminal buds while on the ground. (MA)

Silver fir twigs, 1¹/₂ to 3¹/₂ inches (3.8 to 8.9 cm) long, cut by a Douglas squirrel harvesting the terminal buds. (WA)

These nipped fir twigs were cut by red squirrels feeding on the male cones, which have been removed from the underside of the twigs. (VT)

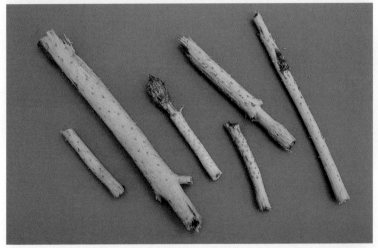

Top: This ponderosa pine is surrounded by countless nipped twigs cut by Abert's squirrels feeding on the tender bark of the outermost limbs. (AZ) *Bottom:* A close-up look at the debarked, nipped twigs of a ponderosa pine stripped by Abert's squirrels. The twigs measured 2 to 8 inches (5.1 to 20.3 cm) long and 1/4 to 5/8 inch (.6 to 1.6 cm) in diameter. (AZ)

terminal buds and the male cones, which in fir trees, look like tiny buds growing on the underside of the branch tips.

Abert's squirrels nip twigs through much of the winter and spring, feeding heavily on the tender bark of ponderosa pines, found on the outermost branch tips. Trees in which they are feeding are surrounded by nipped branches, which dry and brown with time but persist for months after the squirrel has moved on in search of other food sources.

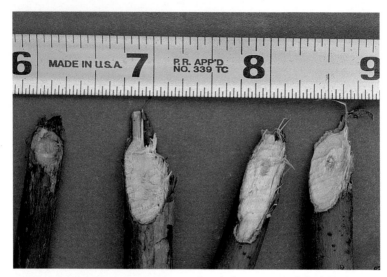

A varied assortment of shrub leaders cut by mountain beavers. These are the remaining ends; the severed portions with characteristic "steps" were carted off and brought underground. From left to right: a salmonberry, an elderberry, and two vine maple stalks. Aplodontia also browse sword fern, devil's club, big-leaf maple, western cedar, and western hemlock. (WA)

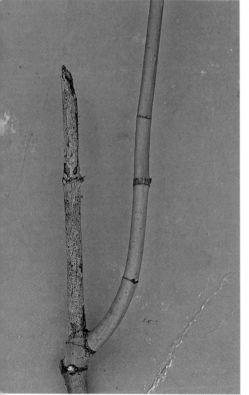

Mountain beavers. Aplodontia nip the leaders and limbs of saplings and shrubs. You may catch glimpses of these severed ends poking out from burrow entrances, but for the most part, you'll find only old signs of them after an animal cleans a burrow. What is common in the woods is the remaining cut trunks of various shrubs and young trees.

Vine maple is often sought by mountain beavers. I quickly learned to scan the woods for this shrub and look for this growth pattern between chest and head height, which is a telltale sign of past feeding by aplodontia and nearby burrow systems. (WA)

Look for the classic angled cut and obvious teeth marks. Most cuts are done between chest and head height, making them easy to find if you're looking for them.

Porcupines. Porcupines nip twigs to gain access to nutritious buds and mast crops that grow at the outer edges of the canopy, where a heavy mammal might break the tree limbs supporting it and plunge to a nasty death. Cutting twigs enables porcupines to bring distant food closer to where they feed and still remain safe on larger-diameter limbs. As an example, consider oak nips. The porcupine pulls in the severed branch and eats the attached acorns. When it's finished, it drops the branch and reaches for another.

Porcupines follow a seasonal clock, in that they tend to feed and create nipped twigs in specific tree species in certain seasons of the year. In the spring, they can be found nipping red maples to feed off buds, as well as aspens and red oaks to feed on leaf shoots and young leaves. They generally take the summer off and turn to herbaceous greens on the ground. In early fall, they cut twigs to feed heavily on mast crops, including acorns and beechnuts. In winter, nipped twigs are created when they feed on the foliage of hemlocks and spruces.

Long after leaf drop, it was obvious that this red oak had had a mast year by the numerous porcupine nipped twigs hanging in the canopy. Twigs nipped while the leaves are still green hold their leaves far longer than the rest of the tree. Nipped twigs also littered the ground and were held aloft by surrounding vegetation. (MA)

The ends of oak twigs cut by porcupines show characteristic steps. Porcupine nipped twigs range from ¹/₄ to 1¹/₄ inches (.6 to 3.2 cm) in diameter and occasionally larger. (MA)

Nipped twigs of eastern hemlock, cut by porcupines feeding on the foliage, carpet the ground. (MA)

Nipped twigs of red oak resulting from porcupines eating the young leaves in spring. (MA)

Red tree voles. Red tree voles nip the twigs of firs and hemlocks, often between 1 and 9 inches (2.5 and 22.9 cm) long. They bring their harvest back to the nest, where they feed on the roof, allowing a buildup of refuse and scats to further weatherproof their home.

Due to the arboreal nature of the red tree vole, we encounter few signs of their presence on the ground. However, the careful observer may find ball-like clumps of discarded resin ducts that have dropped from feeding platforms atop nests. The resin ducts transport sap and nutrients to the foliage and are located

Porcupines continue to feed in a tree day after day, and the subsequent cropping and shaping may be drastic. This is a hemlock after a winter season of heavy attention by nearby porcupines. (MA)

Top: A close-up look at debarked twigs and discarded Douglas fir needle resin ducts collected and eaten by red tree voles. (OR) *Bottom:* Clumps of discarded resin ducts, which can be found at active nests as well as on the ground—definitive proof of resident red tree voles. (OR)

along both edges of every needle. A dining vole carefully removes these resin ducts before eating the central portions of each needle. These resin ducts dry, accumulate, and occasionally drop to the ground; they are also used to line nest chambers. Twigs may also be debarked, but they are very small and are best observed by climbing the tree and looking on feeding platforms.

Juniper twigs nipped by woodrats as they collected the berries and seeds. (UT)

Woodrats. Woodrats also nip twigs to harvest juniper berries and other masts. I've seen this sign on a few occasions, and the work was always done very near nest sites.

Insects. There are many species of beetle that create nipped twigs, and they are divided into two large groups: pruners and girdlers. Rather than the characteristic "stair" pattern of rodent-nipped twigs, oak twig pruners leave a very smooth, clean cut straight through the branch; there is also a characteristic hole down the center of the twig.

Felled Trees

The infamous beavers are responsible for many felled trees and shrubs near wetland systems, which they use in the construction of dams and lodges, as well as for sustenance. Beaver work is unmistakable. They are the only mammal other than humans that invests the time and energy to cut through the base of large shrubs and trees. Literature states that a 5-inch (12.7-cm) diameter willow can be chewed down by a beaver in three minutes. Other rodents are able to fell cornstalks and cattails, but logging woody material is entirely the realm of the beaver. Beaver sculpture is varied and beautiful—from half-chewed trees to stumps of every shape—and is always accompanied by large wood chips, which carpet the work area completely over time.

Logs are then cut into manageable chunks and toted off for winter stores or construction purposes. Only the largest chunks remain, and these are stripped clean of the cambium layer by feeding beavers, leaving intricate incisor patterns that are much larger than those of porcupines or snowshoe hares.

Top: A large birch felled and debarked by beavers. (NH) *Bottom:* Close-up of an impressive oak tree felled by persistent beavers. Note the carpet of large wood chips, which always accompanies the signs of working beavers. (NH)

Numerous birch saplings bent and broken by moose that straddled and walked over them to gain access to the uppermost buds. (MA)

Broken Limbs and Trunks

Branches and trunks are often broken as a direct result of feeding mammals, especially the larger mammals of North America. Both muskox and moose pull foliage and buds down as they feed and often break branches. Deer also break smaller-diameter branches from time to time; I've noted this most often on mountain maples.

Moose also break the trunks of trees and shrubs in another way. Even massive moose cannot reach all the buds on every sapling in the forest, but a bit of ingenuity brings

While a moose was straddling this balsam fir tree to browse the highest limbs, the trunk snapped clean and fell to the snow. (NH)

the tallest tips within reach. Moose either pull a limb to bend and break a small-diameter trunk or straddle the sapling and feed as they walk forward and over the tree, allowing their great mass to pull more food within reach. Often the trunks snap at some point, and the upper trunk is left either hanging limply when the moose moves on or on the ground. Look

Top: This mountain holly was broken by a black bear pulling fruits within reach. Note that there are no teeth marks along the trunk. (NH) *Bottom:* Here are more subtle signs of feeding. This dogwood was pulled down by a black bear harvesting fruits, but there was no observable damage to the trunk or limbs. (MT)

for browsed tips to help differentiate this sign from others, such as saplings broken by marking and feeding bears.

Fishers and bears both pull branches down to their level to obtain food, although on a very different scale. Bears break small-diameter tree trunks when climbing beyond their weight capacity or when pulling down

Top: A broken apple tree after a visit by a foraging black bear. (MA) *Bottom:* A bear "nest" in an American beech composed of numerous branches that were torn and chewed free, pulled close to the bear, and then discarded after all the nuts were eaten. (VT)

A bear nest in a red oak tree. (MN) Photo by Lynn Rogers.

to mouth level food that sits out of reach. Look for apple tree limbs, highbush blueberries, elderberries, and mountain holly trunks broken by bears feeding on fruits, as well as broken aspens, beeches, maples, and others when bears are feeding on buds and leaf shoots. Foraging fishers also pull in and break branches of blueberries and winterberries, leaving a miniature version of bear sign.

"Bear nests" are an exciting find on any foray and are signs of feeding bears rather than resting ones. Bears feed in the canopy of fruit and mast trees, chewing and breaking branches in order to reach food growing farthest out on limbs. Once food has been removed from a limb, the bear throws or pushes the limb downward and may even stand on these limbs as they accumulate in a crotch of a tree, which also improves the bear's footing. Look for this sign in oak, cherry, serviceberry, and beech trees, and occasionally in others.

Marking

Bears. Bears break limbs and trunks of trees and shrubs for marking purposes. Alcott Smith was the first to point out that bears occasionally climb high into conifers and remove the central leader with diligent chewing and pulling. I've found this sign 40 feet (12.2 m) up in hemlocks and firs and as low as chest height while standing on the ground. All the decapitated trees I've found have been associated with wetland edges, which are obviously important feeding areas for bears.

Terry DeBruyn (1999) writes about this subject, having witnessed this behavior on several occasions with one of the bears in his study group. This particular female would chase out a trespassing bear and then, having failed to overtake the trespasser, would climb and decapitate cedar trees in some yet undetermined communication strategy, or possibly as a displacement behavior.

A hemlock tree decapitated by a marking black bear. Note its placement along the edge of a large wetland system. (NH)

Bears also break saplings and shrubs in high-traffic areas, feeding spots, and areas where females leave cubs. The break is usually done with the mouth rather than by pulling at the tree with the front paws, which is generally the case when feeding. Remember to consider the tree species when trying to determine whether sign is feeding or marking, because some trees do not offer bears much sustenance.

Canines. Canines chew various items when playing, as well as when creating comfortable beds and dens. I've found areas where wolves had chewed off all the lower branches

A yellow birch bitten and broken by a black bear, adjacent to an important feeding area. (MA)

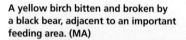

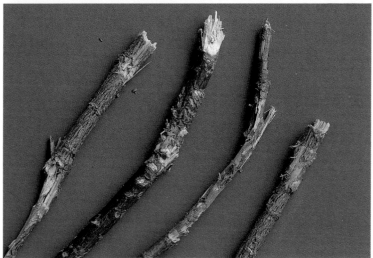

Top: A shrub broken by a playful wolf, next to a regular bedding area likely linked with a rendezvous site. (MN) *Bottom:* Hundreds of chewed sticks like these carpeted a wolf pack's regular bedding area. (MN)

around spruce trees in order to lie comfortably under the cover of evergreen boughs. I've also found chewed and broken saplings in an area of regular bedding, likely a rendezvous site (like an aboveground den), and some saplings that had been chewed into small pieces, which carpeted the area.

A fisher "beat up" this hemlock sapling in a scent marking ritual. Note the broken limbs. (NH) Photo by Sue Mansfield.

Fishers and wolverines. Fishers and wolverines roll on, bite, and "beat up" small saplings and shrubs for marking purposes. Fishers use small evergreen saplings again and again, and signs of wear accumulate, including loss of foliage and broken branches. Little is known about this behavior, and I do not know whether martens also scent in similar fashion.

Chain saw and brush hog. The potential interpretations of a broken or severed limb or trunk are too numerous to count, and many of them are due to human activity. Have they been cut or sliced by a knife, severed or marked by a brush hog or chain saw, or injured by a passing snowmobile? As a tracker, nothing must fail to be of interest—study all signs of human disturbance. That knowledge may come in handy later in what you thought was a remote and inaccessible part of some forest.

3) Sign on Fruit and Mast

Interpreting signs on fruit and mast crops requires the three perspectives. Regardless of whether you are looking at acorns, hickory nuts, or pinecone remains, the contextual clues play a large role in your final assessment. Caching, nipped twigs, scats, hairs, and the location of feeding are all useful things to note.

Caching behaviors vary across mammal species, as do likely spots selected for feeding. Large and medium mammals leave more obvious contextual clues. Bears leave claws marks in the trunks and broken branches overhead if they are feeding before fruits and nuts fall to the ground. If they are feeding after the fall, there is evidence of digging and shuffling in the debris layer, and likely marked trees and scats nearby.

Porcupines also leave plenty of sign. While food still hangs in the trees, they cut and drop nipped twigs after pulling the branch in and plucking nuts. After the fall, they dig and shuffle in the debris, as do hogs, which root massive areas to find and feed on acorns and other crops.

The smaller rodents pose the greatest challenge to trackers. First, where have you found the feeding sign? Was it on the ground, near a cache, or up on a log? The importance of these contextual clues cannot be overemphasized. Most signs on mast crops do not appear where the food was harvested or found; rather, they are found at a cache site where they were retrieved, at a preferred feeding station, or discarded from a nearby burrow or cavity.

Consider the various caching strategies of several common species. Gray squirrels cache hundreds of acorns and other food items all over their home range, each shallow dig holding one to three nuts. It is common to find digs where squirrels have retrieved such caches throughout the winter, with shell remains of nuts right next to the hole.

Fox squirrels often cache in tree cavities and create larger caches of many items. They also cache cooperatively and share the food supply with other fox squirrels.

A single acorn placed in a small dig; the gray squirrel was spooked before he covered his cache. (MA)

Red squirrels put all their eggs in one basket, rather than disperse their food supplies across their home range, as gray squirrels do. Reds tend to create one to three large caches under logs or rocks or in root systems, burrows, and occasionally tree cavities. The feeding remains, the midden, are near the cache, to minimize commuting. Whereas the signs left by gray squirrels often consist of just several nuts, the signs of feeding red squirrels may be an accumulation of dozens or even hundreds of shells, cone scales, and cones. Also be aware that the midden of a red squirrel and its cache may be the same pile. Harvested cones are sometimes cached in the accumulated middens from previous years. Midden piles keep new cones moist, cool, and closed until squirrels are ready to eat them.

Chipmunks and some ground squirrels store food and eat in the burrow, so the sign does not appear until a cleaning, and then it is often scattered to help camouflage the burrow entrance. These species either hibernate or slow their metabolism so that they need less food than if they remained active throughout the year. Yet Sutton (Wilson and Ruff, 1999) reported a cache of an alpine chipmunk containing 68,000 items and weighing 6.7 ounces (190 g).

Southern flying squirrels also cache thousands of items through the fall, often in nest cavities, but also on the ground in smaller caches, much like gray squirrels. You'll find significant accumulations of feeding sign under nest cavities, as well as signs of the retrieval of smaller caches while following their trails on the ground in winter.

Mice store food in any available cache, hollow, and cavity. I have come across caches under logs, in cavities, and behind loose bark. I once found a mouse cache of acorns behind stacked pictures leaning against the wall and among blankets in the loft of an old apartment. Mice also store mast crops in abandoned bird nests—quite common in thrush-sized nests found in thickets and shrubs in and around fields.

The place where an animal is feeding reflects strategies for survival and also provides useful clues to species identification. Certain squirrel species are comfortable feeding at ground level; the fox squirrel wanders far from cover to feed. Others prefer to be raised up on a perch to watch and listen for predators. Red squirrel and fox squirrel sign accumulates under their favorite perches on tree limbs, logs, or boulders. Gray squirrels, in contrast, vary their perches and often feed on the ground. Chipmunks almost always eat on an elevated perch such as large a rock or tree stump to maintain a vigilant watch for predators. Chipmunks tend to vary their perches more than red squirrels do, so the accumulation of sign at any one site is significantly less.

White-footed mice (*Peromyscus* species) employ a very different strategy. These mice tend to drag food under cover—beneath a rock, log, or other shelter. Sign atop the rock has likely been made by chipmunks

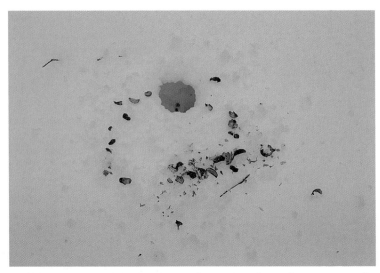

The remains of several acorns retrieved and eaten on the ground by a gray squirrel at its cache site. (NH)

or by a bird that needed an anvil, whereas sign below the same rock has probably been made by a mouse.

Cavities and burrows are also wonderful aids in interpreting feeding sign. For example, a red squirrel's underground cache is often very close to a midden pile, and sometimes in it. Sign also accumulates beneath cavities commandeered by southern flying squirrels, which discard food remains throughout a winter season. This is useful in two ways: as a sign to confirm a flying squirrel's cavity, and as a cavity to support flying squirrel sign.

A brush mouse's midden of piñon pine nuts under the protection of this large rock. (TX)

The incisor marks of meadow voles cover this wild pear fruit. Meadow voles relish all sorts of windfallen fruits. (NY)

Apples and Other Large Fruits

Apples, pears, and other large fruits are popular fare among many bird and animal species. Larger mammals, from fishers to bears, tend to eat fruit in its entirety. Smaller mammals, such as meadow voles and chipmunks, leave obvious incisor marks in the flesh of fresh windfalls. Birds leave clear beak marks and feed on apples in particular ways.

A papaya opened and eaten by a young coati. The young animals tended to feed in the trees, and the adults tended to carry the fruit to the edge of the plantation and feed near or in protective cover. (Mexico)

Crabapple seeds split and eaten by a southern flying squirrel. (NY)

Acorns

The incredible nutritional value of acorns has been acknowledged and well documented for thousands of years. Where there are acorns, birds compete with numerous mammals, including humans, in annual harvests. Richard Ketchum (Rupp, 1990) tracked 15,000 acorns produced by one tree in an incredible bounty. His work showed that 83 percent of the acorns were harvested by mammals, 6 percent went to insect predators, 10 percent were naturally defective, and less than 1 percent actually sprouted, half of which died while still seedlings.

The acorn, which varies widely in shape and size, offers a compact package of fats, starches, and proteins just in time to store for the winter months ahead or to speed weight gain before the lean season. The thickness of the shell varies among oak species, as well as among individual trees. The thickness of the shell greatly influences how acorns are opened, and thus is a factor in interpreting feeding sign. With experience, you will learn the subtleties of interpretation.

There is one more important variable to consider when studying acorn sign: Was the acorn dry or green when it was opened? A cached, and therefore dry, acorn responds differently to teeth than a moist acorn does. Dry acorns split more easily, and the shrunken and hardened nut meat is easier to remove. It doesn't take long to be able to differentiate between opened green and dry acorns. Also consider the implications of green versus dry acorns with regard to caching behaviors. Hogs and bears love acorns and feast on them in the fall and sometimes into early winter, but are they likely to store acorns in underground burrows or to

Top: Acorns opened by a white-breasted nuthatch show typical avian feeding signs. (NM) *Bottom:* California ground squirrels eat large quantities of California black oak acorns. Here they are feeding on the immature nuts in early summer. (CA)

be found retrieving acorns from a cache in a tree cavity? (Yes, bears occasionally raid underground nut caches, but these were originally made by rodents.) How about southern flying squirrels? Mice?

Acorns crunched by deer and porcupines can look like those opened by crows, but contextual clues will clarify things. Deer pick up acorns from the ground, and there are likely to be signs of shuffling debris or digging. Porcupines feed in the canopy before acorns drop, after which they continue to feed on the ground. But if porcupines have been eating acorns in the tree, you won't miss the numerous nipped twigs that have been cut to pull the outermost acorns within reach of their sharp incisors.

Rodents often leave teeth marks in the nut meat and around the hole in the shell. Small mammals scoop with their upper incisors while grip-

Top: I found large quantities of acorn "cups," all with the same characteristic cut, near California ground squirrel burrows in late fall. The acorns were removed and stored underground. (CA) *Bottom:* The remains of mature California black oak acorns eaten by California ground squirrels. (CA)

ping the outside of the nut with their lower incisors. These lower teeth leave tiny, white indentations and marks along the outside edge of the hole, which trackers call *chatter*. Any evidence of chatter immediately rules out the possibility that the signs were left by feeding birds.

Other mammals eat the whole acorn, but shell remains reappear in scats. I've found acorn shells in both bear and fisher scats. Yet on occa-

Top: Scrub oak acorns eaten by dusky-footed woodrats. (CA) *Bottom:* Shin oak acorns eaten by white-throated woodrats. (TX)

sion, fishers and bears separate the shell from the nut. My work confirms assertions made by Alan N. Emond that bears and other animals take advantage of natural catches, where mast crops roll or are blown and accumulate, and are therefore good places to look for sign.

There are countless oak species across the country, most of which fall within either the white oak or red oak group. The trees in these two groups vary in form, leaf structure, and seed composition and strategy. White oak acorns have only about half the fat (dry weight) of red oak

Top: Acorns *(Quercus* sp.) opened by a brush mouse. (TX) *Bottom:* White oak acorns opened by a porcupine. (MA)

acorns and thus provide less of what a squirrel wants, but they also contain one-half to one-eighth the tannins of red oak acorns, making them far easier to digest and metabolize.

White oak acorns germinate in the fall before winter begins, while red oak acorns wait until spring. At the time of germination, energy and food resources are funneled into growing, and the nutritional value of the acorn drops. It is for this reason that Steele and Smallwood (1994) hypothesized that white oak acorns are almost always eaten by gray squirrels immediately where they are found, whereas red oak acorns are often carried away and cached. This is certainly what I have observed in the field in New England. When an equal bounty of white and red oak acorns fills squirrel territories, signs of feeding on white oak acorns sprinkle the area during the fall, while signs of feeding on red oak acorns are more prevalent after the onset of winter.

Steele and Smallwood (1994) also report the following fascinating behavior: They observed gray squirrels nipping the embryos within white oak acorns before caching, which prevents germination. In this way, they ensure that the nutritional value of the acorn is not jeopardized by growth and are able to cache the acorn for winter use without the risk of returning to find a seedling instead of an acorn.

Many animals that eat acorns also eat any acorn weevils (insect larvae) they discover in infested acorns. By fall, weevils have reached maggot proportions and provide a boost of protein for those that eat them. Some mammals and birds open acorns only to eat the weevil, while others, such as gray squirrels and white-footed mice, eat the weevil and

Massive burr oak acorns opened by a gray squirrel. (MO)

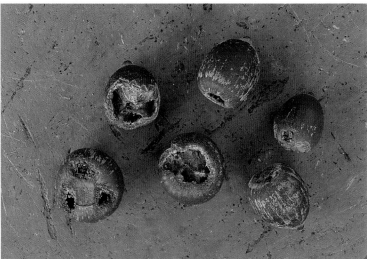

Top: Acorns opened by a rock squirrel. (CO) *Bottom:* White-footed mice opened these northern red oak acorns to harvest the acorn weevils (insect larvae) within. They may or may not follow up by eating the acorn. (MA)

then cache the acorn for later consumption. The dark areas where the weevil lived, as well as the mealy brown frass (excrement) left in its wake, can help you determine whether you have found an infested acorn. The following illustrations compare numerous mammal species feeding on the acorns of the northern red oak (*Quercus rubrus*).

Northern red oak acorns compared

Northern red oak acorns: porcupine. (MA)

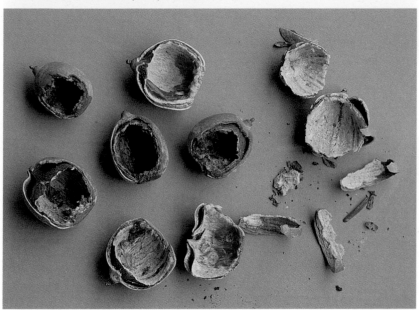

Northern red oak acorns: southern flying squirrel. (MA)

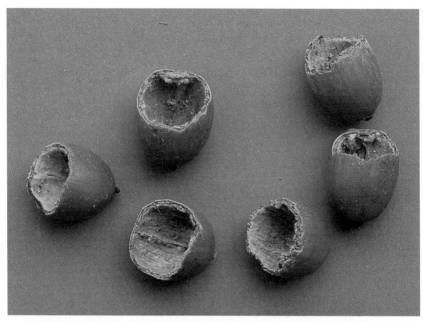

Northern red oak acorns: deer mouse. Note that the acorns were dry. (NH)

Northern red oak acorns: eastern chipmunk. (NH)

Northern red oak acorns: red squirrel. (MA)

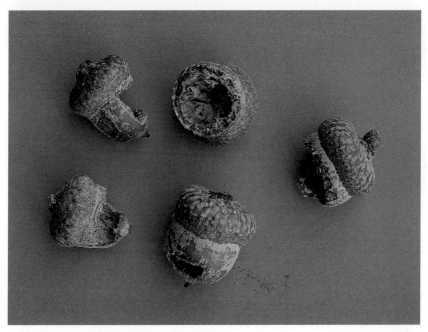

Northern red oak acorns: deer mouse. (MA)

Northern red oak acorns: gray squirrel. (NH)

Northern red oak acorns: fisher. (MA) Photo by Paul Rezendes.

Northern red oak acorns: white-tailed deer. (VT)

Northern red oak acorns: black bear. (MA)

Hickory Nuts

Hickory nuts are another wonderful source of fats and vitamins ready for harvest in late summer or early fall. Bears, hogs, turkeys, squirrels, chipmunks, and mice are among those that partake in the feast.

Top: Red squirrels open hickory nuts in several ways. This is the most prevalent method I find in the field: They enter the nut from both sides, creating large jagged holes. Look for incisor marks on the hickory's midrib. (NH) *Bottom:* This is the second most common method I find: The squirrels chew a groove around the entire nut until it splits into two perfect halves. The beveled edges are characteristic. (MA)

When mature, hickory nuts have a much harder shell than acorns, and the nuts of certain species, such as the shellbark hickory, require sharp incisors and determination or a good hammer to open. Yet mammals feed heavily on hickory nuts as they drop, and masses of them are stored for winter use.

Sign on hickory nuts is clearer and often easier to interpret than sign on acorns. Each mammal has a unique way of obtaining the nut meat,

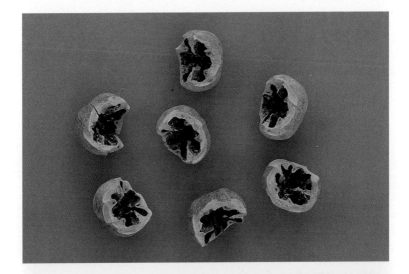

Top: Another variation of red squirrel sign: The beveled edges help differentiate this sign from the work of eastern chipmunks. (MA) *Bottom:* Red squirrels open hickory nuts in a fourth variation. (MA)

Hickory nut remains: southern flying squirrel. Southern flying squirrels typically enter the nut from a shoulder and make one smooth, circular hole from which to extract the nut meat. The midrib is cut. They may also make several round holes and attack the nut from several angles; this sign looks similar to that created by mice. (NH)

Look carefully for the carrying notches chewed by southern flying squirrels into hickory nuts for transportation purposes. Imagine the squirrel gliding back to its cavity with a massive hickory nut sticking out the front of its mouth—the equivalent of holding a football in your teeth. (NH)

so their sign is easy to differentiate. Chipmunks and red squirrels use several methods to extract the nut. It is interesting to note that although red squirrels have several characteristic methods of opening a hickory nut, certain techniques are more common, and each individual squirrel tends to choose only one method and stick with it. Thus, when you find a midden of hickory shells discarded by a red squirrel, they have almost always been opened in the same way.

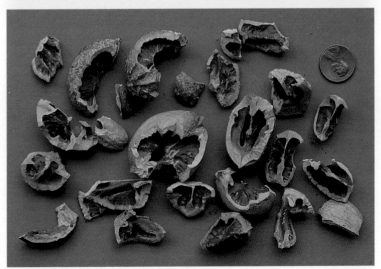

Top: Shagbark hickory nut remains: gray squirrel. (NH) *Bottom:* Shellbark hickory nut remains: gray squirrel. (MO)

Shagbark hickory nut remains, harvested while the rinds were still green: eastern chipmunk. (NY)

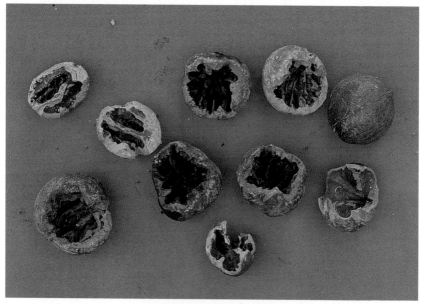

Shagbark hickory nut remains: eastern chipmunk. Note the jagged, circular holes. Eastern chipmunks also chew carrying notches, less obvious than those of southern flying squirrels, for transportation purposes. (NH)

Hickory nut remains: deer mouse. Note that mice do not cut the midrib and often enter from multiple sides. (NH)

Walnuts and Butternuts

Like hickory nuts, walnuts and butternuts offer fats and other nutrients just in time for the coming cold months. They also have very hard shells that require a great deal of effort to open. However, these tough shells show more clearly than other mast crops the characteristic signs of the mammals that opened them.

Black walnuts opened by gray squirrels. (NJ)

Butternuts opened by red squirrels. (MA)

Beechnuts, American Lindens, and Maples

Many mammals eat beechnuts (22 percent protein, 50 percent fat) in their entirety, and the small, shredded husks slip beneath leaf litter quickly and are difficult to interpret. I am not always sure what type of animal fed on the opened beechnuts I encounter in the woods. I stick with the contextual signs—most importantly, the place selected for feeding. I have also found the hulls of beechnuts in bear, red fox, coyote, and fisher scats.

American beechnuts: white-footed mouse on left with penny, porcupine on right. (MA)

Beechnuts: Red squirrel at left, common grackle right above, blue jay right below with penny. (VT)

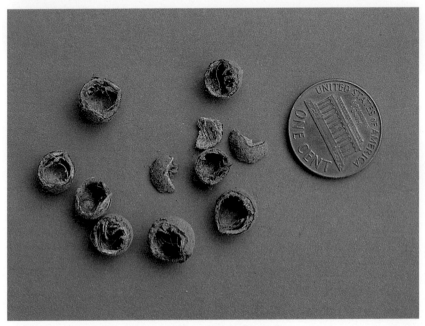

American linden mast opened by eastern chipmunks. (MA)

Compare these maple seeds opened by red squirrels (NY) with . . .

. . . these maple seeds opened by white-footed mice. (MA)

Hazelnuts

Each year, there seems to be a race to collect and eat the popular hazelnuts. Many animals harvest them, and signs are sprinkled about the landscape. Chipmunks and larger squirrels split them open, but I have limited experience interpreting hazelnut sign and so rely heavily upon contextual clues. Mice, however, chew characteristic holes, as they do with many nut crops.

Black bears crack the green-beaked hazelnut hull and remove the nut in its entirety, often without severing the fruit from the limb at all. (NH) Photo by Sue Mansfield.

American hazelnuts opened by eastern chipmunks. (MA)

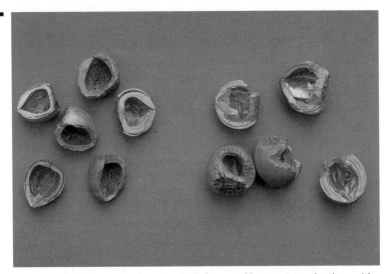

Compare the California hazelnuts on the left opened by acorn woodpeckers with those on the right opened by western gray squirrels. Note the characteristic groove cut by the incisors on the nuts opened by squirrels. (CA)

Pine Nuts and Cones

Pine nuts are an invaluable source of food for wildlife around the world. Regardless of the type of pine, there will always be a bird or mammal harvesting the nuts and cones, which vary enormously in size and shape. Single-leaf piñon pine nuts offer 39 percent fat and 54 percent carbohy-

Red squirrels harvest and consume conifer cones in a three-step process. First, the cones (Douglas fir) are cut free from the canopy and dropped to the ground. (MT)

Top: Second, cones are gathered and cached in available cavities, burrows, or middens. (MT) *Bottom:* Third, cones are retrieved and dismantled at favorite perches. (MT)

drates, and a pound of Colorado piñon pine nuts is good for nearly 3,000 calories. Spruce, fir, hemlock, and larch cones have similar structures to pinecones and are used in much the same manner.

Depending on the maturation of the cone, different species are able to harvest the rich pine nuts. Initially, the cones are tightly closed while the seeds slowly mature within. When the cone has fully matured, it begins to dry out, forcing the cone scales to separate with an audible "pop" or "snap" and allowing the dried seeds to fall and be dispersed by the wind or moved by wildlife. The winged seeds of certain pines catch the wind and disperse as far as the gusts allow. Other pines have not evolved winged seeds and rely solely on birds and mammals for seed dispersal.

Top: A red squirrel's large Sitka spruce cone cache. (AK) *Bottom:* For comparison, a large red squirrel midden (composed of feeding remains). This one measured an impressive 18 by 19 feet (5.5 by 5.8 m) and 10 inches (25.4 cm) deep. (AK)

It's interesting to note the seed dispersion strategies used by many fir species. Fir cones grow, mature, disperse seeds, and disintegrate without ever falling to the ground. Therefore, almost every fir cone you find on the ground has been cut free by an animal; look closely for signs of which species is responsible.

Top: White pinecones dismantled by foraging red squirrels. (MN) *Bottom:* Sitka spruce cone remains: red squirrel. (AK)

Jeffrey's pinecone remains: California ground squirrel. (CA)

Red spruce cone remains: southern flying squirrel. Cone remains are found on the ground at cache sites, where the squirrels forage, and occasionally under cavities. Similar red squirrel signs accumulate at their regular feeding perches. (NH)

Green, immature cones of ponderosa pines: Abert's squirrel. (AZ)

Mature ponderosa pine cone remains: Abert's squirrel. (NM)

Western hemlock cone remains: Douglas squirrel. Chipmunks tend to leave more of the stub that secures the cone scale; the sign on the cone stem is therefore bumpier than on cones foraged by red squirrels. (WA)

For comparison, study the feeding signs of foraging piñon jays on this piñon pinecone—beaten cones, but still intact. (AZ)

Close-up of red pinecone remains, dismantled by a red squirrel. Note the horizontal lines left by the incisors where each cone scale was severed. (MA)

Piñon pinecone remains: cliff chipmunk. (AZ)

Top: Piñon pine nut remains: brush mouse. (TX) *Bottom:* Piñon pinecone remains: rock squirrel. (UT)

Whereas birds often remove pine nuts from cones and carry them to another spot to feed, most signs of mammals feeding on pine nuts are accompanied by cone remains. The signs of cone remains are somewhat easier to interpret than those of nut remains, especially if the pine nuts of the species you are assessing are small. Birds leave ample sign on the cone, such as shredded or split cone scales, but they generally leave the cone intact. Mammals almost always chew through cone scales, dismantling the cone as they feed, or cache nuts in cheek pouches.

Rosehips

The fruits and seeds of roses are eaten by a variety of wildlife. Larger mammals eat them in their entirety—I've found marten scats composed completely of rosehips. Smaller animals often choose the seed or fruit, and associated signs are often necessary to confirm interpretation. Be aware that numerous bird species also feed on rosehips.

Top: Rose hip remains: red squirrel. (MT) *Bottom:* Rose hip remains: yellow pine chipmunk. (MT)

Rose hip remains: deer mouse. A midden formed deep within the protective cover of the rosebush. (NY)

Junipers and Manzanitas

The fruits and seeds of junipers and manzanitas, found in the West, are eaten by many species. Like cherry and tupelo, these fruits are often eaten in their entirety by larger mammals, but smaller rodents leave more obvious signs of feeding in the remaining seeds.

Juniper seed remains: desert woodrat. (CA)

Juniper seed remains: Ord's kangaroo rat. (UT)

Manzanita seed remains: dusky-footed woodrat. (CA)

Manzanita seed remains: mouse (*Peromyscus* sp.). (CA)

Small Fruits

Domestic and wild cherries are relished by wildlife. The berries are small enough to be swallowed whole by most mammals, so the only sign on the tree or bush is the absence of fruit. Eastern chipmunks feed on the fruits and discard the seeds—with obvious incisor marks in the fruit that remains attached to the pit. Signs of cherries can be seen in the scats of numerous species, including birds, such as American robins,

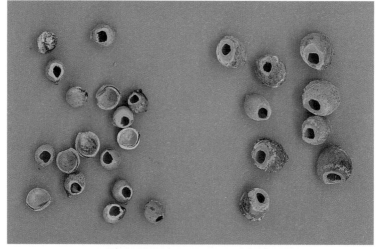

The feeding signs of deer mice opening wild cherry seeds (smaller) and beach plum seeds (larger) are very similar. Occasionally, mice split the seeds as well. (NH, MA)

and mammals, such as bears, coyotes, fishers, raccoons, foxes, opossums, and even striped skunks.

You may also encounter sign on cherry pits. White-footed and deer mice gather and store great numbers of wild cherry and the larger beach plum seeds for winter use. Amusing signs to look for are the cherry scats of bears and others, where all that remains are the fruit skins and pulp—

Top: Tupelo seeds opened by deer mice. (MA) *Bottom:* Mountain ash fruits harvested by yellow pine chipmunks. (MT)

A bird nest full of bittersweet fruits, stored and eaten by a deer mouse. (NH)

mice have stolen and carried off all the seeds. A large bear scat must provide a wonderful opportunity for the tiny mice, as the fruits and seeds have already been separated and collected in quantity in one convenient location. Dan Gardoqui has also documented split cherry pits in southern flying squirrel cavities, similar to the split crabapple seeds presented earlier.

The fruits of tupelos are also eaten by many mammal species and are small enough to be swallowed in their entirety. Coyote, bear, and fox scats are filled with tupelo seeds when they are in mast. Also, as with cherries, signs of seeds opened and stored by mice are common.

Winterberry and blueberry are among the many other fruits eaten by mammals that leave little sign other than remains in scats. Consider broken branches in your assessment of bushes. Both bears and fishers break the branches of these species as they gorge and feed.

Deadwood

Live trees offer much to animals. They are browsed, debarked, and marked; buds, nuts, and fruits are eaten; and they provide shelter for many species. Trees also continue contributing in death. Jon Luoma (1999) writes about research in the Andrews Forest of Oregon, where it was discovered that there is actually more life in biomass in a dead tree than in a living one. Wildlife use a tree while it lives and continue to do so when it dies—as a snag (standing deadwood), as a log (fallen deadwood), and as a hummock in the dynamic landscape, which is what trees left on their own are destined to become over time.

At each of these stages of disintegration, the tree becomes a different ecosystem, utilized by different insects, birds, and mammals. Sapsuckers and red squirrels may tap a young tree, and voles, hares, and porcupines may remove layers of bark and cambium for food. As the tree matures, mast crops may be collected, or fruits or buds. Bears may break branches while feeding, and raccoons may scratch up the bark when climbing after nesting birds. A fisher may capture a squirrel that has built a drey high in the upper limbs. Over time, cavities are created by birds, and limbs are broken or die. Flying squirrels and mice move into the interior. Martens and ringtails may raise young in larger openings.

The tree eventually dies and then becomes alive with different insects and bird species. Holes for nesting and winter roosting continue to be drilled by woodpeckers. Mice and squirrels collect the drying cambium layer for nesting materials. More birds and mammals move in, finding shelter from wind, rain, and snow. Fishers check the tree more often, removing roosting birds, nesting mice, and resting flying squirrels.

When the tree begins to crumble and stands at only a fraction of its previous height, a downy woodpecker may excavate a winter roost. Eventually, the tree falls and becomes a bridge for squirrels and raccoons and cover for shrews and voles. Bears rip at its sides to expose insects, and seedlings begin to germinate along its upper side, held above the suffocating leaf litter on the forest floor. And as some trees rot away, cottontails and grouse bathe in the decomposing wood.

Eventually, earth covers the tree remains, and a new forest grows directly from what was contributed by the decomposition of the tree. Although this is an extreme simplification of an intricate and amazing process, the importance of snags and logs in a healthy ecosystem cannot be overemphasized. Vital to all wildlife, snags and logs enrich the environment long after a tree has died.

A black bear tore into this standing snag to feast on the ants working within. (MA)

Barking of dead big-tooth aspen bark by gray squirrels. (NY)

Barking

A common sign found on trees and saplings that have recently died, or on windfallen limbs that have recently dropped, is that of rodents and birds collecting the fibrous, drying inner bark for nesting materials. Certain shrub and tree species yield much more fibrous, stringy bark than others. Among the best are linden, maple, oak, and hickory. Look for teeth marks in the deadwood and strips of cambium and inner bark missing from branches and small-diameter trunks. Mice, woodrats, and all squirrel species collect nesting materials in this way, and their sign is common in woodlands. These

Barking of dead scrub oak branches by a dusky-footed woodrat. (CA)

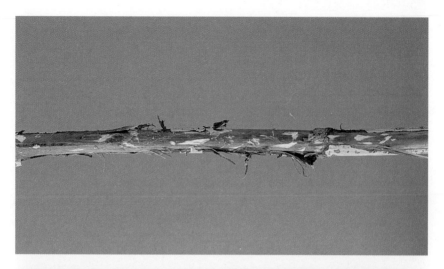

Top: A dead striped maple twig stripped by a white-footed mouse. (NH) *Bottom:* Dead hickory bark harvested by a red squirrel. (MA)

animals continue to improve their nests as the winter progresses, and I've seen fresh barking sign in midwinter.

This sign is also seen on green limbs and live shrubs and trees from time to time, but it is far more common on dead or nearly dead vegetation.

Left: Closer inspection of the dieback—the dead branch—on this high-elevation tree along a hiking trail in Glacier National Park revealed tufts of grizzly fur and other signs of rubbing. (MT) *Right:* The dead spruce with the reddish foliage was girdled by a black bear feeding on the spring sapwood months before. (WY)

Snags as Sign

Trees die for numerous reasons, including old age, poor genetics, salt from roads, pollution, high or low water levels, disease, defoliation, and as a direct result of mammal behavior. The more recently a tree has died, the easier it is to determine whether a mammal was responsible.

Girdling by mammals is a common cause of death in trees and shrubs. If the cambium layer is severed all the way around a trunk or limb, any plant growth beyond that point will cease and die back, and the stress on the overall organism may be too much to allow any further growth. Entire shrubs and trees are often killed by girdling, whether the cambium is cut by vigorous antler rubs, horned trunks, debarking, incisor scraping, or a chain saw run round the trunk.

Any area where bark is removed presents the opportunity for a fungal, bacterial, or insect predator to move in and attack the tree. Bark feeding now can cause a tree's demise many years later, or it can adversely affect the health of the tree for the remainder of its life. Often, the effects of mammal signs are not apparent until long after the animals have moved on.

Heavy browse obviously suppresses growth, but if it's continued over time, it can kill shrubs and trees. In areas with excessive deer populations, forests become open and devoid of saplings and undergrowth, which die back or are suppressed by continuous browsing. Bears and moose break trunks and limbs while feeding and moving about, which may also lead to the death of woody plants.

High water kills many trees. When beavers move into an area and build a dam, the result is often a pond created by rising water levels. Beaver ponds are frequently filled with snags of similar age, all of which died due to excessive water when the dam was completed. In turn, these snags provide all sorts of habitat for insects and birds, and the entire area becomes incredibly rich in wildlife as the soil below the pond surface become saturated with nutrients.

Scratching and Scent Posts

Snags and stumps are often used for marking and communication. It seems reasonable to assume that rotting wood would absorb and hold urine better than other surfaces, thus preserving scent communication longer. Perhaps this is why stumps are favorite scent posts of foxes, coyotes, wolves, bobcats, lynx, fishers, and many others. Stumps also provide elevated surfaces for those that prefer to leave scats above ground level. I have found, among others, fox, fisher, marten, otter, raccoon, mink, weasel, swamp rabbit, and red squirrel scats on stumps and logs.

Stumps, snags, and logs are also used by felines for scratching posts, as described earlier in the chapter.

Logs

Raccoons, coatis, skunks, and bears all tear at old stumps and logs to expose insects found within or beneath them. Bear sign is certainly the easiest to recognize in the field and is often found in clumps. It is

A stump opened by a black bear feeding on ants and other insect larvae. (MN)

Top: A grizzly rolled this large log in search of insects. (MT) *Bottom:* A black bear ripped open this log in search of insect larvae and ants. (MT)

usual to find many logs ripped apart in a given area, rather than just one. Differentiating grizzly from black bear sign on logs is difficult. I tend to see more obvious claws marks in the wood when grizzlies tear open logs, but this is not a reliable differentiation. I rely heavily on ecological clues and associated signs such as scats, tracks, and marked trees.

Other Signs of Feeding **7**

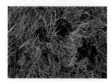

While collecting data for the annual Bear Sign Survey in Glacier National Park, we worked in teams of four or more. Grizzlies have been known to charge and maul single hikers, pairs, and occasionally groups of three, but never four or more—at least, not yet. Four remains the magic number.

On one particular trip, four of us moved into a drainage on the west side renowned for its bear activity. We moved with the confidence of seasoned hikers and were aware of the protection afforded by our group of four. After watching a grizzly sow and two cubs move with purpose and speed downhill across the lake, we paused for lunch after a morning of recording the position of marked trees, scats, and rubbed trees on annual transects. It was a good day.

With our bellies full, we strapped on our packs and began the journey up the drainage, where, after collecting data all afternoon, we planned to spend the night. We'd walked for only a few minutes, still trying to establish our rhythm, when Thad yelled out, "Okay bears, here we come." Many believe in the make-lots-of-noise theory of bear avoidance: They hear you coming and get out of your way. In this case, it certainly worked.

The words were barely out of Thad's mouth when there was a burst of commotion trailside and a grizzly leaped onto the trail just ahead of us. He stood, allowing us to study him from the side and making his great bulk all the more apparent; he was a very large bear. No one moved at first, and then I noticed that Thad and I were slowly walking backward. My heart pounded at the base of my throat so loudly that I was sure everyone could hear it. The two behind us must have been moving backward as well, for we never collided.

After what seemed like endless scrutiny by the bear, he turned and dashed uphill through thick understory. We stood staring after the thunderous noise of breaking brush until the sounds faded and were replaced by the calls of chickadees in the canopy. The magic number still held.

The fresh carcass of a black bear, recently killed by a grizzly. Note the earth and debris that were collected to cover the front end of the carcass in an attempt at caching. (MT)

After we all had a good laugh, relived the experience a few times, and regained our composure, we proceeded up the trail. Twenty-three yards had separated us from the bear. After pacing the distance out, I looked down to where the bear had been bedded and saw something amazing. "Steve, he was eating a black bear!"

Steve, the head biologist for the project, happened to be with us that day. Suddenly we were afraid again. A bear on a fresh carcass in the fall had good reason not to run away, being reluctant to leave all that protein and fat for its competition to steal. The bear had run, but he certainly would not go far; he would be back soon to reclaim what he had left behind.

We pulled out our bear mace, which suddenly seemed to be the equivalent of holding a water pistol or toy gun. Three of us stood guard while Steve went to verify the carcass. He returned soon enough and told me to have a look and to snap a few pictures. My camera had been hanging at my side all day long and had never been raised during our stare-down with the bear.

At the scene, vegetation was compressed for 20 yards around the carcass. Bear beds were evident in a few areas, and a few scats were left like mines on the crushed grass. The black bear lay on its stomach, as if caught in midstride running from the grizzly. The grizzly had caught the black bear on the back, clawing deep and tearing it open. Colorful internal organs were still visible, hanging limply, only partially consumed. Dirt and vegetation from the immediate vicinity of the carcass had been scraped inward and thrown over the front side of the black bear, helping to hide scent and visual cues that would lead potential competitors, such as wolves, other bears, or wolverines, to the site. This kill was incredibly fresh.

I snapped two shots and quickly returned to the trail, with fear filtering what I'd been able to see and interpret. We moved farther up the trail and stopped to discuss our options. Steve had the insight to consider our next day's agenda—which was to hike down the same trail, past the carcass again, and out to the road. The bear might not run the next time. And then there was the issue of others' safety. Should some lone hiker come upon this bear and carcass, the results could be fatal.

Staying close together, and yelling to the bear, we passed the carcass site again and began our hike out. The next day, we posted the trail and had the drainage closed to hiking for a week. That would give the bear enough time to clean the carcass and move on in search of other food.

Digging and Rooting

Digs of every size and shape will be encountered in your explorations, all presenting a challenge. Determining why a dig was made by what was removed is the best place to begin when analyzing and interpreting digs. Without an understanding of why it was made, a dig is just a hole in the ground. And knowing that a false truffle was eaten or recognizing the remains of a ground squirrel nest considerably narrows the list of poten-

tial mammals responsible. Again, an ecological perspective helps when interpreting signs in the field.

What follows are categories differentiated by the possible reasons for the dig. Caches of mast crops are not discussed here, as they often accompany the remains of nuts; digs associated with mast are discussed in chapter 6. Caches of meat are discussed later in this chapter.

Truffles

False truffles (*Elaphomyces, Endogone, Rhizopogon* species), or underground mushrooms, are popular fare for many animals. Deer create large, flat digs, more like scrapes. Porcupine digs are more conical,

In the lowest points of coastal dunes— spots hollowed out by winds—coyotes dig down to fresh water. Three watering holes were dug by coyotes along the expanse of this dune system, and crows, deer, and other mammals all took advantage when the coyotes were away. (MA)

A false truffle dig by a porcupine. Look closely for the circular impression left by the truffle, visible near the center of the dig. Porcupine digs tend to be 6 to 12 inches (15.2 to 30.5 cm) across. (MA)

The remains of a large false truffle, excavated by a northern flying squirrel. Note the incisor marks along the rim. (WA)

A false truffle dig of a white-tailed deer. (MA)

although these animals often uncover a large area until their noses tell them exactly where to dig. Flying squirrels create small, neat, conical digs just large enough to extract the truffle, as do Uinta chipmunks. Beavers and voles have also been documented digging for truffles, and other squirrel species may eat them as well.

All truffle digs are differentiated from other digs by locating the spot where the truffle sat in the earth. At the bottom of the dig, you will find a circular impression with very smooth, firm walls, ranging from 3/8 to 1 1/2 inches (.95 to 3.8 cm) in diameter.

Roots and Bulbs

Bears, deer, muskrats, voles, and peccaries reliably dig up roots and bulbs, and rabbits and rodents occasionally dig up garden bulbs and root crops. Feral hogs root for their roots and bulbs. Loose soil often holds a track, claw or hoof marks, and other ecological clues that are a great help in interpretation. Many holes are proportionate in size to the animal, but some are not. The countless tiny digs of singing voles digging up roots are proportionate, as are the root digs made by muskrats. The shallow digs of grizzlies feeding on glacier lily bulbs look like someone was preparing a garden by turning over the earth. Conversely, bear digs can be incredibly small and clean—as if the roots and tubers were just plucked from the earth.

Whereas digging involves shoveling and moving earth and debris with paws, hooves, and claws, rooting is excavation with the snout and

Deer create flat, shallow digs to feed on the roots of many sedges and grasses. (MA)

Collared peccaries dig up the roots and tubers of numerous plant species, and their signs can be dramatic and deep. (TX)

Muskrats have created substantial sign while digging for roots and tubers on a coastal island. (ME)

Grizzly bear digs for pea vine roots are common on overgrown riverbeds of the far north at the end of spring. (AK)

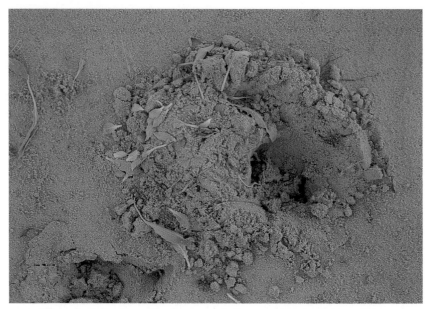

The mark of a hog's muzzle where a small tuber was rooted and eaten. (TX)

A substantial rooted area where hogs have been feeding. Look carefully to distinguish between fresh, dark brown rooting and the lighter rooting that occurred several weeks earlier. (NC)

Grizzly digs for glacier lily bulbs are especially common in autumn. (MT)

teeth. Many animals use the head when digging, but rooting often brings to mind feral hogs and other pigs. The signs of rooting are much the same as those of digging and can be difficult to differentiate. Signs of claws and hooves are helpful, but they are not always evident in digs, especially if they are not fresh. Hogs are known to do extensive rooting, and you may find massive areas overturned by a family group or even an individual.

In Debris

The debris layer is rich in insect life, and at certain times of year it holds the annual drop of mast crops and fruit relished by many. Deer, bears,

Debris displaced by coatis looking for insects. (AZ)

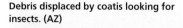

A bear continues to shuffle debris in shallow snow in search of fallen beechnuts. (NH)

porcupines, fishers, hogs, peccaries, and numerous bird species are among those that annually shuffle debris in search of acorns, pine nuts, hickory nuts, fallen apples, and numerous other mast crops. Deer, bears, and hogs can turn over expansive areas while feeding, leaving behind what appears to be the work of a rototiller; in fact, all three species can be found together. I've followed bears into areas where deer are digging and feeding, and vice versa. Chipmunks, squirrels, other small mammals, and birds tend to forage in smaller areas and leave much smaller digs.

Skunks, raccoons, and others also shift debris in search of insects. Even if you rely on associated sign to interpret these scenarios, you may not be able to determine with complete certainty what was responsible.

Coatis move a tremendous about of debris in search of insects. I once followed a troop in southeastern Arizona, and the members continually used their snouts to overturn leaves and debris as they went. Occasionally they would stop to scratch the earth with their claws as well, but much of their digging was done in the debris surface.

In Snow

Snow covers the landscape in the North through the winter months, but many mammals remember what lies on the ground or was hidden in earth or debris before the snowflakes began to fall. And snow can be moved, if the rewards are worth the energy expended.

Many mammals dig in snow to feed on windfallen mast crops, such as acorns and hickory nuts, as well as to retrieve caches made before

Left: Deer continue to dig through snow in search of acorns. Note the acorn remains dropped along the edge of the dig. (NH) *Right:* Elk have been digging down to graze on grasses. (MT)

the snowfall. Deer, porcupines, and bears all dig through the snow layer to continue feeding on acorns and hickory nuts. I once followed a number of fisher trails into an apple orchard where a series of digs and tunnels had been created to feed on windfallen apples through 2 feet (61 cm) of snow in January.

Some grazers also dig through snow to feed on still green or dried grasses. Elk and bison dig as deep as necessary, using both hoof and head as shovels. White-tailed jackrabbits also dig down to continue feeding on grasses through the winter. On a number of occasions, I've found bison and elk digging in the very spots they were bedding, where the snowpack had been compacted and warmed by the body. Mule deer also dig to browse on sage, and I've found black-tailed jackrabbits digging 2 feet (61 cm) down to feed on prickly pears in southern Idaho.

Predation for Insects, Mollusks, and Other Invertebrates

Bears, raccoons, and skunks are all known to dig up and eat ground hornets, or yellow jackets. Unlike honeybee nests, which are opened to get at the honey, ground hornet nests are opened to eat the hornets themselves and their pupae. The remains of the nest make identification easy, although the papery nests dissolve quickly when exposed to moisture and rain, and sometimes little remains to interpret at all. Honeycomb construction is much sturdier, allowing signs to persist longer.

Differentiating raccoon and bear digs for ground hornets can be difficult. Often the entrance created by a raccoon to remove a nest is smaller, more like a tunnel or burrow, than the larger, wider dig made by a bear. When nests are close to the earth's surface, the digs may be more difficult to separate. Associated sign is always helpful, including whether there are other open nests in the same area. I found a spot worked by a black bear where there were eight opened wasp nests within an acre.

Raccoons, skunks, armadillos, and bears also dig for other insect species. Skunk digs are conical, and the dirt throwback is very short and

Left: A hornet's nest excavated by a raccoon. (MA) Photo by John McCarter.
Right: A yellow jacket nest excavated and opened by a black bear. (NH)

Left: Every rock in this photo was turned by a grizzly bear searching for insects. (MT) *Right:* A hooded skunk dig, foraging for insects. (Mexico)

kept near the hole. Raccoon digs tend to pull all the debris and soil in one direction and keep buildup farther from the hole. Armadillo digs vary tremendously. Most often, they are small, conical, and similar to those made by other medium-sized mammals. However, armadillos also excavate great areas. In the dwindling sabal palm habitat in the southern tip of Texas, many of the oldest trees are leaning due to incredible armadillo excavations around their roots. But what appears detrimental to the trees is actually saving them, for the armadillos are feeding on parasitic beetles and their larvae, which would certainly overtake and kill the last remaining trees. Armadillos also dig often—look for a series of small digs in close association.

Crabs, crayfish, clams, and mussels are also popular fare for many mammals. I use associated signs to interpret most digs for these species. Raccoons, skunks, muskrats, rice rats, otters, and bears are among the potential predators. Consider the amount of sign you've found in one place. Bears dig and eat clams on the spot. Raccoons feed on crayfish as they move. Muskrats and rice rats form larger middens at feeding stations, and otter sign accumulates at favorite haul-outs and roll areas. Additional information on feeding signs is found in the Kill Sites section.

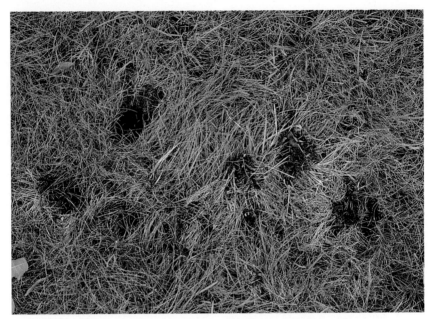

A striped skunk's small digs are a sure sign of grub infestation in yards. They'll continue foraging until the grubs are killed or move on. (NH)

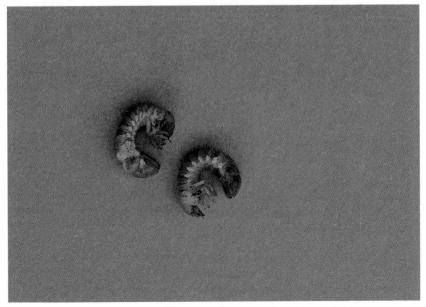

Grubs removed from an area where skunks were tearing up lawn. (NH)

Typical armadillo dig. (TX)

A raccoon has excavated this crayfish burrow in the hope of eating its inhabitant.
(FL)

A brown bear's digs and subsequent clam remains at low tide. Numerous digs are visible in the distance. (AK) Photo by Lynn Rogers.

Predation for Small Mammals

Numerous predators excavate burrows and earth in the hope of capturing some small mammal. Brown bears search out ground squirrels and pocket gophers, leaving gaping holes. Bears double their efforts to find ground squirrels as summer comes to an end and fall begins, when squirrels move more slowly and may be trapped in their hibernacula. Even black bears dig up occasional small mammals when the opportunity presents itself.

Look closely for the remains of an arctic ground squirrel's nest in the center of this grizzly bear excavation. The dirt may be thrown up to 6 feet (1.5 m) when grizzlies are digging for ground squirrels.

A black bear removed this vole nest, which was just below the surface. In most of their range, small mammals and fawns are the extent of black bears' predatory hunting. (MN)

A pair of coyotes has been digging for kangaroo rats; they eat the entire animal, so signs that confirm success are difficult to find. (TX)

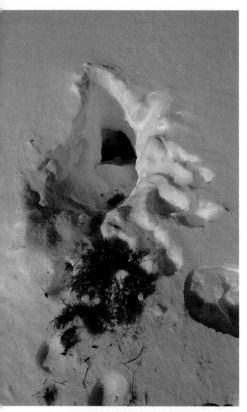

A small field held 11 digs made over the course of a week when a red fox dug through more than 3 feet (90 cm) of snow to remove vole nests. (ID)

Foxes and coyotes dig up voles, pocket mice, and other small mammals year-round. I've found red foxes digging through 3 feet (90 cm) of snow to remove vole nests made at ground level—probably to eat the young, which do not run. I've also found many instances in which gray foxes trapped red squirrels in their burrows and successfully dug from several entrances, leaping back and forth until the squirrel was revealed. Kit foxes, too, are tremendous diggers and are more carnivorous than other foxes, relying heavily on catching kangaroo rats and pocket mice out in the open or digging them out from their burrows.

A kit fox dig, hunting kangaroo rats. (CA)

Badgers are notorious for digging up small mammals, and their sign often accumulates over time, leaving a great expanse of large holes and throw mounds. I've also found spots where the related fisher has dug up red-backed voles, shrews, and other small mammals.

Black-footed ferrets dig in a unique fashion: They do not throw dirt between their legs but rather pull out loads of dirt held in the front paws while walking backward out of burrows. Not everything is understood about such digs. Some people theorize that this is part of prey acquisition, while others believe that it is related to denning. Either way, the unique furrows created by ferrets walking backward are easily identifiable in a prairie dog town and are sure signs of their presence.

Predation for Turtle Eggs

Whenever you find the remains of soft, leathery turtle eggs, you can be certain that they have been preyed on. When turtles hatch naturally, they do so underground, where the female had so diligently dug out an area to lay her eggs. When hatching turtles burst forth above the earth's surface, they leave their eggshells hidden beneath the soil.

I have found it difficult to determine what mammal has preyed on turtle eggs when studying only the eggs themselves; corvids and other birds add to the confusion. Raccoons, coatis, and skunks dig up and poach turtle eggs whenever the opportunity presents itself. In each instance, eggs are strewn about the nest site, and an inspection of eggshell remains reveals small punctures, which are the canine teeth. I rely on associated signs to identify the culprit.

I was unable to determine with certainty what preyed on this turtle's nest. (MN)

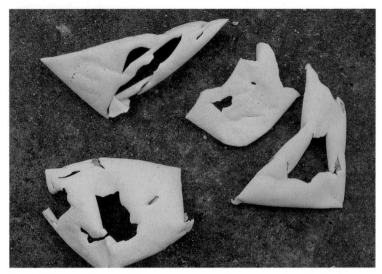

Hawksbill sea turtle eggs with punctures created by a raccoon's teeth. Tracks confirmed the predator. (Mexico)

Kill Sites

Within the realm of tracking, the term *kill site* is often used to describe an area where the signs of a predator taking prey are left behind. Some people think that kill sites must be very dramatic, involving large prey and predators, but I believe that places where small prey are taken—even insects, amphibians, and mollusks—still constitute kill sites. I also want to emphasize that a kill site is often much larger than the immediate area of the prey's remains. Smaller prey tend to leave a small effect on the landscape, but large prey may be responsible for concentric rings of sign.

Consider the illustrated example, which a friend and I explored on a frozen lake in northern Minnesota. A white-tailed deer was killed by a wolf pack, but the actual place where the deer was killed was at the center of numerous stories ringing the area. What really constitutes the kill site? Is it only the actual place where the deer was pulled down and the wolves fed?

1. This was the location of the takedown and initial feeding. All that remained were scraps of fur, bone chunks, and a hoof. The area was 20 yards (18.3 m) across, including the drag marks of blood and rumen contents. Wolf and raven tracks carpeted the entire area. A bald eagle trail led from where it had landed 20 yards (18.3 m) away from the carcass straight into the site; then it was lost in

the chaos of other tracks. A red fox had visited and revisited the site, leaving a scat near the stomach remains.

2. Windblown deer hair carpeted the frozen snow under an eagle's perch—an old snag—where bits of carcass had been fed on. There was a fox trail winding through the hair, searching for tidbits, and a scat was left just under the perch.

3. There was a second eagle perch and more windblown deer hair; in each spot, the plucked fur covered a good 30 yards (27.4 m) of ice.

4. The first wolf roll was substantial and very close to the carcass.

5. The first bedding area consisted of four separate wolf beds, all in close proximity under the cover of mixed woods, but still very close to the lake surface.

6. In this area, a raven had carried and fed on carcass remains—a bit of blood and hair remained.

7. This was a second area where a raven had carried and fed on carcass remains—a bit of blood and hair remained.

8. This was a cache site, where large bone fragments, fur, and hooves were sprinkled across an area covering about 5 or 6 yards (4.57 or 5.5 m). There was a wolf scat near the dig, composed mostly of internal organs and meat. The red fox had been here, too, and had left a scat high on a small boulder. A marten had passed through and investigated the area. Raven tracks were common. There were also two wolf beds nearby.

9. Further wolf rolling occurred in several spots near the cache site.

10. Wolf trails came together and interacted. There were four additional wolf scats in close proximity.

In what Jack Childs refers to as a "typical first feeding of a jaguar," an ear and the tongue were eaten. (Brazil) Photo by Matt Colvin.

11. A marten backtracked a pair of wolves that had just come from the kill site, likely smelling the carcass and hoping for a free meal. However, the marten did not dare cross the large expanse of ice to the island.

Note: Wolf trails are represented by dotted lines. The chase before the white-tailed deer was caught is represented by dashes and dots.

The combination of all these accumulating signs was the kill site. All the additional animal feeding signs, as well as the bedding, caching, and rolling wolf behaviors, were a result of the initial interaction between wolves and one deer. Without the kill, the wolves would have passed through, the red fox would have invested time elsewhere, there would have been little raven sign, and the eagle would have perched at another lake. Kill sites influence the landscape and all its inhabitants in magnificent ways; all we need to do is look.

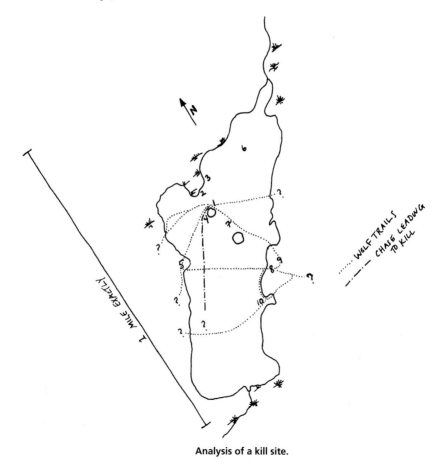

Analysis of a kill site.

The Predator's Teeth

When a mammal attacks, kills, and eats another animal, all the teeth are used. The canines hold the victim and make the kill. The carnassials break the skin and open the carcass. Incisors and canines pull skin flaps back to expose meat and pluck feathers from birds. The carnassials shear manageable chunks from the carcass and shear feathers from prey. The molars soften and pound edible portions before swallowing.

Measuring the distance between punctures made by upper or lower canines on a carcass can be a useful clue when trying to determine the predator.

	Distance between Upper Canines	Distance between Lower Canines
Gray wolf	$1^3/_4$–2 in. (4.4–5.1 cm)	$1^3/_4$–2 in. (4.4–5.1 cm)
Coyote	$1^1/_{16}$–$1^7/_{16}$ in. (2.7–3.7 cm)	$1^1/_8$–$1^1/_4$ in. (2.9–3.2 cm)
Red fox	$^{15}/_{16}$–$1^1/_8$ in. (2.4–2.9 cm)	$^3/_4$–$^7/_8$ in. (1.9–2.2 cm)
Black bear	$1^{11}/_{16}$–$2^1/_2$ in. (4.3–6.4 cm)	$1^{11}/_{16}$–$2^1/_4$ in. (2.7–5.7 cm)
Cougar	$1^5/_8$–$2^1/_{16}$ in. (4.1–5.2 cm)	$1^3/_{16}$–$1^7/_8$ in. (3–4.9 cm)
Wolverine	$1^1/_8$–$1^3/_{16}$ in. (2.9–3 cm)	1–$1^{11}/_{16}$ in. (2.5–2.7 cm)
Bobcat	$^9/_{16}$–$1^1/_{16}$ in. (1.4–2.7 cm)	$^9/_{16}$–1 in. (1.4–2.5 cm)
House cat	$^1/_2$–$^9/_{16}$ in. (1.3–1.4 cm)	$^7/_{16}$–$^9/_{16}$ in. (1.1–1.4 cm)
Fisher	$^{11}/_{16}$–$^{13}/_{16}$ in. (1.7–2.1 cm)	$^5/_8$–$^3/_4$ in. (1.6–1.9 cm)
Marten	$^7/_{16}$–$^5/_8$ in. (1.1–1.6 cm)	$^3/_8$–$^9/_{16}$ in. (1–1.4 cm)
Otter	$^3/_4$–1 in. (1.9–2.5 cm)	$^1/_2$–$^{15}/_{16}$ in. (1.3–2.4 cm)
Long-tailed weasel	$^3/_{16}$–$^5/_{16}$ in. (.5–.8 cm)	$^5/_{32}$–$^1/_4$ in. (.4–.6 cm)
Mink	$^3/_8$–$^3/_4$ in. (1–1.9 cm)	$^3/_8$–$^5/_8$ in. (1–1.6 cm)
Striped skunk	$^7/_{16}$–$^1/_2$ in. (1.1–1.3 cm)	$^7/_{16}$–$^1/_2$ in. (1.1–1.3cm)
Ringtail	$^3/_8$–$^7/_{16}$ in. (1–1.1 cm)	$^3/_8$–$^7/_{16}$ in. (1–1.1 cm)
Harbor seal	$^3/_4$–1 in. (1.9–2.5 cm)	$^5/_8$–$^{15}/_{16}$ in. (1.6–2.4 cm)

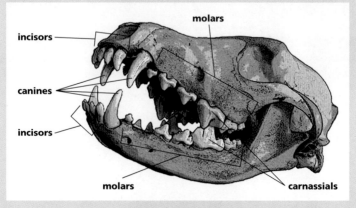

Eastern coyote skull.

Compare the snails opened by white-footed mice on the left with the yellow snails opened by crows on a coastal island on the right. Shrews, mice, and chipmunks will all chew snails in the same manner, starting at the entrance and winding backwards until the prey is secured. (NY, ME)

A freshwater mussel midden accumulates at a muskrat's favorite feeding perch. (MA) Photo by Paul Rezendes.

Crab carapaces in a muskrat midden near a burrow entrance. (ME)

pace almost untouched, while muskrats tend to chew the undersides, leaving just the upper shell. If crab claws are found, gulls enter from one side, whereas muskrats enter from an end. Muskrats tend to eat the smaller legs as well, but gulls generally discard them.

Raccoons discard crayfish heads and claws in shallow water, so their signs are often overlooked. Often they eat smaller prey, such as mole crabs, in their entirety. Along coastal beaches in Oregon, I often found river otters exploring the tidal pools at low tide and feeding on crabs. Although I never took a picture of the remains, I remember that the otters ate the crabs almost in their entirety. I've also watched minks running with massive crayfish in their mouths, but I've never been able to find feeding remains.

The remains of freshwater mussels opened by mammals are common in appropriate habitats. When opening mussels, otters break a small rectangular chunk out of one side of the shell and leave the remains to accumulate at favorite haul-outs. Muskrats creates even larger middens at favorite feeding perches. Amazingly, the shells of mussels opened by muskrats often show no obvious signs of forced entry. Raccoons also eat mussels.

Mammals Eating Fish

Fish are most often eaten in their entirety, or the remains slide back into the water and are overlooked by trackers. I've watched numerous otters eating fish and have only once found any remains other than blood and a bit of guts—they start with the head and eat the whole thing. Paul

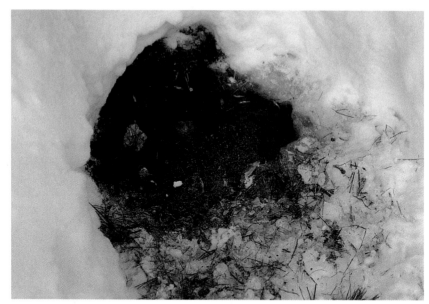

This hole was originally dug by a coyote, which broke the thin ice at the edge of a pond where tiny fish were congregating. Coyotes returned repeatedly to feast, and a red fox visited a few times too. Look closely for the fish. (MA)

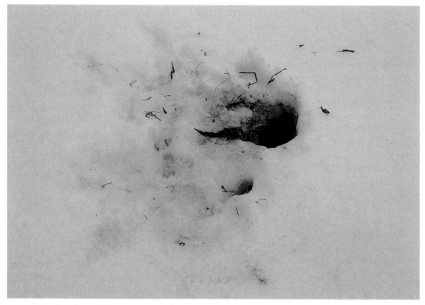

The haul-out of an otter on a frozen pond. I watched an otter eat three fish in succession at this spot, and nothing was left except stains in the snow. (NH)

A mink's hole, trail, and cache of sunfish, revealed during a warm spell when the snow melted. (MA) Photo by Paul Rezendes.

A brown bear ate only the nutritious brain of this spawning salmon. (AK) Photo by Lynn Rogers.

Rezendes found fish heads left behind on one occasion, and I once found tails. Minks, too, seem to eat the entire fish, but unlike otters, they cache in times of plenty.

Fish remains left by feeding bears vary, depending on the quantity of fish available, the ease of capturing them, and the weight and health of the bear. Sometimes they eat the whole thing. At other times, especially during the salmon run, bears become more selective, eating only the brain and the nutritious eggs if they've caught a female. Charles Russell (1994) wrote about a wolf pack feeding on the brains of salmons. They severed the heads of the fish cleanly and left their untouched bodies sprinkled along stream banks.

Mammals Eating Mammals
Large Prey
Analysis of large prey remains can be a sticky business, but contextual clues aid in interpretation. The earlier large prey remains are found (within two to three days is best), and the less the predator has fed on the

carcass, the easier it is to interpret the clues left behind. With time, scavengers and competitors appear on the scene, and carcass remains are quickly scattered to the four winds. Coyotes, ravens and their relatives, eagles, and small rodents clean a carcass completely, leaving little but confusion for the tracker. It is incredibly difficult to identify with certainty the original predator at an old kill site when scavengers have been there.

Begin by determining whether you are at an actual kill site or whether the predator was scavenging. Animals die for so many reasons, and predators often take the opportunity to scavenge a carcass they encounter. Also consider the following questions: Are you at the

Lots of blood covers the distance between a deer's bed and where it was killed by several coyotes. The deer had been wounded by a hunter. (MA) Photo by Paul Rezendes.

Jon Young's Carcass Analysis:
North American CyberTracker Sequence

Jon Young's kill site analysis is full of pointers about all the components of carcass interpretation. He divides the tracker's attention into three areas: (1) site disturbance patterns, (2) carcass disbursement, and (3) carcass conditions. Carcass conditions are subdivided into categories of assessment. Each note asks the tracker to assess something specific— these are signposts that tell you where to look and smell and how to think when considering carcass remains. This sequence is a wonderful start to carcass analysis.

1. Site Disturbance Patterns
- Carcass drag marks?
- Body prints?
- Substrate thatching?
- Pulling tracks?
- Vegetation killed by fluids or gut piles?
- Vegetation dead zone?
- Digs?
- Disturbance: None? Small? Moderate? Great?
- Buried carcass?

2. Carcass Disbursement
- Primary carcass length and width?
- Disturbance area length and width?
- Kill site length and width?

3. Carcass Conditions
A. General Description
- Flies? Fly eggs? Maggots?
- Eyes clear, clouded, shriveled, or missing?
- Fresh and limber? Stiffening or very stiff?
- Carcass bloated?
- Carcass odorless, or a vague, strong, or intense odor?
- Carcass whole/intact?
- Opened but mostly intact, or stripped of meat?
- Stripped of viscera?
- Bones of leg exposed? Ribs exposed?
- Parts missing?
- Just a dried-up hide and bones? Mostly skeletonized? Just old bones? Little bits of fur and bone? Only a dark spot on vegetation?
- Femur and marrow conditions?
- Coat condition?

B. Points of Entry
- Rear/rectal area?
- Rear legs?
- Viscera/intestines?
- Viscera, liver, heart, and lungs?
- Skull and brains?
- Nasal area?

(continued on page 718)

C. Parts Consumed
- Skull and brains?
- Neck?
- Shoulders?
- Rib flesh?
- Lungs?
- Heart and liver?
- Intestines?
- Front legs?
- Hind legs?
- Rump?
- Hide, fur, or feathers?
- Stomach contents?
- Bones?
- Paws, hooves, or feet?

D. Bone Conditions
- Whole/intact and wet?
- Whole/intact and dry?
- Whole/intact and brittle?
- Marrow bones cracked?
- Bones missing or dispersed?
- Rib ends chewed?
- Rodent chews on bones?

E. Parts Missing
- Eyes?
- Skull?
- Brains?
- Skin on head?
- Neck?
- Right or left shoulder?
- Right or left front leg?
- Right or left foot/hoof?
- Right or left wing?
- Rib cage?
- Hide covering ribs?
- Internal organs?
- Right or left hind leg?
- Right or left hind foot/hoof?
- Tail?
- Hide from hind legs?

F. Detailed Forensics
- Hairs?
- Hairs from predator or scavengers?
- Feathers?
- Grid analysis?
- Other?

G. Prey Age
- Fetal or newborn?
- Juvenile, adolescent, or adult?
- Old?
- Nestling or fledgling?
- Precocial or altricial?
- One, two, three, four, or five or more years old?

original kill site, or has the carcass been moved? Are there signs of a chase or struggle? Are there signs of blood? Mammals do not have to be dead long before their blood congeals and no longer runs. Also consider the position of the legs. If the animal is on its side and the legs are straight out, this supports a kill, whereas a carcass with several or all of the legs tucked under the body might indicate an animal that died in bed.

Next, consider how the carcass was entered. Was it from the rump, or just behind the rib cage? Are there any scratches across the carcass from claws or teeth? Are there any clear bites to the rump, ears, back of the neck, or throat? Has the carcass been cached or covered in any way? Have the remains been scented? Are there scats and nearby beds to consider?

Those who want to study carcasses in more detail can skin the remains and examine the body tissues. Hemorrhaging will be readily apparent where tissue was deeply clawed or bitten—especially by the canines of the killing bite. Bruises from swats or other contact will also be visible—confined areas of colored tissue. Punctures made by teeth will be more apparent, and therefore the location of bites can be determined more easily; measurements between canines can be taken, which aid in identifying the predator.

Wolves. Wolves tend to attack the rear end of their intended prey first, while another wolf tries to grab the nose; this allows others to follow up with attacks to the flanks and sometimes the shoulders. Fresh kills show slashes and cuts where wolves bit and held on to the prey during the pursuit. Look closely at the nose, flanks, rear, neck, and shoulders of the victim. Generally, once the prey is dead, the abdomen is torn open—much as a cougar enters a carcass—and the organs are consumed by the alpha pair. Others eat from wounds inflicted during the chase. On very large prey, wolves may begin feeding before the prey has died.

In short order, the carcass is stripped, dragged about, and cut into pieces. Depending on the state of the pack, the wolves may eat absolutely everything except for the stomach contents and intestines. One wolf can consume just over 20 pounds (9.1 kg) of meat in a sitting, so even a car-

Wolves had recently killed and fed on this elk. (ID) Photo by Kevin Jarvis, Shikari Tracking Guild.

After several days, this was all that remained of a white-tailed deer killed by wolves: some hide, a few bones, a hoof, the smeared stomach contents, and blood-soaked snow. (MN)

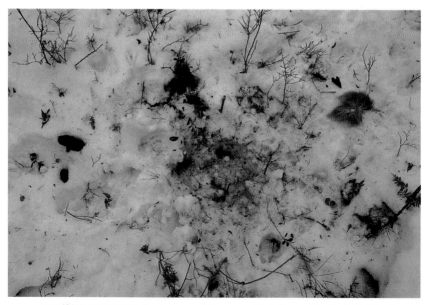

A wolf has returned to feed at one of its caches. Note the scat to the left side of the hole. (MN)

Bone chunks found at the cache site. Few predators can crush bones as efficiently as wolves. (MN)

cass of considerable size can disappear quickly if there are many wolves in the pack. When they are full, pack members cache food for later consumption; it is not unusual for both coyotes and wolves to regurgitate food chunks into caches, as well as drag or carry pieces of the actual kill to be buried nearby.

Wolves' feeding schedules depend on the size of the prey they hunt and the size of the pack. A general estimate is that wolves need to eat every 7 to 10 days, but there are many variables that must be considered, depending on where you are tracking. Some researchers believe that each wolf in a pack requires 15 to 20 deer per year to survive. Wolves have a varied palate and are known to eat deer, moose, elk, mountain sheep, bison, muskox, mice, squirrels, birds, beavers, and snowshoe hares. They also kill and eat livestock.

Cougars and Jaguars. Cougars hunt and kill predominantly mule and white-tailed deer, but they also eat elk (most often calves), bighorn sheep, porcupines, peccaries, coyotes, bobcats, beavers, rabbits, ground squirrels, and occasionally domestic calves or sheep. Cougars are not mass killers of large prey; in fact, they live rather precariously on fewer deer than one might expect. Researchers across the country have found that cougars kill far less frequently than imagined. Ackerman (1982), who studied cougars in Utah, states the following numbers for females: A solitary female needs to kill a deer every 16 days, one with 3-month-old kittens needs to kill every 9 days, and a female with 15-month-old kittens (just before dispersion) needs a deer every 3 days to keep the family in top form.

Above: A spike buck killed by a cougar. Note the fur ball, sheared by the cat before opening the carcass, which was incorporated in the attempt to cover the carcass. Ribs are sheared, and internal organs have been consumed. (ID) *Below left:* The trail of a cougar dragging a freshly killed deer carcass. (WY) Photo by Michael Sanders. *Below right:* A close-up of the area on a deer carcass where a cougar "plucked"—actually sheared—fur before breaking the skin to feed. Photo by Sue Morse.

A deer carcass cached by a cougar. (WY) Photo by Jim Halfpenny.

When skinning the carcass, look for hemorrhaging at the base of the neck and skull. Cougars tend to bite and sever the spinal cord by forcing vertebrae apart in the neck or at the base of the skull, or they reach around and bite the throat, strangling the victim. Look for canine teeth as well as claw marks along the back, sides, and shoulders, where the cougar may have gripped the victim before making the killing bite. Cougars kill quickly and often drop victims in short order.

Jack Childs (1998) studied jaguar predation on cattle in Brazil and documented two features of jaguar kills that he has yet to see during decades trailing cougars in the southwest. First, jaguars often bite and hold the nose of prey when attacking, leaving obvious signs of canines. Second, they often enter one side of the prey's face to remove and eat the tongue.

Cougars tend to drag their prey under a low-hanging tree or rock overhang, or sometimes into a cave. After feeding, they cover the remainder of the carcass with available materials. If they are in unsuitable habitat without debris, there are often signs of attempting to cover the carcass anyway. Cougars may also drag the carcass between feedings (up to 1,000 feet [300 m], and sometimes straight up vertical rock), and several cache sites may be found in the vicinity of the carcass. Occasionally, cougars do not cover a kill, most often in the rare circumstance of a mass killing; in this case, only one or two animals are covered, and the others are left exposed.

First, cougars (and bobcats) "pluck" hair from the area where they will enter the carcass. Sue Morse researched this behavior and found that cats aren't actually plucking at all. Rather, they are using their lower

A cougar killed this coyote and ate much of the carcasss, including the brains. (TX) Photo by Greg Levandoski.

incisors to shear the brittle ungulate fur from the skin. An investigation of the entrance area should reveal hair stubble; the roots are left intact where the cats have sheared the fur away. Also look for balls of hair near the carcass, which is the fur removed from the entrance site. Often this fur is reused when gathering materials for caching.

The carcass is entered from just behind the rib cage, and the internal organs (liver, lungs, and heart) are eaten first. Sometimes, only these organs are eaten before the cougar moves on in search of fresh food. Ribs are sheared away and may be eaten. Next, the larger leg muscles are eaten from the inside of the leg out, and sometimes the brain of the victim is eaten as well. John Laudré, a cougar researcher in Idaho, often finds sites where cougars have eaten the entire skulls of mule deer. Its common for cougars to abandon a kill before completely cleaning the bones, but a female with kittens is more likely to stick around. She may even feed, then leave the remainder of the carcass to the kittens while she goes off to find another deer.

Cougars protect their kills, and it is well documented that they attack and kill coyotes that venture too close. Wolves will also kill coyotes that wander too close to kills.

Bears. Brown and black bears tend to prey on smaller prey than do other large carnivores, including deer fawn, elk and cow calves, and occasional sheep. Claw marks are not often seen on the back or shoulders, as with cat-killed animals, and the bite to the spine may be made either on the neck or just behind the shoulders. Lynn Rogers has watched numerous black bears kill and eat deer fawns and reports that they bite anywhere they can grip the animal; on occasion, they even begin to feed before the fawn has died. Fawns are most often eaten in their entirety. Black bears have also been documented feeding on the udders of lactating ungulates they have killed.

Grizzlies may start at the head and shoulders to enter a carcass, or enter to feed on viscera and hindquarters. All bears invert carcasses as they feed, pulling the skin over the head, to avoid eating the fur and skin, although smaller carcasses may be eaten entirely. An inverted carcass, inside out, is definitely a bear kill. On one occasion, I stumbled upon a grizzly eating an elk. When I returned after the bear had finished feeding, I found that the elk's hide had been expertly skinned by the bear, rolled up neatly, and placed to the side of the carcass.

Black bears and grizzlies drag carcasses into better cover for feeding or caching. Black bears may or may not cover the carcass, but grizzlies nearly always do so. These cache sites often include bedding areas and plenty of fresh scats, all of which must be considered in your interpretation. Please be aware that a possessive bear could return at any time, so staying close to a cache may be dangerous.

Should you skin the carcass, look for hemorrhaging on the neck and back, as well as bruises where the bear swatted the animal. Bruises appear as confined areas of discoloration, which shouldn't be confused with any changes due to sun exposure or decay.

Bears are notorious scavengers, so be sure to determine whether a bear killed the prey or found it dead. Long-dead carcasses are occasionally eaten, and bears may make a meal of the maggots themselves. Scats filled with maggots often indicate scavenging rather than predation.

Fawn remains, killed and partially consumed by a black bear. (MN) Photo by Lynn Rogers.

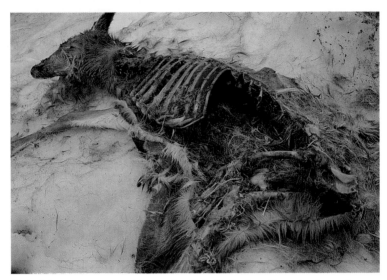

Typical deer carcass opened by coyotes. Note the broken ribs and entrance from behind. (NH)

Coyotes. Like wolves and dogs, coyotes tear at their prey during the chase, biting flanks, head, and neck and sometimes shredding the ears of smaller animals such as fawns. Coyotes tend to open a carcass from the rear and then move into the ribs and cut out the internal organs. They often remove the rumen right away; this may be an indicator of the original kill site or the place where the carcass was encountered. Within a short time, the carcass is dragged and moved several times, and it is cut into smaller pieces and dragged in different directions by different coyotes seeking a spot to feed in solitude. Older kill sites are a scattering of bones and fur.

Coyotes also cache nearby, especially if they find a fresh carcass and are early on the scene. Other coyotes are sure to show up eventually, and caches can be turned to when competition at the carcass becomes too fierce. Like wolves, coyotes cache whole pieces or, on occasion, swallow food and regurgitate it into holes for later use. Also look for areas in nearby vegetation or snow where muzzles were rubbed and cleaned; this sign is also found at wolf kills.

Dogs are responsible for killing many deer, other ungulates, and smaller game. These carcasses are typically mutilated—more so than when coyotes or wolves take down prey—and the dogs may do little feeding at all. Foxes will also strangle fawns on occasion.

Bobcats. Bobcats, especially males, take deer and other large prey. Like cougars, they tend to either stalk and surprise or wait and surprise their prey in a given area. The killing bite is to the back of the neck or to

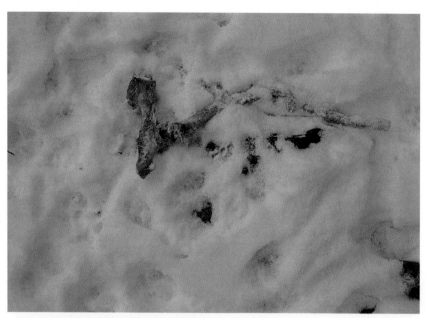

Carcass remains scented by a coyote. (VT)

A young deer killed and partially consumed by a bobcat. Note that no large bones have been broken. (NH) Photo by Sue Mansfield.

the throat, suffocating the victim. Lynx have also been documented killing deer on several occasions.

Bobcats cover their prey and often move the carcass and recover it on successive nights. They appear to be unable to break the large bones of mature deer, so they sever and separate them from the carcass at the joints as they feed. A cleaned carcass with intact large bones is a good indicator of a bobcat kill.

Vampire bats. Three species of vampire bat are found in North America, although only one lives far enough north to inhabit the southern tip of Texas; vampire bats are a Mexican experience. All three species have been documented feeding off large mammals, but the principal prey of the common vampire bat *(Desmodus rotundus)* is the cow; it also feeds on other livestock. The remaining two vampire bat species feed more often from avian prey.

With their modified, razor-sharp incisors, vampire bats slice prey, and the anticoagulants in their saliva keep the wound from clotting. They lap up the flowing blood with their tongues until they are bloated, and then return to their roost until the following night. Signs of their feeding can be quite common in areas where they are abundant—look for cows and other large mammals with blood-soaked shoulders and rumps or blood dripping down their sides, dying their coats.

Look closely at the neck of this cow for the bloodstains that mark the spot where a vampire bat fed. (Mexico) Photo by Merlin D. Tuttle, Bat Conservation International.

The last remains of a porcupine killed and fed on several times by a bobcat. (MA)

Medium Prey

The smaller the prey, the more difficult it is to distinguish the predators and interpret carcass remains without contextual clues. Teeth marks can be analyzed, but tracks, scats, and caching become more important factors in the interpretation.

Bobcats and lynx. Bobcats and lynx both cover their caches, but they often make a meal of smaller prey in one sitting. In one unusual cache I found the remains of half a raccoon, an entire gray squirrel, and a mink's tail. I've found spots where bobcats had killed gray squirrels, and all that remained was the tails. Like fishers, bobcats successfully kill porcupines by attacking the nose, and they harvest a long list of other medium prey.

When lynx eat hares, they often leave the intestines and stomach, a foot or two, and a skin flap from the back. These remains are sometimes cached, but lynx are unlikely to return for them unless times are hard.

Foxes and coyotes. Foxes and coyotes often eat smaller prey in their entirety. I have found fox-killed cottontail remains—one or two feet, the intestines, and a flap of skin and fur left behind.

Canines cache in natural hollows and cavities and often dig when the substrate is suitable. They dig with their paws and claws, keeping the soil and other debris neatly piled next to the hole—very different from the flying dirt sent by cartoon canines caching bones. Then the nose, not the paws, is used to carefully replace the soil removed from the hole to cover the cache of eggs, meat, bird, or whatever. They add sticks and natural materials to match the surrounding ground. Their ability to camouflage the cache is incredible. Noted red fox researcher J. D. Henry

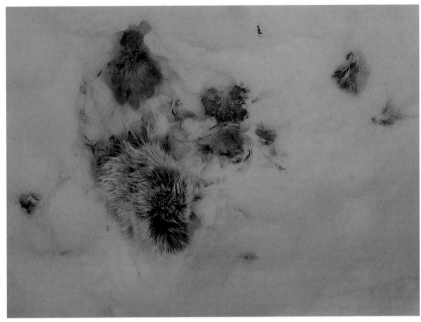

The remains of a snowshoe hare killed and eaten by a lynx. (ME)

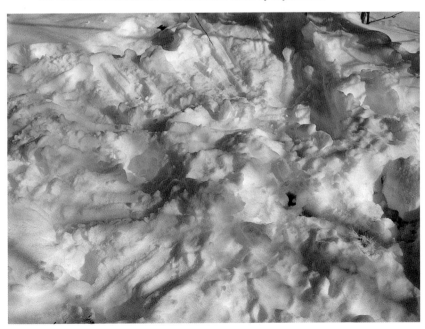

A lynx's cached snowshoe hare remains. (ME)

(1993) reports that it is nearly impossible to find fox caches, even when he has just watched them being made.

Arctic foxes are notorious cachers, creating large larders that can sustain them for months. Olaus Murie recorded the contents of several caches while exploring the Arctic. The first held 103 petrels, 6 tufted puffins, 4 auklets, and 1 guillemot. The second held 107 least auklets, 18 crested auklets, 3 tufted puffins, 1 horned puffin, 1 murre, and 7 petrels. Another researcher, Alwin Pederson, found a cache of 36 dovekies, 2 murrelets, 4 snow buntings, and numerous dovekie eggs.

Foxes often remember exactly where they cached prey and return later. They may also stumble upon or follow other foxes and fishers and pilfer their caches. But what comes around goes around, and they are likely to be the victims of such thievery sometime down the road.

Coyotes, which work in teams, tend to cache when they discover a carcass, more to hide resources from other coyotes than to keep food for later. When a carcass is cleaned, a coyote that had arrived early and made nearby caches can turn to those additional stashes to continue feeding.

Fishers and martens. Fishers and martens take prey their own size and larger and tend to eat them in their entirety over time, except for the stomach contents and intestines, which are discarded. Killing bites are often made to the back of the neck, but carcasses are entered from various locations.

An exception to the neck bite is the fairly rare circumstance when a fisher kills a porcupine. Two strategies seem to be employed to kill this

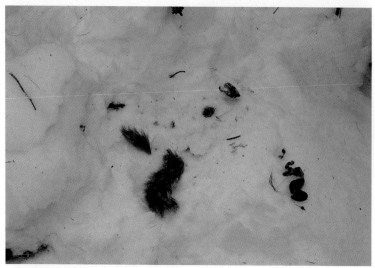

The remains of a gray squirrel killed and eaten by a fisher. (MA) Photo by Paul Rezendes.

well-defended animal. One is to catch a porcupine out on a tree limb and force it to move too quickly, causing it to fall and be injured or killed. The second is to catch a porcupine out in the open and to run around it quickly, slashing at the vulnerable nose and allowing the porcupine to bleed and weaken to the point where it stops defending itself. Then it is flipped on its back, and the carcass is opened from the spineless belly. I have seen many porcupines successfully keep a fisher at bay, and I know of remarkably few times when a fisher killed a porcupine. Certainly, fisher do kill porcupines from time to time, but the literature overemphasizes this behavior.

These animals cache in hollows, tree cavities, dug holes, tree crotches, and abandoned bird nests. I once followed a fisher trail up a tree and found the remains of a raccoon in a bird nest. Caches are often scented with rolling, urine, scat, or a combination of these strategies. Fishers are also found following fox trails and digging up their caches.

Small Prey

Many large and medium predators eat small mammals and leave no trace at all—occasionally a spot of blood or a scattered grass nest. When a bobcat kills a gray squirrel, often only the tail remains, and on several occasions I've found just trickles of blood where red squirrels had been killed and eaten. House cats leave only the tails of southern flying squirrels they catch and eat, and fishers leave only the tails and intestines of gray squirrels they eat.

Voles and mice are eaten by foxes, coyotes, bears, and felines in their entirety. I've watched both coyotes and red foxes feeding on voles. A crunch or two with the carnassials, and then they are swallowed.

Small predators leave sign on proportionately small prey. Often

This is the stomach of a small mammal that was traveling beneath the snow layer when a bobcat pounced, killed, and ate it on the spot. (MA) Photo by John McCarter.

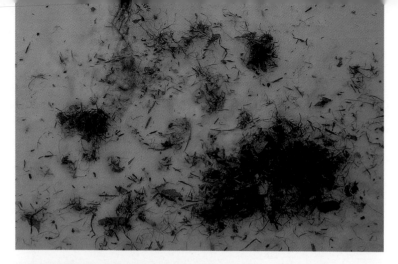

Top: The nest remains of a flying squirrel, pulled from a rotting snag by a hunting fisher. (NH) *Bottom:* An ermine killed this white-footed mouse and ate only the brain. (OR) Photo by Chris Maser.

weasels and other small mammals, such as chipmunks, eat only the brain of smaller prey. It is a theory that well-fed weasels eat only the most nutritious portion of their kills and leave the rest behind. Chris Maser (1998) also noted that a long-tailed weasel can kill prey by biting the base of the skull without puncturing the skin. I too have found carcasses cached by weasels that had no punctures created by the canine teeth at the base of the skull.

A surprising variety of small mammals take the opportunity to feed on one another or at carcasses. Grasshopper mice attack prey by biting the neck at the base of the skull—look for sign of incisors rather than canines. Chipmunks have been recorded killing and eating mice, and

Nancy Birtwell watched a mole cleaning this chipmunk carcass, which had originally been killed and left by a house cat. (MA)

shrews and mice are well known to attack and eat other small mammals. These signs are very difficult to distinguish from one another without associated signs.

Mammals Eating Birds

From time to time, I am lucky enough to find kill sites where feathers still linger. The context surrounding these kill sites, as well as the arrangement and condition of the feathers, aids in the identification of the predator. Is the kill site under a low-hanging branch, near a wetland, or out in the open? Have the feathers been dropped from a perch? Is there scat or a day bed nearby? Has the carcass been moved or cached, or was the entire bird consumed in one place? There is a lot to consider before moving in to look at the feathers themselves.

Also consider the size of the bird that was eaten. If an ermine takes a chickadee, there will be feather remains. If a fisher takes a chickadee, the bird will be eaten in its entirety. The size of the prey certainly says something about the size of the predator. Naturally, this applies to large prey as well. The remains of a wild turkey would not rule out fishers but may be large enough to rule out ermines. This is only common sense, but it is still an important consideration.

An examination of the quills of individual feathers and of clumps of feathers offers even more information. Although this is not an exact science, and there is variation in the way quills are damaged by a single animal, there are useful categories of sign that help narrow the list of possible predators.

Top: A long-tailed weasel's cache holds the remains of two ruffed grouse and an entire common merganser. (NH) *Bottom:* The clipped ends of blue jay feathers from a bird killed and eaten by a fisher. (MA)

If the tip of the shaft proximal to the body has been cut, a mammal is the predator responsible. Inspection of the back teeth of predators reveals the carnassial teeth, which are used for shearing food into manageable chunks. In canines, these teeth are well developed, and this behavior is easily witnessed when a domestic dog is given a hunk of food. It slides the chunk to the back of the mouth and chews to one side, using the back teeth. This is exactly what is found in the case of feathers. Canines shear

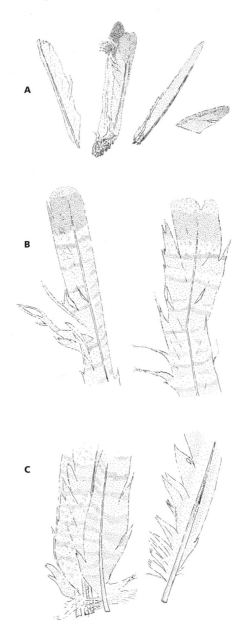

A Junco feathers sheared by a long-tailed weasel. (NH)
B Ruffed grouse feathers plucked by a red fox—note the holes in the plumage made by the canine teeth. (NH)
C Ruffed grouse feathers sheared by a red fox. (NH)

Top: A close-up look at this coyote's kill site shows that mourning dove feathers were both sheared and plucked with the teeth. *Bottom:* A junco killed and eaten by a long-tailed weasel near a bird feeder. (NH)

feathers off large feathered prey. And remember, size is relative among predators—what is large for a fox is not large for a wolf.

When canines shear feathers, you often find clumps of feathers at the kill site. Sections of feathers are sheared off together, and the saliva of the mammal may help these clumps stick together. Look for the angle of the shear to be constant across the entire clump of feathers—this is crucial in separating canines from other mammals. Weasels also shear off sections of feathers, but the shear is short, and if the shearing continued, the angle would vary with each bite. This is why the junco feathers pictured were sheared in a circular fashion—there were multiple bites involved. Alternatively, the overall appearance of the sheared edge may be ragged. Bobcats, which have less developed carnassial teeth than canines do,

A rock dove killed and eaten by a feral cat in the safety of a hay barn. (NY)

leave much more ragged sign, and the clumps are much smaller than one would expect for such a large animal. The appearance is one of chewing through feathers rather than cleanly shearing them.

House cats, foxes, coyotes, and others pluck feathers as well. Rather than damage to the quill, as occurs in feathers plucked by raptors, the sign is higher on the feather. The quill may show signs of handling near the top, but look for holes or impressions in the plumage itself, where canine teeth bit down and the feather was pulled. I have found house cat kills in which all the remaining feathers were pulled. In red fox and coyote kill sites, it is common to find both bitten-off feathers and plucked feathers together. Tail feathers seem to be plucked by foxes more often than bitten.

Mammals Eating Bird Eggs

Eggs are popular fare throughout the world, eaten by both birds and mammals, humans included. Eggs are also damaged for reasons other than feeding, and a discussion of these signs is presented as well.

There are several important variables to consider when you find the remains of eggs. First, did the eggs hatch naturally? As soon as the young have hatched, parents carry the eggshells and drop them a suitable distance from the nest, or at least push them out of the nest itself. Eggshells may act as visual and olfactory attractants to the nest, endangering the young.

The shells of eggs that have hatched naturally are in two separate pieces, or halves. The membrane, which lines the inside of the egg, is folded inward, which is a good indicator of successful hatching, and it separates easily from the hard outer shell. Young birds also move in such a way that one half of an eggshell may end up within the other half—this is a sure sign of a natural hatch.

Other variables to consider when assessing egg remains are the size of the egg and the number of eggs involved. The size of an egg influences how it is opened by predators. Weasels and skunks are constant threats to egg clutches. In general, if an egg is large relative to the preda-

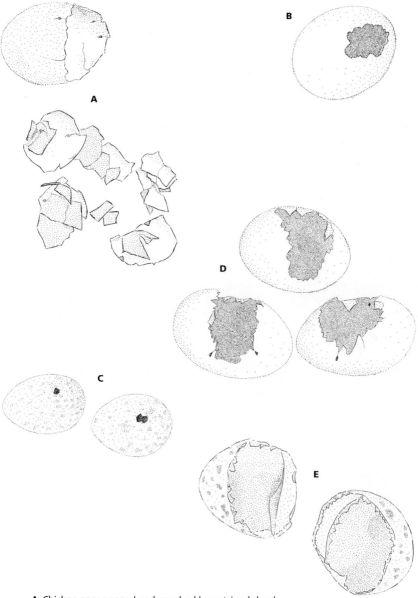

A Chicken eggs opened and smashed by a striped skunk.
B Chicken egg opened by an American crow.
C House sparrow eggs "beaked" by a house wren.
D Mallard eggs preyed on by a mink—note the holes made by the canine teeth.
E Cliff swallow eggs that have naturally hatched—note the folding of the internal lining.

A Mourning Dove Nest

While attaching shade cloth to a large wooden frame 15 feet (4.6 m) off the ground, I spooked a mourning dove off her nest, and the shock nearly threw me to the ground. She returned quickly enough and perched only 5 feet (1.5 m) from where I crawled across the wooden framework. What synchronicity to arrive at that place at that very moment!

I crawled over to have a look at the nest, and as I peered down, one egg began to move, then another, and then the third as well. The first to move was also the first to crack, and I watched the entire amazing process as a tiny mourning dove emerged from her egg and entered our world. She was black from beak to rump, with fine black fluff and soot black skin, with the exception of a bright white lump sitting atop her upper mandible—the egg tooth, which she had used to puncture and cut the shell in two.

The nearby female was becoming quite upset, pacing back and forth along one of the wooden beams, so I moved 10 feet (3.05 m) from the nest and continued to watch. She returned to watch as the other two eggs hatched, and she quickly began to organize them. The first chore was to remove the eggshells, which might attract predators through either scent or sight. One half at a time was gripped in her beak, and off she flew, well beyond sight. She did not pause until they were all gone, and then she settled in to keep her young covered.

This is why we find egg remains in what seem to be unlikely circumstances. Birds drop them in parking lots, in the middle of fields, in streams and lakes, and in other unusual places far enough from the nest to prevent them from being tracked or traced by potential threats to the new family.

tor, it is opened at the pointy end—which is the method used by skunks to open chicken eggs. If the egg is small in relation to the animal, it is likely to be opened from the side, leaving roughly squarish, ragged openings, such as when minks eat mallard eggs. The key indicator is evidence of the canine teeth in the shell, which consists of tiny holes near the entrance. If you can pair up a jaw's canines, then estimating the size of the animal is easier. The quantity of eggs also comes into play. For example, a single egg eaten by an opossum may be cleaned of its contents, and then the shell may be consumed. In the case of many eggs, opossums tend to leave the shells behind as evidence of the crime.

Many rodents, from mice to chipmunks to squirrels, eat eggs as well as attack and eat the hatchlings. Foxes, raccoons, and opossums are also notorious nest raiders. Based on my limited experience, foxes and opossums eat eggs in their entirety—shell and all. I watched an opossum crack open an egg, slurp up the contents, and then return to eat the entire shell. I've been told that raccoons do the same, although the number of eggs is a factor. A full turkey's nest would be a challenge for any animal to finish in one sitting, especially when ingesting the shells as well.

Mammal Remains 8

At the invitation of Charlie Perakis, tracker and friend, I visited his island sanctuary off the coast of Maine as winter was fading into spring. Before we had walked from the dock, across the green, and to the cottage, we came upon the first snowshoe hare remains—an exposed spinal column attached to both furry hind feet. As I wandered the small island over the next several days, these remains were duplicated under every circumstance. Spines and attached feet were found cached in root mounds, out on the rocks just above the high-water mark, under spruce trees, and in grassy meadows. They were found among the buildings that had seen no one for months and on the most remote corner of the island. Again and again, spines with attached rear feet. They were classic avian kill sites, and that was the only possibility, as there were no mammal predators on the island at all.

We also found massive pellets, up to 6 inches (15.2 cm) long, most often on the rocks next to the pounding surf. They were all filled with huge bones, including the vertebrae of hares. These signs all spoke of large owls, which wintered on the island. Skulls and bones carpeted the island, and within hours my standards for collection raised significantly—from any skull to only complete skulls with all their teeth and lower jaws intact.

Charlie knew of three large raptors that used the island: bald eagles, ospreys in summer, and snowy owls in winter. The eagle had nested on the island just the year before, high up in a dead spruce tree. But what we were finding could only be the signs of snowy owls.

One afternoon I made my way to the east end of the island and found myself watching eiders from the rocky shore. I sat in a spot that held the sun and kept the winds at bay to better absorb the power that surrounded me. I closed my eyes and focused on the pounding surf for some time, which reverberated through my body with each new surge of water.

When I stood to make my way along the coastline, a ghost-white form rose up from a nearby perch on the rocks. Had he been there all along or

A classic snowy owl kill, and the typical remains when feeding on snowshoe hares. (ME)

just arrived? I'll never know. He lifted effortlessly, without haste, and was soon joined by a pair of nearby gulls that began to lazily harass him and escort him out to sea. The snowy owl looked very small by the time the gulls returned to roost, and I began hopping from rock to rock, moving north and west around the island, grinning from ear to ear.

During a recent winter, I spent many a day following a particular black bear that denned late in the year—so late, in fact, that it was actually early the next year. One fine day, I followed him from bed to feeding area to second bed, and even onto a third and fourth bed—he was beginning to slow down. Between second and third beds he moved up a drainage, exploring laurel thickets and other impenetrable vegetation. Stubborn and determined, I followed the trail and was rewarded mid–laurel patch with a dig in the snow and debris. The bear had removed and discarded a large deer antler, likely cast the winter before.

I'm no antler man. In all the hours, days, and months I've spent exploring wood and field, I've found impressively few antlers. Yet friends of mine are like magnets and collect antlers on nearly every hike they take. I was particularly excited by this find.

The antler had colored with age, taking on green and brown hues, no doubt influenced by the surrounding debris layer and all the molds and fungi that grow within. Several tines were completely gone, chewed by tiny incisors into nothing. Squirrels and even smaller animals such as mice or voles had worked the antler extensively, eating between a third and a half of its entire bulk—which must have been impressive when whole. How many animals had been to visit this antler, dropped by a large buck so long ago? Mice and squirrels long past, a bear most recently, but I wondered how many other stories it had to tell.

The remains of mammals are found in every circumstance. Mammals emerge into this world, feed and grow with available resources, and eventually die, returning a portion of what they have taken in life to the continuous cycle of chemical processes that sustain all living things. Hair, antlers, and claws are also shed while the animal is still alive.

Hair

Mammal hair can be found in myriad circumstances across the land-scape—blowing freely or caught on barbed wire, thorns, and fence posts. Hair appears where bears and cats have rubbed, where moose have scratched, and where squirrels have massacred a mossy knoll in a scenting behavior. Hair is gathered for nest building and to cushion winter roosts. Hair is also a common component of scats and speaks to us about predator-prey relations.

While leading a workshop, I once followed a bobcat trail to a spot where he'd pulled a vole's nest from beneath the receding ice and snow during a winter warm spell. The vole latrine was evident inside, but what was truly amazing was the nest itself. The entire shelter was con-structed from hair, skin, and quills scavenged from a nearby porcupine carcass earlier in the season. And the quantity of scat in the latrine was testament to the fact that the vole had been successfully living in the prickly fortress for some time.

Quills, claws, and toenails are all hair, adapted and changed with evo-lution. All are useful clues of an ani-mal's presence. Quills in particular are dropped by porcupines all the time and are often evident in runs and carpeting areas where they hole up to rest. Be careful when handling quills, but remember that they also

Using a white surface as a background helps bring out these black bear hairs on a rubbed tree. (NH)

The cells responsible for antler growth are the fastest growing cells known—faster than cancer cells. Consider moose to get a better sense of their amazing potential. In 150 days, moose antlers grow from bump to fully exposed bone. Antlers may weigh up to of 80 pounds (36.3 kg) (the average is about 50 [22.7 kg]). Some simple math shows that 80-pound antlers would result from an average of just over half a pound (230 g) of growth per day!

Antlers offer some offensive and defensive benefits to the wearer. Yet researchers state that antlers are designed to minimize the chance of injury during conflicts and were created for sparring, not spearing, competition. Antlers not only aid in scent communication but also visually display the health and vigor of prospective mates. In moose, animals with smaller racks never challenge ones with larger racks. After constructing incredibly large antlers for himself, Anthony Bubenik put this to the test with Alaskan moose. When he joined the courting arena, the males quickly backed off, and Bubenik was unexpectedly confronted with numerous receptive females.

Moose, elk, deer, and caribou antlers are more easily differentiated from one another than are the antlers of the two deer species of North America. White-tailed deer grow antlers in which single tines grow from a central beam, whereas the central beam in mule deer antlers quickly forks into two, and each successive branch then forks to create a greater number of tines.

The size of an animal's antlers varies from year to year, and the annual drop ensures that the current condition of the male is advertised to

Porcupine incisor marks are clearly visible on this moose antler. (MN).

Both wolves and coyotes eat moose and caribou antlers. Look closely for the clear canine tooth impressions on this moose antler, chewed by a coyote. (NH)

females. Old and diseased animals grow less impressive racks and thus lose the opportunity to mate. The greatest antler potential comes with a combination of age, health, nutrition (diets high in calcium, phosphorus, and protein), and genetics. This ensures that the strongest DNA packages will be passed on, thus contributing to the continuation of the species overall.

The antler itself is a sign of the animal from which it dropped, but more often than not, it also wears signs of other animals. Bones and

Many smaller rodents chew available antlers and bones. (NH)

antlers offer a wonderful source of calcium in a compact package, and numerous mammals take advantage. The first to do so are often the antlered animals themselves, especially after such a calcium-depleting exercise as growing a set of antlers. Elk and caribou can be observed chewing each other's antlers just after the rut, when hormones have calmed and males begin to spend time together. Look for tines that have been chewed off, leaving a ragged, rough nub.

Rodents of every size eat all sorts of bones and antlers. Porcupines down to mice will have a chew, and to some extent, the size of the incisors helps the tracker differentiate among them. Coyotes and wolves also eat moose and caribou antlers, and the imprints of canine teeth are common on the antlers of both these species. Their feeding is concentrated in the softer central portion of the dish, to which the tines attach. You can find moose antlers with just the tines remaining because the entire central portion has been eaten.

Dead Mammals

Animals die for numerous reasons. Certainly human-related factors such as poachers, cars, and habitat loss are among the leading causes. Millions of deaths are also caused by alien species, including house cats and rats. Hunters and trappers also influence populations, but to a much less degree than the above-mentioned causes. Animals also die because of starvation, predator-prey relations, disease, genetics, old age, weather, exposure, and so on.

Shrews are often killed by predators and then abandoned. (MA)

Left: This red fox died under unbelievable circumstances. While pouncing, he somehow caught a rear leg in the shrubbery above; he struggled to free himself, dislocating his leg, and eventually starved to death. The maggots, which entered at the anus, may have killed him first. (MA) *Right:* The remains of a red-backed vole, killed and eaten by a kestrel. Identifying mammal remains is an important skill. (MA)

A neighbor watched a fox walk into his yard one night and curl up to sleep on the lawn. When it hadn't moved on by the next morning, he investigated and found that it had died during the night for unknown reasons. Occasionally we find such animals, dead for no apparent reason. These are some of the greatest mysteries for trackers.

Tissue and muscle return to the earth with time, sliding from the skeleton and disappearing into the soil. Other mammals, birds, and numerous insects speed this process along. Eventually, all that remains are the bones. The skull and bones are the last tracks left by an individual animal. The bones themselves are sign of mammals long past, but they are also eaten by other mammals that need the calcium within.

An elk skull hidden in tall grass. (WY)

The bones and skull of a snowshoe hare. (ME)

Studying skulls and bones is a rewarding and addictive pastime and has a useful application to tracking. You may come across bones from animals long dead, and they also turn up during scat analysis and when working with bird pellets. Three resources to consider, all listed in the bibliography, are Burt and Grossenheider's *Peterson Field Guide: Mammals,* Jones and Manning's *Illustrated Key to Skulls of Genera of North American Land Mammals,* and Gilbert's *Mammalian Osteology.* These will get you started.

In Closing

Tracking is like dancing, because your body is happy. It tells you hunting will be good. You feel it in the dance. It tells you when you love tracking and dancing, you are talking with God.

!NGATE XGAMXEBE, BUSHMAN TRACKER, FROM THE DOCUMENTARY *The Great Dance*

Many of my most cherished moments in tracking came during the years I devoted my field time to the woods next to my home. I would pick one animal to track for an entire snow season. I began with a red fox, followed by a fisher, then two years on a gray fox (I'd learned so much the first year), then a bobcat, and so on. For those who are intent on honing their tracking skills, this may be the best strategy for learning on a deeper level. It has been several years since I've done this, but I look forward to reestablishing this intensive commitment to an area and an animal as soon as possible. Following is a story from my season spent following a male fisher.

I was living along a narrow road on a small horse farm in southern New Hampshire. The abandoned railroad tracks behind my house led east into woods filled with vernal pools, beaver ponds, streams, and great boulders left there long ago. After an early snowstorm, I tromped out in heavy, knee-deep snow and discovered his trail loping along the far side of the near beaver pond and then paralleling the stream down into some rocks. I knew immediately that I would track this fisher as often as possible as long as the snow lasted and beyond. His tracks were the largest—still are the largest—fisher tracks I'd ever seen. He was like a small wolverine loose in New England.

Nobody else walked the land I tracked four to six days a week, a terrain consisting of private lots, a granite quarry, the abandoned railroad tracks, and a poorly managed tree farm, all sprinkled with ponds, streams, and boulder fields. Just 1 mile (1.6 km) to the north was a scenic "nature reserve" with ponds and picnic tables. But I'd say that the nature reserve had only one-fifth the wildlife activity of my woods. Although the ponds were beautiful and nice to canoe, the animals preferred the edge of the quarry, the slashed trunks and tops of the tree farm property, and a string of vernal pools among boulders on the adjacent hillside.

I followed this fisher for endless hours and countless miles. Two females maintained separate ranges within the great area roamed by the male. Luckily, he chose to spend more time with the female that lived close to my home, and he also concentrated his hunting forays nearby. I've read that a fisher can cover 18 miles (28.96 km) a night on a vigilant hunt for food, with periodic naps during its rounds. What my source failed to mention was that these 18 miles are often within 2 square miles (3.2 sq km) or less—thus, while tracking a fisher, you are likely to cross your own trail more than once over the course of a day.

This fisher maintained relationships with three other species: porcupine, raccoon, and red fox. It was these animals the fisher scented and followed for short distances as he traveled. It is a misconception that fishers live entirely on porcupines. Fishers are relentless hunters of incredible tenacity and skill, and they have a varied palate. Porcupines are not easy prey, and many other animals can be secured without such risk to life and limb. I have often seen fishers scenting, following, and killing raccoons, and this fisher was no exception. Over the winter, he pulled two drowsy raccoons from tree cavities, and I found the remains of a third cached in a bird nest, although I'm not sure where it originated. That year, the male and the closer female denned in a set of rocks not 30 yards (27.4 km) from boulders used by a large porcupine four or five days a week. The porcupine split its time between the boulders and a massive hemlock tree that stood precipitously on a dramatic cliff over the rock quarry about half a mile to the northeast.

The male fisher regularly visited the porcupine's lair. The first time I followed him into the porcupine's safe haven was quite alarming. I readied myself for a study of the strewn quill and bone remains, sure that this was what I'd find after a visit from such a barbarous feeder. I ducked inside and instead found the porcupine staring directly at me, quite surprised by my visit in the middle of the day. He ran straight for me, and I jumped up through a hole in the ceiling of the cave—the space created where the great boulders touched—avoiding a potentially painful encounter in the nick of time. Apparently, the low ceiling behind me was a better hiding spot in which to bury his unprotected nose and turn his back against predators like myself.

Heart racing, I returned to the cave and carefully moved around the bristling porcupine. In the center of the open area was a large rock, on which rested a fresh fisher scat. And as the season continued and the snow deepened, so did the carpet of porcupine droppings in the cave and the accumulation of fisher scats on the central stone platform, which relayed some message I wish I could interpret.

My fisher, as I affectionately referred to him, also heavily scented red fox trails. These two animals had an unusual relationship, raiding each other's food caches. But the fisher certainly held the upper hand in all encounters. I tracked him chasing the fox on a number of occasions, stretching out to his full length in an attempt to narrow the distance between them. The fox always escaped. Fishers are known to kill foxes, but I also know people who have watched a red fox fight off a fisher. Apparently, there is no sure winner when the two species tangle.

I followed this male for months, prying into every part of his personal life. I picked apart caches in trees and buried under snow. I found the remains of one of the neighbor's chickens, a house cat, several raccoons, grouse, snowshoe hares, and gray, red, and flying squirrels. He dug up windfallen apples, nibbled at winterberry, and picked at road-kills. Fishers are efficient hunting machines; their rear feet can turn 180 degrees, so they can run up and down trees at the same speed. Nothing is safe.

After several months, he suddenly took an interest in a fourth animal species. He began to scent and follow my old trails as he crossed them on his rounds. We had entered into a relationship. I had taken notice of the fisher, and now the fisher took notice of me. He'd likely watched me poking about in his woods on several occasions, but I'd never even glimpsed him. In fact, I had never seen a wild fisher at all.

All winter, four evenings a week, I attended university courses. And each time I drove my little winding road—a road I knew the fisher crossed on a regular basis, sometimes 10 times a night—I'd turn off the radio, click on the high beams, and think to myself, maybe tonight's the night I'll see my first fisher. Winter was coming to an end.

On a night no different from the rest, I reached to turn off the radio and thought to myself, he'll hear your car, not the radio. So I left it on. I turned onto my road, and as the forest arched in from both sides, I had that gut feeling I've come to cherish and trust. Something was different, something I was supposed to notice. Driving down the road, winding through the forest and into the open until I reached the gate of my driveway, I waited. Nothing. I couldn't believe it. I'd never had that feeling without something happening.

I turned into my long, wide gravel drive, which sloped up toward the end and was surrounded on the left by the house and by horse fields straight ahead and to the right. But as I turned, something jumped in front of the car. It flowed smoothly up the drive and seemed to float up the hill at the far end. I did not think but allowed my body to absorb recognition. The animal followed the top of the incline east and entered the horse fields. I kept turning my car, keeping the beautiful, loping fisher in my headlights, and watched as he faded into the darkness.

His tracks covered the first few steps to my house. He'd never visited the horse fields before, and in my experience, fishers always avoid large, open areas. To my knowledge, he never visited the area again.

Never forget the trail, look ever for the track in the snow;
it is the priceless, unimpeachable record of the creature's life
and thought, in the oldest writing known on the earth.

ERNEST THOMPSON SETON

APPENDIX: RESOURCES

Tracking Courses

Marcelo Aranda
arandam@ecologia.edu.mx
(Marcelo has been teaching tracking courses in Mexico and
other regions for 20 years.)

Boulder Outdoor Survival School
Josh Bernstein, David Wescot
PO Box 1590
Boulder, CO 80306
(800) 335-7404
(303) 444-9779

Tom Brown's Tracking, Nature,
Wilderness Survival School
PO Box 173
Asbury, NJ 08802-0173
(908) 479-4681

Earth Skills
Jim Lowery
1113 Cougar Court
Frazier Park, CA 93225
(661) 245-0318

Mark Elbroch
markelbroch@yahoo.com

Alan N. Emond
Little Cree Spy Excursions
12 Wilson Hill Road
Colrain, MA 01340
(413) 624-5115

In This Place
Paul Wanta, Heather Lenz
PO Box 217
Wendell, MA 01379
(978) 544-2399

Keeping Track
Sue Morse, Research and
    Program Director
Wolfrun Field Office
(802) 899-2023

John McCarter
89 Sampson Road
Bolton, MA 01740
(978) 779-0117

A Naturalist's World
Dr. Jim Halfpenny
PO Box 989
Gardiner, MT 59030
(406) 848-9458

Nature and Vision
  Tracking School
Charles Worsham
760 Thomas Road
Madison Heights, VA 24572
(804) 846-1987

Ndakinna Wilderness Project
Jim Bruchac
PO Box 308
23 Middle Grove Road
Greenfield Center, NY 12833
(518) 583-9980

Paul Rezendes Programs
  in Nature
Paul Rezendes, Mark Elbroch,
  John McCarter, Alcott Smith
3933 Bearsden Road
Royalston, MA 01368-9400
(978) 249-8810

Shikari Tracking Guild
www.shikari.org

Alcott Smith/Upland Fauna
PO Box 897
Hanover, NH 03755
(603) 448-6352

The Teton Science School
PO Box 68
1 Ditch Creek Road
Kelly, WY 83011
(307) 733-4765
www.tetonscience.org

The Tracking Project
John Stokes
PO Box 266
Corales, NM 87048

Tracks and Trees
  Learning Center
N7597 County Highway Y
Watertown, WI 53094
(920) 699-3217
www.tracksandtrees.com

White Pines Programs
Dan Gardoqui, Matt Wild
PO Box 665
Cape Neddick, ME 03902
(207) 676-9499
www.whitepineprograms.org

Wilderness Awareness School
Kamana Naturalist Training
  Program
PO Box 5000, no. 5-137
Duvall, WA 98019
(425) 788-1301
www.NatureOutlet.com

Wilderness Youth Project
Warren Brush
3905 State Street
Suite 7-518
Santa Barbara, CA 93105
www.wyp.org

Additional Resources

Acorn Naturalists
17821 East 17th Street, #103
PO Box 2423
Tustin, CA 92781-2423
(800) 422-8886
www.acornnaturalists.com
Specializes in science and
environmental education
resources.

Beartracker's Animal Tracks Den
www.geocities.com/Yosemite/
Rapids/7076
A website containing tracking
instruction and resources.

CyberTracker International
Louis Liebenberg
PO Box 1211
Noordhoek, 7985
Cape Town, South Africa
+27 (0)21 949 2171
www.cybertracker.org

CyberTracker Shikari
Warren Brush, Kevin Jarvis
www.cybertrackershikari.org

In This Place
(See contact information above)
Publishes *The Tracking Way*,
a quarterly full-color
magazine devoted to sense of
place, cultural celebration,
nature awareness,
and tracking.

International Society of Profes-
sional Trackers Newsletter
PO Box 654
Stevenson, WA 98648
www.ispt.org
Contains a long list of tracking
resources and contacts all
over the continent.

Keeping Track, Inc.
(See contact information above)
Markets all sorts of tools for
citizen scientists conducting
tracking surveys, as well
as scientific workshops
on cougars, bears, bobcats,
and Canada lynx.

Clare Walker Leslie
76 Garfield Street
Cambridge, MA 02138
(617) 547-9128
Naturalist, artist, illustrator,
author.

The National Wildlife
Federation
8925 Leesburg Pike
Vienna, VA 22184
(703) 790-4100

The Natural Resources
Defense Council
40 West 20th Street
New York, NY 10011
(212) 727-2700

OWLink Media
www.OWLinkMedia.com
Produces and markets
  Jon Young's audiotapes,
  curricula, and select books.

Society of Primitive Technology
David and Paula Wescot
PO Box 905
Rexburg, ID 83440
(208) 359-2400
www.primitive.org
The *Bulletin of Primitive Technology* is a periodical devoted to wilderness skills.

WildEarth: The Journal of Wildlands Recovery and Protection
PO Box 455
Richmond, VT 05477
(802) 434-4077

Wilderness Way Magazine
PO Box 621
Bellaire, TX 77402-0128
(713) 667-0128
www.wwmag.net

The Wildlands Project
1955 West Grant Road,
  Suite 145
Tucson, AZ 85745-1147
(520) 884-0875
http://www.twp.org

The Yellowstone to Yukon
  Conservation Initiative
710 9th Street, Studio B
Canmore, Alberta T1W 2V7
Canada
y2y@banff.net

BIBLIOGRAPHY

Abbey, Edward. *Desert Solitaire: A Season in the Wilderness.* New York: Simon and Schuster, 1968.

Ackerman, B. "Cougar Predation and Ecological Energetics in Southern Utah." Master's thesis, Utah State University, 1982.

Ackerman, B., F. Lindzey, and T. Hemker. "Cougar Food Habits in Southern Utah." *Journal of Wildlife Management* 48 (1984): 147–55.

Allaby, Michael. *A Dictionary of Zoology.* 2nd ed. New York: Oxford University Press, 1999.

Aranda, M. *Huellas y otros rastros de los mamíferos grandes y medianos de México.* Xalapa, Mexico: Instituto de Ecología, 2000.

Armstrong, David. *Mammals of the Canyon Country.* Moab, UT: Canyonlands Natural History Association, 1982.

Bang, Preben, and Preben Dahlstrom. *Collins Guide to Animal Tracks and Signs: A Guide to the Tracking of All British and European Mammals and Birds.* English trans. London: Collins Sons, 1974.

Bass, Rick. *The Ninemile Wolves.* Livingston, MT: Clark City Press, 1992.

———. *The Book of Yaak.* Boston: Houghton Mifflin, 1996.

Baylor, B., and P. Parnall. *The Other Way to Listen.* New York: Aladdin Paperbacks, 1997.

Beavers, S., and F. Ramsey. "Detectability Analysis in Transect Surveys." *Journal of Wildlife Management* 62, no. 3 (1998): 948–57.

Benyus, Janine M. *The Field Guide to Wildlife Habitats of the Eastern United States.* New York: Fireside, 1989.

Bouchner, Miroslav. *Animal Tracks.* English ed. Prague: Aventinum, 1998.

Brown, R. W., and M. J. Lawrence. *Mammals Tracks and Signs.* London: Macdonald, 1983.

Brown, R., M. Lawrence, and J. Pope. *Hamlyn Guide: Animals Tracks, Trails, and Signs.* London: Hamyln, 1982.

Brown, Tom. *Tom Brown's Field Guide to Nature Observation and Tracking.* New York: Berkeley, 1983.

————. *The Science and Art of Tracking.* New York: Berkeley, 1999.

Brown, Tom, and W. Watkins. *The Tracker.* Englewood Cliffs, NJ: Prentice-Hall, 1978.

Bruchac, J. *Roots of Survival: Native American Storytelling and the Sacred.* Golden, CO: Fulcrum, 1996.

Brunner, Josef. *Tracks and Tracking.* New York: Outing, 1909.

Burnham, K., and D. Anderson. "The Need for Distance Data in Transect Counts." *Journal of Wildlife Management* 48, no. 4 (1984): 1248–54.

Burt, William, and Richard Grossenheider. *Peterson Field Guides: Mammals.* Boston: Houghton Mifflin, 1976.

Caduto, Michale J., and Joseph Bruchac. *Keepers of the Animals: Native American Stories and Wildlife Activities for Children.* Golden, CO: Fulcrum, 1991.

Carson, Rachel. *Silent Spring.* Boston: Houghton Mifflin, 1962.

Chadwick, Douglas H., and Joel Sartore. *The Company We Keep: America's Endangered Species.* Washington, DC: National Geographic Society, 1996.

Childs, J. *Tracking the Felids of the Borderlands.* Self-published, 1998. For ordering information: (520) 883-4029.

Corbett, Jim. *Jungle Lore.* London: Oxford University Press, 1953.

Davis, W., and D. Schmidly. *The Mammals of Texas.* Austin, TX: Texas Parks and Wildlife Department, 1994.

DeBruyn, T. *Walking with Bears.* New York: Lyons Press, 1999.

Drengson, Alan, and Duncan Taylor, eds. *Ecoforestry: The Art and Science of Sustainable Forest Use.* Gabriola Island, BC: New Society Press, 1997.

Eastman, John. *The Book of Forest and Thicket.* Mechanicsburg, PA: Stackpole Books, 1992.

Eberhardt, L. "Transect Methods for Population Studies." *Journal of Wildlife Management* 42, no. 1 (1978): 1–31.

Elbroch, M. "Trail Markers." *Northern Woodlands* (summer 1999): 50–51.

————. "Beyond Words: Tracking with the Body and Imagination." *Wilderness Way Magazine,* vol. 7, issue 3 (1999): 48–50.

Elbroch, Mark, with Eleanor Marks. *Bird Tracks & Sign: A Guide to North American Species.* Mechanicsburg, PA: Stackpole Books, 2001.

Fair, J., with L. Rogers. *The Great American Bear.* Minnetonka, MN: Cowles Press, 1994.

Falkus, Hugh. *Nature Detective.* London: Victor Gollanz, 1978.

Forrest, Louise. *A Field Guide to Tracking Animals in Snow.* Mechanicsburg, PA: Stackpole Books, 1988.

Franck, Frederick. *The Zen of Seeing.* New York: Vintage Books, 1973.

Gamberg, M., and J. Atkinson. "Prey Hair and Bone Recovery in Ermine Scats." *Journal of Wildlife Management* 52, no. 4 (1988): 657–60.

Gilbert, B. M. *Mammalian Osteology.* Columbia, MO: Missouri Archaeological Society, 1990.

Gregory, M., and G. Cameron. "Scent Communication and Its Association with Dominance Behavior in the Hispid Cotton Rat." *Journal of Mammalogy* 70, no. 1 (1989): 10–17.

Griffin, Donald R. *Animal Minds.* Chicago: University of Chicago Press, 1992.

Halfpenny, James. *A Field Guide to Mammal Tracking in Western America.* Boulder, CO: Johnson Books, 1986.

————. *Scats and Tracks of the Rocky Mountains.* Helena, MT: Falcon, 1998.

Hanratty, Tom. *Tracking Man and Beast.* Milwaukee: Medicine Hawk Publications, 1997.

Hansen, K. *Cougar: The American Lion.* Flagstaff, AZ: Northland, 1992.

Hanson, Roseann, and Jonathan Hanson. *Basic Essentials: Animal Tracks.* Guilford, CT: Globe Pequot Press, 2001.

Heinrich, Bernd. "Maple Sugaring by Red Squirrels." *Journal of Mammalogy* 73, no. 1 (1992): 51–54.

————. *The Trees in My Forest.* New York: HarperCollins, 1997.

Henry, J. D. *How to Spot a Fox.* Shelburne, VT: Chapters, 1993.

Hildebrand, M. "Analysis of Asymmetrical Gaits." *Journal of Mammalogy* 58, no. 2 (1977): 131–41.

Hildebrand, M., and G. Goslow. *Analysis of Vertebrate Structure.* 5th ed. New York: John Wiley and Sons, 2001.

Hoogland, J. *The Black-tailed Prairie Dog: Social Life of a Burrowing Mammal.* Chicago: University of Chicago Press, 1995.

Howe, R. "Scent Marking Behavior in Three Species of Woodrats *(Neotoma)* in Captivity." *Journal of Mammalogy* 58, no. 4 (1977): 685–88.

Jaeger, Ellsworth. *Tracks and Trailcraft.* New York: Macmillan, 1948.

Johnson, M. "Tent Building in Mountain Beavers." *Journal of Mammalogy* 56, no. 3 (1975): 715–16.

Jones, J. K., Jr., and R. W. Manning. *Illustrated Key to Skulls of Genera of North American Land Mammals.* Lubbock, TX: Texas Tech University Press, 1992.

Joyal, R., and J. G. Ricard. "Winter Defecation Output and Bedding Frequency of Wild, Free-Ranging Moose." *Journal of Wildlife Management* 50, no. 4 (1986): 734–36.

Kellert, Stephen R., and Edward O. Wilson, eds. *The Biophilia Hypothesis.* Washington, DC: Island Press, 1993.

Kricher, John, and Gordon Morrison. *Peterson Field Guides: Ecology of Eastern Forests.* New York: Houghton Mifflin, 1988.

————. *Peterson Field Guides: Ecology of Western Forests.* New York: Houghton Mifflin, 1998.

————. *Peterson Field Guides: Rocky Mountain and Southwest Forests.* New York: Houghton Mifflin, 1993.

Lawrence, Gale. *A Field Guide to the Familiar: Learning to Observe the Natural World.* Hanover, NH: University of New England Press, 1998.

Lawrence, M., and R. Brown. *Mammals of Britain: Their Tracks, Trails, and Signs.* Poole, Dorset, UK: Blandford Press, 1967.

LeCount, A. *Black Bear Field Guide.* Phoenix, AZ: Arizona Game and Fish Department, 1986.

Leopold, Aldo. *A Sand County Almanac.* London: Oxford University Press, 1968.

Leslie, Clare Walker. *The Art of Field Sketching.* Dubuque, IA: Kindall/Hunt, 1984.

Leslie, Clare Walker, and Charles E. Roth. *Keeping a Nature Journal*. North Adams, MA: Storey Books, 2000.

Liebenberg, Louis. *The Art of Tracking: The Origin of Science*. Cape Town, South Africa: David Philip, 1990.

———. *A Field Guide to the Animal Tracks of Southern Africa*. Cape Town, South Africa: David Philip, 1990.

Lord, R. D., A. M. Vilches, J. I. Maiztequi, and C. A. Soldini. "The Tracking Board: A Relative Census Technique for Studying Rodents." *Journal of Mammalogy* 51, no. 4 (1970): 828.

Luoma, Jon R. *The Hidden Forest: The Biography of an Ecosystem*. New York: Henry Holt, 1999.

MacCraken, J., and V. Van Bellenberghe. "Age- and Sex-Related Differences in Fecal Pellet Dimensions of Moose." *Journal of Wildlife Management* 51, no. 2 (1987): 360–64.

MacKintosh, G., ed. *In Defense of Wildlife: Preserving Communities and Corridors*. Washington, DC: Defenders of Wildlife, 1989.

MacMahon, James A. *Deserts*. New York: Alfred A. Knopf, 1985.

Marchand J. *Life in the Cloud: An Introduction to Winter Ecology*. Hanover, NH: University Press of New England, 1987.

Martin, Alexander C., Herbert S. Zim, and Arnold L. Nelson. *American Wildlife and Plants: A Guide to Wildlife Food Habits*. New York: Dover, 1951.

Maser, Chris. *Mammals of the Pacific Northwest*. Corvallis, OR: OSU Press, 1998.

Matthiessen, Peter. *Wildlife in America*. New York: Penguin Press, 1987.

Mech, D. *The Way of the Wolf*. Stillwater, MN: Voyageur Press, 1991.

Mech, D., U. Seal, and G. Delgivdice. "Use of Urine in Snow to Indicate Condition of Wolves." *Journal of Wildlife Management* 51, no. 1 (1987): 10–13.

Merlin, Pinau. *A Field Guide to Desert Holes*. Tucson: Arizona Desert Museum Press, 1999.

Miller, Brian. "Using Focal Species in the Design of Nature Reserve Networks." *Wild Earth* 8 (winter 1998–99).

Miller, K., R. L. Marchinton, K. Forand, and K. Johansen. "Dominance, Testosterone Levels, and Scraping Activity in a Captive Herd of White-tailed Deer." *Journal of Mammalogy* 28, no. 4 (1987): 812–17.

Miquelle, D., and V. Van Bellenberghe. "Impact of Bark Stripping by Moose on aspen-Spruce Communities." *Journal of Wildlife Management* 53, no. 3 (1989): 577–86.

Mitchel, John Hanson. *A Field Guide to Your Own Back Yard*. Woodstock, VT: W. W. Norton, 1999.

Morgan, Lewis. *The American Beaver*. Toronto: Dover, 1986.

Morse, S. "Cougar Conundrum." *Northern Woodlands Magazine* (summer 2001): 19.

———. "Is the Lynx Missing?" *Northern Woodlands Magazine* (spring 2001): 19.

Murie, A. *A Naturalist in Alaska*. New York: Devin-Adair, 1961.

Murie, O. *A Field Guide to Animal Tracks*. New York: Houghton Mifflin, 1954.

Muybridge, E. *Animals in Motion.* New York: Dover, 1957.

Nelson, Richard. *The Island Within.* New York: Vintage Press, 1989.

———. *Heart and Blood: Living with Deer in America.* New York: Vintage Press, 1997.

Ormond, Clyde. *How to Track and Find Game.* New York: Outdoor Life, Funk and Wagnalls, 1975.

Ough, W. "Scent Marking by Captive Raccoons." *Journal of Mammalogy* 63, no. 2 (1982): 318–19.

Parker, G. *Eastern Coyote.* Halifax, NS: Nimbus, 1995.

Peterson, D. *Racks.* Santa Barbara, CA: Capra Press, 1991.

Peterson, R. *The Wolves of Isle Royale.* Minocqua, WI: Willow Creek Press, 1995.

Powell, R. *The Fisher.* Minneapolis: University of Minnesota Press, 1993.

Quinn, D. *The Story of B.* New York: Bantam Books, 1996.

Rezendes, Paul. *Tracking and The Art of Seeing: How to Read Animal Tracks and Sign.* 2nd ed. New York: HarperCollins, 1999.

Rezendes, Paul. *The Wild Within: Adventures in Nature and Animal Teachings.* New York: Penguin Putnam, 1998.

Rue, Leonard Lee. *Sportsman's Guide to Game Animals.* New York: Outdoor Life Books, Harper & Row, 1968.

———. *Complete Guide to Game Animals.* New York: Outdoor Life Books, Harper and Row, 1981.

Rupp, R. *Red Oaks and Black Birches.* Pownal, VT: Storey Communications, 1990.

Russell, C. *Spirit Bear.* Toronto: Keyporter Books, 1994.

Ryden, Hope. *Bobcat Year.* New York: Viking Press, 1981.

———. *Lily Pond: Four Years with a Family of Beavers.* New York: William Morrow, 1989.

Sargeant, G., D. Johnson, and W. Berg. "Interpreting Carnivore Scent Station Surveys." *Journal of Wildlife Management* 62, no. 4 (1998): 1235–45.

Seton, E. T. *Animal Tracks and Hunter Signs.* New York: Doubleday, 1958.

Shaw, H. *Mountain Lion Field Guide.* Special report no. 9. Phoenix, AZ: Arizona Game and Fish Department, 1979.

Shaw, John. *The Nature Photographer's Complete Guide to Professional Field Techniques.* New York: American Photographic Book Publishing, 1984.

Sheldon, I., and T. Eder. *Animal Tracks of Quebec.* Renton, WA: Lone Pine, 2000.

Sheldon, I., T. Hartson, and M. Elbroch. *Animal Tracks of New England.* Renton, WA: Lone Pine, 2000.

Skalski, J. "Using Sign Counts to Quantify Animal Abundance." *Journal of Wildlife Management* 55, no. 4 (1991): 705–15.

Smith, Andrew. "The Art of Making Hay." *National Wildlife* 35, no. 3 (1997): 30–35.

Smith, Richard. *Animal Tracks and Signs of North America.* Harrisburg, PA: Stackpole Books, 1982.

Steele, M., L. Hadj-Chikh, and J. Hazeltine. "Caching and Feeding Decisions by *Sciurus carolinensis*: Responses to Weevil Infested Acorns." *Journal of Mammalogy* 77, no. 2 (1996): 305–14.

Steele, M and Smallwood. "What are Squirrels Hiding?" *Natural History* (October 1994): 40–44.

Stokes, D., and L. Stokes. *A Guide to Animal Tracking and Behavior.* Boston: Little, Brown, 1986.

Stokes, John, and Kanawahienton (David Benedict), Rokwaho (Dan Thompson), and Tekaronianekon (Jake Swamp). *Thanksgiving Address.* Six Nations Indian Museum and the Tracking Project. Corrales, NM: Six Nations Indian Museum and the Tracking Project, 1993.

Strachan, Rob. *Mammal Detective.* London: Whittet Books, 1995.

Stuart, Chris, and Tilde Stuart. *A Field Guide to the Tracks and Signs of Southern and East African Wildlife.* Capetown, South Africa: Southern Book Publishers, 1994.

Sullivan, T., and M. Platner. *The Keeping Track Guide to Photographing Animal Tracks and Sign.* Huntington, VT: Keeping Track, 2001.

Triggs, B. *Tracks, Scats, and Other Traces.* Melbourne, Australia: Oxford University Press, 1996.

Van der Post, Laurens. *A Story like the Wind.* London: Hogarth Press, 1972.

Van Dyke, F., R. Brocke, and H. Shaw. "Use of Road Track Counts as Indices of Mt. Lion Presence." *Journal of Wildlife Management* 50, no. 1 (1986): 102–109.

Weaver, J. "Refining the Equation for Interpreting Prey Occurrence in Gray Wolf Scats." *Journal of Wildlife Management* 57, no. 3 (1993): 534–538.

Wessels, Tom. *Reading the Forested Landscape: A Natural History of New England.* Woodstock, VT: Countryman Press, 1997.

Wigley, T., and M. Johnson. "Disappearance Rates for Deer Pellets in the Southeast." *Journal of Wildlife Management* 45, no. 1 (1981): 251–253.

Wilson, Don E., F. Russell Cole, James D. Nichols, Rasanayagam Rudran, and Mercedes S. Foster, eds. *Measuring and Monitoring Biodiversity: Standard Methods for Mammals.* Washington, DC: Smithsonian Institution, 1996.

Wilson, Edward O. *The Diversity of Life.* New York: W. W. Norton, 1992.

———. *Consilience.* New York: Alfred A. Knopf, 1998.

Wilson, D., and S. Ruff, eds. *The Smithsonian Book of North American Mammals.* Washington, DC: Smithsonian Institute Press, 1999.

Wolfson, D. Untitled and unpublished research paper describing the age characteristics of black bear climbing sign on American beech trees.

Woolsey, N. *Coyote Field Guide.* Special report no. 15. Phoenix, AZ: Arizona Game and Fish Department, 1985.

Zielinski, W., and T. Kucera. *American Marten, Fisher, Lynx, and Wolverine: Survey Methods for Their Detection.* (PSW-GTR-157). Berkeley, CA: Pacific Southwest Research Station, U.S. Forest Service, 1996.

Zoller, P., W. Smith, and L. Brennan. "Characteristics and Adaptive Significance of Latrines of Swamp Rabbits." *Journal of Mammalogy* 77, no. 4 (1996): 1049–1058.

Zwinger, A., and B. Willard. *Land above the Trees.* Boulder, CO: Johnson Books, 1996.

ACKNOWLEDGMENTS

I am indebted to the animals who shared their stories with me, so that I could share them with you. Thank you bear, fisher, and fox; thank you mouse, shrew, and badger. I give thanks for the earth that held tracks, for the water that was often necessary for perfect substrate conditions, for the plants and trees that wore signs of animals passing, for the sun that shone brightly, and for the clouds that allowed perfect photography conditions and brought moisture and snow. Tracking has revealed a trail of continuous challenges, mysteries, beauty, personal growth, and questions—it's as if I'm being carried gently but swiftly by something greater than myself. The natural world has nourished me since my birth; it is where I feel at home.

I'd also like to celebrate all the people who share tracking with others across the country. Your work is so important! I give special thanks to Tom Brown, Jr., Jon Young, Paul Rezendes, Sue Morse, Charles Worsham, Louis Liebenberg, and Dr. Jim Halfpenny for sharing their insights into tracking with me and so many others. Tom brought tracking to the masses and also role-models vision, passion, and focus. Jon helped me become a better teacher, continues to demonstrate the "peacemaker principles," and works tirelessly to connect people and teach others. Jon has also gone out of his way to include me further in his own work. Paul taught me photography, gave me greater confidence in what I knew, and allowed me to teach and grow in his school. Paul also encouraged the researcher in me, and this inspiration led to many of the new findings in this book.

Great thanks as well to every person who has written anything on tracking. I appreciate your efforts and experience as I drink up the knowledge you were kind enough to document for the benefit of others. Olaus Murie documented so much in North America, as did Ernest Thompson Seton before him; their work will always be remembered.

I have tracked with countless people over the years, and I thank all of them for sharing their time, energy, and passion for living. Each one taught me much about tracking, awareness, and purpose. Among them are Kayla Sanford, Mike Pewtherer, Jonathan Talbot, Frank Grindrod, Keith Badger, John McCarter, Ricardo Sierra, Walker Korby, Eleanor Marks, Nancy Birtwell, Fred Vanderbeck, Philip Sherwood-Berndt, George Leoniak, Kurt Rinehart, and Raychelle Harris. Keith, Eleanor, Nancy, and Fred have especially supported me and this work in every way possible. Kayla Sanford was the one who suggested I start shooting slides of the tracks and signs I was finding so that they could be shared with others. And, Raychelle Harris volunteered her time, energy, cooking, resources, affection, and cheer to help create an environment in which I could focus on this work. In the last weeks before the manuscript was due, she also helped by typing revisions and labeling slides, saving me days of work. And thanks to my students of tracking—you have all taught me so much.

Numerous people aided me in the research for this book. Sue Morse, John McCarter, and Sue Mansfield shared their tracking research and notes. Doug Wachob of the Teton Science School allowed me to handle and study the track casts and scat collection of Olaus Murie, made so many years ago. Dave Erler and Sue Clarke of the New Hampshire Science Center provided space and time for me to coax their southern flying squirrels onto track plates. Qanangaq and Jon and Barbara Zebrowski shared a wolf den they had found in Minnesota. Mircea G. Hidalgo of the Instituto de Ecología, AC, shared research methods and included me in his work in Mexico studying small and medium carnivores in dry tropical forests; he also carted me about on my personal adventures. Jim Lowery shared his video cuts of animals in motion and his enthusiasm. Tom Maier of the U.S. Forest Service and tracker Keith McCormick allowed me to join and expand their existing research on small mammals with my own work with track plates. Shawnee Riplog-Peterson, curator, and Peter Siminski of the Arizona–Sonora Desert Museum helped me get tracks from captive jaguarundis. Doug Alberton, biologist for Badlands National Park, offered to bring me into the field to search for ferret sign, but when poor weather conditions intervened, he provided pictures that his team, including Greg Schroeder and Darren Johnson, had taken in the field. Ranger Aaron Kaye helped burn the images onto a CD. John Guetterman of the Oregon Bureau of Land Management, Coos Bay District, was tremendously kind, sharing what he had learned about red tree voles, as well as samples of feeding sign collected from active nests in the field. Jennifer and Adam Vashon provided lodging, food, and good cheer while I visited and participated in lynx research in northern Maine, overseen by Craig McGlaughlin, another generous biologist. Bill Steiver, biologist for Great Smoky Mountains National Park, pointed the way to wild hogs. Greg Levandoski shared his knowledge of lechugilla plants. Jessica Perkins shared her studies and samples of hazelnuts opened by western gray squirrels. Paul Houghtaling shared an aplodontia scat. Alcott Smith provided instructive discussions on anatomy and evolution and helped me better understand the structure of mammal feet. Drs. Colleen McDonough and Jim Loughrey generously shared research and armadillo fecal samples. The mammal training team at the New England Aquarium worked hard to collect a scat sample from one of their sea otters before it dissolved and sank to the bottom of the tank. Thanks also to Frank Grindrod for introducing me to Alan N. Emond, who freely shared experiences and sign collected from black bears eating acorns in western Massachusetts. And Mike Pewtherer and Craig Holdrege of the Nature Institute both shared their skull collections with me and Jen and John Badger shared a moose antler they had found.

Several top-notch trackers reviewed the manuscript. Thank you to Keith Badger, Dan Gardoqui, Walker Korby, John McCarter, and Jon Young for sharing what they've learned in the woods over the years and for their good advice. Kate Davies generously found the time to review the manuscript with a critical eye and share her gifts for language and writing. Walker Korby also shared his skills with pen and computer graphics and contributed the mammal silhouettes found on the last few pages. Custom Slide Service has consistently developed my slides professionally over the many years I've photographed.

I traveled widely to create this guide. Cheers to my Nissan truck which took me where I needed to go. And several folks suffered my personal agenda and schedules while traveling with me: Nate Ripperton joined me for a trip to Big Bend, Philip Sherwood-Berndt traveled and tracked across Alaska with me, and Raychelle Harris tolerated numerous field trips across the country, most of them in the discomfort of my truck. Matt Macdonald also joined me for a quick trip to Minnesota.

So many people provided stories, laughter, showers, warm food, and hospitality in every sense and shared local tracking spots across the country. Their generosity and spirit made traveling more enjoyable. Thank you to Jonathan Talbott, Julie Stonefelt, Greg Levandoski, Lynn Rogers, Rayanne Harris, Raylene Harris, Ray Harris, Rachel Stone, Mark and Lisa Moulton, Kevin and Cissi Jarvas, Doniga Murdock, Jon Young, and Mike and Diane Pewtherer.

Although I'd like to list every spot I've ever tracked, I'll only list those that were especially generous while I did research for this book. For these places I am incredibly grateful, and for every patch of ground that has supported me while I've tracked across this continent. Some of the areas are Quabbin, Valdez, Pillsbury, Fudd Hill, Pack Monadnock,

Chamela, Pisgah, Connecticut River, my favorite rock quarry, Lamar Valley, Glacier, Big Bend, Alligator, Padre, Denali, Monahans, Mojave, Cuyama, Death Valley, Cordova, Sawtooth, Baggs, and Route 160. This project would not have been possible without the full support of my family. My grandfather introduced me to nature and birds many years ago among the hedgerows and fields of Suffolk, England. Since then, every member of my family has not only suffered with but also supported and encouraged my obsessive interest in wildlife, birding, and tracking. My parents supported this project in every way possible, and my father deserves special recognition for patiently sharing what he knows of scanners, art programs, and computers. Liz Gorst, my grandmother, has always been supportive and enthusiastic and kept me safe while I explored off-trail with her continual prayers; in addition, she lent me a considerable sum to extend the research trips for this project. Without these funds, this book would have been far more limited in scope.

And none of this would have happened without the faith, vision, and opportunity offered by Mark Allison of Stackpole Books and the subsequent organization and perseverance of Amy Wagner, Mark's right hand.

INDEX

Abrasions on bark or cambium,
611–15
Acorns, 644–55
Amble, 49
Antilocapridae, 244–45, 492–93
Antler rubs, 595–99
Antlers, cast, 745–48
Aplodontia or mountain beaver
burrows, 439–40
castings and eskers, 384
debarking, 587, 589
feeding signs, 574
nipping of twigs, 625–27
scat, 494
tracks, 83, 254–56
Armadillo, nine-banded
burrows, 440–41
digs, 699, 701
scat, 471–72, 534
tracks, 91, 117–19
Artiodactyla
bison, goat, muskox and sheep
(Bovidae), 245–54
boar (Suidae), 226–28
deer and relatives (Cervidae),
231–43
javelina or peccary (Tayassuidae),
229–31
pronghorn (Antilocapridae),
244–45

Badger, American
burrows, 444–45
predation of small mammals, 705
scat, 480, 535
tracks, 99, 181–83
Barking, 615, 682–83
Bat, 473, 515
Bear
American black, 107, 151–53, 395,
448, 477, 547–48, 554
beds, 394–96
breaking of limbs/trunks, 635–36
brown or grizzly, 110–11, 154–56,
396, 448–49, 477, 549–50, 554
claw marks, categories of, 614
dens, 448–50
digs, 691, 693, 695, 697, 698,
699, 702
feeding signs, 581, 591, 595,
685–86, 715, 716
gait, 46–47, 50
kill site analysis, 724–25
marking, 606–10, 636–38
polar, 46–47, 112–13, 157–59, 396,
449–50
predation of small mammals,
702–3
runs, 376–77
scat, 477, 547–50, 554

ABOUT THE AUTHOR

Mark Elbroch has maintained a home base in central New England for the last seven years, but search for signs of him along muddy stream banks in remote areas near you. He has contributed to numerous research projects in North America, including monitoring collared black bears, capturing and collaring cougars, live-capturing and censusing small mammals, inventorying carnivores in dry tropical forests, participating in Glacier National Park's Bear Sign survey, and documenting fisher and marten presence in remaining old-growth stands, in addition to undertaking many personal projects while tracking across the continent. He is the coauthor of *Animal Tracks of New England,* is lead author of *Bird Tracks & Sign,* and has written articles for periodicals and other publications on tracking. He is a supporter of the Shikari Tracking Guild, a group of trackers working to preserve and teach tracking widely to ensure that our tracking knowledge expands with each successive generation, and is involved in creating an evaluation standard for North American trackers in conjunction with Louis Leibenberg's CyberTracker Conservation in Africa. He also teaches workshops throughout New England, continues to track and travel widely, and works as an American Sign Language/English interpreter.

RELATIVE SIZES OF NORTH AMERICAN MAMMALS

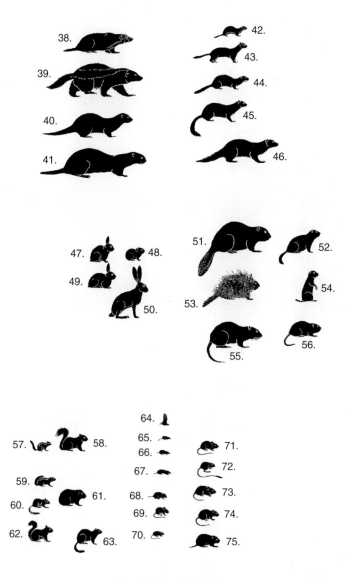

Drawings by Walker Korby

Relative Sizes of North American Mammals

Drawings continued overleaf

Relative Sizes of North American Mammals

Key to Relative Sizes of North American Mammals

1. Polar bear, *Ursus maritimis*
2. Grizzly bear, *Ursus arctos*
3. Black bear, *Ursus americanus*
4. Feral hog, *Sus scrofa*
5. Peccary, *Pecari tajacu*
6. Elephant seal, *Mirounga angustirostris*
7. Harbor seal, *Phoca vitulina*
8. Moose, *Alces alces*
9. Bison, *Bison bison*
10. Muskox, *Ovibus moschatus*
11. Deer, *Odocoileus* sp.
12. Caribou, *Rangifer tarandus*
13. Elk, *Cervus elaphus*
14. Pronghorn, *Antilocapra americana*
15. Mountain sheep, *Ovis* sp.
16. Mountain goat, *Oreamus americanus*
17. Gray wolf, *Canis lupus*
18. Red wolf, *Canis rufus*
19. Coyote, *Canis latrans*
20. Red fox, *Vulpes vulpes*
21. Gray fox, *Urocyon cinereoargenteus*
22. Kit fox, *Vulpes velox*
23. Arctic fox, *Alopex lagopus*
24. Jaguar, *Panthera onca*
25. Cougar, *Puma concolor*
26. Ocelot, *Leopardus pardalis*
27. Lynx, *Lynx canadensis*
28. Jaguarundi, *Herpailurus yaguarondi*
29. Bobcat, *Lynx rufus*
30. Opossum, *Didelphis virginiana*
31. Armadillo, *Dasypus novemcinctus*
32. Raccoon, *Procyon lotor*
33. Coati, *Nasua narica*
34. Spotted skunk, *Spilogale* sp.
35. Striped skunk, *Mephitis* sp.
36. Hognose skunk, *Conepatus* sp.
37. Ringtail, *Bassariscus astutus*
38. Badger, *Taxidea taxus*
39. Wolverine, *Gulo gulo*
40. River otter, *Lontra canadensis*
41. Sea otter, *Enhydra lutris*
42. Weasel, *Mustela* sp.
43. Black-footed ferret, *Mustela nigripes*
44. Mink, *Mustela vison*
45. Marten, *Martes americana*
46. Fisher, *Martes pennanti*
47. Cottontail, *Sylvilagus* sp.
48. Pika, *Ochotona* sp.
49. Snowshoe hare, *Lepus americanus*
50. Jackrabbit, *Lepus* sp.
51. Beaver, *Castor canadensis*
52. Woodchuck, *Marmota* sp.
53. Porcupine, *Erethizon dorsatum*
54. Prairie dog, *Cynomys* sp.
55. Nutria, *Myocastor coypus*
56. Muskrat, *Ondatra zibethicus*
57. Chipmunk, *Tamias* sp.
58. Gray squirrel, *Sciurus* sp.
59. Antelope ground squirrel, *Ammospermophilus* sp.
60. Flying squirrel, *Glaucomys* sp.
61. Aplodontia, *Aplodontia rufa*
62. Red squirrel, *Tamiasciurus* sp.
63. Ground squirrel, *Spermophilus* sp.
64. Bat, *Myotis* sp.
65. Shrew, *Sorex* sp.
66. Short-tailed shrew, *Blarina* sp.
67. Mole, *Parascalops* sp.
68. Vole, *Microtus* sp.
69. White-footed mouse, *Peromyscus* sp.
70. Pocket mouse, *Perognathus* and *Chaetodipus* sp.
71. Rice rat, *Oryzomys* sp.
72. Kangaroo rat, *Dipodomys* sp.
73. Cotton rat, *Sigmodon* sp.
74. Woodrat, *Neotoma* sp.
75. Pocket gopher, *Thomomys* and *Pappageomys* sp.

Drawings continued overleaf